THE
PRICE
OF
DEPENDENCY

ALSO BY ROBERT M. O'NEIL

Free Speech: Responsible Communication Under Law

Civil Liberties: Case Studies and the Law
(with Donald Parker and Nicholas Econopouly)

A Guide to Debate
(with Russel Windes)

THE
PRICE
OF
DEPENDENCY

Civil Liberties in the
Welfare State

ROBERT M. O'NEIL

E. P. Dutton & Co., Inc.
New York
1970

Grateful acknowledgment is made to the following for permission to use copyright material:

Atheneum Publishers, for an excerpt from *Privacy and Freedom*, by Alan F. Westin. Copyright © 1967 by The Association of the Bar of the City of New York. Reprinted by permission of Atheneum Publishers.

The Duke University School of Law, for portions of "The Privacy of Government Employees" by William Creech. Reprinted, with permission, from a symposium, "Privacy," appearing in *Law and Contemporary Problems* (Vol. 31, No. 2, Spring 1966), published by the Duke University School of Law, Durham, North Carolina. Copyright,©, 1966, by Duke University.

The Harvard Law Review Association, for material from "Developments in the Law—Academic Freedom," appearing in 81 *Harvard Law Review* 1130 (1968). Copyright © 1968 by The Harvard Law Review Association.

Fred B. Rothman & Co., for a portion of "The American Welfare System by J. M. Wedemeyer and Percy Moore, appearing in *California Law Review*. Copyright,©, 1966, *California Law Review*. Reprinted by permission.

The Regents of the University of California, for quotations from "Public Assistance and Social Insurance—A Normative Evaluation, by Jacobus Ten Broek and Richard B. Wilson, appearing in 1 *U.C.L.A. Law Review*, 237-302. Copyright,©, 1954, by the Regents of the University of California.

Washington Law Review, for portions of "Constitutional Rights in the Public Sector: Justice Douglas on Liberty in the Welfare State," by Hans A. Linde, appearing in *Washington Law Review*, Vol. 40. Copyright,©, 1965, by the Washington Law Review Association.

To my father,
Walter G. O'Neil
and
To the memory of my mother,
Isabel M. O'Neil

CONTENTS

PREFACE

AND

ACKNOWLEDGMENTS

This book began as a paper prepared for a conference on the Law of the Poor at Berkeley in the spring of 1965. The topic was suggested by the conference director, the late Professor Jacobus Ten Broek, who from the unique perspective of his sightless world gave thousands of students and colleagues the insight and conviction necessary to write about the plight of disadvantaged groups in twentieth-century America. Before and after the conference, he reviewed this paper and made sensitive, invaluable critical comments. These comments, and his observations at the conference, laid the groundwork and provided the initial inspiration for this book.

The work that Ten Broek and others began a quarter century ago has been kept current and refined by a corps of younger legal scholars. Notable among them are Professors Hans Linde of the University of Oregon, Charles Reich of Yale, and William Van Alstyne of Duke. My indebtedness to each of them for particular thoughts and insights has been selectively recognized throughout this volume; the general debt owed to these three colleagues by any-one working in this field must be acknowledged here because it transcends particular footnotes and citations.

To Professor Linde I owe a very special debt, or perhaps several debts of different kinds. When we were colleagues at Berkeley during the troubled winter of 1964–65, we talked frequently about problems that were the concern of his seminal two-part article in the *Washington Law Review,* and later became the focus of this book. His critical, thoughtful reading of the entire manuscript for this volume elicited countless suggestions for reorganization of structure, sharpening of analysis, and clarification of expression. His were the kinds of comments that any responsible author needs from some source; I was most fortunate to have so able and generous a colleague laboring in the same field. In many ways this book really is a joint effort; Hans Linde is due much credit for whatever may be its strengths, while I properly accept the blame for its weaknesses.

Two persons with whom I have worked in recent years—mentors rather than colleagues—have significantly aided my understanding of these problems and strengthened my resolve to write about them. Mr. Justice William J. Brennan, Jr., whose law clerk I was during the 1962 Term, gave new meaning to the doctrine of unconstitutional conditions through an opinion he wrote for the Court in 1958. During the next decade, he consistently applied legal precedent and tradition to protecting the rights and interests of government beneficiaries with whom this book is concerned. More recently, I have served in several capacities with President Martin Meyerson of the State University of New York at Buffalo; my work with him has been profoundly educational in ways that transcend the law and the lawyer's competence, but bear directly upon the relations between law and society. I am indebted to Justice Brennan and President Meyerson in ways that a formal acknowledgment cannot adequately express, but may simply indicate.

The preparation of this manuscript reflected the care and skill of Mrs. Lillian Bousma, formerly of Buffalo and now of Cleveland. She was much more than a typist and collator, though she did perform these two vital roles with perfection. She was a constant source both of reassurance and of criticism as the book began to take shape during the winter of 1967–68. She was aided on occasion by two able and gracious colleagues in the President's Office at Buffalo, Mrs. Phyllis Blendowski and Mrs. Barbara Chelikowsky.

Throughout the writing and revision of this book, my wife, Karen Elson O'Neil, has managed to make this work a family project. She read the entire text at least twice, and much of it a third time in galley. Her substantive contributions have been so basic and so harmonious that I cannot easily recall what was my own original thought and what was the result of her refinement. She has made the most vital contribution of all—a patience, a sensitivity, an understanding far beyond even the reasonable expectations of matrimonial loyalty.

Robert M. O'Neil

Berkeley, California
November, 1969

THE
PRICE
OF
DEPENDENCY

I

A REVOLUTION

OF RISING

EXPECTATIONS

In today's welfare state, most citizens receive government benefits at some time in their lives. In 1969, slightly over half of all high school graduates went on to college. Two out of three of them attended publicly supported institutions. A substantial portion of those enrolled in private colleges depend upon federal grants, loans, or work-study payments, or upon state scholarships to finance their education. Roughly one out of every six Americans engaged in nonagricultural employment works for the government at the federal, state, county, or municipal level. In addition, several million persons are employed indirectly by government in business firms that are under government contract.

Some 2.2 million persons live in the 600,000 units of public housing built under federal subsidy since the program began in 1937. It is in the welfare field that government benefits are most comprehensive. About nine out of ten salaried workers and wage earners in the United States are eligible for Social Security. Some 83 percent of civilian payrolls are covered by workmen's compensation programs, and a slightly lower percentage comes under state unemployment insurance. Over six million Americans receive veterans' benefits. Nearly five million persons receive aid for families with dependent children, a half million receive aid for the permanently and totally disabled, another half million are served by vocational rehabilitation grants and programs, and so on. The list could, of course, be made much longer, but these examples will suggest how extensive are the government's subsidies.

What is distinctive about these beneficial relationships between government and the recipients? First, the arrangement is technically voluntary on both sides. Nothing compels the government to offer such benefits to any particular person, or to anyone at all. The individual, in turn, is theoretically free to take the benefit or to leave it. The welfare applicant may be hard pressed by circumstances to find some source of aid, but the law does not compel him to resort to welfare; private charity is often available as an alternative. Second, the relationship involves some formal application for the benefit and results in an agreement between the government and the recipient—if only through the processing of the application and the making of payments.

Third, the benefits of these programs are not available to all persons, but only to those who meet certain prescribed qualifications. Scholarship applicants must typically show they are not only students but are in financial need, and often that they have some promise of achievement. Public housing applicants must have low incomes; welfare mothers must show they have dependent children and are without other means of support; and a Social Security claimant must have reached a certain age. Thus the benefit constitutes a special, rather than a general or indiscriminate, relationship between the individual and the government. Fourth, the subsidy is usually substantial and important to the beneficiary. For many persons, indeed, the benefit provides the sole source of support, as in the case of most welfare programs; or, as with free higher education or college scholarships, it is a prerequisite to advancement.

These characteristics suggest how government benefits differ from other relationships. Benefits are easily distinguishable from various involuntary relationships involving appropriation of government funds for the support of individual citizens. The room, board, and wage given to persons inducted into the armed forces do superficially resemble benefits, but must be excluded because of the involuntary basis of the relationship. Support of prisoners or persons committed to mental institutions is distinguishable on similar grounds. Support of elementary and secondary education (at least through the age of sixteen) likewise creates no government benefits because school attendance is compulsory.

Second, benefits should be distinguished from myriad government regulations of individual conduct. Most licenses—to drive a car, run a certain kind of business, or practice a profession—look like government benefits but really are not. Licensing serves simply to restrict entry and to regulate or control conduct, or set uniform standards where the participants would otherwise be free to act on their own initiatives and desires. Much the same can be said of passports; the government does not bestow a right to travel by issuing a passport—although such a document may in fact be necessary for an American citizen to enter many foreign countries. The passport, like many other types of regulation, is a form of license.

Third, true benefits should be distinguished from incidental opportunities afforded by government to all persons. Anyone (including an alien) is free, for instance, to travel upon highways and roads built with public funds and maintained at government expense. Recreational use of parks and forests is equally and readily available to all persons. A host of government services and facilities are automatically accessible to anyone who seeks them. These relationships are quite voluntary, of course. But there is no procedure for application or qualification, no agreement between government and individual, nothing special about the status of beneficiary. Such opportunities, moreover, are seldom essential to the recipient, save possibly for the costly services performed for special groups such as farmers, private airplane pilots, and owners of small craft. Thus it seems appropriate to exclude these opportunities from a discussion of government benefits.

Finally, benefits must be distinguished from certain individual rights inherent in a democratic constitutional government. The franchise, for example, is an opportunity provided by government to all citizens, and has some of the character of a benefit. But the right to vote, like the right to speak or to worship freely, the freedom to marry and raise a family, and other comparable liberties, is so central to democracy that government cannot abridge it except under the most extreme circumstances. (Convicted felons and illiterate persons may be denied the franchise, and one may not speak or worship in a way that endangers the lives of his fellow citizens. But the exceptions are few, extraordinary, and temporary.) Thus the basic attributes of citizenship clearly are not benefits in the sense in which that term is used here. They are too vital to be deemed an exercise of the government's dispensing power.

Yet despite the extent of our dependence upon government, American attitudes toward public subsidy reflect an archaic sense of self-sufficiency. We refuse to recognize the reality of relations between government and the citizen. Characteristic is the ambivalence of the merchant or manufacturer who inveighs against "big government" and espouses a Darwinian model of competition, but insists that his business cannot survive without government largesse—whether in the form of a protective tariff or outright cash subsidy. Like many others who depend on the government but do not like to admit their dependence, the businessman may actually believe that government benefits go only to those who are helpless or lazy, or both.

Equally prevalent is an assumption that the government can take away, qualify, or condition whatever it gives. This view is understandably prevalent among the middle and upper classes, who resist recognition of their own dependence upon the government. What is surprising is the extent to which the poor—those for whom welfare and public housing are a way of life—accept the government's power to encumber and to withdraw at will the benefits it extends. The result is a pervasive reluctance to find any claim of right in, or entitlement to, government benefits—a reluctance that shapes the attitudes of the dependent as well as the independent or semidependent.

The American legal system reflects and perpetuates these assumptions. Until very recently, the courts held that government employment, attendance at a state college or university, and public housing occupancy were bare "privileges" that could be subject to almost any conditions or qualifications. The terminology has changed a bit in the last decade; courts seldom use the language of "privilege" today. But the results in the cases have not changed radically, despite the more benign view of the beneficiary's interest. And the courts pass upon only a tiny fraction of the arbitrary denials or callous withdrawals of government benefits. The worst cases probably never even reach the courts—for the simple reason that people who are most heavily dependent upon the government for subsistence are least likely to fight its decisions.

The cases that do reach the courts are usually judged by a double standard. There is a striking disparity between the protections afforded a person who is on trial for a crime, and the government beneficiary whose government job, scholarship, or welfare payments are in jeopardy. Every schoolchild learns about the constitutional safeguards assured in a criminal trial. The defendant is entitled to notice of the specific charges against him, to a trial by an impartial jury of his peers, and to representation by counsel—with the state required to provide an attorney if he cannot afford to hire his own. Evidence obtained through an illegal search cannot be introduced against him, and he may not be compelled to testify against himself. He has a right to appeal his conviction, and to have a copy of the trial transcript prepared at public expense. These and other safeguards must be followed before a court can commit a person to prison or levy a fine.

Few of these safeguards are found in a contest over the denial or withdrawal of a government benefit. (Government employees, for instance, can still be fired without a hearing unless civil service regulations or academic tenure provisions require one.) The double standard rests on the assumption that the criminal trial and penalties are so much more serious that wholly different and far more sensitive procedures should be followed to convict than to take away a benefit. This assumption is fundamentally unsound, as resort to common sense and general experience will readily suggest.

Often the loss of a government benefit constitutes a "punishment" far more serious than a criminal sentence. A state university student may be willing to risk arrest and payment of a substantial fine or even a rather stiff jail sentence for a sit-in or demonstration. But that same student will take a quite different view of expulsion or dismissal from the university for the same offense. The opportunity to continue a higher education at public expense is of substantially greater value to most students than the $100 he might be fined, or even staying out of jail.

A driver for a municipal bus company can afford to pay a heavy fine for a traffic offense much more readily than he can risk the loss of his job for the same infraction. The job is of substantially greater value to the employee than avoidance of all but the most serious criminal punishment. And the collateral consequences of dismissal may be far more serious: while he cannot easily get another driving job after a serious traffic offense, a criminal record is far less likely to hurt his chances in other lines of work than is an involuntary loss of employment. (Much the same can be said of the college student: expulsion from one school will affect the student's eligibility for admission to another institution much more seriously than will a sit-in conviction.)

A tax-exempt foundation can accept a court order against certain activities, or even the criminal conviction of one of its officers, much more readily than it can risk loss of its tax exemption or its charter. The foundation can still function even with the president in prison, so long as the exemption survives.

A layman would, therefore, expect the legal system to protect the interests of the government beneficiary at least as rigorously as those of the person charged with crime. One would assume that benefits should ordinarily not be withdrawn or denied for reasons that would not support a criminal conviction.

The purpose of this book is to suggest why and to what extent the layman's assumption does not accord with the legal reality, and to show what is being done in the courts to abolish the double standard. For at no time in the history of government benefit programs has this double standard come under such bitter and persistent attack as today.

The dimensions of the government benefits problem have only been hinted at. In order to appreciate the real significance of the pervasive double standard, a random survey or catalogue of incidents may be helpful. The one that follows is illustrative rather than definitive.

A baby froze to death in Arlington, Virginia, because its parents had recently arrived in the state and were not yet eligible for welfare under the one-year-residence requirement. A mother on welfare in Chicago confessed to a serious crime after police threatened to remove her and her children from the welfare rolls if she did not cooperate with them. An unmarried welfare mother in Santa Barbara was offered probation after conviction for a narcotics crime, but only on condition that she agree immediately to a sterilization operation.

A graduate student in Westchester County, New York, married and the father of two children, lost his draft deferment because he told his local board of his support for Dr. Benjamin Spock, then on trial for antidraft conspiracy. A Maryland man applied for a notary public's commission but was rejected because he refused to swear that he believed in God.

Public school teachers in Seward, Alaska, Lockport, Illinois, and Susanville, California, were discharged for making public statements critical of local school board policies. Public housing tenants in Newark, Durham, and Sacramento received eviction notices shortly after being elected to head anti-administration tenants' unions.

A jobless worker in Ohio was denied unemployment compensation because he refused to swear he did not advocate the overthrow of the government. A model hired to pose for a junior college art class in Walnut Creek, California, was denied her modeling fee when she refused to sign a similar loyalty oath.

A welfare caseworker in Oakland, California, was fired for refusing to take part in a series of surprise predawn raids to check the homes of some of his clients. Also in Oakland, a career public health doctor was discharged under a county rule forbidding partisan political activity; he had organized a speakers' bureau in another county for a gubernatorial candidate.

The security clearance of a geologist in New York was revoked after he protested city police handling of an antiwar demonstration. An American Peace Corps volunteer in Chile was dismissed because he wrote a letter to *The New York Times* that sharply criticized United States policy in Vietnam.

The ashes of a World War II veteran, who had won the Distinguished Service Cross in Pacific combat, were denied a last resting place in Arlington National Cemetery because he had once been convicted of conspiring to teach and advocate the overthrow of the government.

An unemployed man in upstate New York was taken off welfare when he refused to cut brush in knee-deep snow. Benefits were denied to a mother of several children in rural Georgia who refused a job as field hand at wages below her welfare payments. A Catholic welfare mother in San Francisco was denied further aid unless she agreed to file a divorce suit against the husband who had abandoned her and her child.

A student editor at a small Southern state college was summarily expelled for publishing an editorial critical of the governor and some members of the legislature.

A Negro civil rights organization in New Orleans was denied use of the municipal auditorium because it would not formally accept the city's "official" policy on segregation. A scheduled community concert in a Long Island high school auditorium was canceled by local officials because the program included controversial folk singer Pete Seeger. The American Nazi Party was denied use of New York's Union Square for a July 4th rally because the Commissioner of Parks feared the speakers' remarks might offend or anger the audience.

These examples are more representative than extraordinary. Many parallel catalogues could be compiled from the daily newspaper as well as from court decisions. A mere parade of horrors does not, however, establish the importance of the subject. Several other factors also attest to the need for a thorough study of conditions and restrictions on government benefits. There are important common elements recurrent in these cases; the profound similarities between government beneficiaries are typically obscured by the more obvious but less meaningful differences. One must probe well below the surface to find the parallels between the case of the welfare mother removed from the rolls because of disapproved sexual behavior and that of the college professor or government engineer discharged for unorthodox political beliefs or associations.

Second, it is worth studying government benefits and the restrictions imposed on them because of the rising volume of government subsidy in almost all sectors. Bare figures will document the mounting importance of the problem. Between 1960 and 1968, the number of federal domestic social (including educational) programs increased from 45 to 435. The budget for these programs rose from just under $10 billion at the end of the Eisenhower administration to slightly over $25 billion at the close of the Johnson years. The growth of individual components of that budget are particularly impressive: federal funds for health care jumped from $3 billion to just under $15 billion during these years; for education, from about $2 billion to $11 billion annually; and there were comparable increases in federal funds for the aged, for the poor, and for children and youth. Although state and local appropriations have grown less dramatically, the overall trends in the sheer volume and proportions of government benefits make imperative a study of qualifications, conditions, restrictions, and procedures for termination.

A third factor is surely relevant, although its bearing may be less obvious. The public sector is far from tranquil these days. The causes of the unrest—protests and disruptions on state university campuses, teacher and sanitation workers' strikes, and welfare client sit-ins and marches—are unclear. But there is a rather close correlation between these manifestations of malaise and the rising levels of government subsidies. The greatest expansion in public higher education has taken place since 1960, so that today about two out of every three college students are on publicly supported campuses. The rise in campus demonstrations, disruptions, and protests has almost paralleled these enrollment trends. The startling increase in strikes by public employees has come at a time when wages for many jobs in the public sector are overtaking comparable private pay scales, and government fringe benefits are often superior. Militancy among welfare clients has had a similar history: the first effective organization of welfare recipients (followed by marches, sit-ins, and "strikes") has accompanied the fastest increase ever in welfare and health care benefits.

It is uncertain whether there is any causal relationship between the improving quality of the fare and the biting of the hand that feeds. The United States may be experiencing what historians call a "revolution of rising expectations." Protests and demands may have been partially a response to the incomplete fulfillment of the goals of the disadvantaged and the dependent, and to frustrations created by the gap that remains. Meanwhile, the improvement in levels, amounts, and scope of benefits may have focused attention for the first time on nonmonetary differences between beneficiaries and other citizens who are independent of government. While the welfare client was worrying about the source or adequacy of his next meal, he had little time to ponder the caseworker's attitude toward an extramarital affair. The college student compelled to work full time to pay the tuition at a private college or to pay off a large loan was unlikely to mount the barricades to protest rules against political activity. The government worker whose main concern was achieving job security through civil service, or reaching a salary grade where he could support his family decently, would probably not balk at signing a loyalty oath or protest a ban on partisan political involvement. But when the monetary levels of benefits have become adequate—and roughly comparable to the levels available from private sources—the beneficiary may well focus on the nonmonetary differences between the public and private sectors. Those differences, long neglected or unrealized because of more pressing monetary concerns, suddenly assume a significance that may go far to explain both the timing and the extent of the malaise in the public sector. While strikers and demonstrators seldom mention such factors as a cause of protest, that omission is not conclusive. The real impact of these differences may, indeed, be more subconscious than conscious.

I. *Types of Conditioned Benefits*

Some mention has already been made of the major types of government benefits. Since these will be the major focus of this book, it seems appropriate to review each in more detail. The five major categories of beneficiaries include government employees, students at state colleges and universities, welfare recipients, tenants in public housing projects, and occasional or incidental users of public property. This listing does not, however, exhaust the broad spectrum of government subsidy. Thus completeness requires a distinct category to cover recipients of such varied benefits as tax exemptions and draft deferments.

CONDITIONS ON GOVERNMENT EMPLOYMENT

Government working conditions and wages may often be superior to those in private business. Yet in a variety of ways, the public employee is subjected to restrictions and disabilities not imposed upon workers performing nearly identical tasks in the private sector. Applicants for government jobs in some forty states have been required to sign loyalty oaths. While some demand only a simple promise to uphold the Constitution and the laws, the oaths of other states have demanded a negative disclaimer of vaguely defined "subversive" political associations.

The government worker is barred—both on and off the job —from a wide range of political activities that could not constitutionally be denied a worker in the private sector. If he publicly calls for a major change in government policy, he may lose his job. Or he may jeopardize his position by refusing to perform what he deems an unconstitutional task; for example, a social worker may be required to conduct a predawn raid on a client's home, or a high school teacher may be required to lead his class in a flag-salute exercise against his religious or conscientious scruples.

In various ways, public employees forego personal privacy which other citizens enjoy. Intake questionnaires and on-the-job surveys may probe, often embarrassingly, innermost feelings and intensely personal experiences. Collection of data by the employing agency may create a kind of "big brother" atmosphere for the staff.

Ongoing surveillance through compulsory lie detector tests or periodic psychological examinations may further threaten the public worker's privacy. Finally, those who work for the government are denied a wide range of labor-organizing and collective-bargaining activities that are legally guaranteed to employees of private firms. Even where public employees are allowed to organize and bargain collectively, the right to strike is denied by law. There is an obvious relationship between the last point and those made previously: in private industry, it is frequently the presence of a strong union, with an effective grievance machinery, that protects the workers from those indignities and disabilities that government officials can usually impose without fear of a strike.

STATE COLLEGE AND UNIVERSITY STUDENTS

Many legislators and educational administrators still consider attendance at a state college or university a "privilege" that can be suspended or withdrawn summarily. Thus they feel admission to college can be conditioned on a surrender of various constitutional liberties.

Despite the general abandonment of the condescending doctrine of *in loco parentis,* vestiges of that governing principle linger. State colleges frequently insist, for example, on unscheduled visits to student rooms in residence halls when a search warrant clearly could not be obtained to inspect an off-campus apartment, even though the college's own rule, rather than the student's choice, may keep him in the dormitory. Student editors of college newspapers and magazines are denied a large measure of freedom of the press which applies off campus. Editors may publish at their peril editorials or articles disapproved by the faculty advisor or other university officials.

The most serious disparity is, however, a procedural one. Until quite recently, summary dismissals or expulsions were the rule rather than the exception. Under pressure of court decrees ordering reinstatement of dismissed students, major universities have begun to reshape their rules of procedure to comport with due process. But the procedures still used by many state colleges would be unacceptable even in a criminal trial for petty larceny.

WELFARE RECIPIENTS

The most heavily dependent group of government beneficiaries is also probably the least protected. The protection of the rights and liberties of people on welfare is so recent a phenomenon that no substantial body of law yet exists. The issues in this field are quite varied and complex. All but a handful of states until recently required an indigent newcomer to the state to wait six months to a year (in one case, five years) before becoming eligible for welfare. Political restrictions are sometimes imposed on welfare recipients; a loyalty oath was originally required of elderly applicants for Medicare but was eliminated after several court tests.

Many welfare restrictions are aimed at the unmarried mother, and thus have a built-in racial bias. Most states have adopted some form of "substitute father" or "man in the house" rule. Under such rules, payments are reduced or denied altogether to otherwise eligible mothers if there is a man living with the family or even associating more than casually with the mother. This policy often applies even though the man may be under no legal obligation to support the children; may not, in fact, have provided any support; and may even have been incapable of supporting them.

Welfare mothers are frequently required to accept any employment that is available and offered to them. These "employable mother" policies tend to force poor women into menial domestic and field work. The onus of these requirements is compounded by removing the mother from the welfare rolls when she either accepts or refuses employment—even though her wages may be substantially lower than the meager welfare check she has been receiving.

The privacy of the welfare recipient's home may be threatened almost as much as his independence is destroyed. Many welfare departments have conducted "midnight raids" or searches to ferret out evidence of welfare fraud or violation. These searches are easy and often successful simply because few welfare clients dare to bar the caseworker. The relationship between caseworker and client is such that explicit threats may be unnecessary to gain entry. The client naturally assumes that his payments will be jeopardized by any resistance on his part.

USERS OF PUBLIC PROPERTY

As government is an employer, educator, and benefactor, it is also a property owner and landlord. In its landholding capacity, government occasionally restricts the liberties of its citizens who lease or license its property. There has been a running battle over the General Services Administration's regulation of newspapers and magazines to be sold on newsstands in Federal Government buildings. Some local transit agencies have restricted types of advertising they will display in buses, streetcars, and subway trains. Although such advertising space is generally available to commercial slogans and political candidates, it has often been denied to controversial and unpopular causes such as opposition to the Vietnam war.

Local governments have hampered free use of municipal and school auditoriums and even staging areas in public parks for controversial political meetings and rallies. Restrictive criteria and disclaimer affidavits have sometimes been imposed as a way of screening applicants. Nowhere have these restrictions been more rigorously imposed than on state college and university campuses. The "speaker ban" controversy has been the cause of more than one major student demonstration. Only gradually have college governing boards recognized that the exclusion of a controversial speaker from the campus altogether may be far harder to defend even than his wildest statements.

PUBLIC HOUSING

The government is also a landlord on a massive scale through the Public Housing Program. In the three decades since enactment of the Federal Public Housing Act, millions of American families have lived and grown up in huge government-owned, often barren and barrack-like, projects. Apart from the psychological and aesthetic tragedy of project life, public housing administration generates substantial legal problems. In many cities, women with illegitimate children are systematically excluded from projects. Frequently, a single serious criminal violation will deprive an otherwise qualified applicant of space in a housing project. Even where the offender is not part of the applicant's immediate family, a fel-

ony record of a close relative may render the family vaguely "unde-
sirable" and therefore inadmissible. In some cities, applicants have
been barred because of juvenile offenses many years ago which
have long since been forgiven for other purposes.

Public housing programs have threatened the political liberties of tenants in several ways. Federal law once required all applicants for project space to sign an "antisubversive" affidavit. That
approach to political conformity has long since been abandoned. In
its place, however, has come a different and subtler form of political control—sanctions against collective protest activities by militant tenants. Leaders of tenants' unions have been evicted soon after emerging as tenant spokesmen, especially during times of tension and conflict between tenants and management.

The rights and liberties of public housing tenants have been
even less well protected by the courts than those of public employees, state college students, and welfare recipients. There is much
less precedent by which to control the discretion of project managers in these sensitive areas. The typical tenant, moreover, has only
the minimal security of a month-to-month lease. Since either party
may end the tenancy by giving a month's notice, and since the management is seldom required by law to grant a hearing, there is little
opportunity for the tenant to prove that an eviction violated his constitutional rights. The applicant who is barred at the threshold is, of
course, in an even weaker position. He cannot require the authority
to respond to his request within a reasonable time, much less to give
him reasons for an adverse decision.

MISCELLANEOUS BENEFITS

These five major categories by no means exhaust the range of
benefit programs encumbered by conditions. Indeed, some of the
most difficult cases have arisen outside of these five areas. The dimensions of this miscellaneous category may be illustrated by several problems concerning scholarships, draft deferments, and tax
exemptions. Significantly, only one of these three government benefits involves the payment of money to the beneficiary—although
all three meet the definition of a government benefit set forth earlier
in the chapter. Their inclusion here is both appropriate and necessary to complete the survey of the topic.

For the state college student, the opportunity of a higher education largely at public expense may well be the most important benefit. But for the private university student (and the very needy state student), access to government scholarships, fellowships, and work-study payments may be almost as vital. Government assistance to students has long been a target for the indignation of conservative legislators who see students as the most dangerous and least grateful of public beneficiaries.

Within recent memory, government and higher education have come about as close to a standoff over the National Defense Education Act loyalty oath as over any issue. The oath requirement, attached to NDEA loan appropriations in 1958, applied to all students receiving loan funds under the Act. Many colleges and universities (including most of the Ivy League) so deeply opposed the attribution of disloyalty to their students and the intrusion into internal university affairs that they refused any NDEA funds. A larger number of institutions continued to accept NDEA loans, but protested strenuously until the oath requirement was repealed in 1962.

Recent restrictions on scholarships and fellowships have raised again the specter of political tests for students. After the wave of campus disturbances in the spring of 1968, Congress provided for withholding federal aid to student demonstrators. The precise language varied somewhat from one measure to another. Under some programs, aid must be terminated upon proof that the student "wilfully refused to obey a lawful regulation or order" of the University, and after a hearing on the question. Another student aid law penalized only students convicted of crimes on the campus involving (in the words of the statute) the "use of force, disruption, or seizure of property under control of such institution" where the crime "was of a serious nature and contributed to the substantial disruption of the administration of the institution. . . ." By the fall of 1968, almost every graduate and undergraduate student receiving federal funds was subject to one or the other (or both) of these disabilities.

If financial aid is one government benefit which a college student can ill afford to lose, the other benefit upon which the male student depends is his Selective Service deferment. This benefit has also proved highly vulnerable to political pressures and restrictions. In the fall of 1965, Selective Service Director Louis B. Hershey urged that deferments be denied to or taken away from students who demonstrated against the war and the draft. When a federal court in New York upset a reclassification of two students who had taken part in a sit-in at a Michigan draft board, the General simply withdrew to await the next encounter. By the fall of 1967, he was ready to revive his earlier mandate. In a directive to all local draft boards, Hershey suggested that students involved in demonstrations or protests against military recruiting—at least where the activity was unlawful—should be reclassified at once as "I—A Delinquent" —and thus moved to the top of the induction list. The Justice Department opposed the Hershey policy on the ground that criminal sanctions should be the sole punishment for such conduct; the informal deliberations of the draft boards should not be substituted for the due process of the courts—particularly where freedom of speech might be at stake. Despite numerous attacks within and without the government, however, Hershey refused to alter his recommendation to punish antiwar demonstrators by canceling their deferments.

It soon became clear that the Hershey directive was no idle threat. Several dozen students and one Catholic chaplain lost deferments after they returned or burned draft cards during the 1967–68 school year. A student at Oberlin College was reclassified because he had taken part in a campus demonstration against a Navy recruiter; only after frequent appeals by the student and the college administration was the deferment restored. A married graduate student with two children was reclassified and ordered to report for induction after sending to his draft board a "letter of complicity" sharing guilt for the antidraft conspiracy for which Dr. Benjamin Spock and others had been indicted.

Finally, tax exemptions for foundations and other organizations have been restricted and conditioned for seemingly political goals. In the spring of 1966, California's Sierra Club—a conservation group with some forty thousand members, including a half dozen United States congressmen—campaigned publicly against construction of two dams that would flood much of the Grand Canyon. The Club ran full-page ads in *The New York Times* and the *Washington Post* condemning plans for the dams. Four days later, internal revenue officials publicly questioned the Club's eligibility for tax-deductible contributions and began an audit of its books. The announced purpose of the investigation was to determine whether the exemption had been lost by engaging in lobbying activities; federal tax regulations provide that attempts to influence legislation may not constitute a "substantial part" of an exempt organization's activities. A finding that the organization has engaged "substantially" in lobbying will cancel the exemption—regardless of the objectives of the campaign. After an administrative hearing, IRS did withdraw the exemption because of the Grand Canyon battle.

II. *The Rationale of Conditions*

It is clear enough why government bestows benefits. Far less apparent are the reasons for attaching conditions and restrictions to these benefits. Any study of the conditioning process must understand these reasons, for a restriction on a government program cannot be reviewed by a court without some knowledge of why the responsible legislators or administrators initially imposed it.

The reasons for imposing conditions on benefits are infinitely varied, complex, and even conflicting. Easy explanations are rare—if only because of the diverse rationale of any legislation enacted by a large body of members with differing constituencies and personal philosophies. One example may illustrate the difficulty of identifying a single purpose for a seemingly simple restriction on a benefit program. At one time, the Federal Job Corps program excluded all applicants with criminal records. There never was a public announcement or explanation of this restriction, although it must have been communicated through the usual internal machinery to those who screened candidates.

The most obvious reason for such a restriction would be a judgment that former delinquents might disrupt the training camps. Equally, however, those in charge of the program might have felt, in allocating a limited number of places, that preference should be given to applicants with clean records. Or the restriction may have been imposed by the Job Corps because of the greater difficulty anticipated in placing former delinquents in steady jobs. An equally plausible explanation is the deterrent effect which such a policy might have: if word got around that a single offense would keep one out of the Job Corps, then potentially eligible youth might be careful to stay out of trouble. In this way the Job Corps could discourage crime and promote good citizenship while serving the primary mission of providing job training. Finally, there is a simple but appealing explanation for the restriction: when an agency is faced with a difficult selection process, any simple device that will reduce the eligible population and make the screening easier is always welcome. Here is a ready-made self-selector, which bears at least a tenuous relationship to the goals of the program. Yet there is no assurance that any of these factors, or any combination of them, really explains the Job Corps exclusion policy.

The recently imposed "riot-ban" restrictions on federal aid to college students further illustrate the difficulty of identifying catalysts. If one reads the legislative history of these restrictions added to appropriation bills in 1968 and 1969, one purpose emerges clearly—to punish students who engage in disruptive conduct on college campuses, and to deter other students from such activity in the future. But below the surface, there are at least two other concerns. To some legislators, never overly supportive of student aid programs, these restrictions may have offered an opportunity to cut back the scope and coverage of the college aid programs in a way that was politically acceptable. (Direct curtailment of benefit programs, particularly in the areas of education and welfare, is seldom popular; indirect curtailment through antiradical restrictions may be quite palatable.) For Congressional liberals, some of whom supported the restrictions, there was clearly a third concern: to give strife-torn universities and their administrators an added weapon in dealing with nihilistic students. Unlike the NDEA loyalty oath, these restrictions did not superimpose a system of penalties onto the university's disciplinary system, but simply added another, albeit external, sanction to the university's own rather bare arsenal.

There is one pervasive explanation for many conditions that cannot be dignified as a legislative purpose or goal. Many government programs reflect the middle-class stereotype of the beneficiary who is too lazy, too weak, too old, or too young to fend for himself and must therefore be supported by the tax revenues from his fellow citizens. Legislators who begin with that assumption about the nature of government benefits are unlikely to bestow any government subsidy—at least to the poor—without exacting some price to underscore the "inferiority" and the dependence of the recipients. Many conditions on government benefits represent a *quid pro quo* of this sort whether in the form of a loyalty oath, a waiver of some interest in personal privacy, or the stripping of one's assets.

The legislator or administrator who views the beneficiary in this light is reluctant to give with the left hand unless the right hand has either held back a slice of the bounty, or soured its taste enough to make the recipient conscious of his dependence upon his more industrious and self-sufficient benefactors.

Against this background, we may begin to identify the purposes or objectives of the conditions most frequently attached to government benefit programs. Some conditions may be traceable to only one of these purposes; others may well reflect a composite or amalgam of several objectives.

CONDITIONS DESIGNED TO GATHER INFORMATION OR MAINTAIN RECORDS

The legislature may demand extensive information about the beneficiaries in order to build up accurate and informative records, to evaluate the program, or to facilitate development of other programs. This end will usually be served by requiring the applicant to fill out various forms, or to supply information subsequently. He may even be required to answer questions under oath, or to have his replies checked with a lie detector. Questions or requests for information may not at first seem to constitute conditions on the benefit; yet if the benefit is denied to one who withholds information, the restrictive effect of the inquiry is clear enough.

Most questions on application forms that are asked only for information purposes seem innocuous enough. But where the inquiry probes into the applicant's political views, or his sexual behavior, or his religious beliefs, it can become highly intrusive. Indeed, serious objections have been raised in Congress and in the press to some rather personal questions on the 1970 census form about family incomes and sharing of bath facilities. These questions may well be intrusive *per se*—even though no information given could incriminate the respondent. Clearly, there are hazards even in those questions that are asked to build up general government data files or to evaluate benefit programs.

CONDITIONS DESIGNED TO ENSURE THE ELIGIBILITY OF BENEFICIARIES

Conditions may seek primarily to ensure that benefits go only to persons for whom the program was designed. Every government benefit program contains conditions that are really no more than eligibility criteria. It is appropriate to require a scholarship applicant to prove that he is a student; or to demand evidence that a Social Security claimant has in fact reached the retirement age; or that an applicant for second-class mailing privileges does regularly publish a periodical.

Such conditions as these sound innocent enough in most areas of benefits. But when one moves to the welfare field, the matter becomes far more complicated. People who are fully capable of supporting themselves clearly should not receive welfare payments. Yet, financial need may best be determined by a detailed examination of the applicant's assets and income. In addition, many states require more than a simple disclosure of information. The applicant may be required not only to prove that he is poor, but to make himself even poorer—typically by divesting himself of all but minimal savings and possessions—before he can receive welfare. Eligibility criteria of this kind not only measure poverty; they may actually create it in some cases.

CONDITIONS DESIGNED TO CONTROL OR RESTRICT THE SCOPE OF THE PROGRAM

Conditions on government benefits may often reflect simply a legislative desire to save money. In a time of rapidly rising welfare, education, and public housing costs, parsimony is a wholly plausible explanation for restrictive conditions. Economy can be achieved, of course, simply by comprehensive reductions in benefit levels—but that approach is likely to be politically unpopular. The same savings may be much more subtly and palatably effected by using conditions and restrictions to reduce the class of eligible beneficiaries.

Economy of another sort may explain certain essentially protectionist conditions imposed on government programs. The United States foreign aid program restricts the use of funds to purchase American goods, shipped in American vessels, and covered by American insurers. "Buy American" programs at both national and state levels involve a similar use of the conditioning power. The Pennsylvania legislature recently passed a bill forbidding the use in state-financed projects of steel produced outside the United States. But the Governor, acting on the advice of the U.S. State Department, vetoed the bill because of its potential impact on American international trade and its invitation to foreign retaliation.

When a public housing authority rejects an applicant whose record shows a penchant for criminal violence, this decision presumably reflects a concern for the welfare of those who would be his neighbors. And if a government agency will not hire, or a state university will not admit as a student, a convicted arsonist or an aggressive homosexual, the judgment reflects a similar precaution. Administrators probably assume that they would be derelict if they did not impose protective restrictions in cases of this type.

CONDITIONS IMPOSED FOR POLITICAL OBJECTIVES

A pervasive (and usually pernicious) purpose of many conditions on government benefits is the furtherance of political orthodoxy or conformity. At the start of his first administration, George Washington announced that he would not "bring men into any office of consequence knowingly whose political tenets are adverse to the measures the general government is pursuing; for this, in my opinion, would be a sort of political suicide." Many years later, Huey Long expressed the same precept less elegantly in explaining why he had ordered the editor of the Louisiana State University student newspaper taken off the state payroll for running an editorial attacking the Long administration: "I'm not payin' anybody to criticize me." Of course the civil service system has drastically curtailed the power of the executive branch to screen employees according to their political views. In fact, the effort to keep the civil service above partisan pressures has so neutralized the political life of the public worker that in most states and in the federal service he can do little more than vote or express his views to his immediate family. Neutrality or detachment has largely superseded orthodoxy as the political goal of conditions on government employment.

Other types of conditions still foster political conformity. Nowhere is this objective more clearly reflected than in the loyalty oaths and disclaimers that have been attached to many government benefits. Oaths and other antisubversive restrictions may have several purposes, but they are all related to political conformity. Legislators may feel they should give preference in awarding public funds to persons who affirmatively demonstrate their loyalty and support for the government. Or they may believe that there are real dangers in bestowing benefits—particularly employment in sensitive positions—upon persons who may possibly have any ties with a foreign or "subversive" cause. There is also a feeling that government funds, if they get into subversive hands, will strengthen the Communist or anti-American cause in some way, and so should be restricted to applicants of impeccable loyalty.

CONDITIONS IMPOSED FOR MORAL OBJECTIVES

Welfare programs are replete with restrictions directed at extramarital relations, promiscuity, and illegitimate births. Public housing projects, too, sometimes exclude or evict unwed mothers. As with political conditions, these moral criteria probably reflect both a positive desire and a negative deterrent—a conviction, on the one hand, that integral families and monogamous mothers should be preferred in the allocation of scarce resources; and a desire, on the other hand, to discourage promiscuity and illegitimacy by such restrictive policies. Legislators enacting such benefit programs may consider themselves to be the guardians of the public morality much as they have long felt a responsibility for the political security of the country when considering loyalty oaths and other political restrictions.

CONDITIONS DESIGNED TO DISCOURAGE DEPENDENCY

In a sense, all conditions and restrictions probably discourage dependency among persons of marginal need simply because they make the benefit less attractive than it would be if it were unencumbered. But some conditions seek specially to aid—or force—the beneficiary to become independent of the benefit to which they are attached. Welfare rules requiring employable mothers to accept work in lieu of welfare are good examples. Some public housing programs encourage tenants to increase their incomes and thus move out of the project. Unemployment compensation and other income supplements are usually available for a limited duration; while the limit may be designed chiefly to reduce the cost of the program, it also forces the beneficiary to become self-sufficient after a certain time. Whether or not a reduction of dependency is a discrete objective in such cases, there is no doubt that many conditions incidentally promote self-sufficiency.

CONDITIONS DESIGNED TO REALLOCATE RESOURCES

A subtle but increasingly fruitful use of the conditioning power lies in the reallocation of human and material resources. The Federal Government encourages recent college graduates to teach in the inner city—where the need for good teachers is clearly greatest—by offering special forgiveness of NDEA loans and scarce occupational draft deferments. Special tax benefits can draw private capital into the central cities and urban ghettos where indigenous development is most urgently needed. And of course income tax deductions for charitable donations to certain kinds of organizations (and not to others, such as political parties) effect a massive redistribution of individual and corporate wealth. While a deduction may not be a "benefit" (as we have defined the term) to the individual taxpayer, there can be no question about the tax *exemption* by which the recipient assures the donor a deduction for his gift. In these and numerous other ways, government uses conditioned and restricted benefits to channel and reallocate private resources in support of governmental objectives.

CONDITIONS DESIGNED TO ACHIEVE INDIRECTLY
GOVERNMENTAL GOALS THAT CANNOT BE ACHIEVED
THROUGH DIRECT REGULATION

Cutting across many of these objectives—and yet distinct from them—is the increasing resort to conditioned benefits as a way of doing indirectly what the government cannot easily accomplish by direct means. The Federal Government especially has come to appreciate the conditioning power as an alternative mode of regulation, sometimes far faster and more efficient than the direct sanctions on which government has traditionally relied. Conditioning of benefits affords a flexible alternative to criminal prosecution and civil injunction—a carrot in place of the traditional stick.

Desegregation of the public schools points up the contrasting effectiveness of the two approaches. The United States Supreme

Court held in 1954 that racial segregation imposed by law was unconstitutional. During the next decade, when the government relied chiefly on federal court suits brought by individual Negro parents, and later by the Justice Department, barely any progress was made in breaking down racial barriers in Southern school systems. In fact, segregation actually intensified in some areas.

Ten years and a month after the Supreme Court decision, Congress passed the Civil Rights Act of 1964. This law gave federal officials a powerful arsenal of new weapons to deal with racial discrimination. Most potent of these new weapons was the provision (Title VI) that federal funds could no longer be allocated to any program in which racial segregation was practiced. Each agency was to draft and implement its own program for barring discrimination. The Department of Health, Education and Welfare immediately set to work on this task; three years later it had an enforcement unit of some three hundred persons and an elaborate set of desegregation guidelines applicable to districts receiving federal funds.

Vastly more important than the creation of the machinery, however, was the measure of its accomplishment. By summer of 1967, HEW and Civil Rights Commission officials noted with obvious satisfaction that more progress had been made in three years by threatening to cut off federal funds from recalcitrant Southern school districts than federal court lawsuits had achieved in a decade.

Comparable progress was made in desegregating other federally assisted programs. Alabama welfare officials, after stubbornly resisting direct federal pressures to end segregation in state-supported health and nursing facilities, eventually (if reluctantly) yielded to a threat of withdrawal of federal funds for the state's welfare programs.

The Federal Government has also invoked indirect solutions to the persistent problem of finding adequate jobs for minority groups. The 1964 Civil Rights Act banned discrimination in hiring and promotion by most private firms employing over twenty-five workers. An Equal Employment Opportunity Commission was created to enforce the new law; the Labor Department and other branches of the Federal Government gave it high priority during the next few years. But unemployment rates for nonwhites remained roughly twice those for whites, despite a steady decline in both through the mid-1960s. The jobless rate for nonwhite teenagers remained alarmingly above that for white youths. Simple enforcement of nondiscrimination in the private sector seemed incapable, by itself, of opening up adequate job opportunities. Nor would that approach meet the even tougher problem of underemployment and subemployment in the urban ghettos, to which the Report of The National Advisory Commission on Civil Disorders drew urgent national attention.

The two years that followed release of the Commission report saw a marked acceleration of induced integration. One major step was the issuance in the spring of 1968 of a Presidential Executive Order banning job discrimination in virtually all federal contracts. The order was quickly followed by Labor Department regulations requiring each contractor and his subcontractors to undertake "affirmative action" programs to ensure at least some black faces and Spanish names on the job. But the major break with tradition was to come a year and a half later when the new Secretary of Labor, George Schultz, announced the highly controversial "Philadelphia Plan." Under its terms, federal contractors in the Philadelphia area were required to set and meet minority group quotas for their work forces in six skilled crafts. The quotas, beginning at 4 percent of the work force in 1969, were to reach 26 percent by 1973. Despite vehement opposition to the quota system from both union and management sectors, the Philadelphia Plan appeared almost certain to be extended throughout the country, at least to major urban areas with substantial nonwhite unemployment.

The Federal Government could not constitutionally compel a private business firm to adopt a minority quota hiring policy. So drastic a step was imposed as a condition on the important benefit of federal construction contracts only because the limits of direct regulation had been reached and found inadequate. It now remains to be seen whether the carrot will succeed where the stick has failed.

This discussion suggests one important principle about the conditioning of benefits that should be apparent by now but deserves specific recognition: not all conditions, by any means, are repressive or intrusive to the beneficiary, or geared to doubtful governmental goals. As the effective use of conditions to promote desegregation and deter discrimination suggests, conditions may be and often are used for ameliorative and quite positive purposes as well. Beautification, for example, has been a vital ingredient of the federal highway program. States seeking funds for road construction must comply with federal billboard control restrictions, including removal of deviant display advertising, or they will lose 10 percent of federal highway assistance.

Some urban renewal and improvement plans have made similar use of the conditioning power. Zoning variances may be disallowed, for example, unless certain aesthetic conditions are met. Where the historical motif is crucial—as on Boston's Beacon Hill or in New Orleans' Vieux Carré—major alterations or repairs may not be undertaken until the building's owner has demonstrated the authenticity and conformance of his plans to the restoration pattern. (Officials in St. Augustine, Florida, planning observance of the city's four hundredth anniversary, offered space in the restored Spanish quarter to a French patisserie—but only on the condition, with which the baker reluctantly complied, that the menu include a selection of Spanish dishes.) Government possesses a vast range of largely untapped power to affect the environment through conditioned benefits.

The conditioning power is clearly a two-edged sword. Not all conditions, by any means, are objectionable. Some conditions (such as the desegregation requirements imposed on Southern hospitals and school districts) may be objectionable to the recipient but are designed to promote the general welfare or serve valid constitutional ends. Yet it is clearly improper to judge the validity of conditions by the goals they seek to achieve. If there are any limits on governmental power, they must surely restrict the means as well as the ends. Government should not be able to bring about desegregation, for example, by forcing Southern school officials to waive the privacy of their homes and personal files as the price of receiving federal funds. There must be some assessment of the validity of conditions and restrictions entirely apart from the goals or ends they seek to serve. Developing a framework for that assessment is the concern of the next chapter.

II

THE POWER

TO WITHHOLD AND

THE POWER

TO CONDITION

I. *The Greater and the Lesser*

A government benefit results from a relationship that appears voluntary on both sides. Why, therefore, should government not be able to give or deny benefits to whomever it wishes, and make them available on whatever terms it deems appropriate? The suggestion has a more than superficial appeal. Some thirty years ago, the case for complete discretion in the dispensing of government benefits was posed in this way: "If I have no ground for complaint at being denied a privilege absolutely, it is hard to see how I acquire such a ground merely because the state, instead of denying me a privilege outright, offers me an alternative, however harsh." If the citizen has no right to the benefit, the argument runs, he has no legal basis to object either to an arbitrary withholding of the benefit, or to the attachment of conditions and restrictions that may put him to a hard choice.

This argument proceeds from the premise that government is not legally required to confer benefits at all. Thus, there is no duty to bestow a particular benefit on any one applicant or claimant. A particular benefit, it is asserted, may therefore be denied to any person at any time for any reason. As a corollary, benefits which need never have been extended or created in the first place may be withdrawn or terminated at any time and on any ground. Or the terms on which they were granted may be changed to suit the desires and needs of the grantor. Since no reason need be given for denying a benefit outright, it follows that no reason need be given for taking away the benefit already granted. Finally, if there is no right to know why the benefit was withdrawn, the beneficiary has no claim to a hearing or other opportunity to contest the termination or to demonstrate his continuing eligibility.

There is another premise at the heart of the argument: since government may at its discretion invoke the "greater" power to deny a benefit outright or to terminate it without explanation, it can exercise the "lesser" power of granting or renewing the benefit subject to conditions or restrictions of its determination. The applicant who cannot complain when the government refuses to grant him the benefit at all can hardly object when that benefit is offered with strings attached, however offensive those strings may be.

This line of reasoning does have a superficial appeal, but will not survive careful analysis. There are two basic and disabling flaws. First, it is far from clear that a "greater" power always permits the exercise of a "lesser" power. Second, there is grave doubt whether the power to deny something outright is in fact the greater, and the power to condition it the lesser.

The argument developed here clearly proves too much. If the existence of a greater power justifies the use of a lesser power, then a criminal defendant subject to execution after conviction could be put to death by slow torture. The answer to this suggestion is found in the constitutional prohibition against punishment that is "cruel and unusual." It is equally clear that a military deserter who could be shot on sight cannot constitutionally be stripped of his American citizenship if he is captured—even though exile would seem clearly to be the "lesser" power within the "greater" power to take the deserter's life. In other areas, too, the courts have refused to accept the argument that a "greater" power justifies "lesser" acts. Although it does not deal directly with governmental power, there is an important analogy in the labor field: the Supreme Court has held that an employer wishing to avoid unionization can go completely out of business, but cannot selectively close down part of his business to blunt the union's organizing efforts. Here again, the Court has quite logically rejected the claim that the "greater" always comprehends the "lesser."

There is an even more basic flaw in the argument. The root assumption—that the attachment of conditions to a benefit is a "lesser" act than outright denial of the benefit—is fundamentally unsound. It overlooks, for one thing, the tension and ambivalence inevitably created by the offer of an attractive benefit encumbered by unattractive strings. The unexplained denial of a benefit will probably alter no conduct except that which would have been made possible by the benefit itself. But where conditions or restrictions are imposed, the natural response of the person who wants or needs the benefit badly enough is to change his behavior (or even his beliefs) to suit the grantor's demands.

Thus the very attachment of conditions may well influence human conduct far more significantly than the unexplained withholding or withdrawal of a benefit. Frequently, therefore, the power to condition may actually be the "greater" of the two if the test of importance is the impact upon present and prospective beneficiaries. Yet the two powers really are not related in this way at all; the question which is the "greater" or the "lesser" misses the point badly. "The power to impose conditions," one commentator has said, "is not a lesser part of the power to withhold, but instead is a distinct exercise of a power which must find its own justification." The inquiry into such justifications for conditions is one we have already begun and will pursue in later chapters.

The argument for unlimited use of the conditioning power proves too much in another respect. The notion that government may impose whatever restrictions it wishes upon a benefit would support the conclusion that benefits could be categorically denied to Protestants, or to whites, or to blacks, or to people with blue eyes. The Fourteenth Amendment of the United States Constitution, repository of the equal protection clause, will not allow such distinctions in any governmental programs, regardless of the importance of the benefit. Government may not use racial, religious, or ethnic differences as a basis for bestowing benefits any more than for imposing burdens.

It is true that a legislature or agency may decide not to launch a benefit program because Negroes or Catholics or some other group would profit disproportionately. Such a decision not to enter the field at all would presumably be unimpeachable in the courts, whatever the motive. But it is quite another matter to say that once the program has begun, government may withhold enjoyment of it from certain persons and groups along lines incompatible with the equal protection clause. Once government acts at all, and discriminates in doing so, the constitution has been violated. Thus there are clearly some conditions and restrictions that government may not attach to even the most incidental of its benefits.

Other branches of the law, quite unrelated to government benefits, have recognized a vital distinction between complete inaction and action promised or taken. For centuries, the common law of contracts, property, and torts (wrongs) has held that reasonable reliance by one person upon the unsolicited offer of another may create an obligation the volunteer did not seek and may not even realize he had incurred. One who stores someone else's goods free of charge (a "gratuitous bailee" in property law) assumes minimal responsibilities toward the property and may have to compensate the owner if his willful lack of care causes its loss. Under the law of contracts, if one person gratuitously offers to renew a friend's insurance policy but neglects to do so until after the policy expires, his oversight may make him the friend's insurer in the event of a loss that would have been covered by the policy.

The law of torts also imposes liability upon the good samaritan who abandons or botches a rescue effort. The traveler who has no legal duty to stop to aid an injured person may, by doing so, assume a legal responsibility to minister to the victim with reasonable care. The doctrine rests on two premises. First, the volunteer who does stop may deter other passersby who would have offered aid had they not supposed the victim was cared for. Second, the victim himself may have relied to some degree upon the samaritan; a drowning man will sometimes stop trying to swim to shore if a rescuer starts out after him.

It would be anomalous if the law of government benefits wholly disregarded these principles so clearly recognized in other sectors of the law. Yet the traditional "greater-includes-the-lesser" reasoning simply assumes their inapplicability here. To argue that government may terminate a benefit at any time since it was under no initial obligation to confer the benefit is rather like saying that a person can neglect the property he keeps without charge, or fail to renew the insurance policy his friend entrusted to him, or abandon the rescue effort when he is halfway out from shore. The duty created by the beneficiary's reliance upon a benefit once promised or conferred closely resembles the interests of others who accept gratuitous undertakings or volunteer assistance. No matter how casual or generous may be the initial offer of the benefit, the acceptance of that offer may severely restrict the governmental options in administering the program. Our discussion to this point has assumed that benefits do indeed constitute voluntary arrangements between government and citizen. If the government is legally required to bestow a particular benefit, then of course the whole picture changes radically. There is a growing body of law supporting the claim of entitlement or "right" to benefits under special circumstances. We must examine that development, but will defer it until a later stage of the book. For the analysis that follows, we assume, consistent with the threshold definition of "benefit," that government is not legally required to create welfare programs, construct public housing, provide jobs, or maintain state colleges and universities.

II. *How the Theory of Unconstitutional Conditions Evolved Historically*

Most of the law about conditions before 1900 had nothing to do with government benefits as we have defined them. The early cases dealt with corporations chartered in one state seeking to do business in other states. The other states would frequently charge a high fee or impose burdensome conditions on an out-of-state company—partly to protect local business, and partly to induce the "foreign" corporation to incorporate there. Since a state could exclude out-of-state business from local commerce, it was assumed that any conditions could be imposed as the price of access to local markets and resources.

In 1869 the United States Supreme Court upheld Virginia's exclusion of a nonresident insurance company which had refused to pay a required license fee for doing business there. Virginia's power to condition entry was as absolute as (and grounded upon) its power of total exclusion: admission of a foreign corporation "may be granted upon such terms and conditions as . . . states may think proper to impose. They may exclude the foreign corporation entirely; they may restrict its business to particular localities, or they may exact such security for the performance of its contracts with their citizens as in their judgment will best promote the public interest. The whole matter rests in their discretion."

The 1870s brought a rash of such cases. Among them was a decision upholding Wisconsin's ouster of an insurance firm which had breached a condition of entry by removing to the federal courts a lawsuit filed against it in the state courts. The Supreme Court re-affirmed that a nonresident corporation "has no constitutional right to do business in that state; that state has authority at any time to declare that it shall not transact business there." Given the absolute power of exclusion, the "lesser" act of conditional admission followed *ex hypothesi.*

There were occasional voices of dissent during the last quarter of the nineteenth century. In the Wisconsin case, for example, Mr. Justice Bradley challenged the majority's assumption that "the greater always includes the lesser" and termed "unsound" the conclusion that "if the state may exclude the . . . [corporation] without any cause it may exclude them for a bad cause . . ."

The majority view prevailed, however, until the 1920s. Then the earlier precedents were suddenly swept aside with one stroke of the judicial pen: ". . . a state may not in imposing conditions upon the privilege of a foreign corporation's doing business in the state exact from it a waiver of the exercise of its constitutional right to resort to the federal courts, or thereafter withdraw the privilege of doing business because of the exercise of such a right, whether waived in advance or not." Thus for the first time, the Court denied to the state the authority to exact from a foreign corporation, as the price of doing business within the state, a waiver of federal constitutional rights. The state may, of course, continue to exclude out-of-state business altogether; but if it permits any access to local markets, ". . . the power of the State in that respect is not unlimited; and one of the limitations is that it may not impose conditions which require the relinquishment of constitutional rights."

The law which was being made in the foreign corporation cases poured over slowly into the field of individual rights and liberties. In 1897, the Supreme Court upheld a Boston city ordinance requiring a permit from the mayor for any rally or public address on the Common or Public Garden. Although the ordinance prescribed no standards for the mayor's exercise of this power, none were constitutionally required: "The right to absolutely exclude all right to use necessarily includes the authority to determine under what circumstances such use may be availed of as the greater power contains the lesser."

Mr. Justice Holmes, who had written the opinion of the Massachusetts court in that case, saw no important constitutional difference between a city's total refusal to open its parks for speeches and rallies and conditioning such use upon a permit granted by the mayor in his unfettered discretion. Nor did Justice Holmes see any constitutional vice in a city's ban on political activities by public workers. A New Bedford policeman who had been fired for partisan activities found no redress in the Massachusetts courts. The officer might, said Holmes, "have a constitutional right to talk politics, but he has no constitutional right to be a policeman."

Yet, it was also Justice Holmes who first announced a more sensitive view of the individual interests affected by conditioned benefits. When the Court held in 1921 that fourth class mailing privileges could be conditioned or withdrawn at will by the Post Office, Holmes warned: "The United States may give up the Post Office when it sees fit, but while it carries it on, the use of the mails is almost as much a part of free speech as the right to use our tongues. . . ." His fellow dissenter, Justice Louis D. Brandeis, was even more explicit: "Congress may not through its postal police power put limitations upon the freedom of the press which, if directly attempted, would be unconstitutional."

A quarter century later, the Holmes-Brandeis philosophy became the prevailing constitutional doctrine. When the bulk mailing privilege issue returned to the Court in a slightly different guise, the majority adopted the view of the conditioning power that had commanded only two votes in the 1920s: "Grave constitutional questions are immediately raised once it is said that the use of the mails is a privilege which may be extended or withheld on any grounds whatever . . . Under that view, the second class rate could be granted on condition that certain economic or political ideas not be disseminated. The provisions . . . [of the statute] would have to be far more explicit for us to assume that congress made such a radical departure from our traditions and undertook to clothe the Postmaster General with the power to supervise the tastes of the reading public of the country."

The old doctrine died hard. As late as 1951, the Supreme Court observed while upholding a New York loyalty oath, that public school teachers "may work for the school system upon the reasonable terms laid down by the proper authorities of New York. If they do not choose to work on such terms, they are at liberty to retain their beliefs and associations and go elsewhere." Mr. Justice

Douglas refused, in dissent, to "accept the recent doctrine that a citizen who enters the public service can be forced to sacrifice his civil rights. . . ." But he spoke almost alone on that occasion.

Since the early 1950s, the Supreme Court has become increasingly sensitive to the claims of the government beneficiary. In 1960, the Court stopped short of declaring Social Security benefits a "right," but insisted that the claimant had a sufficient "interest" in his benefits to warrant substantial safeguards. While the Court has declined to classify public employment as either a "right" or a "privilege," recurrent statements recognize that "constitutional protection does extend to the public servant whose exclusion pursuant to a statute is patently arbitrary or discriminatory." Similar protection has been extended to such lesser government benefits as a notary public's commission, admission of an attorney to the bar, property tax exemptions, and unemployment benefits.

An unemployment compensation case in 1963 showed how far the Court had come since Justice Holmes's cavalier dismissal of the Boston common orator and the New Bedford policeman. The case arose because a Seventh Day Adventist in South Carolina could find no employment that permitted her to take Saturdays off. Since Saturday was her day of worship, she rejected all offers of six-day work. When she filed an application for unemployment compensation, state officials told her she was deemed "unavailable for suitable employment" and accordingly denied her claim. She carried the claim through the state courts—which upheld the commission's finding of ineligibility—and eventually to the Supreme Court.

By a 7–2 margin, the justices reversed the state court's judgment. The majority held the woman could not constitutionally be compelled to choose between the practice of her religion and her only available source of income. Since her disqualification for employment (and consequently for unemployment compensation) resulted solely from the exercise of a religious liberty guaranteed by the First Amendment, it was clear the state had attached an unconstitutional condition to its unemployment benefits program: "Governmental imposition of such a choice puts the same kind of burden upon the free exercise of religion as would a fine imposed against [the woman] for her Saturday worship." So cruel a choice might be justified by a "compelling state interest," but South Carolina had demonstrated no such interest.

Occasional traces of the old "greater includes the lesser" doctrine persist in the lower courts. A federal district judge recently characterized a welfare payment as "a grant, . . . not the fulfillment of a contractual obligation," with the result that "Congress may surround the grants with reasonable requirements and prescribe the categories of persons to whom grants shall be given." Seldom is language so clearly deferential to government discretion found in contemporary cases. Yet as we have noted earlier, the revolution in terminology may obscure the realities of much more gradual change in the results of the cases.

Two important matters now seem beyond dispute: first, the case for unrestricted use of the power to condition government benefits is logically untenable, and is incompatible with basic legal principles developed long before the inception of most government benefit programs. Second, the courts have gradually come to question the greater-includes-the-lesser argument, and some have flatly rejected it. What is lacking is a well-developed and clearly defined body of law to replace the ancient doctrine of virtually complete discretion. The following analysis suggests a set of criteria that may help to resolve difficult contests over the interests of government beneficiaries.

III. *Constitutionality of Conditioned Benefits: A Framework for Analysis*

Courts have struck down conditions on government benefits, as we have seen, with increasing frequency. But with the exception of the California Supreme Court and a few others, they have proceeded into this treacherous field more on hunch and instinct about basic fairness (or unfairness) than by predetermined principle or criterion. Standards are badly needed and long overdue, particularly in view of the rapidly mounting volume of cases involving attacks on conditioned benefits. The criteria suggested here are not those typically invoked by courts in benefit cases, although they are consistent with the general approach of the most thoughtful tribunals. Taken together, they may furnish a working model for the analysis of contests over the constitutionality of conditioned benefits.

HOW IMPORTANT IS THE BENEFIT TO THE BENEFICIARY?

There has been much discussion about the distinction between "right" and "privilege." Most of that discussion has been pointless and misleading. There is, in fact no benefit so sacred or inalienable that it is immune from all conditions and restrictions (that is, an absolute "right"); nor is there any benefit so insubstantial or gratuitous as to be subject to any and all conditions. (Certain governmental acts, notably the making of appointments by the President of the United States, may in fact be unreviewable in the courts; but their insulation from attack does not mean that arbitrary or discriminatory use of these powers is legally unobjectionable.)

There is, in fact, a scale of benefits ranging from the most protected to the least—a continuum that makes impossible the marking of any artificial distinction between "right" and "privilege." At one end of the scale are such basic attributes of citizenship as the franchise and freedom of expression, which, although they are not really benefits as we have defined that term, can still be conditioned and curtailed under extraordinary circumstances. At the other end of the scale are gratuitous bestowals of government bounty such as veterans' bonuses, Christmas gifts for government employees, prize awards for state university students, and the like. Even such incidental benefits as these cannot be categorically denied to Negroes, or Jews, or Catholics.

The superficially appealing dichotomy between "right" and "privilege" is thus no more than a convenient (though misleading) means of placing a particular benefit along the continuum of protection. It has had a quite pernicious influence, however, because it has foreclosed or deterred much critical analysis and thought that would otherwise have been applied to problems of government benefits. It is so convenient to call something a "privilege"—as some courts still do—and then assume that the label obviates further analysis of the beneficiary's interests. These labels should be discarded in any serious study of government benefits. We should instead recognize a very broad continuum of benefits of varying importance and entitlement to protection.

The related question—how important is the benefit to the beneficiary—now assumes a new meaning. Sometimes the answer is relatively simple. A promotion to civil service status or the achievement of academic tenure is clearly more important than a Christmas bonus. Even objective standards will determine that much. But subtler distinctions quickly unfold, and one must resort increasingly to subjective criteria to assess the importance to the particular beneficiary of acquiring (or losing) a given relationship with government. It is not only subjective variations in needs and perceptions that affect this judgment. In addition, the passage of time, differences in location, age, race, and many other factors will influence the relative importance of a benefit.

The changing character of Social Security benefits may illustrate the subjective nature of importance. In the 1930s, Social Security might have been regarded as a bare gratuity (at least if one overlooked the investment each claimant had built up during his years of employment). During the last thirty years, however, patterns of individual saving and insurance have undoubtedly changed in reliance upon the very existence of Social Security to cover emergencies and contingencies that once had to be met from private sources. A similar shift will probably occur with regard to medical care of the elderly as the Medicare program is increasingly influential. Thus, a court now called upon to weigh the importance of Social Security or unemployment benefits to the beneficiary should evaluate critically the changes which reliance upon the very existence of such programs has brought about on the part of present and potential beneficiaries. In addition to direct reliance by beneficiaries themselves, there may have been equally important reliance by persons who would be obligated to support the beneficiary if government aid were unavailable. Such contingent expectations and collateral reliance should be weighed in the balance, too, in assessing the importance of the benefit.

ARE ALTERNATIVE BENEFITS AVAILABLE IN THE PRIVATE SECTOR?

The importance of the benefit to the recipient is greatly influenced by the availability of similar opportunities from nongovernment sources. A professor who declines to take the loyalty oath required by a state college can typically find employment at a private university. But similar alternatives are much less readily available to teachers in the elementary and secondary schools. Even if one includes the dwindling number of jobs in church-affiliated and other independent schools, the private share of total employment in precollege education is very small.

Primarily, even exclusively, public branches are developing in many professions that were once confined almost wholly to the private sector. It is no answer to a public health physician, for example, to point to the door of private practice if the door to state employment is barred by an unacceptable condition or restriction. The fact is that many types of public health work are carried on only by the government—even though most physicians still practice in the private sector. As the public sector's share of the total work force increases, moreover, the availability of private sector alternatives will steadily diminish. As the beneficiary's range of choice thus narrows, the growing importance of opportunities in the public sector is obvious.

Paradoxically, alternatives in the private sector are probably least available to beneficiaries at the top and the bottom of the socioeconomic scale. At the top there is the atomic scientist, the government economist, the big city school superintendent or state university administrator, who may well have worked his way up through the public sector so far that he has priced himself out of the private market. (At least in the Federal Government, salaries are occasionally higher at the top levels for career civil servants than comparable salaries in private business, industry, or education—even where comparable positions exist.)

At the bottom of the scale the process of transfer is equally restricted, though for opposite reasons. Self-sufficiency is one of the lowest priority goals of the welfare system. In fact, as we have already observed, welfare standards of many states require the applicant to make himself even poorer than he already is, by divesting himself of all assets over a few hundred dollars, before he can even apply for assistance. When welfare recipients earn more than a pittance, they are typically docked that amount on their welfare checks—or in some states, they are cut off welfare entirely, even though the wages they earn may well be below the level of their benefits. Thus there is little incentive to reach the level of near-sufficiency at which one could effectively move from dependence to independence. Transfer may thus be as hard for the welfare client at the bottom as it is for the atomic scientist or university president at the top, though for wholly different reasons.

There is another necessary caveat about private sector alternatives for those at the bottom of the system. Alternatives that exist in theory may be unavailable in practice. For middle and upper class senior citizens, private medical insurance has always been readily available. But for others—especially those who will profit most from Medicare—the cost of premiums has always placed private insurance out of reach. Thus the mere existence of private sector programs, or even their extensive use, does not necessarily constitute workable alternatives for every member of the eligible class. A more discriminating analysis is required to determine whether particular barriers to such alternatives greatly increase the beneficiaries' dependence upon the government sector. Special care should be taken in judging a condition or restriction when the beneficiary or applicant has no feasible alternative to the program which imposes it.

IN WHAT WAYS DOES THE CONDITION INFLUENCE THE BENEFICIARY'S JUDGMENT?

A welfare applicant does not approach benefits, or conditions, with the same psychological set as the executives of a nonresident corporation. Whatever the cost, the corporation need only sacrifice economic interests in order to gain access to the local market. Conditions imposed upon public housing tenants and welfare recipients often exact a price that is different in kind as well as degree: the demand to sign a loyalty oath or list one's political affiliations or declare his belief in God directly affects liberties of conscience and expression which obviously have a higher psychological value and should enjoy greater legal protection than the corporation's economic interests.

COULD THE OBJECT OF THE CONDITION BE ACHIEVED BY DIRECT MEANS?

It is sometimes argued that government may not achieve through the use of conditions any objectives which it could not reach through direct regulation. This principle may well be valid where the conditions are used in lieu of direct regulation that would be patently unconstitutional—for example, because it involved explicit racial discrimination. But beyond these simple cases, the soundness of the proposition is doubtful. For there are many cases of conditions that attempt to deter or encourage behavior that government clearly could not reach through direct regulation. We cannot simply assume that all these indirect approaches are therefore unconstitutional.

It is very doubtful, for example, whether the Federal Government could constitutionally conscript prospective teachers for service in the public schools after they finished college. But those doubts do not seriously undermine the "forgiveness" provision of the National Defense Education Loan Program. Under that provision, students may be relieved of their indebtedness to the Federal Government in proportion to the number of years they agree to teach (up to 50 percent forgiveness for five years' service). Presumably the absence of direct government power does not preclude the use of indirect methods.

Nonetheless, indirect inducement or subtle coercion through conditioned benefits should be viewed with some suspicion where direct regulation would be unconstitutional. The very resort to indirect means may suggest some reluctance on the legislature's part to expose its regulatory purpose to the scrutiny of the courts. Conditions imposed on benefits are usually more difficult to attack than direct criminal sanctions. The question "Could it be done directly?" is therefore still relevant—even though a negative answer should not be conclusive.

HOW RELEVANT TO THE BENEFIT IS THE CONDITION OR RESTRICTION?

Relevance is another deceptively simple criterion. It is often assumed that a condition is unconstitutional if it bears no direct relationship to the purposes of the benefit program. This factor does indeed deserve some place in the balance. But undue reliance upon the criterion of relevance tends to obscure other equally important questions.

The relevance of the condition to the benefit does, of course, have some bearing on the constitutional analysis. A security check might be tolerated more readily when imposed on applicants for top secret defense jobs than when it is imposed on applicants for public housing or on an art model seeking employment. Similarly, a test of professional competence is a quite appropriate criterion for admission to legal or medical practice; but as Mr. Justice Douglas has cautioned, "Nothing in a man's political beliefs disables him from setting broken bones or removing ruptured appendixes safely and efficiently."

One might refine the issue of relevance by posing two further questions about a conditioned benefit: (1) How strong is the government's interest in the benefit program? and (2) How strong is the government's interest in the activity governed by the condition? These questions cannot realistically be separated. Government undoubtedly has a stronger interest in ascertaining the professional competence of public health physicians than in discouraging immorality among public housing tenants. But it makes little sense to say abstractly that the government's interest in licensing professional practitioners is stronger or weaker than its stake in providing low-cost shelter for needy citizens. Nor can one say abstractly that government is more concerned about determining professional competence than in promoting morality. These comparisons acquire meaning only when a particular condition is judged in relation to a particular benefit. Neither the importance of the benefit program nor that of the condition can be evaluated in isolation.

If the condition is not directly relevant to the benefit program, that should not end the inquiry. A further question should be posed: Is the condition relevant to some other valid government purpose? If it is, then the lack of relevance to the benefit program may be unimportant. To illustrate: When government funds are given to local school boards to help end segregation in the public schools, the condition that racial discrimination be avoided in the use of such funds is obviously relevant to the program. But when federal funds are given for school building or hospital construction or any of a variety of other state and local programs, the condition of racial nondiscrimination—which now applies to every federal grant or loan program—is usually related tenuously (at best) to the program's central objective. Yet that lack of relevance is certainly not disabling so long as the condition furthers *some* valid government purpose—for example, ensuring equal treatment for minority groups.

WHAT ALTERNATIVE MEANS, IF ANY, WOULD ACHIEVE THE SAME END?

Where a condition or restriction on a government benefit exacts a heavy toll of the beneficiary's political liberty or privacy, it seems reasonable to inquire whether government could not accomplish the same end through less offensive means. For example, it is highly doubtful whether a prophylactic ban on political activities by civil servants is essential to any legitimate governmental interest. If the real evil is the danger of civil servants being pressured by their superiors into contributing to or working for partisan causes, then direct criminal sanctions against such improper pressures would seem sufficient. Several courts have, in fact, so held. It has frequently been required that the more drastic, more sweeping restriction be abandoned wherever less onerous methods of regulation are available. The government bears the burden of proving that such alternatives are either unavailable or ineffective.

IN WHAT FORM IS THE CONDITION IMPOSED?

The form in which a condition or restriction is imposed may bear centrally on its validity. Sometimes the nature of the condition and the consequences of its breach are clearly explained to the applicant at the time the benefit is offered. Other conditions, however, remain obscure, and withdrawal of the benefit because of a breach may take the beneficiary largely by surprise.

There is a special danger inherent in conditions that are imposed after the benefit has been offered or accepted. Illustrative is the case of a political deportee's forfeiture of Social Security benefits, recently upheld by the Supreme Court. The beneficiary, a Bulgarian, entered the United States before the Social Security laws were enacted. He joined the Communist Party briefly during the 1930s at a time when party membership was neither illegal nor a ground for deportation. For twenty years, he and his employer contributed regularly to the Social Security fund. Shortly before his retirement, Congress decreed that any person deported from the country because of Communist Party membership (which had since been made a ground for deportation) would forfeit all Social Security benefits. After the Bulgarian had been deported, his wife (who remained in the United States) tried unsuccessfully to obtain Social

Security from his account. The federal courts upheld the administrator's decision that the denial of benefits was constitutional.

In this case, the government's action was vulnerable chiefly because of its threat to freedom of political association. In addition, the *procedure* was faulty because it took the beneficiary by surprise in two respects: first, there was no warning at the time he first came under Social Security that his political activities might someday jeopardize his claim. Second, at the time he became a Communist, he had no reason to fear loss of benefits. (He could not, in fact, have withdrawn from Social Security so long as he worked in covered employment, even if he knew all the consequences. But so long as some jobs existed outside of the Social Security system during the entire period—for example, under state employee retirement contribution systems—meaningful alternatives were apparently available to him.)

In addition to the adequacy and timing of notice, the language in which a condition is couched may be relevant. Recent Supreme Court decisions have indicted the vagueness and looseness of language characteristically used in public employee loyalty oaths. States may still demand such oaths of government workers, but "the measure which purports to define disloyalty must allow public servants to know what is and what is not disloyal." Though courts have not yet required that conditions be stated with the same precision required of the criminal law, a compelling case can be made for at least as high a standard in judging conditions affecting future conduct as in judging criminal sanctions.

Finally, adequate notice requires not only an understanding that *something* will happen if the condition is breached, but a full appreciation of the actual consequences. Thus, one who lists his political affiliations in applying for government employment may be willing to risk being rejected if an organization to which he belongs is unlawful, or being discharged if it is later proved he falsified his application. But he may not be willing to allow the list to be circulated among his colleagues or superiors, or turned over to a legislative investigating committee, for whatever reprisals may follow such wider dissemination. If the applicant is not adequately warned of such collateral consequences, then the whole conditioning process is particularly vulnerable.

WHAT PROCEDURES ARE PROVIDED FOR DETERMINING
A BREACH OF THE CONDITION?

When government uses direct regulation—criminal prosecution or injunction—it must follow carefully prescribed and formal procedures. But the beneficiary often fares much less well. If a state university student steals a book from the campus library, he has presumably violated the general criminal law and also incurred campus discipline. If the offense is serious enough, he may even be denied his student status. On the one hand, he cannot be jailed or fined—the direct form of regulation—without a criminal trial before an impartial judge and perhaps a jury, nor without the right to be represented by counsel, protection against self-incrimination, an opportunity to confront his accusers, and the right to appeal. Yet for the same act, indirect sanctions—possibly expulsion—may be imposed through informal procedures, and perhaps even without any hearing.

Although indirect regulation is seldom accompanied by safeguards required in the criminal courts, the protections actually available to the government beneficiary vary considerably. To return to the case of the state university student, for example, courts and educational administrators alike are requiring increasingly strict procedures before expulsion or suspension can take place. Perhaps a university that guarantees every student a full trial-type hearing for disciplinary proceedings should be able to impose more onerous conditions upon attendance than the college that retains the right to eject students summarily. In practice, of course, the institution with the fairest and most scrupulous disciplinary procedures is also likely to be most enlightened in its approach to student conduct.

Another relevant aspect of procedure is the allocation of the burden of proof. A decade ago, the United States Supreme Court struck down California's qualified property tax exemption for veterans on the rather narrow ground that the eligibility provision required the applicant to demonstrate his loyalty. The placement of the burden of proof, the Court held, might deter constitutionally protected speech and political activity: "The man who knows that he must bring forth proof and persuade another of the lawfulness of his conduct necessarily must steer wider of the unlawful zone than if the State must bear these burdens." The Court did not preclude

California from denying tax exemptions to disloyal veterans. The state could even continue to require veterans to file loyalty oaths as the condition of claiming the exemption—so long as the state bore the burden of proof in any contest over the validity of the declaration. The decision turned, then, on the quite narrow but important ground of burden of proof.

Finally, some attention should be given to the availability of court review. Direct regulation is preferable to conditioning of benefits partly because the former can usually be challenged directly in court on its merits. But the immunity of conditioned benefits to attack in court is not inherent. Congress has begun to open the door to judicial review by providing for "test suits" in the federal courts to challenge aspects of benefit programs. The Supreme Court opened the door wider by overruling a forty-year-old decision that barred a suit by a taxpayer seeking to challenge government expenditures for welfare programs. Any taxpayer now has legal standing to bring such a suit seeking, for example, to enjoin use of federal funds to support church-related institutions. Yet the reviewability of claims of welfare recipients remains uncertain. Further legislation may be necessary to open the doors of the courts wide enough to reach conditions attached to such benefits.

This framework suggests a model for constitutional analysis of conditioned benefits. Some conditions may be clearly invalid on the basis of one of these criteria. More often, the question can be resolved only by the application of several criteria, and will remain a close one even after the list has been exhausted. Of course constitutional decisions regularly demand careful accommodation between conflicting governmental interests. Indeed, it is the essence of controversy over the use of the conditioning power that such an accommodation be made in each case. Without an accommodation, the legitimate and beneficial uses of conditions cannot be legally distinguished from those that impair constitutional liberties.

III

THE PARADOXES

OF THE

PUBLIC SERVICE

The United States has never developed an occupational subculture comparable to the civil servant classes of many European nations. Indeed, civilian government work has, throughout much of American history, been a rather mediocre and lackluster occupation. Only recently has the career civil service attracted college graduates and professional personnel with ambition and idealism.

Several trends have helped to improve the status of the civil service. One factor has been the phenomenal growth of public employment. In 1930, the nation's three million public employees constituted about 10 percent of the nonagricultural work force. By 1966, the number exceeded ten million and approached 20 percent of the nonfarm labor force.

The most dramatic expansion has occurred at the state and local levels. Since 1955, federal employment has grown only about 9 percent, while state and local employment jumped some 65 percent. Two groups, women and nonwhite workers, have benefited disproportionately from this expansion. The percentage of black persons in the federal civil service, for example, is roughly double the share in private business and industry. Certain occupational groups have benefited more than others. There has been a growing trend toward professionalization of the civil service, particularly at the federal level—with major infusions of lawyers in the 1930s, physicians and economists in the 1940s and 1950s, space and nuclear scientists in the last decade.

Salary levels have paralleled (or even spurred) these growth trends. In New York, for example, state workers by 1967 earned as much as or more than their counterparts in twenty-one out of twenty-seven common blue and white collar job classes. In Buffalo and Albany, two of the major upstate cities, pay scales for government work averaged about $1,000 a year higher than comparable positions in the private sector. Between 1958 and 1966, the average salary level of state employees increased 45 percent, while salaries in private business and industry went up between 30 and 36 percent.

Despite these improvements, there is now an unprecedented malaise within the public service. The rapid rise in strikes and walkouts is the most obvious manifestation of this condition. In 1955, there were seventeen strikes by government employees, resulting in a loss of some 7,000 man days. Nineteen sixty brought thirty-six work stoppages. By 1965, the figure had increased only slightly to forty-two. But the number of walkouts shot up abruptly to 142 the following year. The number of man days lost through strikes rose from 71,000 in 1965 to 146,000 in 1965, to a startling 455,000 in 1966. In fact, 80 percent of all man-days involved in public school teacher strikes between 1940 and 1968 occurred during the final year of that nearly three-decade period. And the last two years, 1967 and 1968, brought almost as many strikes by teachers as by all public workers combined in any previous year.

These figures alone are alarming enough. What is more significant is that these strikes were illegal. Some states now allow public workers to organize and bargain collectively, but none extends the right to strike that is universally guaranteed to workers in the private sector. Thus nearly every union that struck against a government employer risked heavy fines, contempt citations, and jail sentences.

The figures also fail fully to reflect the mood of public workers. A *New York Times* reporter, covering a Wallace rally at Madison Square Garden during the 1968 campaign, saw the Alabama Governor as a spokesman for the "deep frustrations and discontents [that] seethe within the ranks of the civil service." There is every indication that the militancy bred by these frustrations will spread rather than diminish. A California labor writer observed that "the men and women who work for government are on the move, in the same way that those in private industry began moving thirty years ago." Although organizing and strikes have been confined to the state and local level, columnist Victor Riesel warns that Federal Government buildings "may soon . . . be picketed by experts—not by amateurish peaceists, but by angry federal employees." A *New York Times* survey in the spring of 1967 concluded that "the once docile public servant has begun increasingly to rely on strikes and unionization to resolve his complaints about lagging wages and arbitrary bosses."

Many factors no doubt account for the mounting dissatisfaction and its militant manifestations within the public service. There are economic grievances, to be sure—despite the disproportionate salary increases for many public positions within recent years. Complaints about working conditions, especially in the public schools and in the menial or routine occupations, are legion. There is mounting pressure for better protection of firemen, bus drivers, and teachers who work in high-crime areas and are subjected to constant physical risks. Many public servants are demanding a stronger voice in the making of policy, notably in welfare and other social service agencies. These complaints also arise in the private sector, but they are especially urgent for the government worker.

Other grievances are unique to the public service and may help to explain the recent growth of protests and strikes. Not least of these special grievances is the absence of the very channels that shunt complaints in the private sector toward the bargaining table rather than the picket line. Strikes may be more disabling in the public sector precisely because they are forbidden by law almost everywhere. Indeed, in many states and cities all forms of collective bargaining or negotiation are denied to public workers. These and other disparities between government and private employment will be the subject of this chapter, particularly where they may have constitutional significance.

So far we have spoken of "public" and "private" careers as though the line separating them were always sharp and clear. That used to be the case in the United States and still is in many other countries. The distinction was clear in the 1920s when American public attitudes toward government work were so disparaging. But recent developments have brought a steady blurring of the line that divides the public from the private sector. Economic activity that was once purely "private" has come increasingly under government regulation of all kinds. And public service has meanwhile assumed many attributes of employment relations in private business. Both trends need to be recognized at the start of this study of public employment.

On the one hand, much government work is being done by private firms on government contracts—in universities, research centers, laboratories, and factories. Five of the seven largest educational recipients of federal research and development funds for the most recent fiscal year were private universities. Much of the work of the space program is done on contract by private firms. Even the employment training of high school dropouts through the Job Corps has been delegated to private companies. Several major research laboratories that started out with a diverse clientele have ended up working exclusively for the Federal Government, sometimes even for a single agency.

Employees of these organizations are "private" in the technical sense that they perform their duties on private property and receive their salaries directly from a private business. But it hardly makes sense to consider them private employees when their entire working day is devoted to government business, and the sole source of their compensation is a congressional appropriation from tax funds. Yet despite the blurring of the once clear distinction between public and private work, the law still treats these employees as clearly "private" for most purposes.

The line has been blurred from the other side as well. Private companies and their workers were once completely free of government regulation. At the turn of the century, the Supreme Court struck down even modest wage and hour laws because they impaired the "freedom of contract" between employer and employee. All that has changed now, of course. Largely as a result of legislation passed during the depression, labor-management relations, wages, hours, and working conditions in the private company are now extensively regulated by federal and state law. Employers and employees must make regular contributions to the Social Security system. And since 1965, even the hiring and promotion practices of the private firm are subject to a strong federal ban against discrimination on grounds of race, creed, national origin, or sex. What was once the employer's own domain and the subject of his unbridled discretion is thus no longer "private." Much of what government can do *for* its own work force, it can also require private employers to do for their workers. The harder question remains, and will be

the crux of this chapter: What can government do *to* its employees
—what conditions and restrictions can it impose upon them—
which it could not do to employees of private firms?

I. *Aliens and the Public Service: Citizenship as a Qualification*

Many government benefits are restricted to citizens, and even
to residents of the state or city which confers them. What geographic and nationality limitations can be placed upon public employment? Many states still require all or a substantial part of the
workers hired on government contracts to be citizens of the United
States and residents of the state. And positions in the civil service
are often restricted in the same way. There has, however, been little
attention given to the issue recently, perhaps because noncitizens
typically enjoy a wide range of opportunities outside the civil service in the states where they are most likely to settle.

A half century ago, this issue was a burning one. Several cases
brought to the Supreme Court the constitutionality of state laws
barring employment of aliens. The Court took a seemingly ambiva-
lent view of the problem. On the one hand it struck down an Arizona law requiring all employers within the state to hire at least 80
percent native-born American citizens. The majority reasoned that
an alien who had been lawfully admitted into the country had a federally protected privilege to live in any state. This privilege carried
with it "the right to work for a living in the common occupations of
the community." A denial of that opportunity would make the freedom of entry and movement guaranteed by the Fourteenth Amendment "a barren form of words." But on the same day, the Supreme
Court sustained a New York requirement that "in the construction
of public works by the state or a municipality, or by persons contracting with the state or such municipality, only citizens of the
United States shall be employed." The Court explained the difference in result: while government could not broadly restrict access of
aliens to private jobs, nor deprive private employers of their freedom to hire noncitizens, government's power to restrict access to its
own employment roster was virtually unlimited.

The views of the Court in these cases were much criticized; but
the early precedents have never been overruled. The controversy
was, in fact, virtually dormant until a Santa Barbara, California,

Superior Court in late 1967 ruled unconstitutional a state labor law provision which forbade employment of noncitizens by the State of California and its counties and cities. The law had been on the books since 1915 but was never formally tested; its validity was presumed on the basis of the old New York case. Many intervening developments persuaded the trial judge that such a restriction was incompatible with current Fourteenth Amendment doctrines. In 1948, for example, the U.S. Supreme Court had struck down a California law denying commercial fishing licenses to alien Japanese residing within the state. (Technically, the prohibition was against "persons ineligible to citizenship"—but in practice this was clearly and obviously directed at the Japanese, the only substantial resident group ineligible for citizenship.)

The majority of the Court found this law incompatible with the guarantee of the Fourteenth Amendment "that all persons lawfully in the United States shall abide 'in any state' on an equality of legal privileges with all citizens." Those parts of the Amendment which guarantee the equal protection of the laws and which ensure against deprivation of life or liberty without due process of law extend to "any person," alien as well as citizen.

In addition to the fishing license case, the Supreme Courts of three states had struck down laws which forbade aliens to own land. These decisions turned also upon the Fourteenth Amendment's guarantee of the equal protection of the laws—the clause that has been the cornerstone of the legal attack on school segregation and other forms of racial discrimination. Most recently, the California Supreme Court went a step further by striking down a law that denied the right of inheritance to a resident alien from a nation whose laws did not protect the inheritance of property by resident American nationals.

In accord with these precedents, the California Supreme Court agreed that the alien employment law could no longer stand. The court relied primarily upon the latent conflict between the state's bar against aliens and the need for exclusive federal regulation of matters of immigration and naturalization. But the court added that the law created an irrational classification, and was therefore suspect under the equal protection clause as well. Insofar as the statute sought to measure a taxpayer's stake in the disbursement of public funds, it incorrectly assumed that all aliens were newcomers to the state (or nontaxpayers), while all citizens were long-term residents. To the extent the California law sought to protect citizens from competition by alien labor, it was even more clearly unconstitutional; "such a purpose," said the court, "constitutes prima facie discrimination for its own sake . . ."

The California decision is quite clearly consistent with recent developments defining equal access to government benefits. Closing public employment to aliens not only creates a discrimination between citizens and noncitizens that is difficult to support by reference to any governmental interest; it also imposes a quite arbitrary distinction between aliens' access to public and private jobs. If there are certain tasks that aliens simply are not qualified to perform for the state (none has been suggested), then specific disabilities would quite adequately serve the governmental interests without broadly restricting the economic opportunities of a large class of residents on a criterion that is unrelated to skill or competence. Moreover, the Federal Government has a special interest in ensuring uniform treatment for aliens legally resident in the United States. If the states impose special disabilities and restrictions on the opportunities of aliens, the federal interest in uniformity may be seriously jeopardized.

II. *The Disability of a Criminal Record*

There are various laws or regulations that expressly bar former criminals from public employment. Such exclusion is also often accomplished through informal policies. Several recent developments may illustrate the gravity of this threat to the status of public employment. Reference has already been made to the Job Corps, administered by the Office of Economic Opportunity, which is said to have systematically rejected applicants who have criminal records. Even the Peace Corps has continued (despite vigorous opposition from civil liberties groups) to ask applicants for their arrest records and for all information about convictions more serious than traffic offenses. In January 1968, the Office of Economic Opportunity warned a Chicago antipoverty program—the Woodlawn Organization of the South Side—that it might lose its million dollar federal poverty grant if it continued to employ as teachers certain street gang members who faced criminal charges.

For five years the American Civil Liberties Union sought to

eliminate a question about the applicant's criminal record from the standard Federal Civil Service Commission form. There was evidence that in some cases the disclosure of a mere arrest—with no attempt to judge the severity of the charges—had disqualified otherwise eligible applicants. The ACLU argued that some convictions—particularly those for demonstrations and other political protests—should not be used as a basis for disqualification. To draw an unfavorable inference from such a record might infringe the applicant's liberties and could deter prospective applicants from protest or demonstration. In 1966, the Civil Service Commission agreed to abandon the question. The change was designed, in the words of the Commission's chairman, "to prevent the summary rejection of applicants on the basis of unevaluated arrest records." (There was, of course, an intermediate option: to determine on an individual basis whether the gravity of the particular offense warranted disqualifying the applicant for the particular position.)

Scarcely had this disability been expunged from the record when another took its place. Tucked away in a back corner of the Omnibus Crime Bill of 1968 was a provision that deserves far wider notice than it has received: any person sentenced for a year or more as a result of participating in a riot is barred from all federal employment for five years thereafter. While this bill was on the President's desk, the House Post Office and Civil Service Committee was fashioning an even harsher collateral punishment. It amended another bill to deny federal employment to "any person convicted of committing an unlawful act which is directly or indirectly related to a riot or civil disorder." This disability, observed *The New York Times,* "would rule out a teen-age looter caught with a bottle of pop."

There was a tragic irony about the timing of this Congressional wrath against rioters. These disabilities were imposed at the very time the administration was making massive efforts to induce private firms to hire disadvantaged and hard-core unemployed youths, among whom riot convictions were disproportionately high. For Congress to close the door of government employment, warned *The New York Times,* would "encourage private business to follow suit—exactly the opposite policy from what is necessary and desirable."

There are few court decisions defining the scope of government's power to ask questions about, or reject, an applicant because of a criminal record. Two recent events indicate a tempering of this disability. The City of Detroit has decided to abandon its traditional prohibition against bringing anyone convicted of a felony onto the police force. Applicants must still reveal criminal records, but past convictions will be evaluated on an individual basis according to their seriousness. This major change in policy was designed primarily to expand hiring of nonwhite applicants by Detroit's police force (only 5.7 percent of which is Negro in a city with a black population exceeding one third).

The other pertinent development is a California Supreme Court decision admitting to the practice of law one Terence "Kayo" Hallinan, despite several misdemeanor convictions. Although Hallinan had passed the bar examination and met all the other qualifications for admission, the Board of Bar Examiners rejected him for failure to demonstrate "good moral character." The State Supreme Court, which has final review of all bar admission cases, studied the criminal record carefully. Most of the convictions grew out of sit-ins and other civil rights demonstrations, which clearly did not evidence moral turpitude. While recognizing the appropriateness of criminal penalties for unlawful demonstrations and protests, the Court concluded that such a record should not necessarily keep one out of the legal profession: "If we were to deny to every person who has engaged in a 'sit-in' or other form of nonviolent civil disobedience, and who has been convicted therefor, the right to enter a licensed profession, we would deprive the community of the services of many highly qualified persons of the highest moral courage."

The employment of youths with criminal records became a political issue in New York City's bitter 1969 mayoral campaign. Opponents charged that Mayor Lindsay had unwisely hired ten or more young black men to serve as youth counsellors in a Harlem Afro-American Culture Center. Lindsay defended the charge not only in terms of hopes for rehabilitating the youths in question, all of whom had been suggested by the police as having some leadership potential despite their troubles with the law. In addition, he argued, such youths might help others in the community, and enhance the city's service to the poorest and most crime-ridden areas by extending the credibility and the effective reach of the agencies by which they were employed.

In the absence of any conclusive court decision, two questions emerge: First, what power does government have to ask about prior criminal activity; and second, to what extent may information obtained by such questions provide the sole ground for rejecting an applicant? To begin, information about mere arrests has doubtful relevance for any government job; charges which are later dismissed or never prosecuted should never even come to the attention of a prospective employer. What then of charges which do result in conviction?

Some government jobs are so sensitive, or demand so high a degree of integrity, that even a minor criminal record might disqualify an applicant. And there are certain crimes—homicide and rape, for example—that might reasonably cause rejection of an applicant for most positions in the civil service. Other kinds of governmental judgments are much more difficult to evaluate: What interest, for example, does a government agency have in restricting public positions to applicants with clean records because it wishes to deter crime? And if jobs are in short supply and high demand, with many applicants roughly equal on other grounds, might the presence of a criminal record tip the balance? Any concession in this sensitive area must be quite narrow, for once the door to an applicant's criminal record has been opened even for a limited purpose, irreparable harm may have been done.

If access to applicants' criminal records is permitted at all, there should be much more rigorous insistence upon identifying the purposes for which the information is sought. The questions should be confined to offenses that are directly relevant to the particular position. Ordinarily, even adverse answers will simply be taken into consideration in the processing of the application, but will rarely disqualify the candidate. Finally, in cases in which an adverse inference is drawn from the disclosure of a prior criminal record, some opportunity should be given—presumably through an adversary hearing—for the applicant to explain the context of the conviction. Such an opportunity for explanation seems essential lest a youthful transgression—perhaps idealistically impelled—permanently mar the employment record of a person whose qualifications may be impeccable in all other respects.

III. *Privacy in the Public Service: The Lie Detector at the Office and the Spy in the Bedroom*

Privacy of the public employee may be threatened at three distinct points: by questions asked of an applicant for a government job; by general surveillance of an employee's affairs (both on and off the job); and by specific investigations that may force the employee to testify or lose his job. It is true, of course, that threats of the first two types are frequent—indeed perhaps more prevalent —in certain private firms and corporations. But there are two critical differences between intrusions by public and private employers: first, all actions of government, no less as an employer than in any other capacity, are subject to the limitations of the Fourth Amendment and other constitutional guarantees of privacy; and second, government agencies can call upon a far more powerful and versatile arsenal of investigative resources than are available to private industry. The F.B.I., for example, does security checks only for other branches of the *government*. And the Justice Department can prosecute only a *public* worker for lying.

PROBING AT THE THRESHOLD: INTAKE QUESTIONNAIRES AND TESTS

Probing personality tests have been widely used as a screening device both in the public and private sector. For those government positions covered by Civil Service, such tests may no longer constitute so serious a problem. Alan F. Westin reports in his comprehensive study of privacy: "A sample survey of Civil Service Commissions of eleven states, one territory and four municipalities shows that state and local governments reject personality tests for general Civil Service appointment and promotion, but do use them for a few situations of special public importance or employee stress." Yet it was only in January 1967—and under great pressure both from the American Civil Liberties Union and a powerful congressional investigating committee—that the Civil Service Commission discontinued the use of a searching medical history questionnaire for civilian federal employees and job applicants. The "report of medical history" (Form 89) asked about bed-wetting, pregnancies, homosexuality, and whether blood relatives had committed suicide, had been insane, or had ever suffered from hives.

The Senate Judiciary Subcommittee on Constitutional Rights had discovered that in certain agencies (the National Security Agency, Small Business Administration, Housing and Urban Development Department, and Library of Congress) information obtained from answers to Form 89 had been used as a basis for dismissing or disciplining employees for nonmedical reasons. "It was by no means clear," reported the *Christian Science Monitor,* "that access to these forms would be strictly limited to medical staff. If they were made available to personnel or security officers, answers irrelevant to physical fitness might well have resulted in exclusion from government service." If the information got into the wrong hands, there was a further risk, at least as serious as the prospect of humiliation or denial of employment: information about drug or narcotic habits, excessive drinking, and homosexual experiences might subject a federal employee to criminal liability though he had been compelled to give the answers in order to complete his application.

Form 89 has now been abandoned. But not all personality testing has been terminated. The Defense Department continues to use such forms. Applicants for air traffic control positions within the Federal Aviation Agency must, for example, still answer a "sixteen personality factor test" exploring in detail their political, racial, and religious opinions or associations. The American Civil Liberties Union has charged that this test, too, threatens the applicant's privacy: sensitive, conscientious job seekers may either forego the position to which the test is a prerequisite, or may give up the activities and associations on which the questions cast suspicion.

More serious invasions of privacy lie beyond the jurisdiction of the Civil Service Commission. The State Department, reports Westin, "began using personality tests in 1949 with the creation of its Medical Division. Tests were used when individuals displayed concrete emotional or psychological disturbances and when an examining psychiatrist felt (and the Medical Division agreed) psychological testing was called for in the judgment of the case. . . . The State Department also gives personality tests to all code clerks and communications personnel because of the need for emotionally stable persons in such 'highly sensitive' work.

"Several 'exempt' federal agencies rely heavily on personality tests. In 1964, the Department of Labor used a personality test for 22,000 persons applying to be trained as youth counselors for work with state employment services under operation CAUSE. The test included questions such as, 'I think Lincoln was greater than Washington'; 'I feel there is only one true religion'; 'When a man is with a woman he is usually thinking about things related to her sex'; 'I often go against my parents' wishes'; 'I hardly ever get excited or thrilled.' Under pressure from some Congressmen, the Department of Labor announced that it would not administer such tests in the future for operation CAUSE."

Perhaps the sharpest controversy has surrounded the use of personality tests and questionnaires for Peace Corps volunteers. Peace Corps officials explained to the Senate Constitutional Rights Subcommittee that such tests were required by the situations of special stress to which volunteers were subjected. Identification of possible personality disorders was thus of central importance in the selection of applicants. The Corps thus decided to administer the Minnesota Multiphasic test to all volunteers after they had been received for training, some nine thousand persons each year. This test demanded true or false responses to such statements as, "I feel sure there is only one true religion," "My sex life is satisfactory," "There is very little love and companionship in my family as compared to other homes"; and "There is something wrong with my sex organs." Testimony before the congressional subcommittee raised serious doubts about the need for and value of the Minnesota test. Peace Corps spokesmen did cite a few cases in which possibly unsuited applicants had been rejected on the basis of test results. Thereafter the Peace Corps agreed to waive the test requirement for any applicant who wished not to take it.

Despite the danger to privacy, selection for certain jobs may warrant use of psychiatric examinations and personality tests. The hiring of police officers for large cities may afford the best justification. Roughly three fifths of big city police departments now employ some form of personality screening. Police candidates in Los Angeles are interviewed by a psychiatrist during the regular medical examination. New York City administers a "standard personality test" to all probationary patrolmen and prison correction officers. Very careful interviewing of all applicants for the Omaha police force by two staff psychiatrists systematically eliminates those with personality disorders that might impair their effectiveness as officers. Yet Fletcher Knebel reports that "imposing physique is more highly prized than emotional stability" and that "few units require psychiatric tests to spot racial bias, sadism or panic response under stress." Where such tests are used, he notes that the rate of rejection is high; in Portland, Oregon, for example, a quarter of the recruits fail the test. Knebel bolsters the case for psychological screening:

> Attitude samplings show . . . that [the typical police-man] is prejudiced against Negroes and other minority groups and that he tends to be tougher in his dealings with nonwhites. He has little appreciation of the psychology and culture of the poor minorities or juveniles. He is aware that some fellow officers treat minority citizens with rudeness, abuse and even physical roughness. He opposes full integration of his own police department.

There may be certain government jobs in which the applicants' interest in privacy should be outweighed by the need to reduce the risk that insensitive or disturbed persons will be hired for such highly sensitive work as policing the urban ghettos. Ironically, however, government policies have nearly reversed the priorities. The incidence of personality testing has probably been highest in rather routine, bureaucratic jobs that involve little contact with people other than fellow employees. Where the need is greatest because the tension is highest, as in law enforcement, intensive psychiatric screening has been used far less systematically.

Personality tests have not been the only threat to privacy of government job applicants. Polygraphs and lie detectors have also intruded from time to time. "One report has it," testified the former Chief Counsel and Staff Director of a Constitutional Rights Subcommittee, "that the nonsecret federal agencies possess over 500 polygraph machines and that in one recent year, over 20,000 lie detector tests were administered to government employees and job applicants." During the Subcommittee's investigation, Senator Sam J. Ervin, Jr. (the Subcommittee's Chairman) argued: "Polygraph tests operate on the basis of emotional responses which a brazen liar might successfully dissemble while a timid man would fail."

Despite mounting criticism, the use of polygraphs on federal job applicants appears to be increasing. It began with the National Security Agency in the early 1950s. In 1964, both the NSA and CIA reported they administered a polygraph test to every job applicant. As many as five thousand persons annually may be screened in this fashion. Westin reports: "The Army and Navy informed the Moss Committee that they both used polygraphs for 'personnel screening.' The Army gave 4,600 tests for this purpose in 1963, and the Navy listed 1,200 tests (without further breakdown) for personnel screening, security, criminal investigations, and misconduct. The Army gave 3,494 additional personnel screening polygraph tests in 1963 for a special program of enlisting Cuban refugees into U.S. Army service."

Largely on the basis of this testimony, elicited through lengthy hearings, Senator Ervin introduced a bill "to protect the civilian employees of the executive branch of the United States Government in the enjoyment of their constitutional rights and to prevent unwarranted governmental invasions of their privacy." The Bill passed the Senate by an overwhelming 79–4 vote, then bogged down in the House Committee on Post Office and Civil Service. Its provisions cover most of the issues and abuses we have considered here, and others as well. This proposed charter would make it unlawful to compel an applicant for or holder of a civil service position to take a polygraph test "designed to elicit from him information concerning his personal relationship with any person connected with him by blood or marriage, or concerning his religious beliefs or practices, or concerning his attitude or conduct with respect to sexual matters." The bill also forbids inquiries into the financial affairs of civil servants or their relatives, save for special categories of employees; and even of the latter, inquiries must be confined to "specific items tending to indicate a conflict of interest" in the performance of official duties. In addition, the bill contains important procedural safeguards. No interrogation or investigation for alleged misconduct within the civil service may take place without the presence of counsel, where the employee requests counsel, if disciplinary action might result. An applicant or employee "affected or aggrieved by a violation or threatened violation" of the bill may bring a suit in the federal district court to enjoin the intrusive official action. Yet the Ervin bill is not fully comprehensive. It makes no mention, for example, of physical surveillance, or of the subtler problems of data and computer surveillance. Despite these deliberate omissions, there is no doubt this proposed law would afford a vital new source of protection for the liberties of Federal Government workers and applicants for federal employment. It would, of course, have no direct effect on state and local governments, where most public workers are employed. But perhaps an example of this sort set by Congress would cause many states and cities to emulate.

SURVEILLANCE OF GOVERNMENT EMPLOYEES— ON THE JOB AND OFF

Once the applicant has passed the tests and got the job, there is no assurance that his life will be entirely his own. Objectionable practices that threaten privacy persist at all levels of government. The Post Office Department has, for example, used various techniques to keep tabs on the activities of employees during the work day. Recently the Chief Postal Inspector testified: "The need for surveillance of postal activities in order to keep depredations on the mail at a minimum has been proven over the long history of the Post Office Department. The lookout or observation galleries now in use for that purpose have been time tested . . . Employees do not, of course, generally know when the galleries are being used by inspectors for observation purposes." A far more objectionable Post Office practice—posting secret lookouts in employees' men's rooms—was discontinued as recently as late 1964.

Public school teachers have been actual or potential victims of a particularly abhorrent form of surveillance. The former Chief Counsel of the Senate Constitutional Rights Subcommittee reports: "Monitoring of classroom activities and conversations without the consent or knowledge of teachers, parents or students has become a common problem. The practice is justified as a means of evaluating teachers' performance by direct observation." Dr. Carbone, writing in the *Phi Delta Kappan,* adds:

> Some "professional" educators have for years used electronic devices to tell them what is going on in classrooms. . . . Anyone who has frequent contact with teachers can collect testimonials concerning the use of these intercom systems to "observe" teachers in action. There is ample evidence that some principals use it [intercom] for such purposes without the knowledge or consent of teachers.

Most school intercom systems can be activated from the office without alerting classroom teachers to the fact that someone is listening. There are no lights or warning buzzers to indicate when the device is on.

Governmental concern with employees' private lives may have the most serious consequences. Several years ago, the Federal Bureau of Investigation touched off a national controversy by firing a young, unmarried agent because he had spent a night or two in a young woman's apartment. A Civil Service Board in San Francisco upheld the dismissal of a postal clerk, also a bachelor, for living with a woman to whom he was not married. The Board cautioned that "moral standards have not yet reached the level where men and women may with public approval live in husband and wife relationship without benefit of marriage." A junior college teacher in Los Angeles was dismissed from a permanent faculty position because he lived with a former student who had been married to another man; the teacher thought the woman's Mexican divorce, obtained before they cohabited, was valid. A bachelor New York City policeman was dismissed for bringing "adverse criticism" on the Department by sharing an apartment with his girl friend, a divorcée. He charged that his superiors had found out about his extracurricular activities only by using a "peeping Tom."

An Ohio court did, however, reinstate a public school teacher who was dismissed for "immorality" after he had sent several "gross, vulgar and offensive" private letters to a former male student. In defining "immorality" for this purpose, the court warned: "The private speech or writings of a teacher, not in any way inimical to . . . the welfare [of the school community] are absolutely immaterial . . ."

Matters of dress and physical appearance also raise difficult questions about the extent of government's power over the employee's personal affairs. Not surprisingly, a disproportionate number of these cases have arisen in San Francisco. The city's probation department dismissed James Forstner, a career probation officer, in 1964 because he refused to shave off his beard. After two years of litigation, a California appellate court assured his right to follow his own tonsorial preferences. Another California court upheld the right of a Pasadena school teacher to sport a beard on the job. It was, said the judges, "an expression of his personality" that could no more be suppressed than could oral expression, which clearly enjoyed constitutional protection. The United States Post Office Department has refused to hire or retain "hippie" mail carriers. "Some of the men had hair down to their shoulders," complained the Assistant Postmaster General after a San Francisco inspection tour. "They were wearing everything from bearskin coats to dungarees. Some wore sandals, and some simply went barefoot." The new directive barred carriers from making their rounds in unkempt beards, psychedelic beads, or bare feet. Only after extensive sparring did the American Civil Liberties Union's Northern California branch establish the right of postal workers in San Francisco even to wear peace buttons on the job. An exception had to be made to a Post Office regulation barring "partisan displays" by employees.

In the case of the bearded Pasadena schoolteacher, the court suggested a useful formula for resolving such constitutional claims to "privacy" in the matter of an employee's dress, appearance, and other personal attributes: does the importance to the employing agency of the particular restriction—measured against whatever pertinent experience is available in that or other similar agencies —outweigh the individual's interest in self-expression or nonconformity? Where the personal conduct includes a serious law violation that directly affects the employee's competence or his relations with fellow workers or parts of the general public with whom he deals, then dismissal may be warranted, even necessary. (Where a school teacher carries on an adulterous relationship with a minor student, for example, the breach of professional standards seems obvious.) But where the activity neither violates the criminal law nor impairs the employee's ability to perform his job, the government's interest is attenuated. (For example, obesity has been deemed disqualifying for a physical education instructor but not for an English teacher; for a police officer but not for a police department telephone operator.) There are occupations in which a beard or long hair or strange clothing is truly incompatible with the needs of the public service. But the occasions for penalizing such idiosyncracies should be far fewer than the recent rash of cases might suggest.

There is little constitutional law restricting government's reach into an employee's private or extracurricular affairs. One Supreme Court decision does, however, afford some guidance in resolving these questions. The case concerned an Arkansas statute—

passed in the wake of federal court orders to integrate the Little Rock schools—requiring each public school teacher to file annually with the state education officials an affidavit listing every organization to which he had belonged or regularly contributed within the past five years. A majority of the Supreme Court struck down the statute as an infringement of the employee's First Amendment freedom of association.

Justice Stewart found there was apparently no relationship between the information sought and a teacher's fitness or competence for his classroom duties. Thus a "comprehensive interference with associational freedom goes far beyond what might be justified in the exercise of the state's legitimate inquiry." The threat was heightened by the absence of any guarantee of confidentiality. While a teacher in the North might with impunity report his membership in the NAACP, it would be quite another matter for a Southern teacher to do so. The nontenure teacher in Arkansas thus faced three choices: he could give up his job; he could conceal his political associations; or he could drop out of any organizations that might jeopardize his position. The Court concluded that the state could not exact so harsh a choice of its teachers as a condition of employment. While the state does have a valid interest in preventing teachers from overcommitting their extracurricular time to the detriment of their classroom duties, that interest must be served through less probing means.

An interesting sidelight is provided by the case of the bachelor FBI clerk discharged for spending several nights with a young lady. He petitioned the federal court for reinstatement, claiming that he had engaged only in the sort of "bundling" that was condoned even in Puritan New England. The Court of Appeals did not reach the merits, but held he was entitled to have a jury decide whether he was adequately warned these off-duty social pursuits would cost him his job. The Court did wonder about the strength of the FBI's interest in imposing so stringent a standard of morality on its employees. In any case, an employee must be strictly apprised whether he has to meet "not only the general standards of the community, but also the special standards of the lady from Dubuque."

Finally, government inquiries designed to prevent conflicts of interest or fraud may impair an employee's privacy. The typical federal worker must periodically report his entire financial activities and those of members of his immediate household to allay any suspicion about conflict-of-interest transactions. Testimony before the Constitutional Rights Subcommittee indicated, however, that such detailed financial information has been required of thousands of public employees whose positions "raise no substantial possibility of such conflicts." The Subcommittee's Chief Counsel has urged that because of its breadth and its deep reach into private affairs, the use of this inquiry "should be strictly limited to persons in positions of particular importance such as those persons empowered to award contracts or compromise claims. Surely the form is a questionable device at best since it requires persons to demonstrate periodically their innocence of violations of the numerous federal laws governing conflicts of interest."

Two important cautions are suggested by this comment: first, inquiries should be made only of those government employees whose positions or responsibilities make the answers relevant to an important governmental interest; and second, the questions should never be posed in such a way as to place on the employee the burden of proving his innocence when no evidence of wrongdoing exists. A third principle of general importance should be added: information should never be sought through questionnaires and inquiries if it could be obtained in a less offensive way—for example, from documents that are already on file with the agency or elsewhere.

"A WITNESS AGAINST HIMSELF": THE PUBLIC EMPLOYEE AND THE RISK OF SELF-INCRIMINATION

A host of constitutional cases have considered the extent to which a public employee may be compelled to answer potentially incriminating questions. The first cases arose from legislative investigations in the early and mid-1950s. A tenure faculty member at Brooklyn College who refused to tell a Senate Internal Security Subcommittee about certain past political associations was immediately discharged from his position. A city charter provision made dismissal automatic for any employee who invoked the privilege against self-incrimination to avoid answering a question relating to his official conduct. By a narrow margin the United States Supreme Court held that such a dismissal violated the teacher's constitutional rights since it operated automatically and arbitrarily to discharge every public employee who invoked a constitutional privilege. "In practical effect, the questions asked are taken as confessed and made the basis of the discharge." Moreover, the questions which the professor refused to answer "were admittedly asked for a purpose wholly unrelated to his college functions." While recognizing that no person had a constitutional right to public or academic employment and that a proper inquiry might well "show [the teacher's] continued employment to be inconsistent with a real interest of the state," there had in fact "been no such inquiry here." Such a summary dismissal therefore violated due process of law.

Two years later, a pair of Supreme Court decisions sharply qualified the Brooklyn College case. Both involved public employees—one a New York City subway conductor, and the other a Philadelphia public school teacher—who had refused to answer questions asked by their respective superiors about their political associations and activities. Both were discharged summarily and their dismissals were affirmed by the State Courts. The Supreme Court, finding these cases different from the Brooklyn professor's case, upheld the lower courts. Here the basis for discharge had not been the employee's resort to the Fifth Amendment, but his unwillingness to cooperate with his own superiors. In the Philadelphia case, the Court explained: "By engaging in teaching in the public schools, [the teacher] did not give up his right to freedom of belief, speech or association. He did, however, undertake obligations of frankness, candor and cooperation in answering inquiries made of him by his employing board examining into his fitness to serve it as a public school teacher . . . [He] blocked from the beginning any inquiry into his Communist activities however relevant to his present loyalty. The Board based its dismissal upon [the teacher's] refusal to answer any inquiry about his relevant activities—not upon those activities themselves. It took care to charge petitioner with incompetency and not with disloyalty."

Two years later, the Court's majority reached the same conclusion in a case involving Los Angeles County recreation employees who had refused—despite orders from their superiors—to answer questions about their political activities asked by a state legislative investigating committee. The Brooklyn College case was distinguished again: "The test here rather than being the invocation of any constitutional privilege is the failure of the employee to answer." The dissenters found this case indistinguishable from the Brooklyn College case; to them the city's reliance upon "insubordination" as the basis for the discharge was a transparent device to dilute the constitutional rights of public employees.

The law governing the public worker's obligation to testify has been clouded still further. The Supreme Court held in 1967 that New York could not disbar an attorney who refused, on grounds of self-incrimination, to produce financial records or to testify in person at a judicial inquiry into his alleged professional misconduct. The Court invoked the dormant authority of the 1956 Brooklyn College case. Since the plea of self-incrimination was the sole reason for the lawyer's disbarment, the court made clear that a professional license could not be withdrawn as punishment for resort to the Fifth Amendment. The majority intimated nothing about the rights of public employees.

In a brief concurring opinion, however, Mr. Justice Fortas suggested the issue would be quite different if the petitioner had been a member of the State Civil Service rather than of the bar: ". . . I would distinguish between a lawyer's right to remain silent and that of a public employee who is asked questions specifically, directly and narrowly relating to the performance of his official duties . . . This Court has never held, for example, that a policeman may not be discharged for refusal in disciplinary proceedings to testify as to his conduct as a police officer. . . . But a lawyer is not an employee of the State. He does not have the responsibility of an employee to account to the State for his actions because he does not perform them as an agent of the State." Apparently Justice Fortas was alone in sensing—and trying to resolve—the tension between the new self-incrimination cases and the earlier public employment decisions.

A companion case held that New Jersey could not by threat of dismissal secure incriminating evidence from a public employee. Evidence obtained from policemen called to testify about suspected misconduct was ruled inadmissible: "The choice given [the police officers] was either to forfeit their jobs or to incriminate themselves. The option to lose their means of livelihood or to pay the penalty of self-incrimination is the antithesis of free choice to speak out or remain silent."

The question that remains unanswered is whether government can still dismiss an employee for "noncooperation" if he refuses to answer incriminatory inquiries. But the Supreme Court moved one step closer to an answer the following year in a pair of cases from New York. As a result of political scandals in the 1930s, the state constitution and the New York City Charter provide for dismissal of a "public officer" who refuses to testify about his official conduct or who refuses to waive immunity from prosecution growing out of the inquiry—that is, to give up his privilege against self-incrimination. The New York courts have consistently upheld these requirements. "Although people in public office and on the public payroll may not be compelled to surrender their constitutional privilege against self-incrimination," declared the state court of appeals in the latest case, "they have no constitutional right to remain in office when they refuse to discuss with frankness and candor whether they have faithfully performed their duties."

This theory overlooks, or discounts, the acute dilemma that the public employee faces under interrogation. He can answer the questions, of course, if he is sure he has nothing to hide. But if for any reason he fears the consequences of full disclosure, he is caught either way. If he claims, or refuses to waive, the privilege against self-incrimination, he will be automatically fired under the mandate of the law. If he does waive his privilege, then he risks a series of questions that may uncover admissions fatal to his continued employment anyway. Under one option, there is a choice between loss of employment and criminal prosecution; but under the other option the public worker may face both penalties. And, as we have seen before, loss of public employment is frequently the more serious of the two sanctions.

Thus it is not surprising that the United States Supreme Court found the New York laws unconstitutional. A public worker, when summoned by his superiors, cannot be compelled to waive immunity. Since public employees continue to enjoy the privilege against self-incrimination, they cannot be compelled to choose between surrendering the protection of the privilege in advance of the interrogation, and forfeiting their jobs. The particular employee had been discharged, noted the Court, "not for failure to answer relevant questions about his official duties, but for refusal to waive a constitutional right." If, by contrast, he had been asked specific, job-related questions and had refused to answer, his claim of privilege would have given him no immunity against dismissal.

The private life and personal affairs of the public employee are subject to various official intrusions. His lot is not always worse than that of the man who works for private business or industry. But the very fact that one works for the state and the other does not is still a crucial difference, in practical if not constitutional terms. Recent changes in federal civil service policy have eliminated the most intrusive aspects of applying for a government job and have reduced the reach of official surveillance. Some state agencies have followed this lead. But in many areas of the public service, the lack of individual privacy, and reprisals for idiosyncratic dress or behavior, do much to perpetuate the differences that make public employment a second class occupation.

IV. *The Public Employee and the Unconstitutional Duty*

The problem of compelled, possibly incriminating, testimony by a public employee is really a special facet of a much larger issue: Can a public employee refuse to carry out an order or perform an assigned task because he believes the command is unconstitutional? As a result of increasing opposition to the Vietnam war within the armed forces, several officers have been court-martialed for refusing to carry out orders. Captain Howard B. Levy was cited for refusing to train Green Beret medical aides for service in Vietnam because of his conscientious opposition to the war. Captain Dale E. Noyd of the Air Force refused for similar reasons to train flight personnel for service in Vietnam. In neither case, however, did the military courts even consider the legality or constitutionality of the war itself. They went no further than to find the existence of a formally valid order, and refusal by an officer to carry it out. Since these are the elements of the offense under military law, the inquiry stopped there. (Although the Supreme Court has reviewed Noyd's case, it did not reach this issue.)

The civilian courts have, however, been more sensitive. The case of California social worker Benny Max Parrish suggests a humane response. In November 1962, supervisors of the county for which Parrish worked ordered the welfare department to conduct a series of unscheduled visits to welfare families, between six thirty and ten thirty on a Sunday morning. The principal purpose of these visits was to search for evidence of welfare fraud—for instance, absent parents or unauthorized males in the homes of recipients of Aid to Needy Children. As a control, some target homes would be chosen on the basis of the caseworkers' suspicions, others purely at random. The caseworkers were to travel in pairs. The worker known to the welfare recipient would present himself at the front door of the recipient's home and request admission. As soon as he entered, the caseworker would immediately go to the back door and admit his colleague who had been deployed to the rear of the building. Then the two would conduct a thorough search of the premises.

Parrish refused to take part in this program. He claimed the raids would violate not only the constitutional rights of the welfare clients, but professional standards of social work as well. He was dismissed for insubordination and appealed his case through the California courts. The state supreme court upheld Parrish's claim that the raids were unconstitutional, and agreed that a public officer could not be fired for refusing to violate someone else's rights as a condition of his own employment. Surely a government employee can be discharged for true insubordination, including most deliberate refusals to carry out orders given within the scope of his job. But where his orders encroach on the liberties of others, the employing agency cannot achieve one unconstitutional end by a condition imposed on another benefit.

A similar question has arisen regarding public school teachers who refuse to lead their classes in saluting the flag or pledging allegiance. From time to time teachers have been censured and even discharged for such refusals, but the question has seldom if ever reached the courts. There is one decision, however, which may shed much light on this question. It arose when Seymour Jacobs, a high school teacher in New York City, was suspended for refusing to lead his home room class in the pledge of allegiance. He claimed that the pledge was coercive and that his refusal was based on valid "reasons of conscience." When Jacobs petitioned for reinstatement, therefore, the Board of Education granted a hearing, and assigned as hearing officer Bethuel M. Webster, an adviser (and former law partner) of Mayor Lindsay, and former President of the Association of the Bar of the City of New York.

After a lengthy hearing, Webster recommended to the Board that Jacobs be reinstated. It was clear to him that the teacher's "constitutional rights [had] been infringed." If the Board wished to instill patriotism in its classes, concluded Webster, it must then "adopt means for promoting student patriotism that do not impair the personal liberties of teachers."

This decision, although it is not the judgment of a court and is not binding on the Board of Education, creates an important precedent for public school teachers across the country. Taken together with Parrish, this case suggests that a teacher cannot constitutionally be compelled to search student lockers or desks, to maintain surveillance on students through one-way mirrors or peepholes; or even disclose to school officials information which students have given to him in confidence (even though such information clearly enjoys no legal privilege should the grand jury or the district attorney demand it). In most states, of course, there is no law that bears even indirectly on these questions. The few cases there are do, however, suggest an increasing solicitude for the teacher caught in a dilemma between mandate and conscience.

As the Parrish and the flag-pledge cases suggest, many of the problems raised by conditions on public employment are political in character. We have excluded political restrictions from discussion here only because they deserve the more extensive focus of a separate chapter.

IV

POLITICS

AND THE

PUBLIC SERVICE

The more familiar restrictions on public employment relate to political activities and associations. Four types of restrictions have been particularly controversial: loyalty oaths or disclaimers, bans on partisan political activity, reprisals for criticism of government policy, and prohibitions against strikes by government workers. These restrictions have roots deep in American history, although they have only recently become the subject of controversy and litigation.

A major goal of both regulation and protection of the American civil servant has been eradication of the harmful effects of the "spoils system" that once plagued government at all levels. The pendulum may well have swung too far, however. What started out as neutrality appears to have become sterility; the present regulations seem to go substantially beyond the precautions necessary to insulate the civil service from partisan pressures. The character and validity of these restrictions will be the focus of this chapter.

The first major court decision involving the political liberties of a public employee is a good starting point. We have already mentioned the case of a police officer named McAuliffe who patrolled the streets of New Bedford, Massachusetts, in the 1890s. In his spare time, McAuliffe became involved in local party politics. A rule of the Police Department forbade political activity by its officers. McAuliffe was accordingly dismissed when his superiors discovered his infraction. He then brought suit against the mayor and other officials of New Bedford to regain his position, claiming that the ban on political activities was unreasonable and unconstitutional. The Massachusetts court rejected his claim, but in the process, it announced some legal principles that have reached far beyond the Commonwealth. Justice Oliver Wendell Holmes (who was still ten years away from the U.S. Supreme Court) wrote the opinion of the Massachusetts court. He answered McAuliffe's argument in this fashion: ". . . There is nothing in the Constitution or the statute to prevent the city from attaching obedience to this rule [the ban on political activities] as a condition to the office of policeman, and making it part of the conduct required. The petitioner may have a constitutional right to talk politics, but he has no constitutional right to be a policeman. There are few employments for hire in which the servant does not agree to suspend his constitutional rights of free speech as well as of idleness by the implied terms of his contract. The servant cannot complain, as he takes the employment on the terms which are offered him. On the same principle, the city may impose any reasonable condition upon holding office within its control. This condition seems to us reasonable, if that be a question open to revision here."

I. *The Public Worker and the Oath: The Stigma of Disloyalty*

No major cases involving the public worker and politics arose for fully a half century after the McAuliffe case. When the conflicting claims did reach the courts again, the battleground was loyalty oaths and disclaimers. Although these restrictions on public employment are widely associated with the McCarthy era, they have much earlier origins. Indeed, the closely analogous religious test oaths were so prevalent in prerevolutionary times that the framers of the Constitution thought it wise to include an explicit prohibition to rid the new American government of them: ". . . no religious test shall ever be required as a Qualification to any Office or public Trust under the United States." Political test oaths, too, have a long if undistinguished history that should be recounted at the outset.

The first disclaimer oath made its debut roughly a century ago. Several Reconstruction governments in the 1860s imposed test oaths on applicants for employment and various other positions, including the ministry and the practice of law, to exclude former Confederates from office or influence. The validity of these oaths reached the Supreme Court in 1868. The Court struck down these restrictions as bills of attainder; they represented a legislative judgment of guilt without a trial or hearing.

Throughout most of American history, government has relied upon the simple oath of allegiance as a test for office—a commitment to uphold the Constitution and laws or to perform the duties of the office to the best of one's ability. By the mid-1950s, however, so deeply had the McCarthy era made its impact that fully half the American states had added new tests of loyalty to the regular qualifications for public employment. These new oaths came in many forms. Often they involved a disclaimer by the applicant of past or present political activities—"I do not now advocate or attempt and have not attempted to bring about, or advocated, the violent overthrow of the government." Sometimes the oath required a similar renunciation for a future term of employment: "I will not seek to bring about or advocate the violent overthrow of the government so long as I am employed by the state." More sweeping were oaths which reached political associations and affiliations—"I have not been and am not now a member of any association or organization which advocates or seeks the violent overthrow of the government." Sometimes—as in Maryland (1949) and California (1952)—all these ingredients were combined in a single oath demanding a promise that the applicant had not been, was not now, and would not so long as he worked for the state be or become a member of any "subversive" organization.

An additional seven or eight states required the applicant to promise that he would "by precept and example promote respect for the flag and the statutes of the United States and of the State of————, reverence for law and order, and undivided allegiance to the government of the United States of America." Finally, there were loyalty tests and oaths that appeared innocent enough on the face, but held hidden traps for the unwary public worker. Arizona, for example, had long demanded a simple oath of allegiance. Under a gloss added to the oath in 1961, a public employee would be deemed to have defaulted on his simple oath of office if during his employment he knowingly and willfully became or remained a member of the Communist party or "any of its subordinate organizations" or "any other organization" having as one of its purposes the overthrow of the government of the state or a local subdivision.

These oaths were enforced in a variety of ways. Typically, the applicant would be kept off the payroll until he had signed. Sometimes he might also be discharged even though he was willing to go on working without pay. In extreme cases, one who was found to have falsely sworn the oath might also be criminally prosecuted.

Statutory preambles afford little insight into the objectives of such oaths. Inference suggests four likely legislative goals (apart from currying favor with an ultraconservative constituency) for imposing these conditions on public employment. First, there has been an honest concern to keep subversive and dangerous persons out of influential positions in government. Second, there has undoubtedly been a desire simply to punish those who have suspect political affiliations, whether or not they personally engage in dangerous activity. Third, there is in most oaths a deterrent character, a feeling that others may be dissuaded from joining political fringe groups, or induced to leave them, if government takes a hard line on subversive activities. And fourth, there has been a concern that a few political rotten apples may not only spoil the public service barrel, but give it a bad image as well.

The application of loyalty oaths is, however, seldom as discriminating as these apparent purposes. It must be recalled that in California a model could not be paid for an hour of posing nude before a junior college art class until she signed the loyalty pledge. And a professional boxer could not enter the ring in Indiana unless he had taken an antisubversive vow. Where loyalty oaths have been imposed, in fact, few exceptions have been made. Part-time and temporary employees, some private workers on government contract, and even foreign visitors briefly employed by the state have been forced to sign before they could be paid.

One pervasive question must first be answered before stating the case against the oath: Why would a loyal American have any hesitation about signing a pledge of loyalty? California's Chief Justice Roger Traynor has answered: "There are some who refuse to make the required declaration, not because they advocate overthrow of the government but because they conscientiously believe that the State has no right to inquire into matters so intimately touching political belief. Rightly or wrongly, they fear that such an inquiry is the first step in censorship of unpopular ideas." Two psychologists who studied the impact of the oath upon American college and university faculties concur: "Men and women who oppose communism may find it quite degrading if they feel forced to reiterate their private convictions in order to satisfy suspicious critics. While they agree with the condemnation of communism, they fear they may be setting a dangerous precedent on the broader issue of free expression of opinions. If foreswearing heresy becomes general practice, they may some day find themselves in a precarious position if they should deviate from the prevailing mood of the time." Mr. Justice Douglas has suggested a corollary objection— that the loyalty oath "places the burden of proving loyalty on the citizen. That procedural device goes against the grain of our constitutional system where every man is presumed innocent until guilt is established."

The great danger initially posed by loyalty oaths is that sensitive applicants may simply find the price of government employment too high and may therefore retreat to the private sector. The danger to public service morale from the pall cast by an oppressive oath thus seems greater than any morale problem subversive infiltration might pose.

The constitutional infirmities of particular oaths may best be surveyed by reviewing the Supreme Court decisions which have steadily narrowed the reach of government loyalty tests. As many states broadened their loyalty oaths in the late 40s and early 50s, academic freedom and civil liberties organizations were not far behind in filing constitutional test cases. The first law to be tested was a Los Angeles City ordinance requiring municipal employees to swear that they had not within the preceding five years advocated the violent overthrow of the government or joined an organization that did so, and would not while working for the city advocate violent overthrow nor join an organization committed to that end. The majority of the Justices found the city had a substantial interest in probing the political affiliations of its employees, and that the oath reasonably reflected that interest.

The following year the Court sustained New York's Feinberg Law on a similar theory. At the same time the Court struck down an Oklahoma oath because it was not confined to *knowing* membership in subversive organizations; by reaching innocent as well as conscious participation in such groups, it failed to differentiate between political activity the state could prohibit and that which was constitutionally protected.

In 1961 and 1964 the Court struck down loyalty oaths of the

States of Florida and Washington because their central provisions were excessively vague. The Florida law, for example, required an applicant for a government job to swear that he had never "knowingly lent his aid, support, advice, counsel, or influence to the Communist Party." Such a sweeping ban might include a lawyer who had once defended a Communist, or a person who had campaigned for a political candidate also supported by the Communist Party. The Washington oath suffered a similar vice, for it required every public worker to vouch that he was not a "subversive person" and did not belong to a "subversive organization." That term was defined so loosely that it might well have included a scholar who belonged to an international society with headquarters behind the Iron Curtain, or who attended a conference with Communist delegates. The Court concluded: "We do not question the power of a state to take proper measures safeguarding public service from disloyalty conduct, but measures which purport to define disloyalty must allow public servants to know what is and what is not disloyal."

The harshest blow of all was dealt the following year at Arizona's loyalty oath. The Court had previously held that only "knowing" membership could be banned. In criminal prosecutions under the Internal Security Act, the Court had restricted the reach of government power to knowing membership in illegal organizations that was active and included a specific intent on the member's part to further the unlawful ends. Thus a knowing, active member of the Communist Party might still escape punishment if he could show that his reason for joining the Party was to further the cause of civil rights, rather than the violent overthrow of the government (or some other unlawful end). In the Arizona case the Court's majority (5–4) extended this restriction to loyalty oaths: only renunciation of knowing, active membership, with a specific intent to further the organization's unlawful goals, could constitutionally be made a condition of employment.

The premise of the Arizona case was simple and basic: "Those who join an organization but do not share its unlawful purposes and who do not participate in its unlawful activities surely pose no threat, either as citizens or as public employees."

There is another side to the same coin: government must exercise particular care not to sweep within its prohibitions those who may have innocently joined subversive groups. Even FBI Director

J. Edgar Hoover has acknowledged that during the 1930s many Americans "joined [but] did not know what [the Communist Party] was; they were good, fine young men and women, loyal Americans, but they had been trapped into it—because one of the great weaknesses of all Americans, whether adult or youth, is to join something." Because political association and activity on the lawful side of the line enjoyed the constitutional protections of the First Amendment, government must be especially sensitive in drawing that line.

Two practical considerations reinforced these decisions. For one, there was growing doubt whether loyalty oaths actually accomplished their objectives. *The New York Times* chided proponents of such tests: "[Loyalty oaths] are useless; for what genuine subversive would hesitate to swear loyalty if to do so served his purposes? Only the conscientious are likely to be the victims." If loyalty oaths were largely ineffectual, more apposite sanctions were available to meet whatever threat of subversion and anarchy does exist. Those who actually attempt to bring about the overthrow of the government can be prosecuted directly, under a variety of laws already on the books. Where sufficient grounds exist to suspect a particular person of plotting a revolution or coup, ample avenues of investigation already exist. The Supreme Court has said repeatedly that government must use that method of regulation which is least harmful to constitutionally protected liberties. Yet government need not be helpless if compelled to rely on more precise alternative approaches to the problem of internal security. These methods of self-protection would leave the average, loyal citizen undisturbed, and would then focus, when and where necessary, upon the very small fraction of the population the government has substantial reason to fear.

Rounding out the cycle, the Supreme Court in 1967 struck down New York's Feinberg Law and Maryland's Ober Law—both of which it had sustained in the early 1950s. The grounds of decision were similar to those invoked in other recent cases. At the same time, the Court refused to review several lower court decisions which had upheld simple "oath of allegiance" pledges that required public employees only to swear to defend the constitution and laws of the United States and the state for which they worked. Meanwhile, the oaths of California, Colorado, Georgia, Idaho, Texas, Massachusetts, and Kansas were killed by state and lower federal courts. In several states, including New Hampshire and New Jersey, state attorneys general voluntarily sounded the death knell for their loyalty oaths before the matter even reached the courts. In Illinois and a few other states, unsuccessful efforts were made to induce legislatures to repeal loyalty oaths. By the end of 1969, the only disclaimer-type oaths still on the books either lingered through sheer inertia or embodied recent legislative attempts to salvage what few scraps the Court had left of a once tightly woven loyalty fabric.

II. *Public Workers and Partisan Politics*

Most Americans—whether publicly or privately employed —are not aware of the extent to which the political activities of civil servants are circumscribed by law. The best known and most pervasive restrictions are those imposed on federal employees by the Hatch Act, and on state and local government employees by similar laws (often called "little Hatch Acts"). Such laws have deep historical roots which should be traced in order to understand the current issues.

Right after the Civil War, Congress enacted a law which prohibited solicitation of funds for political purposes from any person employed in a Navy yard. Nine years later this injunction was expanded to prohibit political fund raising on the job or from any Federal Government employee. In a test case decided in 1882, the Supreme Court sustained the statute on the ground that no public employee had any constitutional right to further his or anyone else's political cause either by soliciting or by contributing funds during working hours.

The inauguration of the modern civil service system in 1883 as an antidote to the patronage system of public employment included an early regulation that no government officer should "use his official authority or influence to coerce the political action of any person." President Grover Cleveland shortly thereafter warned the Civil Service that "proper regard for the proprieties and requirements of official place will also prevent their assuming the active conduct of political campaigns." The immediate roots of the Hatch Act lie in a Civil Service Rule promulgated in 1907 by President Theodore Roosevelt (a strong supporter of civil service reform):

"In the competitive classified service, while retaining the right to vote as they please and to express privately their opinions on all political subjects, [government employees] shall take no active part in political management or in political campaigns." This rule covered only classified employees in the Civil Service. During the Depression and New Deal, however, charges of political intimidation of relief workers and other unclassified employees generated pressure for new and more comprehensive laws. The Hatch Act, passed in 1939, was the outgrowth of this impetus. Its object was to insulate government employees from partisan political pressures of various types.

Draftsmen of the Hatch Act were presumably concerned about several dangers: first, the possible drain on "company time" if politicking on the job is permitted; second, the possibility of conflicts of interest between superiors and subordinates if the latter can actively and openly campaign to unseat the former; third, the prospect of bullying and exploitation of subordinates for partisan work or financial support; and finally, the need for the Civil Service more than any other profession to remain politically unsullied and neutral.

The heart of the Hatch Act is Section 9A, which forbids most officers and employees of the federal executive branch, and state workers on federally financed projects, to use official authority or influence to affect an election or to take "any active part in political management or in political campaigns." A violation may result in dismissal, or suspension for not less than ninety days. The phrase "taking any active part in political management or in political campaigns" is defined in terms of pre-1939 Civil Service Commission rulings. Among the activities prohibited by those rulings are participation in political conventions; organizing, conducting, or addressing political rallies or meetings; holding office as political committeeman; soliciting, collecting, or otherwise dealing with political funds or contributions; distributing campaign literature; or engaging in any activity at the polls except voting. The only activities clearly permitted are voting, contributing to campaign funds (except in a federal building or to a fellow employee), joining political organizations, attending political meetings, participating in nonpartisan civic organizations, signing petitions, and speaking or writing on political subjects not connected with political campaigns. Hatch Act restrictions have recently been extended to many employees of local Community Action Organizations funded by the Office of Economic Opportunity.

Hatch Act violations are relatively infrequent. The Civil Service Commission received roughly seven hundred complaints during a recent five-year period. Thirty-eight employees were dismissed, and thirty-two suspended as a result of these charges. A brief sampling will illustrate the range of infractions. A Kentucky state employee on a federal project was dismissed for organizing a lottery and contribution scheme among fellow workers in connection with a political party fund-raising dinner. A rural letter carrier in New Hampshire was suspended for mailing out three hundred copies of a political report by Group Research Reports to a list of prominent New Hampshire citizens, as part of his work in a local labor council. Another Civil Service employee was suspended for thirty days for sending out four hundred post cards carrying his personal opinion of a political candidate. Yet a Federal Court of Appeals reversed a Civil Service Commission decision involving a postal worker who was charged with Hatch Act violation for having spoken in support of a particular candidate at a county Democratic Party central committee meeting. The court observed that "the evidence . . . reflects no more than the public expression by an [employee] of an opinion on a political subject, which is actively protected by statute."

The constitutionality of the Hatch Act has been tested in the United States Supreme Court. The case involved a group of civil servants whose claims the Court dismissed because they had not yet violated the Act but only proposed to do so and wanted advice in advance. But the Court did reach the merits in the case of one sheet metal worker in the Philadelphia Mint who had already worked as a ward executive committeeman for a political party. Such activity, the Court noted, "may promote or retard his advancement or preferment with his superiors. Congress may have thought that government employees are handy elements for leaders in political policy to use in building a political machine." The Hatch Act's restrictions were therefore constitutional because Congress had reasonably concluded that partisan activity might "interfere with the efficiency of the public service."

Mr. Justice Douglas dissented. He argued that while restrictions of this kind might be warranted for especially sensitive or vulnerable positions in the Civil Service, no visible dangers justified the "political sterilization" of the entire government work force. Political rights are "too basic and fundamental in our democratic political society to be sacrificed or qualified for anything short of a clear and present danger to the Civil Service System."

While the Hatch Act has received the Supreme Court's imprimatur, parallel state restrictions have fared somewhat less well, particularly on the West Coast. The first case concerned Dr. Joel Fort, a California public health worker who was fired from the directorship of an alcoholism center because during the 1962 campaign he chaired a speakers' bureau helping to reelect Governor Edmund G. Brown. He did the work on his own time and in a county other than the one where he worked. But this activity violated a county charter provision prohibiting a member of the classified Civil Service from taking any part "in political management or affairs in any political campaign or election, or in any campaign to adopt or reject any initiative or referendum measure other than to cast his vote or to privately express his opinion."

When Dr. Fort sued for reinstatement, the California Supreme Court agreed that his political liberties had been violated by an unconstitutional condition on public employment. The Court recognized that a partisan Civil Service could create special and serious dangers. To the extent the legislature's concern was with such evils, "it is, of course, possible to draw a restrictive provision narrowly in order to deal specifically with such abuses." But restrictions on public employees must be no broader than "required to preserve the efficiency and integrity of its public service." A comprehensive ban on political activities could certainly not be justified "merely because the persons affected are public employees. . . ."

A later California case refined and tightened the matrix for testing political restrictions on government workers: "A governmental agency which would require a waiver of constitutional rights as a condition of public employment must demonstrate: (1) that the political restraints rationally relate to the enhancement of the public service, (2) that the benefits which the public gains by the restraints outweigh the resulting impairment of constitutional rights, and (3) that no alternatives less subversive of constitutional rights are available." About the same time, the Supreme Court of Oregon struck down that state's little Hatch Act, relying heavily upon the constitutional stature of political activity.

Apart from the primary constitutional issues, two corollary

arguments support these holdings. In a sense, the Civil Service System has already done its job so well and established so high a level of integrity that a set of restrictions designed to prevent crude political exploitation seems no longer necessary. There are still serious threats to the integrity of the public service—especially during major national election campaigns. But more precise checks against such abuses could be substituted for the present sweeping prohibitions. Short of abandoning the Hatch Act outright, revisions might remove its most oppressive characteristics while preserving its essential goals. First, the political activity restrictions could be confined to working hours, leaving civil servants free to engage in politics on their own time. Second, it might be possible to subdivide the Civil Service, as British practice does, with special restrictions tailored to the needs of each group. Under this approach, employees who perform essentially industrial and "manipulative" tasks (as in the postal service) are as free to engage in politics as are other citizens. An intermediate group, including some clerical employees and minor grades of scientific and technical workers, are partially restricted. A third group—composed of those in the most vulnerable positions—are restricted in their politics by rules similar to those of the Hatch Act. Neither the British experience nor the purpose of its civil service regulations is precisely analogous to our own, of course, but the British approach is nonetheless instructive.

These arguments have already had some impact in high places. Congress appointed in 1967 a Commission on Political Activity of Government Personnel. The Commission held extensive hearings throughout the country and at all levels of government service, seeking to evaluate and find alternatives to the present Hatch Act restrictions. The Commission's report recommended many changes in the existing law, including greater reliance upon direct criminal sanctions against coercion and other clear abuses of public office, and diminished resort to broad prophylactic prohibitions.

Legislation has already been introduced in the Senate to implement these recommendations. The pending bill would permit much broader and more active political participation in partisan campaigns, and would even allow civil servants to run for elective office except where such candidacy would pose a conflict of interest. The proposed legislation would specifically repeal the Hatch Act and replace it with a limited network of narrower restrictions, supplemented by criminal sanctions against the particular abuses

that spawned the Act and its state and local progeny several decades ago.

A final argument against extensive restrictions invokes the
public interest in the public service. There is evidence that many
people—particularly young people during the New Deal and the
early 1960s—have chosen government careers as a way of becoming more deeply involved in public life and affairs. If the cauteriz-
ing effects of the Hatch Act compel them to choose between government and politics, they still may not forego a few years in
Washington after college or law school. But the prospect seems substantially lower that they will make government a career. Any restrictions which dampen the enthusiasm of idealistic and dedicated
young people for public service should be viewed with great concern. For as the *Public Administration Review,* in a summary of a
recent Brookings Institution study, warned after surveying some
"bleaker aspects" of the federal manpower outlook: "The Federal
Government has to compete in the marketplace to fill its manpower
needs. It can no longer spend time in leisurely contemplation of
ways to limit eligibility for appointment. . . . Young people are not
flocking to the flag of the career civil service . . ."

III. *Protest, Criticism, and Libelous Attacks on Superiors*

Few lines of public employment have been more attractive to
politically active young Americans than the Peace Corps. During its
eight years of operation, it has brought into public employment
thousands of college graduates who would otherwise have been unlikely to work for the government. In the summer of 1967, however,
the Peace Corps announced the dismissal of one Bruce Murray, a
twenty-five-year-old volunteer who had protested American policy
in Southeast Asia (particularly the bombing of North Vietnam)
while serving in Concepción, Chile. When Murray wrote a letter to
The New York Times declaring his opposition to the war, he was
formally warned not to identify himself as a member of the Peace
Corps. He was also admonished against publicizing his views in
Chile. Murray went ahead, however, and had the letter published
both in *The Times* and also in *Elsur,* a Chilean daily. In announcing
Murray's dismissal, a Peace Corps official explained: "The Vietnam war is a major political issue in Chile, and it has been the pol-

icy of the Peace Corps not to get involved in any local political issue."

The criticism of Murray's dismissal was immediate and intense. The American Civil Liberties Union telegraphed President Johnson and Peace Corps Director Jack Vaughn expressing support for any volunteers dismissed as a result of antiwar protests. ACLU then learned that fifty-seven Peace Corps volunteers in Chile who had signed a "Negotiation Now" statement about Vietnam had been threatened with dismissal shortly after the Murray incident unless they withdrew their names from the petition. Most of the signers refused to comply. The ACLU's Executive Director urged the Peace Corps to "officially inform American peace corpsmen in Chile that they are free to sign the petition in question and that the government intends no intimidation of the exercise of their First Amendment Rights."

Two weeks later, six Peace Corps volunteers in Ecuador wrote a letter to *The New York Times* expressing deep concern about the effects of reprisals against antiwar statements: "We have been partially deprived of our status as free agents, as representatives of the American people rather than the American government. This has damaged our relations with the people with whom we work. Many of them who strongly distrust the American government had over the past five years come to regard the Peace Corps as a special sort of organization, and volunteers as unusually sincere people . . . [N]ow the distinction between the Peace Corps and other agencies of the United States government has become blurred. We are losing the confidence of many of the people we came here to help." They went on to protest the recent ruling that forbade identification of Peace Corps membership when taking foreign policy stands.

The Peace Corps controversy highlights a rapidly mounting problem—reprisals for protest or criticism by public employees. A brief survey of recent representative cases will indicate the dimensions of the problem. A fireman in Berkeley, California, was suspended for thirty days after he wrote a letter to a local newspaper attacking the City Council's policies toward the Police Department. His action violated a Fire Department regulation that all firemen "shall refrain from adverse criticism concerning the actions of any superiors, and . . . shall not publicly express disapproval of the policies and practices of the Department."

A mechanic at the Brooklyn Naval Shipyard was discharged

because of a letter he wrote to the Secretary of the Navy complaining about promotion and personnel policies at the Brooklyn yard. The letter contained attacks which his superiors claimed were false, indeed defamatory. He was dismissed for making "unfounded statements."

A member of the American police force in the Canal Zone was discharged from his civil service position for distributing a letter and a poem bitterly critical of the Governor's handling of controversial labor and personnel matters. He was charged with "conduct unbecoming an officer"; some of the statements he had circulated were "derogatory and libelous" with regard to the Governor, and were made "in a sarcastic and contemptuous manner."

Several firemen in Cedar Rapids, Iowa, were dismissed in 1964 for releasing to the press critical and allegedly biased statements during labor negotiations with the department. Departmental rules required submission to the chief and his approval before giving out "any information relative to the department, its operations, equipment, etc. . . ." In Hartford, Connecticut, a welfare caseworker was discharged, allegedly because he had made public statements critical of the state's welfare law and its administration. A nontenure teacher at Arkansas Agricultural and Mechanical College was discharged after he made public statements criticizing the treatment of prisoners in the State Penitentiary. (National disclosure of these prison conditions over a year later prompted a *New York Times* headline, "Arkansas Prison: Chamber of Horror.")

There has been little consistency in the disposition of these cases by the courts. While the Berkeley and Cedar Rapids firemen, the Brooklyn Navy Yard worker and the Arkansas teacher were reinstated by the courts, the Canal Zone policeman and the Connecticut caseworker fared less well. In the Berkeley case, the California court warned that reprisals for criticism raised serious free speech issues: "The acceptance of public employment does not demand abandonment of constitutionally protected rights. . . . [A] public employee may speak freely as long as he does not impair the administration of the public service in which he is engaged." In the Canal Zone case, however, a federal court of appeals took a less tolerant view of the employee's criticism—partly because the times had been troubled ones in Panama, and the court felt the Governor's policies, whether right or wrong, were entitled to greater deference than they might have been under tranquil conditions: "While a free society values robust, vigorous and essentially uninhibited public speech by citizens, such public speech by government employees may produce intolerable disharmony, inefficiency, dissension and even chaos. There is a natural and entirely reasonable difference between the kind of discipline and limitation on speech the government may impose on its employees and the kind it may impose on the public at large."

The law remained in this unsettled state until the Supreme Court reviewed two cases involving outspoken public school teachers (one from Seward, Alaska, and the other from Lockport, Illinois). Both teachers had made statements at local meetings and in the press that were intensely critical of school board and administration policies. Both were discharged, their superiors claiming the statements were not only divisive and possibly disruptive, but actually contained false and defamatory charges. Both dismissals were sustained by the respective state courts.

After hearing both cases, the United States Supreme Court unanimously reversed the dismissal of the Illinois teacher, and sent the Alaska case back to the state court for reconsideration under a new standard. That standard was adapted from the context of private libel and slander suits. The Court had held four years earlier that a writer or publisher could not constitutionally be sued for false statements about the official conduct of a public officer unless the statements were made with "actual malice" or in "reckless disregard of the truth." The Court now held that a schoolteacher or other public employee must be free to the same extent to criticize the official acts of superiors; even though false accusations might be made, the critic may not be dismissed unless his statements exceed the bounds of a rather broad constitutional privilege. Since the statements made by the Illinois teacher clearly did not transcend these limits, his dismissal represented an unconstitutional penalty for the exercise of his political rights.

Important though it is, this decision purports only to deal with cases in which the criticism is defamatory. There are at least two other situations—probably much more common, in fact—in which the government's power to discipline dissident employees remains unresolved. The first is the case in which the criticism of official policy or the acts of one's superiors cannot be classified as true or false, and is therefore not susceptible to *The New York Times* test. If, for example, a subordinate charges that his agency head is "a vicious, arrogant, cocky bastard," no inquiry into the parentage or the specific vices of the named superior will be particularly relevant to a contemplated defamation suit. Such acerbic charges as these—be they irresponsible, and possibly quite damaging to the victim's reputation—are probably not actionable as libel and are thus not covered by the recent Supreme Court decisions. The question of the dismissability of an employee who makes such charges out of malice must therefore look elsewhere for an answer. The Panama Canal Zone case is closer to this situation, and suggests a possible test, although its own facts counsel sparing use of a doctrine that might be dangerous to civil liberties in the civil service.

The other case not touched upon by the Supreme Court is that of the public employee who, against orders and quite possibly against the national interest, divulges absolutely true information. If the breach is extreme, of course, it may be either an act of treason or one covered by some other specific criminal law. But there are many instances of factually correct statements by public employees that fall short of giving away military secrets or releasing classified files to the enemy. The occasional leak to the press by someone who is near or has access to the top of a federal agency is a far better illustration of the problem. The balance to be struck in such a case is a difficult one. Surely the government has some interest in keeping the information confidential, or at least postponing its release until a time when it will be least damaging to public confidence. Equally clearly, however, sanctions against public employees who speak the truth should not be lightly permitted. *The New York Times* standard is no more helpful here than in the other context just considered. Perhaps what is required when the charge is one of leaking the truth is a test approximating the "clear and present danger" test applicable to criminal prosecutions against spoken and written attacks upon the government. Thus a dismissal would require proof that divulgence of the information, at the time and place and under the circumstances of its release, did pose a very substantial threat to the security of the state. That would be a difficult burden to meet, but would at least provide recourse in the extreme case.

IV. *Public Employment and the Right to Strike*

A half century ago Calvin Coolidge won national acclaim (and a Vice Presidential nomination) by putting down the Boston police strike. "There is," he insisted in one of his few memorable statements, "no right to strike against the public safety by anybody, anywhere, anytime." The proposition, stated in this fashion, is hard to dispute. Nor has it been eroded by the passage of time or changes in the law of public employment.

Since Coolidge's day, however, two divergent trends have developed. In private employment, the rights to organize, to picket peacefully, to bargain collectively, and ultimately to strike if agreement cannot be reached on a new contract are not only recognized but are legally protected under the Wagner and Taft-Hartley Acts. Meanwhile, in the public sector, penalties against strikes and walkouts have, if anything, been strengthened, although some concessions have recently been made for unionization and collective bargaining. Thus workers performing identical tasks may or may not strike according to whether their employer is a governmental agency. The years since Coolidge's pronouncement have sharply underscored this disparity between public and private employment.

No one who pays attention to current affairs needs to be told of the impact of public employee strikes on state and local government throughout the United States. The crippling effect of walkouts by public school teachers, sanitation workers, social caseworkers and other employees has hit New York City the hardest. But it is mostly in smaller communities that policemen and firemen have struck against their municipal employers, and have jeopardized essential services. In addition to total strikes, the public sector has been plagued increasingly by epidemics of "blue flu" or slowdowns, swollen sick lists and other forms of protest short of walking out. The chronicle of public employee strikes deserves a book by itself; this is not the place to make more than passing reference to the dimensions of the problem and the alarming current trends.

It is worth a bit of speculation to assess the causes of these strikes. Walkouts are almost unknown in the federal civil service. This might be partly the result of the very severe penalties against striking; every federal worker knows that any breach of the no-strike clause to which he is bound will subject him to a year in jail and a $1,000 fine. Yet the penalties against state and local strikes, at least as drastic in many cases, seem ineffectual as deterrents. Where the union members, or their leaders, really want to strike, and the agency is unable (or unwilling) to meet their demands, no threat of injunction, fine, or jail sentence will keep them on the job.

There must then be other reasons for the high incidence of strikes at the state and municipal level. The greatest number of walkouts seem to have occurred in occupations—notably teaching, social work, and sanitation—from which one can least readily escape to the private sector. Perhaps partly because of the paucity of nongovernmental alternatives, wage scales for these jobs seem not to have shared in the general rises in government salary levels. Yet the bitterest disputes have not centered upon compensation. For the New York schoolteachers and social workers the major demands were for greater participation in policy making and job security rather than fatter paychecks. Moreover, the sectors of public employment hardest hit by strikes have probably been the best organized. It is no coincidence that the rapid rise in teachers' strikes parallels the emergence and consolidation of the Federation of Teachers.

Meanwhile, there has been some relaxation of law affecting the organization of public workers. A decade ago, collective bargaining was generally denied to civil servants. In 1962 federal agencies were told for the first time to recognize and enter into agreements with employee organizations. By 1967, eighteen unions had gained exclusive rights to represent over a million federal workers; the number of collective agreements rose from a scant twenty-six to more than six hundred. Similar changes have occurred at the state and local level. Statutes or constitutional clauses in eleven states now provide for collective bargaining with employee organizations over some or all issues. Administrative or court decisions allow bargaining in an additional fifteen states and in the District of Columbia. Within a decade, therefore, the picture has changed somewhat with regard to *bargaining;* the *strike* remains, however, as universally prohibited as it was in Coolidge's time.

This discussion suggests two pertinent legal questions: First, can a public employee be barred from or punished for joining a labor union? and second, can he constitutionally be forbidden to strike? The first question can be answered rather easily; the second is vastly more complex.

Two recent Federal Court of Appeals cases go far to establish union membership—and perhaps some form of bargaining by implication—as a constitutional right of public employees. Both cases involved government workers who were dismissed for joining unions, in violation of unstated local policies. Both sued for reinstatement, claiming abridgment of their civil rights. The courts upheld the employees in both cases, and found dismissal for union membership an unconstitutional condition on public employment. By analogy to the loyalty oath cases, a public worker could not be punished simply for joining a union that was not engaged in illegal activity. Even if the union's aims were unlawful, it would have to be shown that the particular employee was a knowing, active member who joined for the purpose of furthering the illegal ends—or that his membership in the union disrupted the public service in some other way. In the absence of such evidence, said one court, "to allow dismissal of public employees for assertion of their First Amendment rights of association . . . subjects them to unreasonable conditions of employment."

The right of the individual employee to join a union with impunity does not establish the right of the union to strike, or even to demand a place at the bargaining table. State and federal law are still flatly against the public employee strike, as we have seen. But there are indications of a change in public opinion which may eventually reach the legislatures, despite (or perhaps because of) the persistent flouting of the antistrike injunctions. The National Education Association, the major professional society of elementary and secondary teachers, for years condemned teacher strikes as "unprofessional." At its 1967 Convention, NEA suddenly reversed itself. Within a few months, several NEA affiliates seized the strike initiative from the more aggressive American Federation of Teachers.

Other groups have recently reexamined the public sector strike. The National Council of Churches argues, for example, that civil servants should not be barred from striking "solely by virtue of their public employment." Gubernatorial advisory panels in Michigan and New York have suggested that strikes should be permitted under some conditions. In a Louis Harris poll after the 1968 New York teacher walkout, 49 percent felt that "teachers should have the right to strike" (against 41 percent opposed) and 59 percent believed that teachers who did strike had justifiable reasons for doing so. (A later Gallup poll, however, showed only 35 percent in favor of the right to strike.)

The issue now before us cannot be decided by popular opinion. There is a lurking legal question that surfaces infrequently, but which courts are now being asked to decide: Does the public worker have a constitutional right to strike under some (or all) circumstances? There is still not much law on the question. The U.S. Supreme Court declared some years ago that a strike against the government "is rebellion against constituted authority." The highest court of New York has upheld the state's Taylor Law prohibiting public employee strikes. The union argued that even if no person initially had a constitutional right to strike, it was a denial of equal protection to allow private workers to strike but to deny that option to government employees. The court unanimously rejected this contention: "The ability of the legislature to establish priorities among government employees would be destroyed if public employees could, with impunity, engage in strikes which deprive the public of essential services. . . . The consequence would be the destruction of democratic legislative processes because budgeting and the establishment of priorities would no longer result from the free choice of the electorate's representatives, but from the coercive effect of paralyzing strikes of public employees." The Court concluded that the legislature had drawn a reasonable distinction between the public and private sectors.

Only in California has the legal wall opened even a crack. Some years ago a state court found that the legislature had, by ambiguous wording, allowed Los Angeles transit workers to strike. Later the California Supreme Court set aside an injunction against striking and picketing by Sacramento County social workers. The ground was a narrow one, but the court reserved the question whether the right to strike could constitutionally be denied to public workers. Just before the opening day of classes in the fall of 1969, a Los Angeles Superior Court judge refused to enjoin an imminent strike of public school teachers. Such an injunction would, the court explained, violate the teachers' constitutional rights of free speech and association unless the school district could make "the clearest showing of irreparable injury."

Certainly the question is appropriate for discussion here, because denial of the right to strike is one of the major disabilities of public employment. Let us begin with the arguments supporting the prohibition the law now imposes. It was not Calvin Coolidge, but Franklin Roosevelt, who warned that "a strike of public employees manifests nothing less than an intent on their part to obstruct the operations of government until their demands are satisfied." He thought a strike in the public sector, "looking toward the paralysis of government by those who have sworn to support it, unthinkable and intolerable."

At the heart of the case against the public strike is the sovereign character of government. Unlike the private employer who can respond to a strike or strike threat in a wide variety of ways, the government exists to provide free services from an essentially monopolistic position. Governments, therefore, cannot make ordinary economic, marketplace, profit-and-loss decisions. Moreover, decision making about appropriations is widely separated from the bargaining table. Professor Donald Wollett asks: "Can there be meaningful negotiations on salaries (or any other emolument of value), hours of work, or terms and conditions which have budgetary implications with public management that neither knows nor decides the amount of money which it will have during the next fiscal year?" The city can survive walkouts of fire insurance claim agents; but a strike by firemen will create an acute risk that cannot be tolerated for more than a few hours. Public school teachers, hospital aides, social workers, and sanitation men—all these and more, constituting a large share of municipal employees, have become almost indispensable.

Proponents of the right to strike say there is a substantial constitutional issue at stake. Jerry Wurf, President of the American Federation of State, County and Municipal Employees, and chief spokesman for the cause, argues that "one cannot deprive 20% of the work force of the essentials of democracy in employment relations without harming the basic freedoms of all Americans." The practical meaning of the contention is clear: it is unreasonable, Wurf argues, to deny to workers in a municipal power plant in one community the rights to organize, bargain, and strike which their counterparts in a neighboring private power plant enjoy.

The juxtaposition of public and private employees performing comparable or identical tasks suggests that the *total* ban on government strikes is unnecessarily broad. It is true that many public workers perform essential tasks and cannot be allowed to leave their jobs. The right to strike might well be denied to them, just as it is restricted for certain essential private employees (*e.g.,* railroad workers, milk drivers, and public utility servicemen). But the case for partial restriction does not warrant neutralization of the entire public service corps. In reviewing other regulations affecting government employees, the courts have insisted that the prohibition be no broader than absolutely essential to serve a valid public interest. The outer limits of collective action should be no more loosely determined than those of loyalty oaths or bans on political activity.

The economic arguments are more difficult to refute. Yet the proponents of the right to strike point out that full collective bargaining has worked well in industries in which a closely regulated monopolist (*e.g.,* a telephone company, a public utility, or franchised bus company) has little more direct control over profit determination than do government agency heads. Many nations, including the two that are most relevant for comparative purposes, Canada and Great Britain, permit strikes at least by some public workers. A recent study published by the Cornell University School of Industrial and Labor Relations concluded: "In no country where the right to strike is allowed has there been any protracted breakdown in the public services, nor any unusual abuse of the strike weapon."

Indeed, proponents have argued that allowing strikes might improve, not impair, public sector labor relations. The argument proceeds from two premises. First, it is increasingly obvious that antistrike bans are ineffective against major protests. They are heeded by the small and weak government employee organizations, but no sanctions are sufficient to deter a large and powerful union planning a walkout. Leaders of public employee unions have been willing to risk quite heavy civil and criminal antistrike penalties. In New York City, Teachers Union President Albert Shanker was jailed for contempt in 1967 and again in 1968; later sanitation chief John DeLury was also incarcerated for the duration of the strike. Both unions were fined heavily for flouting the antistrike injunction. But both strikes continued until the workers got substantially what they had demanded at the outset. The reason for the breakdown goes to the heart of the present law: there is, observes labor writer A. H. Raskin, "a tendency to view the legal prohibitions as secondary to the necessity for getting things moving again, by giving the union what it wants."

Given the ineffectiveness of present prohibitions, it has been argued that state and municipal employee strikes might well diminish in frequency and duration if they were legalized. New York labor mediator Theodore Kheel contends that the Taylor Law actually invites the very conduct the legislature sought to outlaw: "By prohibiting strikes of public employees, the law eliminates collective bargaining, which implies the right of the buyer or seller to refuse to buy or sell by a strike or lockout. You can't bargain unless you have the right to say 'no deal' and not buy the car."

While these arguments do not resolve the controversy, they do suggest two tentative conclusions: first, the strike ban on public employees who do not perform essential services—or who hold jobs identical to private workers who are permitted to strike—may be unconstitutional because it goes beyond the government's needs. There is no clear First Amendment issue here, as there is with loyalty oaths, restrictions on partisan activity, and punishment for criticizing government policies. The case here rests on the equal protection clause more than on the free speech guarantee. Yet there surely is an element of protected protest in every peaceful walkout, so the case is not wholly dissimilar to those in which the courts have applied a test of governmental necessity. Second, if less onerous restrictions would adequately serve the government's interests—even in the case of essential services—then the case for a preventive approach to strikes is seriously undermined. If, for example, some form of compulsory arbitration could be adapted to the needs of the public sector, the strike ban might become unnecessary. The very existence of such an alternative weighs heavily in the constitutional balance.

V. Remedies of the Public Employee: Right to a Hearing and to Court Review

The job security of public workers is only as strong as the procedural safeguards against arbitrary dismissal or suspension at the whim of an erratic or hostile supervisor. Two classes of public employees—comprising a significant share of the total public work force—enjoy a rather substantial degree of protection, at least in theory. They are tenured university faculty members and holders of civil service positions. Academic tenure protects, of course, only a rather small group—although its gradual extension to schoolteachers makes it an increasingly important guarantor of academic freedom. But the civil service system affords both job security and procedural guarantees to a large share of government employees at federal and state levels. And even where the civil service system does not apply, individual state agencies frequently provide alternative forms of job security.

Two essential characteristics of tenure and civil service systems constitute the source of protection: first, enumeration of the grounds for which an employee can be dismissed; and second, the requirement of a hearing at which the employee can respond to charges against him. Under federal civil service law, for example, employees may be fired only for "such cause as promotes the efficiency of the service . . ." Academic tenure, according to the widely accepted policies of the American Association of University Professors, ensures that a permanent faculty member's term of service can be terminated "only for adequate cause, except in the case of retirement for age, or under extreme circumstances because of financial exigencies." (Universities conferring tenure on their senior faculty often detail the applicability of this general precept and prescribe procedures to be followed in the event of a dismissal.)

Civil service and tenure policies almost universally provide for a hearing before a discharge becomes effective. Under federal civil service, an employee must be given notice by the agency of its intent to dismiss him, after which he may request a hearing. Court review is available to the employee if the hearing upholds the charges. Academic tenure policies contemplate a hearing by a faculty or administrative committee, followed by appeal to the president or chancellor.

Do these provisions adequately protect the rights of public employees? The question is far too broad for a simple answer. But even a superficial study of the terms of tenure and civil service laws suggests there may be a gap between theory and practice. Under civil service, for example, the phrase "such cause as promotes the efficiency of the service" leaves the Commission and other agencies broad discretion. Civil Service regulations have not only failed to particularize this vague phrase, but have effectively expanded its scope by adding a catch-all ground for dismissal—"any other disqualification which makes an individual unfit for the service." Much the same can be said of academic tenure: if a hostile administrator or governing board wants to oust a troublesome faculty member, it is not hard to make a case that his activities constitute "adequate cause" in the absence of more precise language.

The vagueness of the governing standards might well have been curbed by courts petitioned to reinstate dismissed public employees. But the courts typically (in the words of a recent decision) "defer to the agency as the appropriate judge of what is an appropriate cause for discharge as needed to promote efficiency of the service, provided its decision is not arbitrary or capricious." This deference may have been somewhat less pronounced in cases involving academic tenure, though the cases are so few that generalization would be unreliable. The substantive standards of protection are only as strong as the administrators charged with their application make them, or the courts insist they be.

A recent *Columbia Law Review* student Note suggests how far judicial deference has in practice undermined the theoretical protections of the federal civil service law:

"Even workers subject to dismissal only after a consideration of the 'efficiency of the service'. . . may be fired for reasons which are clearly irrelevant to the avowed purpose of the employment decision. This vague statutory standard for discharge has not, under present judicial construction, provided consistent protection; when utilization of questionable information has been characterized by the administrator as promoting the 'efficiency' of the service, the courts, apparently influenced by the constitutional maxim of unlimited executive discretion, have limited their substantive review to—at best—a sterile investigation of *pro forma* compliance with the statutorily prescribed procedures."

There are other shortcomings of judicial review. For the discharged employee, the expense and delay of a suit for reinstatement may be prohibitive, at a time when he can least afford either money or time. After exhaustion of internal remedies, a hearing in the federal district court, and review by a court of appeals, three to four years' time may be required. (In the case of the Panama Canal Zone Policeman, for example, notice of dismissal was sent in February 1964, thus setting in motion a cycle which brought a decision of the Court of Appeals in April 1968. Supreme Court review may well prolong the ordeal to six years.) The expense involved in conducting such proceedings, quite apart from the suspense, may easily exceed the means of the typical civil servant. If the discharged worker takes another job in the interim to meet these expenses, the whole contest is likely to become academic. Thus if his resources are modest at the time he loses his job, he may well have to choose between the survival of his lawsuit and that of his family.

These uncertainties about judicial review suggest that safeguards on government employment must function, if at all, within the agency. The internal hearing must be the principal protection for the worker faced with dismissal. But civil service regulations fall far short of requiring a trial-type hearing. As a Federal Court of Appeals recently observed in upholding the Civil Service Commission's acceptance of evidence against the employee in the form of affidavits—without an opportunity to examine these before the hearing, or to cross-examine their authors—"this is in keeping with the concept that a Civil Service Commission hearing is informal and not a strict adversary proceeding." (It appears, in fact, that the hearing to which a civil service employee is entitled under present law may well be less elaborate than that which due process now guarantees to a state college or university student.)

However inadequate may be their safeguards, civil service and academic tenure do not apply at all to those who probably need such protection most, the probationary and temporary employees. In the University setting, the problem is obvious. It is the young instructor or assistant professor whose political activities are likely to be most controversial, and whose writings and opinions are most likely to cause his elders to bristle. The novice is much more likely than the veteran to need the shield of academic freedom.

Yet tenure is available only as the reward for surviving the probationary period with no scars, or few. The beginner may therefore have to compromise his scruples by keeping quiet, or leave the academic world altogether if he cannot find a faculty that is hospitable to his idiosyncrasies. For the refusal to reappoint a nontenure faculty member is seldom reviewable; only when an invalid or unsupportable reason is publicly stated can the courts get hold of the controversy at all. What is true of academic tenure is equally true of civil service protection: the safeguards do not apply until one has survived the probationary period during which he is likely to need those safeguards the most. Once he has them, he is often out of danger anyway.

The inadequacy of these statutory protections compels consideration of a more fundamental question, which is crucial to a probationary or temporary employee: Is there a constitutional right to a

hearing before dismissal? The Supreme Court has never squarely
faced the constitutional issue. The lower courts have not reexamined it since the McCarthy era's rash of "internal security" dismissals that seriously undermined all civil service safeguards. But
the question is well worth asking, not only because there are gaps in
the statutes and regulations, but because the constitution may well
demand better protection for public workers than current statutes
afford.

The leading precedent for denying a hearing apparently remains intact. At the height (or depth) of the McCarthy era, the Federal Court of Appeals for the District of Columbia split sharply
over the question of a "disloyal" employee's right to a hearing. The
Supreme Court affirmed the discharge without opinion by an equal
4–4 division, one Justice not participating. The particular employee had formerly been under civil service, but had entered a new
position where she had not yet served out the probationary term.
Thus the statutory safeguards did not apply to her. The majority
concluded that an employee was helpless in such a case: "It is our
clear opinion that the President, absent congressional restriction,
may remove from the Government service any person of whose loyalty he is not completely convinced. He may do so without assigning
any reason or without giving the employee any explanatory notice."
The dissenting judge was appalled at the sweep of this deference to
executive authority; he maintained that "dismissal for disloyalty is
punishment and requires all the safeguards of a judicial trial." But
for the majority, the Constitution required no procedures whatever
for dismissal—despite the stigma which a discharge for alleged
disloyalty would leave upon the employee.

This decision has never been squarely overturned, though
there are implicit qualifications. The Supreme Court has consistently held that if a government agency voluntarily provides for a
hearing when the law does not compel it to do so, that safeguard
cannot be selectively withdrawn or relaxed in particular cases. The
case of the Brooklyn college professor suggests more clearly the answer the Supreme Court would give if the question arose directly.
That case involved a New York law requiring automatic dismissal
of a public employee who refused to testify before an investigating
committee. The Supreme Court found the law unconstitutional, in
part because it undermined the Fifth Amendment privilege. But the
Court also stressed the law's procedural deficiency. While acknowl-

edging that "a proper inquiry might well show [the teacher's] continued employment to be inconsistent with a real interest of the state," the fact was that "there has been no such inquiry here." Obliquely, then, the Court suggested that dismissal under such circumstances demands a hearing, an opportunity for the employee to explain the reasons for his refusal to testify—which in this case would have included the constitutional grounds for refusing to answer the Committee's questions.

A lower federal court has extended this doctrine in a recent oath case. Three judges struck down Idaho's loyalty oath law because it gave no chance for an employee to explain his unwillingness to sign. The automatic inference of disloyalty denied the employee due process of law. In such a case, ruled the court, "a hearing is constitutionally compelled"—both to test the individual's relationship to an allegedly subversive organization, and to give him an opportunity to put on the record his reasons for not signing (and thereby rebut the inference of disloyalty).

The first clear recognition of a constitutional right to some form of hearing has come from a federal district court in Minnesota, reviewing the reinstatement claim of a state university maintenance man. University rules promised "a written statement of reasons for dismissal" to any discharged employee within the civil service. The court was willing to assume that this general regulation required, before dismissal, some opportunity for the employee to respond either in writing or by informal appearance. Were the regulation construed to deny such an opportunity, it would deprive public employees of procedural due process. A civil servant threatened with dismissal must have a chance to offer explanations or show mitigating circumstances, prove mistaken identity or demonstrate that he was merely carrying out a superior's command. This is not strictly a constitutional decision, of course. It purports merely to construe and apply a rather elastic civil service rule. But if those who promulgated the rules now say they never meant to provide a right to a hearing, the court has left little doubt the constitution will not permit them to act accordingly.

These developments, together with the mounting insistence of the courts upon hearings for other types of government beneficiaries, suggest an answer to the constitutional issue. At least where political activities or the exercise of an employee's constitutional rights are at issue, some form of hearing seems constitutionally required before dismissal. The hearing should, moreover, meet the essential criteria of due process, even though it need not constitute a full criminal trial. The civil service system can certainly afford this accommodation of its needs with the interests of the accused employee without crippling its efficiency. The ever-present risk of erroneous or groundless dismissals certainly warrants such a constitutional safeguard.

Having said this much about the right to a hearing, one further point should be made. Civil service was designed originally to check the spoils system and reduce turnover of government staffs after elections. Academic tenure was fashioned to protect the controversial or unorthodox professor from political or economic pressures. But the coin has another side: these safeguards hamper the elimination of accumulated "deadwood" in both university and government bureau, and may therefore seriously frustrate reform or slow progress. The double-edged character of professorial tenure has provoked the wrath of academic administrators seeking to reform and modernize their faculties. The University of Denver's Chancellor, Maurice Mitchell, labeled the tenure system "the biggest single force in opposition to change that exists at the university. . . . After the first few years," he remarked, "the faculty has a life contract. I'd like to see any union do better than that."

The "deadwood" problem has also hampered innovation in some city school systems. Those who have tried to reform and modernize the New York City schools, including the State Education Commissioner and Mayor Lindsay, have long advocated a system of administration suitable to the special needs of urban education. But, as Education writer Fred Hechinger reported in *The New York Times:* "The system's strong commitment to civil-service procedures, with special examinations and eligibility lists, designed at an earlier era to eliminate patronage and graft, today largely reinforces conservative personnel policies. It makes the selection process too standardized to feed into the system rapidly enough the kind of unconventional talent needed to cope with the urban slum schools."

Civil service has sometimes thwarted programs to upgrade minority group opportunities in the public sector. Many a training course has succeeded in preparing disadvantaged workers, orienting them to the job situation, and investing them with the requisite skills, only to see them fail the civil service examination and thus remain outside the system. Efforts have been made—in secretarial and construction training programs—to postpone or waive altogether the civil service examination in order to expand substantially and rapidly the share of minority group workers in a particular government agency. Dramatically different types of examinations have been proposed to reflect the special needs and abilities of applicants who have grown up in the inner city and have very different educational backgrounds from those for whom the standard, middle class, verbal-ability exams are aimed. But progress will remain limited, highly selective, and will seem patronizing until some major alternative to the civil service system can be devised. No viable substitutes appear in immediate prospect.

The paradox of civil service and job security remains unresolved. A system designed to protect some may sometimes benefit the people who need the least help and hurt the Negro and the neophyte who need protection most. Meanwhile, the same system thwarts change and frustrates innovation in the public sector, which should generate the inspiration and leadership for reform in the private sector. The net result is paradoxical indeed: while government employees lack many of the liberties and options that private employers could not or would not curtail, the public sector is saddled with a network of safeguards and protections that tie the whole system to the past. Whether the solution lies in substitution of strong unions for civil service and tenure is a question far too broad to be resolved here. But there must be some better way of accommodating those vital national and individual interests that are at stake.

V

METAMORPHOSIS

OF THE

PUBLIC UNIVERSITY

Higher education at public expense is a government benefit of substantial value. Those who are most cavalier about withdrawing that benefit—advocates of harsh policies toward student demonstrators—implicitly recognize its value when they stress the taxpayers' stake in the education of every state university student. The number of students attending publicly supported institutions has more than doubled in a decade, and the national appropriations for higher education have grown even more rapidly.

Yet there has never been such conflict between benefactor and beneficiary. Protests, demonstrations, strikes, and sit-ins are only symptoms of a much deeper malaise that afflicts 10 percent or more of the student body, and is probably spreading. There is some evidence of a causal connection between the rising levels of support for higher education and the mounting tension on the campus. Dr. Bruno Bettelheim, a psychologist who has closely observed several sit-ins at the University of Chicago, suggests that students in the past felt no need to revolt because they could prove themselves by paying their way through college. "Now we pay them all to go to school," he observed recently, "which makes them dependent when they should be, psychologically speaking, independent. And this is a very hard thing to take. Therefore, they try to prove their manhood in totally irrational ways."

Student protest and demonstrations are hardly new, of course. St. Augustine, teaching in Carthage, once complained of students "disgracefully out of control" who "come breaking into a class in the most unmannerly way . . . behaving almost like madmen . . . [committing] disorderly acts which show an incredible stupidity and which ought to be punished by law." Yale University, founded in 1701, was beset in 1704 by a revolt against a tutor who overzealously extracted fines from students for breaking college rules. By the time of the American Revolution, three of Yale's first six presidents had resigned largely because of student protests. And at Princeton, angry students dynamited Nassau Hall three times during the 1850s.

When Thomas Jefferson returned to his beloved University of Virginia after his years in Washington, he hoped for calm and quiet. In the fall of 1825, however, he found himself in the midst of a bitter confrontation, the account of which has a strikingly modern ring. Insults and a physical attack by several students against two faculty members escalated rapidly and sharply divided the campus. The faculty met the following day and condemned the rebellious students. Disciplinary hearings were held, three students were expelled, others were suspended or reprimanded and one was arrested. Yet Jefferson reassured a friend in a letter several days after the incident that "this riot has [not] been more serious than has been experienced by other seminaries. . . ."

Among the leaders of campus protests have been many whose later careers could hardly be called subversive. In 1894, Amherst College was shaken by Gates' Rebellion—a militant student attack upon the college president for expelling a student. (The student in question was admitted to Amherst after his dismissal from another college where his protest over compulsory chapel had brought him to blows with the chaplain.) The student leader of the revolt was Harlan Fiske Stone, later Attorney General and Chief Justice of the Supreme Court. Calvin Coolidge was reputedly among his partisans. In the 1920s, the campus of a small Illinois liberal arts college was almost closed down, and the president locked in his office, by a group of angry students whose leader was sophomore Ronald Reagan. As Governor of California, Reagan has been somewhat less sanguine about student power, though without ever disclaiming responsibility for the uprising in the 20s.

Riots, demonstrations, strikes, and sit-ins are by no means confined to the United States. In fact, if anything, they have been comparatively mild in this country. However violent the Columbia students may have seemed in the spring of 1968, there was little doubt the French and Italian students, and later the Japanese students, made their points much more destructively. Student revolt is truly a worldwide phenomenon; there is hardly a country with a major university that has not been rocked by violent protest in the past five years. While remarkably few institutions in the United States have been shut down by demonstrations, closings are common in Latin America, Africa, and Western Europe. And when the doors of a foreign university do close, they are likely to remain closed for some time, and not to reopen in a few days as Columbia and San Francisco State managed to do.

The prognosis for the future is not encouraging. Early in 1969, a team of sociologists prepared a world survey of student protests for the United Nations Commission for Social Development. Reviewing recent trends in some fifty nations, they found demonstrations during 1968 only a prelude to larger and bolder protests yet to come. "World opinion," the report warned, "is going to become increasingly the opinion of the world's youth and the generational conflict will assume proportions not previously imagined. . . . Young people of all walks of life are prepared to march, to demonstrate and to riot if necessary in support of views which may not be those of the electorate, nor of the majority, nor yet those of government." The task force concluded ominously that youth seemed to have lost confidence "in the capacity of the older generation to guide affairs without some assistance and planning from young people." These projections suggest conditions may become much worse before they improve.

Despite the historical background and foreign parallels, contemporary campus problems in the United States are quite distinct. Columbia is not Colombia, nor is Charlottesville today the same as Jefferson's Virginia. Certainly the *issues* of the present are vitally different. Campuses today become agonized about the problems that torment the nation. Protests are likely to be longer, partly for this reason, and partly because a higher percentage of the student body is probably involved than has been on the barricades at any comparable period in the past. Attitudes both of and toward the police are likely to make the conflict much bloodier if outside law enforcement authorities are called to the campus.

Perhaps the most profound change concerns the legal rights of students. Not so long ago, the student who disobeyed a rule or insulted the President faced the prospect of probation or suspension after an informal conference with the Dean of Students. If he repented, or if his father came and made amends, the sentence might be reduced, or the matter even disposed of with a reprimand. It was assumed in those simpler days that college and university officials made and enforced their own rules in a legal system insulated from the courts. If a student did bring suit to gain reinstatement, or to clear his record, the judge would typically find that college authorities, taking the place of the student's parents, could "make any rules or regulations for the government or betterment of their pupils that a parent could do for the same purposes." Whether such rules are wise or fair "is a matter left solely to the discretion of the authorities or the parents as the case may be." As recently as 1956, a federal district judge thought "the problem of what constitutes an appropriate reason [for expulsion] must clearly be left to those authorities charged with the duty of maintaining the standards and discipline of the school."

A rapid and dramatic change has come over the legal rights of college and university students. A decade ago a Harvard Law School professor found it "shocking that the officials of a state educational institution . . . should not understand the elementary principles of fair play" and equally shocking "that a court supports them in denying to a student the protection given to a pickpocket." (The reference was to a medical student at the University of Illinois who had been expelled summarily on charges of cheating in 1954. When the student brought suit for reinstatement, or for an opportunity at least to confront and cross-examine her accusers, the court held that a state-supported university had no obligation to hold a hearing before expelling a student.)

Ten years later, the President of the National Student Association urged students facing disciplinary charges to "test your rights in the courts [because] the climate is receptive." And Harvard Law professor, Clark Byse, reviewing the metamorphosis in student rights, welcomed "a society and a legal system which insists upon fair play for students." Fearful of this new trend, James A. Perkins, then President of the American Council on Education (also President of Cornell University) spoke with alarm of "a rash of court cases challenging decisions in areas that were once considered the educational world's peculiar province."

I. *Ingredients of Change: Fresh Winds on and off the Campus*

It is remarkable that this change could have come about at all, and more so that it should have occurred so suddenly. It is hard to pinpoint the precise year or month in which student rights became a viable concern of the courts. But one can ascribe the metamorphosis to a period of slightly less than two years. In September 1959 a federal court of appeals in New York refused to look behind the dismissal of a Brooklyn College student; one judge found no jurisdiction whatever in the federal courts, and another found jurisdiction but saw no possible claim on the merits where a student was punished for political activity on campus. (The third judge would have reviewed the merits.) Twenty-three months later, a federal panel in the South reviewed the case of a group of students expelled without a hearing for off-campus civil rights protests that resulted in criminal convictions. For the first time, this court found the disciplinary procedures of publicly supported colleges and universities of concern to the federal judiciary, and held that a student who claimed a violation of his civil rights and liberties could seek redress in a federal forum.

Of course the revolution did not occur within so brief a period, nor is it yet complete. Pressures were building up before 1961 and might well have changed the law a decade earlier if more students had brought more cases to court. But that was the era of the "silent generation," and discipline typically grew out of panty raids or the usual, predictable "sex, beer and cheating" cases. It was not until the political cases of the late 1950s—coincident with the civil rights movement in the South—that proper grist was available for the judicial mill. In addition, several other ingredients combined in such a way that courts could no longer turn such cases away.

THE CHANGING CHARACTER OF HIGHER EDUCATION

Higher education was once the province of the elite. Most institutions were privately endowed and offered only a few scholarships for the needy student. Even the public universities and land grant colleges afforded only limited opportunities for lower class youth; Henry George once described the University of California as "that school where the taxes of the poor go to support the sons of the rich." Since World War II, the balance has swung quite sharply. Through the proliferation of junior colleges and new four-year state colleges, and the doubling or even tripling of enrollment in the older state universities, educational opportunities have penetrated well into the lower middle and lower classes. Most recently, special programs for disadvantaged and minority group students have further expanded these opportunities. For the first time in 1968–69, more than half of all high school graduates (over 40 percent of college-age youth) attend an institution of higher learning.

If college education is more accessible than ever before, it is also far more essential than it ever has been to success in a world of growing complexity and specialization. Christopher Jencks and David Riesman have written, "The bulk of the American intelligentsia now depends on universities for a livelihood and virtually every would-be member of the upper middle class thinks he needs some university's imprimatur, at least in the form of a B.A. and preferably in the form of a graduate professional degree as well." The Regents of the New York State educational system recognized in their 1964 Master Plan that a college degree is as essential today as "high school attendance and a high school diploma were in the past."

The value of a college education can be measured in monetary terms as well. Recent census figures indicate that the holder of a bachelor's degree will earn about $170,000 more during his lifetime than his counterpart who stopped after high school. Graduate work increases the earning potential at least another $80,000.

If higher education returns a tangible profit, it also has rapidly rising tangible costs. During the four-year period 1963 to 1967 federal appropriations for higher education, in the form of direct grants, rose from just over $1 million to $3.3 million. State expenditures for both operating costs and new capital construction have risen commensurately—even faster than the rise in number of students or degrees granted. In addition to the direct costs of higher education, the costs of indirect assistance—through scholarships, fellowships, work-study payments and the like—have risen sharply. From 1940 to 1964, for example, college enrollment about tripled—but the amounts awarded in scholarships, fellowships, and grants increased tenfold.

If college and university attendance in general is a significant benefit, the opportunity to attend a publicly supported institution is especially valuable. The average student attending a private college in the fall of 1968 paid $1,380 in tuition and fees. His counterpart at a publicly supported institution paid less than a quarter of that amount, an average of $299. Thus at a bare minimum, the opportunity to attend a publicly supported institution is worth about $1,100 a year, or $4,400 over the four-year undergraduate course, assuming the differential does not increase. To that figure should be added the value of partially subsidized residence halls and dining facilities, and of course the scholarship and financial aid which many students receive even at institutions that are virtually tuition-free. There can be little doubt of the net value of a higher education at public expense.

Yet these are crude and inadequate ways to measure the importance of staying in school. For the male student, any interruption in his education, whether voluntary or involuntary, may bring induction into military service and quite likely Vietnam. A suspension or expulsion may well mean the loss of financial aid—a scholarship or fellowship—without which the student simply cannot continue. Then there are the collateral consequences of exclusion from the academic community described by a student comment in the *Yale Law Journal:* "Nonacademic expulsion from graduate or professional school is in many ways the equivalent of a license revocation proceeding; as a result of the school's punitive action, the door to a profession is permanently closed. Although he retains what knowledge he has acquired, the expelled student after having expended effort, time and money in his studies, loses both what he has invested towards a degree and its future value . . ."

Thus it is hardly surprising that many students would rather spend a night or even a week in jail, or pay a hundred-dollar fine, than risk expulsion for a demonstration or protest. The wonder is that the courts have been so late and so slow to appreciate the importance of a college education, particularly in a publicly supported institution. Equally surprising is the late realization that has come within the academic community; only rather recently, for example, has the American Association of University Professors broadened its definition of academic freedom to include student rights.

CHANGING CHARACTER OF STUDENT PROTESTS

Several essential observations must be made about the catalysts of student protest, both the issues and the participants. As we have already seen, protest and disruption on the campus are hardly new phenomena. But the causes of the upheaval of the 1960s are dramatically different from those of the 1940s and 50s. And the character of the participants is different, too, in ways that bear directly upon the evolution of the law defining student rights.

Something should first be said about the institutions that are affected by student protest. In the beginning—the Berkeley Sproul Hall sit-in of December 1964—college administrators refused to believe that the malaise could spread to their hitherto tranquil campuses. Berkeley had always been a hotbed of student radicalism; maybe City College of New York, Chicago, Madison, and a few other active campuses would suffer similar afflictions, but there the epidemic would stop.

In fact, the "it-can't-happen-here" attitude probably persisted until the spring of 1969, when it *did* happen at Harvard, in a way that dramatically destroyed the illusion of institutional immunity. To faculty members who had left the battlefields of Berkeley for the calm of Cambridge during the mid 60s, or had chosen "safe" universities in preference to "troubled" ones, the illusion had been shattered. But it was not Harvard alone that broke the spell; equally important was the spread of campus protest during 1968–69 to small liberal arts colleges and seminaries. To be sure, nearly 90 percent of American colleges and universities escaped major protests, but institutions of every type, size, region, sectarian affiliation, and nonsectarian character were to be found in the afflicted 10 percent. At least since Harvard, it is clear that violent student protest can happen anywhere.

The explanation for this rapid and pervasive spread of student malaise must be found in the catalytic issues. They have centered largely about the Vietnam war and the civil rights or minority group questions. Occasional protests against dormitory parietal rules and cafeteria food have been insignificant in the total national picture. (The latter have, however, supplied about the only humor in recent years; the award for lightness of touch must go to the University of Colorado students who seized the cafeteria to protest the quality of the fare, then renamed it after the state's only convicted cannibal, a snowbound miner who devoured his companion to avert starvation in the winter of 1883.)

One of the most sensitive and careful analyses of the causes of student protests was that of the Commission appointed to investigate the 1968 uprising at Columbia. Under the chairmanship of Harvard Law School Professor Archibald Cox, the Commission identified four factors as central: first, the present student generation is "the best informed, the most intelligent, and the most idealistic this country has ever known." Second, these students seem "unusually antagonistic to all forms of restraint and particularly violent in social or political protest," although impatience toward elders and antipathy toward authority are ageless characteristics of young people. Third, the perennial generation gap has been progressively widened by "marked changes in speech, conduct, dress and manners" that have made communication and even understanding increasingly difficult. Fourth, "the size and complexity of the large universities in an urban society increase the alienation of students. . . . One form of response, which must be mentioned among the causes of violent demonstrations, is the romantic reaction against complexity, rationality and restraint, which has become a small but pervasive thread in student life."

These comments have been qualitative only, and something must be said about the quantitative dimension of student protest. Statistical surveys of student involvement abound, but they furnish limited insight. A few figures will suggest how precarious are the estimates. Each year the National Student Association reports that the number of students actively involved in campus protests does not exceed 3 percent—perhaps 2.7 percent or so. A Gallup poll in the summer of 1969 revealed that about 20 percent of the student sample had participated in at least one protest—for most of them, presumably only one. But a recent issue of *Fortune* magazine devoted to the student question identified a much larger corps of "invisible dissidents"—comprising about 40 percent of the campus population. Perhaps 30 percent of the students sampled by *Fortune* could be called sympathetic with the goals of Students for a Democratic Society, although only a small fraction ever mount the barricades when SDS or other radical groups sponsor a campus protest.

The basic weakness of these figures, though, is that the problem is not really a numerical one at all: a few hundred reasonably well-disciplined students bent on destruction or disruption can absolutely cripple a campus. A thousand can close it down or at least force the administration to call large numbers of helmeted policemen. The appearance of police and the predictable bloodshed or chaos will greatly swell the size of the dissident student group, and so on. Thus the number of students initially involved in a protest may be quite small; the critical numerical question is how many other students are sympathetic and can be enlisted if the protest escalates.

These comments bear directly on the changing relationship between the courts and student rights. Student protests are more pervasive, more intense, and involve more serious issues than at any time in recent memory. A student obviously has a far stronger constitutional case when he has been dismissed for protesting against the Vietnam war than against parietal hours or cafeteria food. A student suspended for sitting in to demand racial justice presents a far more appealing case, and a much more substantial constitutional claim, than the student of the 20s or the 50s disciplined for a downtown dance-hall brawl. It is hardly coincidence, therefore, that the courts have shown greater solicitude for students at the same time students have become preoccupied with the vital issues of the day.

CHANGING CHARACTER OF CONSTITUTIONAL LAW

The changing attitudes of the courts toward students have to some extent emulated the changes we have already observed in protection for public employees. The erosion of the old "right-privilege" distinction in the loyalty oath and other cases undoubtedly made a contribution to the evolving law of student rights, although the amount of the debt is somewhat vague. Certainly the insistence on minimal standards of fairness in dismissing students reflects what has happened in public employment.

There was a time when courts would unhesitatingly uphold registration clauses compelling a student to abide by all rules and regulations then in effect and any that might thereafter be adopted. Such covenants typically added that "the student concedes the right to require the withdrawal of any student at any time for any reason deemed sufficient to it and no reason for requiring such withdrawal need be given."

This degree of deference to institutional discretion marked the last Supreme Court case involving college student rights. A group of University of California students had objected on religious grounds to the compulsory ROTC course demanded of all undergraduates. In 1934, the Supreme Court unanimously rejected their claim for an exemption, suggesting that higher education at public expense was a rather marginal privilege: "California has not drafted or called [these students] to attend the University. They are seeking education offered by the state and at the same time insisting that they be excluded from the prescribed course solely upon grounds of their religious belief . . ." Mr. Justice Cardozo, who was usually sensitive to civil liberties violations, added that if the students enroll in "an institution for higher education maintained with the state's monies, then and only then are they commanded to follow courses of instruction believed by the state vital to its welfare." The implication was obvious: if the students did not like the rules at Berkeley, they could always go to Stanford where they would have to pay much higher tuition but would at least be beyond the reach of ROTC.

There is little left of this decision today, although it has never been formally overruled. By the time the recent rash of student cases reached the courts, the underlying constitutional principles had been so altered by decisions involving government employees and other beneficiaries that the ROTC case could be put aside as irrelevant. Some courts still characterize public higher education as a "privilege," to be sure, with the consequence that attendance can be terminated at the discretion of the campus administration and with minimal procedures. But most courts recognize that college and university attendance at public expense, being a government benefit of substantial value, deserves safeguards comparable to those afforded other beneficiaries.

CHANGING BASIS OF UNIVERSITY AUTHORITY

A major reason for judicial deference to acts of university administrators was the assumption that the university stood *in loco parentis* toward its students. Thus college officials could impose whatever restrictions parents could impose on their own children, and enforcement was insulated from court review to the same degree. This doctrine persisted long beyond its useful life, and has been the cause of much misunderstanding.

Professor Henry Steele Commager, the distinguished historian, recently explained why *in loco parentis* once fit the conditions of higher education but no longer applies: "[This doctrine] was transferred from Cambridge to America and caught on here even more strongly for very elementary reasons: college students were, for the most part, very young. A great many boys went up to college in the colonial era at the age of thirteen, fourteen, fifteen. They were, for most practical purposes, what our high school youngsters are now. They did need taking care of and the tutors were *in loco parentis*. . . . All of this is now changed. . . . Therefore, the old tradition of *in loco parentis* is largely irrelevant."

Clearly conditions have changed and the old doctrine must be set aside. As Professor William Van Alstyne notes, *in loco parentis* did have some "superficial appeal, if only because the vast majority of college students were quite young and generally below the age of eighteen. Today, in contrast, there are more students between the ages of thirty and thirty-five in our universities than there are of those under eighteen, and the latter group accounts for only 7% of total college enrollment. Indeed, when apologia of *in loco parentis* were tentatively offered in defense of university restrictions at Berkeley last year, a hasty retreat was taken when it was pointed out that the overwhelming majority of students were more than twenty-one years of age."

This view is now shared by most commentators. Even university administrators have become wary about the responsibility that goes with trying to be a substitute parent to a large and diverse student body. *In loco parentis,* warned the 1967 report of a Cornell University faculty-student commission on campus law, "involves the university in almost limitless obligations of dubious connection with its central purposes, and demeans students as members of the educational community."

With *in loco parentis* discarded as a standard of university authority over students, the courts must face the real issues and fashion a body of law to control the discretion of state college and university officials. If a student can neither be forced to bargain away his rights by signing a registration form, nor have them arbitrarily suspended because the university purports to play the role of his parents, there is a strong basis for the fashioning of legal safeguards.

CHANGING RELATIONSHIP BETWEEN UNIVERSITIES AND COURTS

In part because of the other factors reviewed here, but partly for independent reasons, the courts have seemed increasingly willing to review the decisions of colleges and universities concerning students. One reason has already been hinted at—there are simply many more student cases being filed than ever before; on a percentage basis, if no other, more are likely to reach the trial stage. The rising volume of student cases results partly from the greater incidence and severity of university discipline, and partly from the easier access of legal representation for students. Student associations at several large state universities have actually retained law firms to handle cases of individual students, much as a labor union counsel presses lawsuits for individual union members whose dues contribute to his retainer. And as courts have become more receptive to suits by poor and disadvantaged plaintiffs challenging administrative action, channels have been opened which also prove beneficial to student plaintiffs. The President of the National Student Association knew whereof he spoke when he urged fellow students to "test your rights in the courts [because] the climate is receptive."

Not surprisingly, the growth of student litigation has alarmed some university administrators. Their concern is heightened by the recency and speed of the judicial intrusion into university decision making. Former President James Perkins of Cornell has listed several specific sources of concern. First, there is the prospect that "the academic institution will be prevented from making qualitative decisions about human talent" but that such decisions will be relegated either to "civil laws that must not distinguish between the plumber and the philosopher" or to bickering over legal technicalities, with a grave risk of "permanent damage not only to the sensitive academic processes for judging quality, but indeed to quality itself." A second and "even more fundamental" danger is the threat of judicial intervention to institutional autonomy (and in turn to academic freedom) if academic standards, traditions, and procedures are placed at the mercy of the courts.

Finally, Perkins has expressed practical concerns about judicial review: "There are human rights involved in the time and cost of adjudication. Our judicial system is already overloaded. For every hour that might be spent ironing out conflicts on the campus itself, plaintiffs can wait months and sometimes years for action in the courts. Meanwhile, academic careers and perhaps the institution, too, can be ground to a standstill. The costs of legal procedures can be a nightmare for both the individual and the institution. . . . Further, there is the damage to the student-teacher relationship. If student and teacher must constantly face the prospect of having to testify against each other . . . the spark between them dies very quickly."

What is the legal relationship between court and campus that evokes these dire predictions? Granted, a few courts have actually questioned the very basis of university authority and power. A trial judge in Arizona held that the state legislature's attempt to give the University Regents power to adopt and enforce traffic regulations on the campus violated a constitutional guarantee of separation of powers. Enforcing traffic laws was a function of the courts, held the judge, and could not be given to a university or to any other agency.

Rarely have students sought court review of academic decisions. After graduating from law school, a young man in New York sued his undergraduate alma mater for having wrongfully withheld his B.A. degree. The judge found there had been a misunderstanding about two credits in psychology, and ordered the undergraduate registrar to award the degree. A University of Vermont medical student brought suit in the federal court seeking reinstatement in good standing, claiming he had failed a required course because the instructor was arbitrary and prejudiced against him. The judge acknowledged that courts should generally keep completely out of academic decisions. But "to the extent that the [student] has alleged his dismissal was for reasons other than the quality of his work or in bad faith, he has stated a cause of action. . . . The allegation that [he] was failed by an instructor who had made up his mind to fail him before he completed the course is equivalent . . . to an allegation of bad faith, arbitrariness and capriciousness on the part of said instructor."

For the most part, though, student appeals to the courts have been confined to disciplinary cases. And as a practical matter, review is available only when the punishment is as serious as expulsion, dismissal, or long-term suspension. Where the sanction is less harsh (for example, short-term suspension or probation) the "sentence" will probably have expired and the case become moot before the court can reach the issues. Nor will courts assume jurisdiction where university sanctions are merely threatened but have not been finally imposed; or where internal remedies (such as an appeal to the president) remain open to the student. Thus there are important built-in limits to review: any student is free to file a complaint against university officials. But in practice, only the most serious of charges and penalties will carry the case beyond the university's initial motion to dismiss. (Recall that during the troubled fall semester of 1967, only thirty-two students were actually expelled of the nearly two thousand threatened with disciplinary action for demonstrations and protests.)

A second limitation derives from the narrow and seemingly technical rules of court jurisdiction. In a few states, actions of the state university are treated like those of other state agencies and can be reviewed in court as readily as license revocations by the State Liquor Board. In most states, however, a student may seek the aid of a court only by claiming a violation of his constitutional rights. As we have already seen, most cases are of the "sex, beer and cheating" variety and raise no constitutional issues—unless the university has denied the student any respectable sort of hearing, or discriminated on racial or religious grounds in applying the rules. Thus, quite apart from the procedural hurdles and timing problems, the range of substantive claims that a court will hear excludes all but a tiny fraction of student cases.

Third, even in such cases, the courts reach no further within the walls of the academy than absolutely essential. President Perkins has expressed concern that confidence and trust will be impaired "if student and teacher must constantly face the prospect of having to testify against each other. . . ." The prospect is a most unlikely one. Few of the student discipline cases to date have involved anything approaching an adversary trial. Usually the court reaches one of three conclusions without going much beyond the pleadings: first, the university's decision was sound in terms of both the substantive rule on which the charge was based and the hearing by which the rule was enforced; second, procedural due process was denied because no hearing or an inadequate hearing was held; or third, the student cannot be punished because the substantive rule or regulation was unconstitutional.

In the first situation, no further action is warranted. Cases of the second type are simply remanded to the university with a court order to grant the student a hearing. In the third case, when the substantive basis for the charge is thrown out, the university might dis-

cipline the student under some other rule. None of these three responses requires the court to put anyone—student, faculty
member, or dean—on the witness stand. It is hard to see in this
limited degree of surveillance the "damage . . . to institutional
autonomy" which President Perkins fears from "constant legal
interference." Nor would such occasional judicial intrusion prevent
the university "from making qualitative decisions about human talent"—unless, of course, the qualitative decisions it has been making are so patently arbitrary or unfair that the controlling criteria
should not survive judicial examination.

While President Perkins is not alone in his concern about judicial intrusion into university affairs, other members of the academic community strongly disagree. Professor Clark Byse of the
Harvard Law School, who has served as General Counsel and President of the American Association of University Professors, takes
"pride" in a society and a legal system which insists upon "fair play
for students." In fact, Byse suggests, the courts may not have gone
far enough: "My concern is not that the courts have been too intrusive but that despite some creative judicial decisions in recent years,
the adjudicated cases leave some gaps and there is no assurance that
the courts will continue the wholesome development thus begun."

Byse adds an important point that Perkins overlooks: if students do not have recourse to the courts in cases of real injustice,
they may well take to the barricades. It is unimportant whether one
approves or disapproves of direct action by students or any other
group that feels itself aggrieved. The point is that the absence of a
peaceful avenue of redress may divert energies into a violent one.
"Far better," concludes Professor Byse, "for students to be encouraged to utilize the orderly processes of the courts than to strike, to
sit in, or to engage in other confrontations in which the appeal is in
significant part, if not primarily, to force rather than to reason and
the mind."

Finally, a persuasive claim can be made for judicial review in
the rather small number of cases where it is realistically available.
The two landmark cases defining the constitutional right to a hearing both involved Negro students summarily suspended or dismissed from small Southern state colleges because of constitutionally protected civil rights activities. There have, of course, been
frivolous cases along with the substantial ones. One may well doubt
the value of occupying the time of courts and lawyers disputing a

university's ability to impose a parking or a library fine. Yet even these cases may (like the Arizona traffic case) make important contributions to university law.

In part the need is for colleges and universities to be "kept honest" in their relations with their students—a responsibility which is measurably enhanced by the bare availability of judicial review. More important, the courts have a unique opportunity to enlighten the attitudes of university administrators toward their students in ways that professional societies and student protest groups simply cannot achieve without judicial leverage. If the doctrine of *in loco parentis* is finally interred, it will not be because educational and legal scholars have spoken critically of it. Rather, its final repudiation will come about because courts no longer accept university paternalism as a valid basis for imposing discipline upon errant members of the academic community.

Finally, courts provide a last (sometimes an only) bulwark against politically motivated or bad faith decisions by academic administrators. Occasionally, students are the scapegoats for someone else's error or misjudgment. At other times, students are punished primarily to forestall a legislative or regental inquiry that the administration fears would hurt the institution even more than would an arbitrary expulsion and its aftermath. In such cases, only the courts can impose a principled set of values on the academic community and insist that the popularity of the students or of their activities must play no part in the meting out of discipline.

To the extent that colleges and universities voluntarily provide fair procedures and fashion reasonable regulations on student conduct, judicial review will become unnecessary. The highest goal of the courts is to get themselves out of the business of reviewing academic decisions. Yet the courts stand ready to intervene whenever administrators fall below the minimal standards of substance and procedure that courts have imposed. For these rare cases, judicial review is still a meaningful and important prospect.

II. *The Basis of University Authority: Special Regulatory Interests*

Before considering particular instances of student rights and liberties, it is essential to examine the legal and philosophical bases of university power over student behavior. This might best be done in terms of university interests that justify the adoption of student conduct rules and the meting out of discipline for infractions of those rules. If we agree that *in loco parentis* can no longer be accepted as a source of university authority, and if we are unwilling to accept the fiat of state laws or Trustees' or Regents' rules that delegate certain powers to university officials, then we must formulate more precise reasons why an educational institution should have certain powers over student affairs. These reasons will, in turn, suggest some limits to the exercise of disciplinary authority.

The university shares many functions with other nonacademic institutions and agencies. The large college or university maintains dormitories, athletic fields, libraries, dining facilities, and employs hundreds of secretaries, clerks, accountants, policemen, and other noninstructional personnel. These functions underlie certain of the university's interests in regulating student conduct and behavior. But in other important areas, the university has unique interests that both justify higher expectation about and at the same time demand greater tolerance of student behavior than are appropriate for other institutions.

First, the university derives certain regulatory power from its ownership and operation of buildings and facilities. Parking and traffic regulations, rules against fire hazards and other physical dangers clearly reflect this interest. So does the university's authority to restrict picketing and other forms of protest that may impede the flow of traffic or obstruct entrance to and egress from its buildings. In this respect the university differs little from any other government agency which has incidental responsibilities as landlord.

Second, the university has a special interest in protecting the physical safety, health, and well-being of its students. This responsibility extends primarily to events occurring on the campus, but it may also cover certain events in the outside community. This interest determines, for example, the powers of the university to penalize students or employees who sell narcotics to other members of the university community. The university's responsibility for the health and well-being of its students substantially exceeds that of a typical agency toward its employees or clients.

Third, and most important, the university has special interests in preserving its primary educational functions and responsibilities. This function has some obvious and rather mundane aspects. The university may, for example, prohibit excessive noise in or near its libraries and classrooms because the university shares with public libraries, hospitals, and courthouses a greater need for quiet and calm than is appropriate to public parks or sports arenas.

This central academic interest may carry university regulations beyond the scope of the general criminal and civil law. To preserve its academic integrity, for example, the university may not only punish plagiarism and cheating (which usually fall far short of violating the federal copyright infringement laws), but may also protect the integrity of modern language courses by prohibiting resort to translations of works under study in the original—even though the Constitution clearly prevents government from restricting the reading habits of the ordinary citizen in such a way.

Fourth, the university's special interests also extend to the extracurricular activities of its students. It may restrict the range and nature of these activities (and also protect them from external threats by hostile forces such as professional gamblers); it may also adopt rules designed to prevent some members of the university community from impairing or limiting the extracurricular activities of others.

A fifth interest reflects the responsibility of the university to the larger community. From time to time protests or demonstrations or simple pranks threaten to spill over into the surrounding area. The university's neighbors are likely to look with disfavor upon such exportation of campus affairs, and may threaten or even attempt retaliation. To minimize the friction between town and gown, the university should have special authority to confine certain types of activities to the campus.

On the other hand, fear of retaliation or reprisal from the community—whether it be in the form of a reduction in legislative appropriations, or a crackdown by irate trustees, or a police chief's vendetta—is not an acceptable basis for controlling student conduct. Professor Hans Linde argues persuasively that "university apprehension of public or political restrictions could in any case not justify infringement of *students'* constitutional rights; one state agency cannot plead fear of another state agency or of the electorate in defense of such infringement."

It is not enough that the university's regulatory interests be understood as the general *raison d'être* for student discipline. Not every student behavior that remotely jeopardizes one of those interests warrants punishment. Over a century ago, a Vermont court held that secondary school pupils could be penalized only for behavior outside the classroom which had a direct and immediate effect on the classroom or on the student-teacher relationship. That criterion should once again be the touchstone of university discipline.

A student-faculty seminar at New York University Law School recently developed a uniform code of student conduct grounded on this precept: "University discipline must be limited to misconduct which distinctly and adversely affects the university's pursuit of its educational purposes." Less succinctly, but more precisely, the student conduct code of the University of Oregon announces the same criterion: "The university may apply sanctions or take other appropriate action only when student conduct directly and significantly interferes with the university's (a) primary educational responsibility of insuring the opportunity of all members of the university community to attain their educational objectives, or (b) subsidiary responsibilities of protecting the health and safety of persons in the university community, maintaining and protecting property, keeping records, providing living accommodations and other services, and sponsoring nonclassroom activities such as lectures, concerts, athletic events and social functions."

III. *The Scope of University Authority: University Rules, General Law, and the Location of the Offense*

Clearly there are important differences between what a student does on the campus and what he does away from the university. Yet there has been a tendency, in analyzing the legal issues, to exaggerate the significance of the distinction. On the one hand, some say that whatever a student does, wherever he may be, reflects on the institution with which he is affiliated and is therefore always the university's concern. Conversely, it is argued that the university's power over the student and his behavior stops at the edge of the campus. Geographical bounds are used by proponents of both views to establish deceptively simple tests of university authority.

Apart from the insensitivity of geography to the various special university interests we have just considered, it is not always feasible to differentiate sharply between what is "campus" and what is not. Professor Hans Linde has suggested some of the pitfalls of trying to set physical boundary lines for the range of university authority.

". . . [W]here university interests other than protection of tangible property are concerned, and especially political freedom, property boundaries are hardly the relevant measure of the 'campus.' Consider these concrete examples: The state university buys adjacent residential property for future expansion; pending its use, some of the homes are occupied by existing tenants, some rented to married students, some razed and the land temporarily landscaped or paved for parking. Campus? . . . The university builds an athletic stadium a mile from its academic areas on land owned by it as part of and sharing access and parking with a cultural complex developed in collaboration with local government in the midst of a large open public park. Campus? . . . Yet even the conventional academic campus may contain acres of park land that are in no functional way different from similar parks in other public ownership." Professor Linde concludes that the question is not how problems of this type would be resolved by applying the "on campus— off campus" test, but the much more basic question "whether a theory of university discipline built on that distinction is tenable at all."

Even if a physical line can be drawn distinctly between sites that are on and off the campus, geography still obscures far more pertinent functional considerations. Some student behavior off the campus, even at great distance from the university, is properly of concern to university officials and may warrant disciplinary action, while other infractions on or adjacent to the campus are wisely overlooked. The essential task is to bring to bear other elements that will classify the offense according to the bases and sources of university disciplinary authority.

For this purpose geography does provide a helpful starting point. Another distinction is also useful in launching the analytical grid which may produce workable tests: the distinction between behavior which violates the general criminal law and that which transgresses only university rules. The intersection of these two lines of distinction creates four quadrants—criminal or illegal behavior on the campus and off; and noncriminal behavior (violating only university rules) on and off campus.

NONCRIMINAL ACTIVITY ON THE CAMPUS

A wide variety of student behavior which does not violate the general criminal law may result in university discipline. Most plagiarism occurring on the campus falls far short of the crime of copyright infringement, the only comparable proscription in the general law. Yet plagiarism and other forms of academic dishonesty are very serious offenses indeed, in fact probably the most severely punished of all student transgressions. University rules on use of liquor, visiting students of the opposite sex in the dormitories, etc., are far more stringent than corresponding criminal laws. In fact, it is these "sex, beer and cheating" rules that probably generate about 90 percent of the business of the typical campus judiciary. Few of the students so accused within the campus community could ever be prosecuted in a criminal court—and the few who *could* technically be charged with crime *would* not, as a practical matter, ever be prosecuted.

ACTS ON CAMPUS WHICH VIOLATE BOTH UNIVERSITY RULES AND CRIMINAL LAW

Other student behavior such as that involved in violent protests or demonstrations may well be criminal as well as contrary to university regulations. Where internal and external norms are both transgressed by a single act, the questions that arise are essentially practical: Which authority should proceed first; and if one imposes a penalty, should the other proceed at all? Despite the efforts of some students to claim "double jeopardy" under these circumstances, the interests of the community and of the university are sufficiently different in most cases that both can proceed—even simultaneously—without putting the accused student twice in jeopardy for the same offense. (One federal court in California has so held; the judge refused a student's request to enjoin university disciplinary proceeding being held while a criminal trial was pending, even though evidence developed in the one tribunal might bolster the case against the student in the other.)

The law does not, however, answer the much more troubling policy question. The report of the Cornell Faculty-Student Commission suggests a more sensitive standard: "When university officials apprehend a student for activity in violation of the [university] code and the law, we believe that all but very serious breaches of the law should be handled internally as a code violation." This prescription needs further refinement, however, before it can be operative. First, there is the uncertainty about the key phrase "very serious breaches." Not only is the language rather loose, but the Commission does not indicate whether "seriousness" should be judged by the university's interests or those of the county prosecutor. Second, the university can seldom control the course of the adjudication. If the prosecutor declines to proceed, then of course the decision is up to the university. But if the prosecutor wants to handle the case, and goes first, then little option remains to the university. Third, there is growing doubt in professional circles whether university tribunals, particularly those composed largely or wholly of the offender's fellow students, can meaningfully hear and decide a difficult drug case or a highly controversial political charge.

If it be assumed that the initiative does rest with the university, a disciplinary proceeding seems appropriate where the prosecutor either declines to act or for technical reasons cannot act, and where the offense is "serious" by objective standards. Even where the prosecutor does act and a conviction results, the university may under certain circumstances be warranted in taking independent action for the same offense. This would be so where the penalty exacted by the criminal courts is too light to protect adequately the university's interests. Dual penalties might also be appropriate where the interests of the university and the community at large are fundamentally different. If, for example, a graduate student pirates another's copyrighted work and is found guilty of infringement in the courts, the university is unlikely to feel that its interests in the matter have been fully vindicated. The copyright law seeks mainly to protect one author from misappropriation and unfair competition by his rivals. University rules against plagiarism, by contrast, seek to ensure academic honesty and to warrant that credit and a degree will be awarded only for work that is truly the student's own.

The same analysis would justify dual sanctions for cutting pages out of a library reserve book the night before an examination. Such an excision clearly amounts to petty larceny punishable in the criminal courts. But the university has an independent and important interest in vindicating those students who could not prepare for the examination because they were denied access to the key pages.

The complexity of the problem indicates the folly of generalizing about treatment of the dual offender. All such cases should not be left to the criminal courts, nor should they all be handled on the campus—even if the choice were up to the university in every instance. Each institution should formulate a system of priorities reflecting its own disciplinary capabilities and its views of the local law enforcement machinery, to which exceptions could be made for both practical and humanitarian reasons.

UNLAWFUL ACTIVITY OFF THE CAMPUS

Even more difficult is the question of when the university should punish students for criminal conduct occurring *off* the campus. Two points seem clear at the outset: first, that the campus should not constitute a sanctuary for law violators; one should not receive any immunity from the criminal law simply because he happens to be a member of the university community. Second, the university may feel an obligation, especially where town-gown relations are tense, to see that the student is not discriminated against in the local courts because he is a student or because he is away from home. There is more than a vestige of *in loco parentis* in this posture, but a vestige that is permissible (if not essential) in the eyes of most students as well as administrators who favor student autonomy.

These considerations are peripheral to the central issue of when the university should seek to discipline a student for an off-campus crime—assuming, of course, that the conduct violates a valid university rule. A number of factors should be weighed in making that determination. First, the physical location of the offense is relevant even though hardly conclusive. The university should be less concerned with a student's drunken spree at a European resort than at a bar across the street from the campus. Second, and more important, is the relationship between the offense and other members of the university community. No matter how far away it may occur from the campus, the university can hardly overlook a single sale of "hard" drugs to a fellow student, or an attempt to bribe members of an athletic team to throw a game. An offense which is a serious infraction of the general law is made a matter of grave university concern by the danger to other students, no matter how remote its situs.

The university should also appraise the relevance of the offense to the student status of the offender. The student who steals a ten dollar shirt from a downtown store and a ten dollar book from the library of another college has committed two acts of petty larceny, which will be equated by the criminal courts. His own university would presumably overlook the theft of the shirt, at least if this was a first offense. But theft of a library book so offends the academic community, and is so inconsistent with integrity expected of *students,* that university discipline might well follow despite the small value of the stolen property.

This determinant can be refined even a bit further. The sale of a forged Rembrandt painting is even more serious for an art student than for a student of forestry. Illegal narcotic activity should have even graver implications for a student of medicine or pharmacy than for a student of Byzantine poetry or art. (Indeed, the latter might plausibly advance some professional justification for an occasional puff of hashish during contemplation.) Embezzlement of funds during a summer job is a serious matter for any student, but reflects particularly badly on the character of a law student.

Finally, the student's motive or cause may be relevant to the university. A protest sit-in at a segregated facility or a draft board office may be no less a trespass in the eyes of the criminal law than a drunken entry into a private home in the dark of night. Yet the university should be discriminating enough to judge the two acts differently. The student's political objective surely mitigates the one offense, while the mindless absence of purpose leaves the other unexcused. Civil disobedience of course requires a student to accept at the hands of the law the full consequences of his illegal acts. But nothing in the law or the university's responsibility demands that the consequences be compounded by a separate legal system.

IV. *Means of Enforcement: The University's Internal Sanctions*

A system of rules is only as effective as the means for its enforcement. Some systems can rely chiefly upon persuasion. Not so university codes of student conduct, the enforcement of which must ultimately be coercive. The penalties of the criminal law are unavailable to the university—nor would most institutions wish to impose jail sentences even if they had the legal power to do so. Thus the university is caught between the moral suasion that does not work in serious cases, and criminal penalties which seem barbaric in this context.

The arsenal of intermediate sanctions is poorly stocked. The mildest of regular sanctions is the informal warning or censure, which is little more than admonition that "something" may happen if the student repeats his offense. Next in order of gravity is the formal reprimand, which may go on the student's record and will follow him into graduate school, military service, or employment, but has no immediate consequences.

Placing a student on probation—cutting him off from a particular activity or sector of campus life—is an immediate and significant act, though hardly a deterrent to the persistent campus offender. Considerably more serious is suspension, which involves a total withdrawal of the offender from the university community —either for a prescribed period after which he may return; or for an indefinite period, in which case the penalty is tantamount to termination of the student's relationship. The extreme penalty, expulsion or dismissal, is seldom used. When it is, it may be tempered with an understanding that the student can apply for readmission after a time—an offer which will at least make it easier for him to continue his education at some other institution.

The traditional sanctions are deficient in part because they force a choice between the overly lenient—a warning is only a slap on the wrist—and the excessively severe suspension or expulsion. They are also deficient because they lack any meaningful relation to the broad range of campus offenses. Efforts have been made to devise other more imaginative, more appropriate sanctions. Restitution, either in labor or in money, offers one such alternative when the offense involves destruction of property.

There has also been some attempt to enforce penance as a punishment. A group of students at City College of New York were suspended until each had composed a 5,000-word essay justifying his part in a campus sit-in protesting the construction of new buildings. The Faculty-Student Discipline Committee apparently devised this punishment because it felt standard penalties would be too severe in view of the purpose of the sit-in (to prevent the felling of trees and tearing up of grass to make way for the construction). Yet the Committee also felt the students could not go completely unpunished.

In addition to restitution and penance, several other intermediate penalties are available. There is physical relocation or exclusion of students who have broken rules only in a particular area of the campus. After discovering the use of marijuana by certain dormitory residents, for example, New York University evicted those students from the dorms but imposed no other sanction upon them. This punishment at least enabled the students to complete their semester's course work without interruption.

Surprisingly, the use of therapeutic and rehabilitative sanctions for university offenders is infrequently prescribed—though informal counseling designed to correct rather than punish aberrant behavior is employed by sensitive deans of students. If the narcotics problem continues to trouble American campuses, counseling may be increasingly useful, though relevant even to the more traditional "sex, beer and cheating" cases. The university's primary responsibility in enforcing rules is not so much to deter future transgressions, as to make offenders into useful and constructive members of the academic community.

Finally, selective use of information about students may constitute a sort of "penalty." Student personnel officers say the first question they are often asked by students in trouble at college is, "Will my parents find out about this?" The answer to that question depends, of course, on the university's policy about sending home reports of student infractions. Many institutions feel they are obligated—morally if not legally—to tell parents or guardians about any serious incident resulting in university discipline, at least where the offender is a minor. But where the student is over twenty-one, or married and living off campus, the student should typically make his own decision whether to tell his parents. (Frequently, for obvious reasons, the student will wish to alert his family and seek help from them in a time of trouble, regardless of what the university reports.)

Reporting of information about a student to government agencies can also have a punitive effect. Police departments, FBI agents, and particularly draft boards are keenly interested in gathering and filing such information, and the university must be quite careful about its reporting practices. A recent incident at Cornell University shows what may happen if such care is not exercised. In November 1967 the assistant registrar wrote to a local draft board in the New York City area that a Cornell student registered with that board had burned his draft card during an antiwar protest on the campus. The letter suggested the board might want to reconsider the student's II-S deferment. Before the board had acted, the university's president found out about the communication and reprimanded the registrar for an act he termed "totally unauthorized." The errant official had meanwhile asked the draft board to disregard his letter, and had offered the student a formal apology. The president restated the university's official policy: to make no such recommendations to draft boards or other agencies regarding the draft status of Cornell students. But the incident well illustrates how damaging to a student, and how essentially punitive, can be the careless (or sometimes deliberate) disclosure of such strategic information about him.

V. *Enforcement of the General Law: Police on the Campus*

The sanctions applicable to students clearly include the penalties of the criminal law. No institution of higher education can provide a sanctuary from the criminal law, or shield its members from arrest and punishment when they violate penal statutes on or off the campus. A homicide in a university building must obviously be investigated and redressed as vigorously as one that occurs off the campus, regardless of the offender's membership or nonmembership in the academic community.

The National Commission on the Causes and Prevention of Violence wisely observed in its preliminary report on campus disorders in the summer of 1969: "The belief of many that the civil law should not apply to internal campus affairs . . . is a serious misconception—a residue of the time when the academy served *in loco parentis*. . . . Now that students themselves have finally discarded school authority over their personal lives, they must logically accept the jurisdiction of civil authority. They cannot argue that of all Americans they are uniquely beyond the reach of the law."

To say that the general law extends to the campus does not, however, mandate who is to enforce that law. It is true that only policemen may make arrests (save for the unusual situation in which a citizen may still apprehend a suspect). But there are many different kinds of policemen. At some universities, particularly the large state institutions, the campus police force (which may consist of as many as a hundred officers) is empowered by statute to enforce all laws on the campus by making arrests, filing criminal complaints, obtaining search warrants, etc. Elsewhere the city or town police may patrol the campus and perform necessary law enforcement tasks. Sometimes this role is exercised by the state police. Some universities, particularly smaller private institutions, employ private security guards, who may or may not be deputized to enforce the criminal law. The pattern varies according to institutional size, history, and regional law enforcement practice.

These arrangements usually work well enough except in times of great tension or upheaval on the campus. But when a full-scale riot threatens or breaks out, a handful of campus policemen or security guards, trained to check windows and doors rather than angry crowds, may prove totally inadequate to the situation—and may, in fact, even refuse to enter the fray on the ground that they were not hired for riot duty. It is at such times that the university officials face what may well be the most critical decision of all—whether to summon the "civil authorities," a much-used euphemism for police. Sometimes, of course, the decision may be taken out of their hands. When major disorders erupt on large state university campuses, governors have been known to call out the highway patrol and even the National Guard; usually the president is notified first, but his opinion on the matter may be quite irrelevant. And at other times an overzealous local police force will enter the campus of its own initiative without waiting to be invited.

Where the decision does rest with university officials, however, the dilemma is acute: if the aid of the police is not sought, either the institution or a major part of its operations will be brought to a halt or, much worse, a struggle between opposing campus groups may escalate to a level that the law enforcement resources of the campus are quite powerless to control. On the other hand, as the Violence Commission Report warns: "It is a melancholy fact that even in cases where the need for calling the civil police has been generally recognized, the degree of force actually employed has frequently been perceived as excessive by the majority of the campus community, whose sympathies then turned against the university authorities.

"Indeed, there is reason to believe that a primary objective of campus revolutionaries is to provoke the calling of police and the kinds of police conduct that will bring the majority over to their side."

There is a further constraint: if the police come, they obviously assume command of the battlefield. The decision whether to make arrests—and the manner in which to make them—is typically out of the hands of university officials and in the hands of a precinct captain who may know very little about universities and students. A dragnet arrest inside an occupied building may indiscriminately include innocent bystanders, reporters for the school newspaper or radio station, students attempting to mediate between contesting groups, and foreign students who risk deportation for a single arrest.

An arrest on campus does not always produce a conviction, to be sure. Yet the decision about what follows the arrest is as much beyond the university's control as is the conduct of the police on campus. More than one university official has been unsuccessful in pleading for the dismissal of criminal charges against his students growing out of campus arrests. Courts and district attorneys are quite likely to remind him that, although the university is the formal complainant in the matter, the interests of the state and its citizens have effectively superseded those of the academic community. Such charges may ultimately be dismissed, but not simply because the university wishes they had never been filed.

The consequences of calling the police are so drastic, and so often catastrophic, that many universities have tried to develop "battle plans" in advance of trouble. A responsible president or dean cannot promise the university community that he will never, under any circumstances, call the police to the campus, however much he might wish to be spared that onus. But he can make a major contribution to confidence and understanding by laying down the ground rules well in advance, so that everyone will know when and under what circumstances police *might* be called. Assurance might well be given, for instance, that police would never be called before consultation with student government and faculty leaders (except in the true emergency where police must be called with the speed of a fire alarm).

It might also be provided that a warning be given to persons violating the law—students sitting in a building, for example—before police are summoned at all, and once again before arrests are made. Provision should be made for a corps of impartial observers, drawn from faculty and students, to watch any police action on campus, be alert for evidence of police (or antipolice) brutality, and to provide witnesses in case of court proceedings. Most important, of course, every effort should first be made to restore order by use of the university's own disciplinary machinery. It should be clearly established on every campus that police are called only as a desperate last resort, when all internal resources have proved unavailing despite efforts made in good faith to invoke them.

Even so, no matter how careful the preparations and how clear the ground rules, there is likely to be bloodshed if and when the police are called, and the administration is almost certain to lose support among uncommitted students. Some alternative way must be found to enforce the general law on the campus, when campus law enforcement breaks down. One possible option lies in the temporary restraining order which several universities used during disorders in the spring of 1969. At the State University of New York at Buffalo, a court order was obtained some hours after a student occupation of the administration building. The order directed all persons in the building to "immediately cease and desist from such activity" along with "all persons interfering with the lawful ingress and egress of others at such Campus facilities. . . ." Hundreds of copies of the order were mimeographed within a few hours of the judge's signature, and were distributed to the occupants of the building. The edict also ordered the respondents or their attorney to appear in court the following day to "show cause" why a regular injunction against the illegal occupation should not issue.

The restraining order had its desired effect. The students left the building rather than risk further court proceedings or arrests. The same device was used the next month at Columbia and City College, but with less success. Eight Columbia students who flouted the restraining order were subsequently sentenced to contempt of court and were jailed for the maximum term of thirty days along with a hundred dollar fine. It is doubtful whether service of the writ contributed in any way to the evacuation of the building; more likely, the SDS group simply lacked the general support they had had the previous year, and thus decided to vacate for political rather than legal reasons.

The use of restraining orders has some obvious advantages. Chief among them is the fact that police need not be called to bring the general law to bear on the campus in times of strife. Moreover, the responsible "enemy" ceases to be the university administration and becomes the courts; any decision whether to employ police or make arrests after service of a restraining order is for the judge and not for the president to make. This shift in the locus of conflict seems to have had a tempering effect on student attitudes; one moderate student at City College observed after the restraining order that "none of us want cops on campus, but it's just not the same when they're sent here by the court."

There are other features of the restraining order that make administrators and lawyers uneasy about using this newfound weapon. For one, a narrower range of issues is involved in a trial for criminal contempt than in a prosecution for breach of the peace or trespass. Defenses which might be introduced in mitigation or justification of the latter charges are irrelevant when the only issues are whether a court order was properly served and then was defied by persons who remained in the building. Then too there is a danger that a restraining order may proscribe a range of activities on the campus far broader, and less precisely defined, than could constitutionally be made the target of penal legislation.

Finally, the contempt hearing lacks some of the procedural safeguards that are guaranteed in a regular criminal trial. Thus the Supreme Court has been sparing in its approval of restraining orders, or injunctions, and contempt proceedings for their enforcement, where political activity or expression were affected. Yet despite these limitations and reservations, the more peaceful alternative to open campus warfare that is so badly needed by embattled institutions may lie in a refinement of the restraining order.

The issue of sanctions external to the university has recently been much discussed in another context. Beginning with the winter of 1967–68, congressmen and state lawmakers showed increasing interest in legislation that would punish student protesters who seemed to them immune from campus discipline or criminal sentences. The most obvious starting point was the extensive student loan and grant programs; several provisions, or conditions, were attached to 1969 appropriation bills for higher education assistance. The most significant of these was section 504 of the Higher Education Act Amendments, applicable to National Defense Education Act loans, Educational Opportunity Grants, Work-Study payments, student loan insurance and several other designated programs.

This restriction decreed termination of student aid drawn

from federal funds under two conditions: first, when the institution determined "after affording notice and an opportunity for a hearing" that a student or employee has been convicted of a crime, since the effective date of the new law, "which involved the use of . . . (or assistance to others in the use of) force, disruption, or the seizure of property [of the university] to prevent officials or students . . . from engaging in their duties or pursuing their studies, and that such crime was of a serious nature and contributed to substantial disruption of the institution with respect to which such crime was committed. . . ." Second, when a university determined (also after notice and opportunity for hearing) that a student or employee "has wilfully refused to obey a lawful order or regulation [of the university] and that such refusal was of a serious nature and contributed to a substantial disruption of the administration of such institution. . . ." On either ground the offender is to be denied payments under any of the enumerated federal programs for a period of two years.

The practical significance of these restrictions has been elusive. Early in the Nixon administration, it looked as though they might be vigorously enforced; the President, having learned that 122 of the 540 students arrested in disorders at San Francisco State received federal support, ordered responsible government officials to investigate. Soon thereafter directives went to all college and university presidents reminding them of the institution's responsibility for enforcement. At the same time, there seemed little evidence of compliance in the field—save for obvious cases where students were expelled or suspended for so long a term that they would have forfeited their fellowships even without the statutory mandate. A report by the *Chronicle of Higher Education* noted that despite the strong public statements about compliance, "the executive branch remains essentially unable, and perhaps even unwilling, to push strict enforcement of the restrictions."

Proposals for harsher penalties appeared meanwhile to have strong support in the late winter and early spring of 1969. President Nixon told the U.S. Chamber of Commerce he thought the time had come for college administrators to "have the backbone to stand up against" student disruptions and violence. Within a month, however, the two Cabinet members most directly concerned— Attorney General John Mitchell and Health, Education and Welfare Secretary Robert Finch—both declared themselves opposed to any new legislation aimed at student protesters. Existing laws, they affirmed, were adequate to meet the country's needs. In Congress, meanwhile, support persisted for a statute requiring colleges to draft codes of student conduct before either the institutions or their students would be eligible for federal funds—a compromise provision designed by its proponents to forestall more draconian penalties sought by conservatives. Eventually the President joined the opposition, declaring that the pending legislation was not only unnecessary but "would be just what the demonstrators wanted." Instead, he affirmed, the responsibility for campus discipline should rest with university administrators. Ten days later, by an 18–17 vote, the House Education and Labor Committee killed the proposal for the session.

A similar provision had, however, been adopted by the New York legislature and signed by the Governor. This new law required all colleges and universities chartered by the State to file, not later than July 21, rules and regulations for the "maintenance of public order," along with a program for the enforcement of those rules. Failure to file such a report would make the institution ineligible for state aid. In New York, Colorado, and California new sections were added to the penal laws making it a crime to disrupt or disturb college classes or other activities. The Pennsylvania Higher Education Agency adopted a policy of withholding financial aid from students merely arrested or accused of campus crimes, without awaiting a trial or even administrative hearing. New Jersey meanwhile enacted a novel law permitting students to sue other students who disrupt classes or damage campus property—the successful plaintiff being able to collect up to $100 for each day he is deprived of his education.

Many more proposals were rejected or simply never reached the floor. In some states as many as forty or fifty bills dealing with student protests were introduced during the 1969 session. Few legislatures in states experiencing campus violence failed to pass at least one restrictive measure. Many of the new laws were drafted with far less care and sensitivity than the 1969 federal enactment; for example, state laws denying aid to students convicted of campus crimes seldom require either (a) notice and an opportunity for a hearing by the university; or (b) a finding that the offense seriously disrupted the business of the institution. The state laws are also likely to be more vigorously enforced than the federal restrictions, since state agencies can act more rapidly and directly against individual student offenders.

Punitive legislation against student protesters remains an enigma. Strongly favored by conservative governors and legislators, and endorsed by some moderate lawmakers—either to forestall more drastic restrictions or to appease a hostile constituency—such laws seem as unpopular with the Nixon administration as they were with its predecessor. Moreover, laws aimed specifically at students are almost certain to be either unconstitutional or unenforceable—ineffectual if they contain the procedural guarantees and the limitations found in the present federal restrictions, yet probably invalid if they omit such safeguards.

Finally, there is much evidence to support President Nixon's view that passage of punitive laws "would be just what the demonstrators wanted"—a kind of moral equivalent of calling the police to the campus. The National Commission on Causes and Prevention of Violence, in its campus disorders paper, warned that such legislation would have one (or possibly both) of two effects: on the one hand, a law withdrawing aid to the institution because of riots the administration could not check would punish a great many innocent and needy students in order to punish a few troublemakers. On the other hand, "if aid is withdrawn from even a few students in a manner that the campus views as unjust, the result may be to radicalize a much larger number by convincing them that existing governmental institutions are as inhumane as the revolutionaries claim."

Legislatures may nonetheless be able to make some contribution to the solution of the campus crisis. The Nixon administration and the Violence Commission seem to share the belief that courts (especially the federal courts) could profitably be empowered to issue restraining orders and preliminary injunctions against campus disorder where their authority is now in doubt. To be sure, indiscriminate use of such remedies may jeopardize liberties of expression and undermine procedural guarantees for reasons we have already considered. But surely if legislatures want to do something about campus disorder, this seems a more constructive channel for their efforts than the cumulation of retributive penalties or institutional forfeitures.

VI. *Public Law and the "Private" University*

We have already considered the applicability of university law to the community beyond the campus. It is appropriate to conclude this chapter by inquiring how far the general constitutional law applies to *private* colleges and universities. To one who is not familiar with the intricacies of constitutional law, the question might seem unnecessary. It is important to lawyers, and to those who would understand the law, because of the way the Constitution reads. The Fourteenth Amendment—the channel by which the specific guarantees of the Bill of Rights and the general guarantee of equality are brought to bear upon a wide range of state and local as well as federal acts—begins with the phrase "No State shall . . ."

Originally the courts took a narrow view of this language, and confined its application to actions which were directly those of governments and governmental agencies. This included cities, towns, counties and their branches and divisions, of course, as well as the state governments. But the courts insisted that the Constitution had no bearing upon private or nongovernmental actions—even where those actions might serve to discriminate or segregate on racial lines, to deny freedom of expression or religion, and so on.

In recent years the courts have recognized that certain kinds of nominally "private" institutions exercise essentially governmental powers. Even though they are privately owned and managed, the purpose of the Fourteenth Amendment requires that they be subject to the same constitutional standards as governmental agencies and offices. Thus a corporation that runs a company town for its workers has been treated by the courts just like a public town. A pre-primary election sponsored by a private political organization has been held to be "state action" where it effectively controls the outcome of the later, official primary. Institutions which receive substantial amounts of government funds have sometimes been held accountable to constitutional standards, particularly where a measure of governmental control or supervision goes with the money. In these and other instances, the courts have steadily expanded the range of technically, formally private actions that are treated as "state actions" for constitutional purposes.

Several courts have considered the extent to which the provisions of the Bill of Rights and the Fourteenth Amendment apply to privately chartered and supported colleges and universities. The question first arose in a pair of cases involving Tulane University in New Orleans. A group of black students had been denied admission to Tulane and brought suit in the federal district court, claiming a denial of their constitutional right to equal treatment. Judge J. Skelly Wright found in the students' favor. A careful review of Tulane's original state charter (it was founded as the public University of Louisiana in the mid-19th century), and of the substantial investment of state funds in its early development convinced Judge Wright that subsequent changes in the governance and support of the university had not altered its constitutional responsibilities as a quasi-governmental institution.

Much more important than this narrow holding was Judge Wright's sweeping dictum: "One may question whether any school or college can ever be so 'private' as to escape the reach of the Fourteenth Amendment. . . . No one any longer doubts that education is a matter affected with the greatest public interest. . . . Clearly, the administrators of a private college are performing a public function. They do the work of the State, often in the place of the State. . . . Reason and authority strongly suggest that the Constitution never sanctions racial discrimination in our schools and colleges, no matter how 'private' they may claim to be."

Nine months later, another district judge reexamined the Tulane case (after Judge Wright had left for Washington) and reached the opposite conclusion. Numerous private bequests since the early years had generated a metamorphosis that made Tulane's discrimination a private matter. This difference of opinion between two judges of the same district suggests a recurrent characteristic of cases of this type: each turns on a close study of its particular facts, and courts are likely to decide the issue differently.

The years between 1962 and 1968 saw little progress toward the resolution of the issue laid bare in the Tulane litigation. A federal court of appeals found the University of Tampa to be "public" for admissions purposes because a gift of valuable municipal property had facilitated its inauguration—even though the university was technically a private institution under private control. On the other hand, a district judge in Washington concluded that Howard University was still "private" because of its original private charter in 1867 even though the Federal Government contributes almost the entire operating budget. (This decision was later reversed by the court of appeals on other grounds, without reaching the "state action" issue.)

There was mounting confidence that if the right case appeared, the federal courts would soon extend to the private campus the same guarantees that applied to the public university. In 1968, the right case did reach the courts, and the prognosis proved erroneous. There were, in fact, two cases raising different aspects of the question of "state action." One involved the Columbia University uprising in April and May, and the disciplinary action growing out of those events. The other case came out of a protest at Alfred University against compulsory ROTC for male students.

The students in the Columbia case invoked the protection of the constitution on two grounds; the first, suggested by Judge Wright, being that education (especially higher education) is an inherently public function, even when conducted under private auspices. The argument was stronger in New York State than elsewhere, they claimed, because of the unique control the State's Regents maintain over degree granting and other activities of private as well as publicly supported institutions. The second prop in the Columbia case was the extensive state and federal funds which the University received and which comprised a substantial portion of its budget. (Several federal courts had held financial aid to nominally private hospitals, libraries, and other institutions; sufficient to support a finding of "state action.")

The court rejected both claims and held that Columbia was still, after all, a private university. Higher education was in some sense a public function, of course, but the argument attempted to prove too much. If Columbia was a public institution and its disciplinary measures state action, the court insisted that sectarian colleges must also be deemed public for these purposes, and that would do violence to institutional autonomy. Similarly, if Columbia students could invoke the Bill of Rights, so could its employees, people doing business with the university, and those wanting to use its open spaces for demonstrations. To the district judge (a former member of the Columbia Law faculty) these results seemed unreasonable.

The argument that Columbia became public by receiving substantial government funds fared no better. Most of the precedents on which the students relied involved a degree of interdependence between public and private institutions that was not present in Morningside Heights. Moreover, if an appropriation of government funds alone transformed a private university into a public one, then "all kinds of contractors and enterprises, increasingly dependent upon government business for much larger proportions of their income than those here in question would suddenly find themselves bound by the Bill of Rights too." And that seemed to the court an absurd conclusion.

The Columbia case was followed by one in which the claim of "state action" was far stronger. Alfred University, a private liberal arts college in rural Western New York, plays a unique part in the state's educational system. It is the home of the Ceramics College, a "statutory" unit of the State University of New York, supported by legislative appropriations to the same degree as any of New York's University Centers or State Colleges. Ceramics students take liberal arts courses from the Alfred faculty, and receive an Alfred degree, but pay the substantially lower tuition of State University students. Alfred students in similar numbers take special courses at the Ceramics College. In addition to its annual appropriation for the College, SUNY pays certain of Alfred's incremental costs on a per-student basis. The State, for example, pays a *pro rata* share of the salary of the Dean of Students, who is disciplinarian for the Ceramics as well as the liberal arts students.

In May 1968, shortly after the dust had settled at Columbia, a group of Alfred students were suspended for participating in a demonstration against ROTC exercises. Some of the expelled students were in the liberal arts division, and others in the Ceramics College. They brought suit together, arguing that the affiliation with the State University, and the interdependence thus created, made Alfred's suspensions "state action" even if the acts of the ordinary private college were not. The district court found the case indistinguishable from the Columbia suit, and declined to reach the merits for want of federal jurisdiction. The Court of Appeals approached the case more discriminatingly. The action of Alfred and its dean was state action as to the Ceramics students "for the seemingly simple but entirely sufficient reason that the State has willed it that way." The Ceramics College was in every way a state institution, even though its graduates received Alfred degrees, lived in Alfred dormitories, and attended some Alfred classes.

The court drew a distinction, however, in the case of the liberal arts students. Despite the substantial flow of state funds to the campus, and the operational and curricular interdependence between the two divisions, the disciplinary proceeding was not state action. This was so for several reasons: first, the State and the Ceramics College were in no way involved in Alfred's administration of discipline over its own students; "the state action, not the private action, must be the subject of the complaint," and this discipline was private action. Second, although there was some relationship between public and private activity, this was not a case "where the wholly state-supported activity is so dominant that the private activity could be deemed to have been swallowed up."

Much more could be said about the "public" character of "private" universities that simply did not come out in either the Columbia or Alfred opinions. There is respectable precedent for finding state action—at least where racial discrimination is the object of attack—on the basis of public funds alone, perhaps supplemented by a degree of control that is always present in higher education. The actual interdependence between public and private institutions suggests that the next case may well go the other way. For example, five of the eight universities receiving the largest amounts of federal funds for research and development are private. Government funds for indirect aid through scholarships and fellowships, and direct support in various forms, for both construction and operating costs, are as important to many nominally private universities as to state-supported institutions. The New York legislature, following the recommendations of a study commission on higher education chaired by McGeorge Bundy, appropriated over $20 million for direct aid to the state's private, nonsectarian colleges and universities in 1968–69. Other states are studying the possibility of comparable subsidies. Private institutions are being recognized not merely as needy suppliants at the state capitol, but much more as integral components without which the total state system of higher education simply could not function. (In Massachusetts, for example, professional education in law, medicine, and other fields is still available only at private universities. The District of Columbia would be in dire straits without the Georgetown Medical Center, etc.) The actual interdependence and the recognition of it are likely to increase, and the case for judicial review of private university actions will be correspondingly strengthened.

One final caution is in order. It does make a difference what specific action is under challenge. One act of a private institution may warrant judicial review, while another remains properly beyond reach of the courts. Professor William Cohen of UCLA has observed: "It has not been surprising, given the clear application of the equal protection clause to the arbitrary exclusion of students on racial grounds, that in such cases federal courts have extended the reach of the Fourteenth Amendment even to institutions slightly involved with government. It would not follow that an institution more heavily involved with government would be precluded from using private funds to construct a chapel on the campus. The nature of the question involved gives different judicial perspectives to the state action question."

VI

THE COLLEGE

AND THE

CONSTITUTION

One Saturday afternoon the Board of Trustees of a Midwestern state university met in emergency session to decide how to deal with a sit-in that had troubled the campus for ten days. The demonstration had been touched off by the university's announcement that a young Negro assistant professor of political science would not be rehired the following year. The faculty member was very popular with his own students, and had strong ties with the local black community and its organizations. He was involved in a variety of causes and activities and had represented the university in minority group programs. The trouble was that his publications were meager and gave limited promise of future scholarly achievement. The political science department bent its standards a bit in view of his other contributions, but refused to bend far enough to give tenure to a colleague who had put so little on paper. That decision prompted the academic dean to announce, "with the greatest regret," that the young professor would not be retained.

Both black and white students at once took up the man's cause. A series of rallies and meetings canvassed alternatives of strategy. The students expanded the issues from the immediate concern about retaining the popular young black teacher, to include demands for hiring other minority group instructors, enlarging to 10 percent the school's minority student enrollment—about 3 percent of the total student body at the time—creating an "autonomous" dormitory wing for black students, and granting students an equal voice with faculty in the hiring and promotion of professors.

There was widespread student support for one or more of these demands. Thus the administration was ready for the sit-in when it came, five days after the academic dean's announcement. Some four hundred students moved quietly into the administration building at the close of business that afternoon. The bedrolls, books, and food they carried warned that the siege might be a long one. The leaders confirmed this inference by warning the last secretaries leaving the building that they should not plan to return to work the following day, nor indeed any day until the demands had been granted. The student legion inside the building was clearly adequate to maintain an effective occupation, unless the president called the city police. Past encounters with law enforcement officers, and the presence of many angry students in the building, dissuaded all but one or two hard-line members of the administration from any immediate confrontation. The decision was made to wait things out for at least a week.

When the week ended with many students still occupying the building, mounting demands for firm action from legislators, some faculty members, and trustees convinced the president that he should call the university's governing board into emergency session to review the crisis. The announcement of the meeting planned for Saturday of the second week of the sit-in touched off an angry rally outside the administration building. Not only were militant student leaders talking excitedly about violence and physical destruction for the first time since the sit-in began; equally ominous was a skirmish between demonstrators inside the building and a cordon of football players who had made an unsuccessful sally at the front door. Student spokesmen had indicated they might disrupt classes taught by faculty members who openly opposed their demands. Student support was building on both sides; the campus was, to an alarming degree, a house divided.

The final fuel of the week was added by an editorial in Friday's issue of the student newspaper. (The newspaper, supported substantially by student fees appropriated by the Student Senate, had been moving increasingly to the left and the current editor was a leader of the radical group.) The caption of the editorial—"Fuck the Trustees"—revealed both the political bias and the choice of words in the rather raw piece that followed. The same four letter word appeared several times in succeeding paragraphs, and was accompanied by other epithets deemed acceptable in the locker room but questionable in the parlor. The general thrust of the editorial was that students who supported the sit-in and the underlying demands should mount the barricades on Saturday afternoon and disrupt the trustees' meeting.

At the last minute, the trustees changed the meeting place from their regular room on campus to an undisclosed site (actually a motel) some miles away. Thus the meeting was uninterrupted by angry students, although some trustees, having read the previous day's editorial, maintained an uneasy composure throughout the session, fearing that the students might still track them down.

The agenda for the meeting, drawn up by the chairman of the board, a conservative physician—and over objections from the president—covered the full spectrum of issues related to and arising out of the sit-in:

(1) A motion for immediate expulsion of all students sitting in at the administration building, to be effective Sunday morning.

(2) A motion to expel the editor of the student newspaper, and cut off the paper's subsidy, on grounds of "obscenity" and "insubordination."

(3) A motion to triple the tuition for out-of-state students (in the belief that many of the sit-in leaders were residents of New York and California).

(4) A motion to withdraw recognition and all campus privileges from the university chapter of Students for a Democratic Society, which had taken an active role in fomenting the demonstration.

(5) A motion to reject the specific demands of the students (other than the one relating to the particular faculty member, whose case was to be reviewed separately)—*i.e.,* the demand for expanded hiring of minority group faculty and for a quota of minority students; the demand for an "autonomous" black studies program; the demand for exclusive residence hall space for black students; and the demand for an equal student voice in the hiring and promotion of faculty members.

(6) A motion to permit university officials to enter and inspect any dormitory room at any hour of day or night—a proposal designed to deal not so much with the sit-in as with the rising drug problem on the campus.

(7) A motion to adopt a new and more stringent set of student

conduct rules which had been developed and discussed entirely within the Board, the rules to be effective at once.

The particular events described here are hypothetical, but the scene is increasingly familiar on campuses large and small across the nation. Such a case study provides a scenario by which to consider, in context, the constitutional issues that are of vital importance on college campuses today. Much could be said, of course, about legal questions that once were troublesome but have now passed into history. Within recent memory, there has been dispute about the constitutionality of granting campus privileges to fraternities and sororities that discriminated on racial grounds. Conversely, there have been constitutional attacks on university policies banning all social fraternities, or at least refusing recognition to those that would not sign a nondiscrimination pledge. But the sharp decline in fraternity membership, and the satisfactory accommodation worked out on most campuses, deprive these issues of vital significance in a current constitutional survey. Some of the burning questions today are, however, analogous; the demands for all-black dormitory wings, and requests for recognition of black student associations that exclude whites, must be resolved by reference to the very same constitutional principles that were brought to bear on the fraternity controversy. The novelty of the way the current issues arise should not obscure the relevance of prior precedent and experience.

I. *The Right to a Hearing: Due Process on the Campus*

The first motion on our hypothetical trustees' agenda calls for the expulsion of the sit-ins by the following day. Such a demand contemplates, of course, no hearing or formal proceeding prior to expulsion. Yet it is quite clear under present law that these students cannot be expelled so summarily, and they may in fact not be expellable at all. Two aspects of the question must be considered separately—one having to do with procedures, and the other with substantive rules of conduct. It is better to begin with the matter of procedures, for the discussion of student conduct rules would be meaningless without an understanding of the manner in which they are to be applied.

As recently as the late 1950s, courts would still allow a state college or university to dismiss a student with only a summary hearing, or with no hearing at all. Harvard Law Professor Warren Seavey found this situation "shocking," and concluded that one's "sense of justice should be outraged by denial to students of the normal safeguards."

The condition that troubled Professor Seavey had persisted for several reasons—the relative weakness of students as legal complainants; the use of the "privilege" label to describe higher education, which died hard and rather late; and the noncriminal character of disciplinary proceedings. Perhaps, too, the courts have been reluctant to intervene in internal university affairs even for the limited purpose of seeing that a student receives due process before being expelled. In any event, the situation changed dramatically soon after Seavey's article. Two cases involving students at small Southern predominantly Negro state colleges marked the change. In both cases the students had been dismissed because of off-campus civil rights activity—a lunch counter sit-in in one case, and a freedom ride in the other. Neither group of students received any meaningful hearing on the campus. Both courts found the dismissals unsupportable in the absence of fair procedures, and sent the cases back to the colleges for hearings.

For the guidance of the two institutions, the court of appeals suggested in a case involving a student named St. John Dixon the nature of the hearing to which students were entitled:

> The notice should contain a statement of the specific charges and grounds which, if proven, would justify expulsion under the [college] regulations. . . . The nature of the hearing should vary depending upon the circumstances of the particular case. The case before us requires something more than an informal interview with an administrative authority of the college. By its nature, a charge of misconduct as opposed to a failure to meet the scholastic standards of the college depends upon a collection of the facts concerning the charged misconduct easily colored by the point of view of the witnesses. . . . This is not to imply that a full dress judicial hearing with the right to cross examine witnesses is required. Such a hearing with the attending publicity and disturbance of college activities might be detrimental to the college's educational atmo-

sphere and impractical to carry out. Nevertheless, the rudiments of an adversary proceeding may be preserved without encroaching upon the interests of the college. In the instant case, the student should be given the names of the witnesses against him and an oral or written report on the facts to which each witness testifies. He should also be given the opportunity to present to the Board, or at least to an administrative official of the college, his own defense against the charges and to produce either oral testimony or written affidavits of witnesses in his behalf. If the hearing is not before the Board directly, the results and findings of the hearing should be presented in a report open to the student's inspection. If these rudimentary elements of fair play are followed in a case of misconduct of this particular type, we feel that the requirements of due process of law will have been fulfilled.

Shortly after these decisions, a survey was conducted to determine how closely reality approximated the ideal. Seventy-two state universities responded to a questionnaire concerning procedures they followed in student discipline cases. The results suggested that the federal court decisions spoke more to the future than to the present: as of 1963, 43 percent of the institutions "do not provide students with a reasonably clear and specific list which describes misconduct subject to discipline"; 53 percent do not provide the student with specific written charges; only 17 percent provide such a formal notice at least ten days before the proceeding; and 16 percent "do not even provide for a hearing in cases where the student takes exception to the charge of misconduct or to the penalty proposed." Roughly one half (47 percent) "allow students or administrators who appear as witnesses or who bring the charge to sit on the hearing board if they are otherwise a member." About one third of the institutions "do not allow the student charged to be accompanied by an adviser of his choice during the hearing." One quarter of the sample "do not permit the student charged to question informants or witnesses whose statements may be considered by the hearing board in determining guilt." Eighty-five percent "permit the hearing board to consider statements by witnesses not available for cross-examination." Finally, 47 percent permit the board to consider evidence obtained by methods (*i.e.,* an illegal search) which would compel its exclusion from a criminal trial.

Informal procedures may be permissible—indeed preferable—for the vast majority of university discipline problems. After the close of Berkeley's "year of turmoil" the chairman of the Faculty Committee on Student Conduct, law Professor Ronan Degnan, observed: "Rules of procedure must accommodate primarily the routine case. More than 90 percent of cases before the Committee on Student Conduct need no rules at all; formal rules would merely obstruct and distract. The bulk of cases involves cheating or stealing or general disorderly conduct. The student admits the charges in all but insignificant detail and attempts to explain or justify. There is no need for pleading or charges or cross examination."

Yet these informal procedures were concededly inappropriate for the remaining 10 percent of the cases at Berkeley—the bitterly contested political causes célèbres. Interestingly, this figure of 10 percent corresponds closely to practice in the criminal courts. Some 90 percent of formal criminal charges are typically disposed of on guilty pleas; no more than 10 percent are contested and brought to trial. (The system would be taxed far beyond its capacity if as many as half or even a quarter of the formal charges led to trials.)

What procedural requirements should be met in those cases that are bitterly contested, the 10 percent that warrant formal proceedings? It seems clear that even in the political cause célèbre, the procedures need not be those of the courtroom. It is not possible for the average student offender to be "tried" by a true "jury of his peers." The rules of evidence applicable to criminal trials—which are well understood only by trial lawyers and judges who work with them regularly—would simply cripple the university discipline machinery. There has been no serious suggestion that a full-dress grand jury should be summoned to file a formal indictment against a student offender. These and other specific procedural safeguards, which the Bill of Rights mandates in the criminal courts, would be inappropriate and even possibly damaging to the disciplinary hearing.

What, then, is required for a hearing to meet the test of due process? In determining how far beyond the Dixon decision, quoted earlier, a university should go, a distinction must be drawn between procedures the courts have actually insisted upon, and those that have simply been recommended by interested groups such as the

American Association of University Professors and the American Civil Liberties Union.

The question of the right to counsel provides an illustration. The Dixon case said nothing about the role of lawyers in the hearing. Since 1961, the issue has arisen in several cases. One court has flatly held that universities may properly bar lawyers from appearing with or representing students in discipline hearings. Another federal judge has held, however, that students are entitled to bring attorneys to *advise* them during the hearing, but not to *argue* or *cross-examine* witnesses. Most decisions have simply not discussed the lawyer's role at all.

On the other hand, the model codes of procedure drafted by interested groups evince no doubt about the student's right to counsel. The New York University seminar draft states unequivocally that "a student charged with misconduct . . . has the right to be represented by counsel or an adviser. . . ." The draft code developed by the American Association of University Professors is even more explicit in recognizing "the right . . . to be represented by legal counsel if [the student] wishes." Other model codes of procedure similarly recognize this "right." Thus, whatever the case law may require or permit, an enlightened administrator will think carefully before excluding a student's attorney from the hearing of a serious charge.

There are, moreover, practical reasons why the university may condone or even encourage students to appear with counsel. First, the university will quite likely have its own case presented by a lawyer if the charge is substantial and the consequences grave. Quite apart from the lack of symmetry in having an attorney only on one side, both the appearance and the reality of fairness argue for parity of representation. And as discipline cases become increasingly complex, with subtle points of law involved, the deliberations of the court or hearing panel (typically composed of nonlawyers) will be greatly aided if both sides of the case are professionally presented.

The time may even come when universities will be compelled, by internal pressures if not by court decisions, to provide legal services for students too poor to obtain their own. Meanwhile, student governments are showing increasing interest in the retention of law firms or individual attorneys to represent any student who gets into trouble with the civil or university authorities.

The right to counsel is only one of the ingredients of procedural due process. Other elements—both those that have been required by court decision and others that have merely been recommended as sound policy—should be listed here for the sake of completeness. The catalogue that follows is a brief summary, arranged according to the chronology of the disciplinary proceeding.

Before the Hearing: The current student conduct rules—and the maximum penalties for violation of each—should be clearly published and in the hands of every student. A student who is alleged to have violated a rule should receive written notice of the precise charge against him, citing the rule involved and the time and place of the offense. He should be directed to appear at a specified time for a hearing—a time far enough in the future that he can prepare an adequate defense. The same notice should inform him that he may bring an attorney or other adviser to the hearing.

During the Hearing: The court or hearing body must be impartial, and should be a continuing tribunal of general jurisdiction, rather than an *ad hoc* group convened for the particular case. There should be students on the panel, and ideally a student majority on the court of first instance—unless the case is simply too "hot" for students to handle. The university should assume the burden of proof, so that no penalty can be imposed unless the charge is proved by the preponderance of the evidence. The student should be clearly informed of the evidence against him, and hearsay evidence or statements should be allowed only in the rare case where the witness is unavailable. Cross-examination of witnesses should be allowed. The student should be permitted to introduce evidence in his own behalf. He should not be required to make any self-incriminating statements, particularly if criminal charges are pending for the same offense, and his refusal to testify or answer a particular question should justify no adverse inference.

After the Hearing: A decision should be reached as promptly as possible. The court should decide the case exclusively on the evidence presented, and should not consult with university officials or receive any secret information bearing on the case. A transcript or stenographic summary of the hearing should be made available to the student as well as to the court and the administration.

When the court has reached its decision, the student should be notified at once not only of the result but of the reasoning as well. There should then be an opportunity to appeal to the university president or chancellor, or perhaps to a higher court, composed of persons who have taken no part in the prosecution of the charge initially. If the student wishes to challenge the constitutionality of any rule involved in the case, that question should be referred to a special panel of experts (for example, a panel of law students and faculty members who have a special interest in constitutional law).

One important question about the hearing remains to be considered: *When* must it be held, and can a student be suspended before or while awaiting the outcome of the hearing? Many universities have used so-called "interim suspensions" of student offenders, on the theory that some penalty should be imposed at once, even though formal proceedings might take some time to start. University officials have also argued that certain students pose such a danger to other members of the university community that they should be barred from the campus immediately.

Two federal court decisions in Wisconsin have, however, cast grave doubt on the use of interim suspensions. In December 1968, a group of about one hundred black students were suspended a few days after a violent demonstration on the campus of Oshkosh State College. The students went at once to court, and a district judge enjoined the suspension until the administration issued formal charges and held a hearing on them.

Several months later, after a series of disruptive incidents at Madison, the University of Wisconsin Regents suspended a group of students pending a hearing on charges brought by the administration. The suspension was effective March 6; no hearing was scheduled until March 19. The students at once filed suit in the federal court, challenging the constitutionality of their exclusion from the academic community for thirteen days before an opportunity to dispute their guilt. The district judge found in the students' favor, in what is bound to be a major precedent for campus due process. Interim suspensions might be employed, the court acknowledged, where the university determined that a student's continued presence posed a very substantial danger to the campus community. But even then, there must be a preliminary hearing, at which the student could raise such questions as possible mistaken identity or strongly mitigating circumstances. If it was impossible to schedule such a hearing, then the hearing on the merits of the charge must take place promptly, at the "earliest practical time." Thirteen days was clearly too long to wait, the judge concluded.

Due process, whether in a university, criminal court, or administrative agency, cannot be defined with precision. The university disciplinary proceeding demands an accommodation between the formality of the courtroom and the informality of the dean's office, for neither model is appropriate. The nature of that accommodation will necessarily vary according to the character of different institutions, the type of case, and other factors.

II. *Rules and Regulations: Student Protest and the Constitution*

We return at this point to the hypothetical agenda for the trustees' meeting. The motion for explusion of the sit-ins initially implicated the question of procedures and the right to a hearing. The corollary question is that of rules and regulations upon which a disciplinary charge rests. One might begin with a simple question, to which the answer must be affirmative: "Can a state university punish a student for a sit-in that is disruptive or obstructive?" In the old days, before judicial review of university discipline, the answer was quite simple in every case, since the academy was a legal system within itself. Today the issue is much more complex.

The extent of university authority over disruptive behavior is *not* doubtful because the law condones violence or obstruction, for surely it does not—any more on the campus than in the community at large. Yet one must begin with two propositions that have been repeatedly affirmed and provide the setting for discussion of this matter. On the one hand, dissent and protest must be permitted, indeed must be given the widest latitude, on a college campus. A university more than any other institution should foster the spirit of inquiry and independence that often generates criticism and protest.

It is equally clear, however, that one person's protest may not interfere with the rights and liberties of others, be they fellow students who wish to study or attend classes, professors who wish to teach or conduct research, or administrators and staff who have myriad responsibilities for the operation of a university.

The escalation of campus violence has caused those groups

most committed to upholding the right of dissent to express their deep concern. The American Civil Liberties Union, while vigorously opposing repressive measures against demonstrations, has warned militant students that "protests that deprive others of the opportunity to speak or be heard, or that require physical takeover of buildings to disrupt the educational process, or the incarceration of administrators and others, are anti-civil-libertarian and incompatible with the nature and high purpose of an educational institution." Such tactics, the ACLU cautioned, are self-defeating; they will "breed a counterviolence and backlash that will defeat or set back the very objectives student activists seek to serve and lead to repressive countermeasures."

The question of university disciplinary power is also made difficult by the blurring of the line that separates "legitimate protest" from "violence and disruption." A picket line in front of the administration building may be peaceful one minute, and the next minute may totally obstruct entrances and exits. A sit-in that begins with a corridor for ingress and egress may quickly become disruptive if two or three participants move out of line. These changes are not always the fault of the demonstrators; sometimes it is the acts of counterdemonstrators that transform a peaceful protest into a violent and disruptive event.

The state of the law compounds the difficulty of determining when a university may punish disruptive behavior. We might best approach this new and still developing body of constitutional law with a simple but plausible proposition: the university may penalize student conduct on campus only in situations that would warrant criminal sanctions off campus—unless one of the special university interests has been significantly and directly affected. One example will suggest how these interests may be involved, and their relevance to the scope of university authority. A noisy demonstration by students in a dormitory during examination week may superficially resemble the behavior of a rowdy group of Shriners, Elks, or Lions in the lobby of a hotel they have taken over for their annual convention. Both the university and the hotelkeeper are landlords, and accordingly share a *general* interest (backed by the criminal law) in preserving order and protecting property. But the university has a *special* interest in maintaining calm and quiet so that students may study in the dormitory—an interest which has no counterpart in the case of the downtown hotel.

This is how the basic constitutional proposition operates. Its validity remains to be determined. There are only a handful of court decisions recent enough to reflect the current thinking about university discipline. One federal district court judgment in South Carolina does, however, shed considerable light. The case involved a student at a small state college who had been suspended for leading an unauthorized demonstration on the campus. A college rule required permission from the administration to hold demonstrations, rallies, marches and the like. The judge held the regulation unconstitutional because of its breadth and the dangers of arbitrary action. In passing, the court rejected a proffered distinction between the use of open space on the campus for rallies, and the use of public parks for the same purpose: "In [a Supreme Court case involving another South Carolina demonstration] the Court recognized that assembling at the site of government for peaceful expression of grievances constituted exercise of First Amendment rights in their pristine form. I am not persuaded that the campus of a state college is not similarly available for the same purposes for its students."

Other courts have indicated that higher standards might be appropriate on the campus, whether or not special university interests are affected. One such case was the suit for reinstatement by four Berkeley students suspended for taking part in the "dirty word" incident in the spring of 1965. The California courts held they had properly been excluded from the academic community. The appellate court stressed that "greater freedom and greater restrictions may prevail [on the campus] than in society at large," and that internal norms may be higher than community standards. Such language might well provide support for a higher expectation of campus behavior—save for the fact that the same students were also arrested and convicted under the California Penal Code for the very same offense, and the conviction was affirmed on appeal despite the vigorous intervention of the American Civil Liberties Union. As is frequently the case in law, the results are more important than the words. If one looks at the outcome, the "dirty word" cases can hardly be said to support a double standard.

The recent cases do suggest, therefore, that university discipline and criminal prosecution are governed by similar standards, save when special university interests are affected. This principle has important ramifications. Most significant is its sharp impact on the student conduct rules of many universities that were fashioned in an earlier time and have not been revised or refined. The fact is that many institutions have tried to combat the sophisticated tactics of modern student rebels with blunt tools designed for the old "sex, beer and cheating" cases, oblivious to the possibility of judicial scrutiny. In the dirty word case at Berkeley, a complaint grounded on failure of the students to "adhere to acceptable standards of personal conduct and . . . proper standards of conduct and good taste" barely passed muster. This was about as far as an old-style catch-all rule could be stretched.

Other institutions have responded to new pressures by applying old rules that were specific enough but did not really fit the facts. When students at Boulder blocked interviews with the Central Intelligence Agency recruiter, charges were lodged under an old regulation against hazing and similar pranks. Happily for the administration, the rule did speak about "injury to property" and "interference with the public or private rights of citizens." But the adaptation was fortuitous and awkward. At many other colleges, the first wave of modern demonstrations has evoked charges under rules designed for the era of the panty raid and the goldfish swallow.

It is ironic that one of the largest and most progressive of public institutions, the University of Wisconsin, was the first to be censured by a court for having tried to stretch its old rules beyond the breaking point. As at many other campuses in the fall of 1967, Wisconsin activists were less than hospitable to the Dow Chemical recruiter. A large number of students were suspended or expelled, and many were arrested as a result of the ensuing violence on the campus. Ten of the expelled students petitioned the federal court for reinstatement. They claimed that the regulations applied by the University were unconstitutionally vague and infringed their constitutional liberties.

It would be hard to imagine a case in which the conduct of the students was more clearly disruptive of order on the campus; moreover, the ten plaintiffs in the case were among the ringleaders. Yet the federal district court ultimately ruled that these students had been unconstitutionally expelled and were entitled to reinstatement. The university had based the disciplinary charges on two theories. The first involved a general common law student offense of "misconduct" which, although not specified in the student handbook, was presumed to apply on all campuses. The second ground of the charge was a paragraph in the Laws and Regulation of the University. Under the heading "scope of student freedom," it sanctioned various student political activities, concluding: "They may support causes by lawful means which do not disrupt the operations of the University, or organizations accorded the use of University facilities." The court decided that neither provision would support expulsion.

The vice in the word "misconduct" as the basis for discipline was its vagueness. Without any explanation or illustration in the student handbook, that word standing alone gave neither students nor administrators adequate guidance. If the same word appeared undefined in a criminal statute or ordinance, its invalidity would be clear. Without deciding whether university regulations had to be as precise and specific as criminal laws, the court concluded that the bare "misconduct" test was so vague as to deny due process and invade First Amendment liberties. This judgment applied to campus law a principle that has been basic to First Amendment cases for several decades: Regardless of the particular conduct in the case at bar—however disruptive or obstructive—the actor cannot constitutionally be punished under a rule that might indiscriminately include activity or expression protected by the Constitution. Moreover, a standard as vague as "misconduct" really makes the policeman a kind of legislator-on-the-spot; the law is so general that almost anything the enforcer thinks *should* be illegal can be *made* illegal in his discretion. Vague and imprecise laws not only fail to afford the warning to which prospective violators are entitled; they also allow a range of discretion that may become arbitrary or discriminatory in the wrong hands.

The court reached the same conclusion about the other basis on which the University sought to sustain the charge. The section on "scope of student freedom"—even if read as a prohibition rather than as a declaration of principle—was too vague to support an expulsion. "Neither the element of intention, nor that of proximity of cause and effect," remarked the trial judge, "nor that of substantiality, for example, is dealt with by its language. Nor does it contain even the most general description of the kinds of conduct which might be considered disruptive of the operations of the university, nor does it undertake to draw any distinctions whatever among the various categories of university 'operations.' "

Precision in rule making, and the avoidance of broad discretion, now appear to be prerequisites to university discipline. Looser rules might support milder sanctions than expulsion, though the court did not say so in the Wisconsin case. These recent developments mean that an answer to the question "can a student be expelled for a disruptive sit-in" now depends much more on the answer to another question—"is there a regulation that specifically prohibits disruptive sit-ins"—than upon the disruptive character of the behavior as such.

It is impossible, of course, to anticipate every tactic that student demonstrators may employ. Certainly the precision expected of university rule makers cannot be greater than that demanded of legislators and city councilors. Off the campus, convictions are consistently upheld for "trespass," "breach of the peace," and even "disorderly conduct." But the loose terms of these laws have been amplified either by definitional provisions in companion sections or by a series of pertinent court decisions. As universities build up precedent in student discipline cases, detailed codes of conduct may become less necessary—at least if decisions are indexed and kept available for ready reference. Until such experience and precedent exist, universities would be well advised to determine precisely what conduct they wish to forbid on the campus—blocking doors, interfering with the conduct of classes, destroying university property, breaking up meetings, and the like—and fashion specific rules covering those activities. When the applicable regulations are published in the student handbook, the campus newspaper, or in some other place where conscientious students cannot miss them, such rules can then be enforced in confidence that they will not be overturned by the courts.

A valid rule and a fair hearing are not quite enough, however. There must also be evidence at the hearing sufficient to support the charge. Reviewing courts have recently begun to take a rather critical look at the sufficiency of the testimony against students charged with campus offenses. Two 1968 cases were decided in the favor of dismissed students, in fact, because of the inadequacy of the record. One case involved students suspended from Lincoln University in Missouri for allegedly leading and participating in a demonstration in the school cafeteria. The court reviewed the record critically, compared the evidence with the charges, and concluded that the disciplinary sanction "was not based upon adequate substantial evidence to support its imposition." The defect was due partly to yet

another vague student conduct rule, and partly to an apparent misunderstanding on the part of the discipline committee about the essential elements of the offense. The court did express regret "that
the committee did not have assistance of legal counsel to guide it in
regard to the not uncomplicated problems which arise" in such
hearings. These are increasingly treacherous waters for inexperi-
enced laymen, and even for lawyers who are not up on their cases.

The Supreme Court has seemingly given its imprimatur to this
rather substantial body of law developed by the lower courts. One
must say "seemingly" because the key case—the first student
rights case to reach the Court in thirty-five years—involved a high
school rather than college controversy. Several students at a public
school in Des Moines had been suspended for wearing black arm
bands in violation of a school rule, to express their opposition to the
Vietnam war. Their parents sued for reinstatement, arguing that
this form of political protest was protected by the First Amendment.

The Supreme Court agreed, and reversed the judgment of the
two lower courts. Speaking through Mr. Justice Fortas, the Court
noted that the wearing of armbands under the circumstances of the
case "was entirely divorced from actually or potentially disruptive
conduct" and was essentially "pure speech" at the core of First
Amendment protection. The Court went on to state some important
precepts about the rights of students. These precepts apply, at least
by analogy, to the college context in which most of the student
rights law has developed:

> School officials do not possess absolute authority over
> their students. Students in school as well as out are "persons"
> under our Constitution. They are posssessed of fundamental
> rights which the State must respect, just as they themselves
> must respect their obligations to the State. . . . They may not
> be confined to the expression of those sentiments that are offi-
> cially approved. In the absence of constitutionally valid rea-
> sons to regulate their speech, students are entitled to freedom
> of expression of their views.

The Court noted in passing that this case did not involve regulations of dress or hair style, which might be a quite different matter. Four days before the Supreme Court spoke, however, a federal

judge in Wisconsin had declined to draw just that distinction. In his view, a school rule against long hair worn by male students was valid only if the authorities could show a substantial need for the regulation—for example, if long hair was dangerous to other students, disrupted the order of the classroom, or impaired academic performance. There being no such evidence to support the rule in question, its application violated the student's constitutional rights.

To conclude the discussion of rules of student conduct, one further caution is appropriate. The university administration which suddenly discovers its rules to be archaic and ill suited to protests and demonstrations may hastily draft new rules that single out political activity from other student behavior simply because it is at the center of the current campus stage. The general law once again provides a governing standard: the university may not discriminate against or single out certain acts for harsher treatment because they are politically motivated. While the university, as a landlord, may presumably forbid all banners in dormitory windows, it cannot permit football pennants saying "Beat State" but prohibit signs that read "Beat Nixon" or "Beat the Viet Cong." If bumper stickers can be sold on campus for athletic or charitable causes, they cannot be banned when the cause is political. Where funds can be raised for UNICEF, solicitors for NAACP, SNCC, or CORE are entitled to equal opportunity. There has been a tendency in recent years to apply a double standard to student behavior—to look the other way and remark that "boys will be boys" when fraternity brothers or football players engage in pranks that would cost political radicals their very places in the institution. Demonstrators who sit-in, disrupt meetings, or destroy property surely have no claim to immunity or special treatment because their motivation was political, but neither may they be treated more harshly than a fraternity prankster or an irresponsible athlete on a binge.

III. *Student Organizations: Ban the SDS?*

On the table at the trustees' meeting, the next item called for withdrawal of all campus privileges from the local chapter of the Students for a Democratic Society. The search for the instigator of campus disorders has frequently focused on SDS, and apparently with justification. FBI Director J. Edgar Hoover has called the group "the core of the new left"; this is probably the only opinion of Hoover's with which SDS leaders would venture any accord. There is no accurate way of measuring the strength of SDS, because careful membership records are not kept. But it is safe to assume that on almost all large or politically active campuses (and even some that are relatively small and quiet), there is an SDS chapter with at least ten or a dozen members.

Various efforts have been made to curb the power of SDS. The late Representative Joe Pool, a conservative Texas Democrat, once proposed that federal funds should be withheld from any university which allowed an SDS chapter to function on its campus. "We should not use tax funds for draft resistance," Pool argued at a press conference in the fall of 1967.

Despite the mounting desire of many administrators to see the last of SDS, few universities have even attempted to ban the organization. The University of Colorado briefly considered doing so after the volatile SDS national convention had brought very unfavorable national publicity to the Boulder campus. The Board of Regents first voted to withdraw recognition from SDS, but two weeks later reversed itself. The University's president, who cast the tie-breaking vote at the second Regents' meeting, explained he held "no brief" for the organization, but believed "our campus should be open to their ideas." He reaffirmed the "necessity of the University being open to ideas, even ideas that are repugnant to many who encounter them."

There are practical reasons, too, why few institutions have outlawed controversial political groups. It is naïve to suppose that a formal order from the administration will actually dissolve a designated group or rid the campus of its members and their activities. As a result of various pressures, the leaders of the SDS Chapter at the University of North Carolina suddenly announced they were disbanding the group. The next day there was an organizational meeting of the brand new Southern Student Organizing Committee. To the surprise of few, the old SDS people were prominently involved in the new group. And during the Colorado controversy, one of the Regents recognized the futility of trying to ban a group which would quickly "crop up under another name."

Once a university denies privileges to one controversial group, moreover, an inference of approval arises as to all other groups on the campus. Unless the administration wishes to maintain constant surveillance over the doctrines and activities of all other groups, it cannot avoid the politically damaging consequence of apparent responsibility for the "approved" groups that have survived its censorship. The only safe course is a neutral, nonjudgmental policy that allows all groups to register upon compliance with certain formal prerequisites.

There are also serious constitutional objections to banning political organizations. The original decision of the Colorado Regents had clear implications of censorship; SDS was temporarily the victim of the Regental axe because it had "the announced objective of disrupting and closing down educational institutions." It is unwise, indeed unconstitutional where political expression and activity are involved, to punish an individual or group on the basis of a declared intent to commit an unspecified crime at an indefinite time. With organizations, as with newspapers and controversial speakers, at least "one bite" must be allowed; penalties can be imposed on the responsible individuals after the fact if the law is broken, but the organization cannot be banned in advance.

The controlling constitutional law has emerged from a series of cases involving the Communist Party. Party membership may be made a crime when it is active, conscious of the party's illegal aims, and designed to further those aims. In the absence of such proof, a member is presumed to join the party either without knowledge of its illegal goals, or with a desire to further the party's lawful ends, such as fostering civil rights. The entire organization cannot be outlawed so long as there are any lawful members left. What is true for the Communist Party is surely true for SDS and other campus organizations, and the test should be identical: an individual student cannot be forbidden to join such a group unless his membership is active, aware of the group's illegal aims (if any) and designed solely to further those aims. And the organization cannot be driven off campus—if other political groups are allowed—so long as any lawful members remain.

If student political groups such as SDS cannot be barred from the campus, what control does the university have over them? It seems clear, as a minimum, that every student organization seeking official recognition and campus privileges may be required to register once or twice a year. To make the registration effective, and to permit communication with the organization, the names of the officers or of several responsible student members may be required.

The group may also be asked to deposit a copy of its constitution or bylaws if such a document exists.

Demands for full membership lists represent, however, quite another matter. Once such lists are in the hands of the administration—even in impeccably discreet hands—they loose any immunity from court order or legislative subpoena. And such a transfer may well result in public disclosure of information quite damaging both to individual members—to whom anonymity may be essential—and to the unpopular organization, which has to protect the anonymity of its membership to survive.

Two 1969 court decisions suggest how precarious is sensitive information about students and student groups under these conditions. A California court refused to order Berkeley officials to close to the public files containing the names of officers of campus political (and other) groups, and their stated purposes. The open-file policy was based on the mandate of state law; an earlier court decision had upheld the claim of an Oakland housewife to rummage through the University's previously confidential files to get the names of the leaders of Berkeley's radical student groups.

Meanwhile, SDS members at Columbia tried unsuccessfully to prevent university officials from giving to a Senate investigating committee detailed information about certain radical students and about protest movements on the campus in the spring of 1968. Since the committee had issued a subpoena demanding the information, and since it did exist in the university's files, Columbia officials were powerless to refuse. Thus a federal court dismissed the SDS suit seeking to quash the subpoena, and the files passed quietly out of Columbia's hands into those of the Committee's staff shortly after the end of the school year in June.

IV. *Student Newspapers: Criticism and Obscenity*

The next item on the agenda concerns an editorial in the student newspaper the day before the meeting. Headed "Fuck the Trustees," this expression of the editor's own radical views contained some taboo words and some false statements about the relationship of certain trustees to the "military-industrial complex." Such conflict between administrators or trustees and student editors is a recurrent theme.

Direct intervention by political officials and legislative bodies in the affairs of student newspapers is not unknown. When Huey Long was Governor of Louisiana, he had the editor of the State University newspaper removed on the basis of an editorial attacking the state government. "I'm not payin' anybody to criticize me," he explained to reporters the next day. The climate of freedom in student journalism has probably improved substantially since that time. In one recent survey of college and university presidents, only 3 percent of the 150 respondents said that the content of student publications must be cleared by a board or official before publication. Almost half the institutions had no official policy at all regarding the responsibility of student publications to the administration or faculty. Thirty-one percent noted simply that all student publications have a broad responsibility to a board and/or code of standards; another 13 percent held student publications to "journalistic standards only." In another survey, 225 college presidents were asked to react to the statement "the student press should be free of censorship and advance approval of copy." Roughly three quarters of the respondents agreed with the statement—29 percent without qualification and 45 percent "substantially."

Student editors do not fully share this confidence in the freedom of the campus press. Forty percent of the editors recently surveyed reported that editorials had to be submitted for approval before they could be printed. One third of the sample revealed that they had been privately censured for taking "extreme" stands on controversial issues. Twenty-one percent said that someone had seriously proposed that they or their predecessors be removed from office. In 6 percent of the institutions surveyed, editors actually had been removed on the basis of published material. This survey also revealed that threats to the student press come not only from the administration, but almost as often from student senates and boards that control the subsidy on which the typical campus paper depends. It is only the tiny fraction of college journals that are (like the Harvard *Crimson*) financially independent, where real self-sufficiency and press freedom are to be found.

Only one case, and that very recent, furnishes constitutional guidelines for student publications and editors. In the spring of 1967, Gary Dickey was the editor of the *Tropolitan,* the student paper at Troy State College in Alabama, an institution of some 3,000 students. Dickey wrote an editorial attacking the legislature and the Governor in a dispute with the President of the University of Alabama over a lecture series planned for the Tuscaloosa campus. When the faculty adviser saw the editorial, he told Dickey not to print it. The chairman of the English Department supported Dickey's stand, and he then took the matter to the President. On the basis of a dormant rule forbidding editorials critical of the Governor or the legislature, the President upheld the faculty adviser, who then offered Dickey a column on "raising dogs in North Carolina" to fill the page. But Dickey rejected this alternative, and the issue appeared with white space on the editorial page broken only by the diagonal word "censored."

As soon as the paper was out, Dickey was charged with "willful and deliberate insubordination" and was suspended for the balance of the year. He promptly brought suit in the federal district court, and the judge sent the case back to the college for a hearing that had never been held on the charges. When the hearing reaffirmed Dickey's dismissal, he returned to court for a decision on the merits. The judge ordered his reinstatement the following semester.

College and university rules affecting First Amendment liberties must, held the court, be "reasonable." The regulation invoked by the college president fell far short of that standard: ". . . the maintenance of order and discipline of the students attending Troy State College had nothing to do with the rule that was invoked against Dickey. As a matter of fact, the president of the institution . . . testified that the reason for the rule was that a newspaper could not criticize its owners, and in the case of a state institution, the owners were to be considered as the governor and the members of the legislature."

The court concluded by relating the sanction to the student status of which Dickey had been deprived: "A state cannot force a college student to forfeit his constitutionally protected right of freedom of expression as a condition to his attending a state supported institution . . . [The college officials] cannot punish Gary Clinton Dickey for his exercise of this constitutionally guaranteed right by cloaking his expulsion or suspension in the robe of 'insubordination.'"

This background suggests solutions to the two problems of student journalism with which this section began. It is doubtful that mere criticism of university officials or members of the governing board would constitute sufficient grounds for disciplinary action, such as removal of the editor from his position. The presence of false statements might strengthen the university's case. But censorship is so abhorrent off the campus that a student editor should probably enjoy the same immunity from discipline that a commercial journal enjoys from libel suits, and a government employee enjoys from dismissal based on attacks against his superiors. That is, an editor could be removed or suspended only if statements in the student press concerning a public official were made with actual malice or reckless disregard of the truth. The making of false statements in good faith would not suffice.

The case for a more restrictive view has been argued in a recent survey of academic freedom by the editors of the *Harvard Law Review:* "Public criticism of the administration or the faculty by a student newspaper can undermine the confidence of both the student body and the public in the university, and thereby impair both the quality of instruction and the maintenance of order and discipline. . . . A university might reasonably conclude that in view of the damage that can be done by false reporting, as well as the inexperience or possible irresponsibility of student editors, a rule banning criticism not based on demonstrable fact is justifiable in order to encourage responsible editorial comment."

There are several serious flaws in this line of argument. First, the general government cannot deprive an editor of his position or put him in jail for making false statements; the strongest sanction available off campus is a lawsuit for libel, which is of course equally available to anyone defamed by a student newspaper. Second, a central premise of this argument is one that has been consistently rejected here—that the university's special regulatory interests include self-protection from an angry legislature or a libeled trustee. If such reaction outside the campus will justify muzzling the student press, then it may also justify suppressing student political groups and their activities. Third, resort to so drastic a remedy implies that less repressive alternatives are unavailable. Certainly before removing or suspending an editor, the administration should try to persuade him to make space available for a retraction—if only to spare himself a possibly nasty libel suit. Finally, the administration that finds the official student journal consistently biased or unrepresentative may resort to a quite different remedy that has been used with considerable success on several campuses—the creation of an "opposition" paper to present the other side of campus controversy. There seems little occasion to resort to censorship in defense of institutional autonomy.

The use of "obscenity" in the student press can probably be resolved along the same lines—and would be if administrators and trustees were not so exceedingly sensitive to the tasteless and juvenile use of four letter words. Clearly the flaunting of such language in the student press is not *obscenity,* as that term is now defined in the law. These words, as used in college newspapers, seldom refer at all to sex or sexual behavior, and even when they do, they can hardly be said to arouse the "prurient interest" of readers. Such language is used not to stimulate sexually, but to shock, and to make a point through shock. The words are taboo, and occasionally profane, but very seldom legally obscene. When used in context, to convey a political or social message with emphasis, they enjoy a substantial measure of constitutional protection, however offensive and tasteless they may be. If a university really wanted badly enough to punish their use on campus, it might do what the New Jersey legislature did several years ago, and adopt a regulation reciting seriatim all the forbidden words. (The New Jersey experience was predictable and explains why the effort has not been repeated; within a few days so many curiosity seekers wrote the clerk of the legislature for copies of the bill that the supply was quickly exhausted.)

V. *Keeping Out the "Agitators": High Tuition for Nonresidents*

A fifth item on our agenda, it will be recalled, was a motion to triple the tuition charged to nonresidents of the state. The basis of this proposal was the belief that a large share of the sit-in leaders were from New York and California, and that calm would return to the campus if nonresidents found it less attractive.

The nonresident student already typically pays two or three times the tuition and fees charged to a resident of the state. Two factors, however, mitigate the effects of this differential: first, it is possible for most students to become "residents" of the state in which they attend college after a year or so, and thus take advantage of the much lower fees. Second, there are sharing arrangements in some parts of the country whereby students may study freely in neighboring states, or transfer between institutions belonging to interstate consortia; whatever net difference in tuition charges may exist is made up by the debtor state at the end of the year.

A few students have challenged the nonresident tuition in court but have met with little success. There is a serious threshold problem: some difference in fees is clearly justified by the contribution that the tax dollars of the resident student and his family make to the support of the educational system of his state. Thus it is only the *amount,* and not the *fact,* of the differential that is at all vulnerable. The basis for attacking the monetary gap is a clause of the constitution which guarantees to citizens of one state all the privileges and immunities enjoyed by citizens of other states in which they travel. Under this clause the Supreme Court held unconstitutional a South Carolina licensing law that required nonresident shrimp fishermen to pay $2,500 for a license a resident could get for $25. Although South Carolina might have charged a differential designed to "compensate the state for any added enforcement burden [nonresidents] may impose" or for conservation expenses borne by the taxes of residents, a hundredfold disparity far exceeded any such justifications.

It is not settled that attendance at a state university is a "privilege" under this clause. But if it is, then the tuition question should be resolved much like the shrimp fishing license case. The one court to consider the question on its merits has taken essentially this view. Recognizing that some differential in tuition was clearly an appropriate way to make nonresident students share the costs of the state's system of higher education, the court found "no way . . . to determine the degree to which the higher tuition equalizes the educational cost of residents and nonresidents. . . ." In the absence of an extreme disparity, the amounts involved seemed "a reasonable attempt to achieve a partial cost equalization." Thus it seems unlikely that nonresident tuition charges will be found unconstitutional unless they rise much farther above resident charges than is presently the case.

A more serious constitutional issue is posed by scholarships which are unavailable either to nonresidents wishing to study in the state, or to residents who desire to study in other states. These restrictions clearly curtail the mobility of students, and indirectly impair their constitutional right to move freely from state to state. The privileges and immunities argument, too, might arise in the case of the nonresident student ineligible for financial aid on geographical grounds.

No cases have been brought challenging such restrictions. They are not likely to have much practical significance, except for the student who goes out of state for a special course of study or an unusual degree that is not available at home. But as financial aid derives increasingly from federal rather than state funds, the barriers to student mobility posed by geographical restrictions should cease to be a substantial constitutional issue.

VI. *Separatism and Special Programs for Minority Groups*

Characteristically, the agenda included several demands by and on behalf of black students, notably increased admission of minority students toward a set percentage and the setting aside of dormitory space as a "black wing." Each raises a theoretical question—whether compliance would be unconstitutional—and a practical question—whether alternative ways can be found to achieve the same ends without constitutional hazards.

Consider first the demand for a percentage of minority students to be admitted each year. There is one obvious feature of such a demand that explains the reluctance of minority group spokesmen to seek quotas: a quota can become a ceiling just as readily as it can provide a floor. The group that benefits from a quota one day may find itself the victim of the same quota tomorrow. The courts have also taken a rather dim view of quotas. When a California judge enjoined picketing by a Negro group demanding that a supermarket hire the same percentage of Negro employees as it had Negro patrons, the Supreme Court sustained the injunction on the ground that the picketing was directed to an illegal end. The Court found valid California's desire to bolster its "policy against involuntary employment on racial lines by prohibiting systematic picketing that would subvert such policy." Earlier the Court had held that a Negro was entitled to be tried by a jury in which there has been "neither systematic exclusion nor inclusion" of jurors on ground of race or color.

Objections may persist to the gathering and use of data that identify students on racial or ethnic grounds. Many states have laws—passed not so long ago at the urging of liberals who now seek special opportunities for minority groups—that forbid asking questions about race or keeping racial census information. Yet there has been a sharp departure from the tradition of color blindness in the past two or three years. It is increasingly apparent that only racial surveys will provide any accurate picture of present conditions—of the areas in which progress has been made toward the integration of minority groups, and others where the underrepresentation is most acute. Moreover, special efforts to employ, to recruit, and train minority group members will be ineffectual unless there is some way of identifying applicants on racial grounds. Such data are also essential for the evaluation of special minority group programs.

These considerations have caused the American Civil Liberties Union to abandon its historic opposition to racial surveys and records. In February 1968, ACLU declared its endorsement of "governmental collection or dissemination of race information when it is shown to be necessary to wipe out discriminatory practices." The statement carried an important caveat: careful safeguards must be included to see that such information is not used to the detriment of those minority groups who are the intended beneficiaries of the program.

Something should be said about the morality, if not the legality, of creating special educational opportunities for minority group students. Enough is known about the disparate unemployment rates and levels of educational attainment between whites and blacks that no restatement is needed here. Arguably some preferences are needed now to overcome the effects of decades of discrimination that has withheld or taken away opportunities in higher education even from fully qualified minority candidates. Regular tests or examinations often do not accurately measure the potential of minority students. This is partly because of the heavy verbal emphasis of many of these tests, and partly because of the limited test-taking experience that many minority students have had. Thus special standards may be justified simply in the interests of accurate evaluation.

The use of special criteria to evaluate minority applicants need not "lower" or "water down" the regular admission criteria. What is involved is a process often used for other special groups—the introduction of greater flexibility and broader assessment of human qualities than numerical standards make possible. Most colleges relax or vary the admission criteria to admit applicants with unusual promise of leadership or extraordinary potential in a particular field—not to mention the unabashed waivers of mathematical standards by which accomplished athletes have gained admission to prestigious institutions.

Finally, the underrepresentation of minority groups in higher education represents a vicious circle that must simply be broken somewhere. Only by admitting significant numbers of minority students to colleges and universities that have heretofore been almost totally white can the circle be broken; only under these conditions will there be enough minority students on the campus to relieve some of the isolation and pressure that generate dissension and protest, and jeopardize academic survival. A start must be made in sufficient proportions to constitute a significant breakthrough.

We have reserved the most difficult legal question for the end: If the setting of a minority group *quota* is a violation of the equal protection clause, is there any constitutional impediment to the setting of *goals* toward which to increase the proportion of minority groups in the student body? A literal reading of the Equal Protection clause might cause one to rule out any special preference for minority groups. Yet the legislative history and design of the Fourteenth Amendment manifest its purpose to overcome racial discrimination and segregation. It was clearly intended to ensure equal treatment for the former slaves whose freedom was guaranteed by the Thirteenth Amendment. Consequently any program designed to benefit their descendants rather than to discriminate against them is consistent with the original intent.

The question has often arisen in connection with *de facto* school segregation. A number of Northern and Western states have required (either by statute or administrative order) that local school boards take affirmative steps to relieve racial imbalances. The Supreme Courts of all states in which such requirements have been challenged have sustained their constitutionality. New Jersey's high court noted: "Constitutional color-blindness may be wholly apt when the frame of reference is an attack on official efforts toward segregation; it is not generally apt when the attack is on official efforts toward the avoidance of segregation." The Supreme Judicial Court of Massachusetts concurred: "It would be the height of irony if the racial imbalance act enacted as it was with the laudable purpose of achieving equal educational opportunities should, by prescribing school pupil allocations based on race, founder on unsuspected shoals in the Fourteenth Amendment." Several courts have gone substantially beyond this point and held that such affirmative steps to relieve imbalances are constitutionally *required* as well as permissible under the Fourteenth Amendment.

The question thus comes down to whether the demand is for a quota or for a goal. If the latter is what the students are seeking, then the university would appear free to commit itself to work toward that objective, or even to surpass it, through vigorous recruiting efforts. If, however, the demand is really for a quota, then not only would the institution be unwise and irresponsible to accede, but the students would in fact be undermining their own best interests.

The other demand on our agenda was for exclusively black living accommodations in the residence halls. Just such a request was made by black students at Northwestern University in the spring of 1968. After a sit-in and much negotiation, university officials agreed to set aside such space. Soon thereafter, the University was warned by the U.S. Department of Health, Education and Welfare that such a plan might well cause the forfeiture of substantial federal funds. The director of the education branch of the Office for Civil Rights notified Northwestern that Title VI (the nondiscrimination clause) of the 1964 Civil Rights Act "does bar recipients of federal financial assistance from entering into agreements or promulgating rules . . . which allocate housing or activity space belonging to or controlled by the university on a purely racial basis." After this warning, the University tried to renegotiate the agreement with the students so as to achieve the same goal by other means.

A year later, Antioch College, alma mater of Mrs. Martin Luther King, Jr., and a pioneer in integration of higher education, was in trouble on the same issue. Having created a special dormitory for black students participating in the Afro-American Studies Institute, Antioch officials were accused of fostering segregation, and faced possible loss of the roughly one fifth of the college's budget that comes from federal funds. The Office for Civil Rights in the Department of Health, Education and Welfare, which issued the warning to Antioch and eleven other private colleges with similar programs, was apparently fearful that continued acceptance of such separatism would invite a return to complete segregation by some

Southern institutions whose doors had just been pried open to minority students after a decade of determined federal efforts.

After much discussion and deliberation, the federal agency announced in May that Antioch could operate its black studies institute without risking loss of government funds so long as white students were not excluded solely because of race, color, or national origin. Nonblacks might, however, be excluded from the Institute if the director determined their backgrounds were not "relevant" to its program. And the controversial dormitory wing might remain all black as a result of self-selection, so long as incoming Negro students were not systematically informed that housing was available in a racially homogeneous facility.

The accommodation between Antioch and Washington was an uneasy one. Dr. Kenneth B. Clark, the distinguished Negro psychologist, resigned as a trustee of Antioch in protest against the compromise. Both the college and the government had, he maintained, reversed the trend toward integration and equality by capitulating to the separatist demands of more militant black students, to the detriment of more moderate Negroes on the campus. *The New York Times* editorially shared Dr. Clark's concern, finding in the HEW position "the same hypocrisy used in the past by white segregationists in search of cover-up reasons for the exclusion of nonwhites."

Whether or not it represents a permanent channel for assimilating substantial numbers of minority students in predominantly white institutions, the Antioch compromise at least suggests the resolution of other delicate issues. Chief among them is the dilemma over recognition of Black Student Unions and Associations, and other minority student organizations.

The question of discrimination by student groups was once much debated in the context of Greek letter fraternities. Today that is an all but dead issue, what with declining fraternity membership and the antidiscrimination requirements imposed by many universities. The same basic principles should, however, apply to minority student groups. Discriminatory clauses in charters, constitutions or bylaws should not be permitted, for they represent a clear form of *de jure* segregation. (Of course as a practical matter white students are no more likely to seek membership in the BSA or BSU in large numbers than were black students to want to pledge Sigma Chi.)

There are, in fact, other ways in which minority students can achieve dignity through separatism while remaining within white institutions. Such demands for separatism, whether in living accommodations, dining facilities, or academic programs, may really seek options and choices far more than specific ends. Many minority students seem to want a kind of flexibility they feel has long been denied them as a result of discrimination and segregation. What they really seek is not isolation, but rather a choice between integration and separation on their own terms.

It is quite possible to achieve substantially these ends without formal exclusion of whites. If the dining room in a particular wing serves exclusively soul food, white students may stop by occasionally out of curiosity but they are unlikely to take three meals a day. If the phonograph in the commons plays nothing but soul music, most students who gather around it for recreation will tend to be black. A kind of *de facto* segregation may result which the university is probably powerless to prevent, and might even wish to encourage in lieu of the *de jure* segregation which it may not foster. How far the institution goes in this direction depends partly on its assessment of its obligations and partly—to be quite practical— on the strength and militancy of its black students. There is hardly a major white campus today at which black students do not dominate one or two tables in the cafeteria at lunchtime, making space for an occasional congenial white. The process of separation has either begun, or has continued from earlier times, and it would be folly to try to halt it completely.

VII. *The Dormitory Room: How Much of a Castle?*

The trustees' agenda also contained a proposal to make students' dormitory rooms open for inspection at all hours. The recommendation had little to do with the current sit-in, although many of the trustees thought there was a high correlation between radical politics and illegal drug use on the campus. They also believed the only way to crack down on narcotics—hopefully before a police raid of the campus created disastrous publicity—was to conduct unannounced spot checks of the rooms of students suspected of drug traffic. Thus the most natural and logical approach seemed to be to make explicit that the door was always open to university officials for inspection purposes. (The trustees were aware that drug use was much higher in off-campus apartments than in the residence halls, but knew inspections could not be authorized beyond university premises.)

The validity of such an inspection policy depends to some extent on the student's freedom to choose where he lives. The practice at universities varies considerably with regard to student residence. In a recent survey conducted by the National Association of Student Personnel Administrators, 86 percent of the institutions reporting (154 in all) had some policy restricting the student's choice of living accommodations. About a third of the sample (34 percent) required all undergraduates, except those living at home with parents or a spouse, to live in the residence halls or in approved off-campus housing. An additional 27 percent compelled all freshmen and some upperclassmen, except commuters, to live on the campus. The balance required only freshmen women, or students under a certain age, to take dormitory rooms.

Such requirements may themselves raise constitutional issues. Courts have generally acknowledged that colleges may prevent students from living off campus, or in other than college-approved housing, where such rules stem from solicitude for student welfare. But a federal district court in Louisiana has recently suggested that the case may be different if the source of the college's concern is its own financial health rather than the well-being and safety of its students. In such a situation, it will not do to require only a part of the student body—in the particular case, unmarried women under twenty-one—to live in the dorms simply to ensure profitable operation. "Since the obligation is essentially monetary, then all must pay or none"; otherwise, the requirement unfairly discriminates against the students subject to it.

Even if the student is not required to live on the campus, he still has some legal claim to privacy in the residence hall. The extent of his protection has only recently been defined by the courts. There are now two cases, both decided in 1968, which seem to be in direct conflict. Both involved searches made by university officials and local policemen, suspecting narcotics in the room, and in both cases the suspicions were verified by marijuana discovered on the premises. In one case the student was in the room and objected to the entry; in the other case, the students were out but their permission was not sought. There were a few minor discrepancies in the facts.

The only major difference between the cases, however, was the way in which the privacy issue arose. The first case was a suit for reinstatement by students expelled from the same small Alabama state college that was involved in the Dickey case. In the other case, students at Hofstra College in New York asked a state court to exclude from a narcotics trial the marijuana seized from their dormitory room during the search.

This important procedural distinction may partly explain the quite different outcomes of the two cases, but there is also a difference in tone and spirit. The federal judge in the Alabama case refused to order the students reinstated, or to find their constitutional rights had been violated. Although it was clear neither the university nor the police had "probable cause" to obtain a search warrant, there was "reasonable cause" to suspect that some crime was afoot within the room. Entry under such a lower standard of suspicion was justified because of "the special necessities of the student-college relationship" and the noncriminal character of disciplinary proceedings. The college has special responsibilities as an educational institution that do not apply off the campus. Thus, "a reasonable right of inspection is necessary to the institution's performance of that duty even though it may infringe on the outer boundaries of a dormitory student's Fourth Amendment rights."

Both the result and the language of the New York decision are markedly different. Although it was a criminal case, the judge had to decide essentially the same question involved in the Alabama case—whether college officials could enter the room without the occupant's permission or over his objection to conduct a search when the available evidence of crime would not have justified a search warrant. In holding that the "probable cause" standard of the Fourth Amendment must be met, and that a search of a dormitory room could not be validated by evidence it unearthed, the New York court characterized the student's interest in dormitory privacy quite differently: ". . . the dormitory room of a college student is not open for entry at all times for all purposes. . . . University students are adults. The dorm is a home and it must be inviolate against unlawful search and seizure. To suggest that a student who lives off campus in a boarding house is protected but that one who occupies a dormitory room waives his constitutional liberties is at war with reason, logic and law."

One additional factor may explain the contrasting views of these two courts. The federal court in Alabama relied rather heavily upon a 1967 decision upholding routine searches of high school students' lockers in quest of contraband. The judgment happened to be that of the New York Court of Appeals, and would thus have been influential to the trial judge in the Hofstra case—although either court should have recognized the substantially greater privacy interest of a mature college student in his dormitory room. In the month between the two decisions, the United States Supreme Court reversed the locker case and sent it back to the New York court for reconsideration in light of a search-and-seizure decision a few weeks earlier. Thus when the Hofstra case came on for decision, not only was the locker case no longer binding, but the Supreme Court had indicated its disapproval of a cavalier search policy even in the high schools. The rights of college students seemed all the more clearly entitled to constitutional protection.

This resolution of the question might suggest that a university is powerless to detect and control crime in the residence halls. There are, however, internal remedies that can be followed without infringing students' Fourth Amendment rights. As a practical matter, most students will consent to searches at any reasonable hour, and will be deterred from keeping or using drugs in the dorms simply by the possibility that a proctor or resident assistant may knock at any time, and would be suspicious if entry were refused. Periodic, announced inspections of which students have ample warning might also be carried out over students' objections, pursuant to the university's landlord function. If unannounced inspections are to be made, and students refuse entry at a reasonable hour, some procedure should exist whereby the head resident can obtain a university search warrant sooner than one could be procured from a court downtown. A student judiciary or interresidence council might be empowered to issue campus warrants, provided they applied the same standard of "probable cause" that courts would demand of an applicant for a judicial warrant. Thus the internal judicial machinery would enable university officials to act promptly but would at the same time protect the constitutional liberties of students to the degree they would be protected in off-campus quarters.

VIII. *Where Will It End?*

People used to ask "Can universities survive?" only to amuse
or to provoke. In the condition of deep despair that has beset the
American academic community, the question is now asked in dead
earnest. Those who pose it do not mean to imply that universities
will actually close their doors, or that higher education will cease to
exist. Rather, the prospect that haunts them, and seems an increasingly plausible one, is that of the continually embattled, irrational
and chaotic Latin-American university, where student power rules
with a vengeance, and the battles of the campus are indistinguishable from those of the streets. This fear is reinforced by the conviction that the Latin-American model is the one most attractive to
many of the more militant student leaders.

The most pessimistic observers feel that universities will remain battlegrounds between the generations at least for the duration of the issues that anger, arouse, and alienate students. Peace
and order cannot be restored to the campus, they argue, until the
Vietnam war is over and dramatic progress has been made toward
racial equality. Meanwhile, universities can do little more than try
to ride the crest of the wave.

Others are more optimistic. They find universities largely to
blame for their own troubles, and thus see remedies at least partly
within the institutions' own control. Health, Education and Welfare
Secretary Robert Finch takes this view, and argues that a major
overhaul of university structure is long overdue. President Martin
Meyerson of the State University of New York at Buffalo shares the
conviction that "the most major reformation is now called for" if
American universities are to remain effective and viable institutions; he maintains that universities have changed less than almost
any other type of institution in the twentieth century. Among proponents of this view, there are predictable disagreements on the
course that reform should take, and on the likelihood that internal
restructuring will restore order and reason.

Meanwhile, whatever happens to university structure, the law
may have a modest contribution to make. As a start the clear and
precise codification of student conduct codes seems essential. The
Commission on Violence has observed, five years after the first

Berkeley sit-in, that "few schools have explicit rules either defining the boundaries of permissible protest or stating the consequences if the boundaries are crossed." This is an intolerable situation—as much for the administration that risks being told by a court that its vague rules are unenforceable, as for the students who lack clear guides to how they may and may not protest.

Much also remains to be done on the matter of procedures. The Violence Commission notes that some universities "have very loose rules for disciplinary proceedings [and that] others have diffused disciplinary power so widely among students, faculty and administration that effective discipline is difficult to impose, and is seldom imposed quickly enough to meet an emergency." Here, too, much study and understanding of the law is called for.

The vital question about lawmaking and law enforcing on the campus is not so much *what* is done, as *how* it is done. It is increasingly clear that students—moderates as well as radicals—simply will not accept regulations that are decreed by administrative fiat or ukase. There is also a growing insistence that the same laws should apply to all members of the university community—to faculty and staff as much as to students—and that students should have some remedy against faculty "misconduct" just as faculty members can bring disciplinary charges against lawless students.

The realization of these goals depends upon the involvement of students, faculty, and staff in the common task of campus lawmaking and law enforcement. The issue is usually characterized as one of *"student* participation"; the label merely underscores the partiality of professors' and administrators' perspective. For students, the need is at least as great to find channels for *faculty* and *administrative* participation in a shared enterprise. In any case, such mutual sharing of responsibility must be achieved soon, because the courts are close to saying that rules made without the participation of a major campus constituency cannot be enforced against members of that group. No court has yet so held, but the foundations of a constitutional right to participate in university governance have already been laid.

Participation by students in the making and enforcement of campus rules is a form of "student power," but it is not what the radicals mean or administrators fear when they use that phrase. Indeed, there is much evidence that militants do not really want participation, and will decline invitations to sit on boards, committees and the like; acceptance of such positions would only blunt the force of any efforts to show the rigidity and insensitivity of the university. Thus it may not be possible to devise channels of participation that will include the full spectrum of student political opinion.

There are also some serious practical obstacles to effective participation. First, the primary mission of students is to get an education, and for many (particularly those who must hold part-time jobs) there is little time left in the day for extracurricular activities. Moreover, spending long hours sitting on a rule-making or judicial tribunal may rank rather low on the list of priorities for allocation of whatever time is available.

Second, even the most sincere efforts to achieve participation may appear to many students as "tokenism." It may be felt that the really important decisions—faculty promotion and tenure, curriculum, university investment policies, construction and location of new facilities, admissions policies and many others—still reside where they always did, while students are involved only in issues that do not significantly affect the course or character of the institution. Or students may feel they are simply being exploited to ratify and thereby legitimize decisions that they cannot influence—when, for example, faculty and administrators comprise the majority of the committee.

A third problem derives from the transient nature of students as members of the university community. It is literally impossible for every student generation to participate in making the rules by which it is governed. One class may feel their interests are inadequately represented by the spokesmen for predecessor classes. Yet there must be some stability: the law cannot be remade every time a new group of students arrives. The most that can be hoped for is meaningful participation by a group of students at one time, with the understanding that students will also be centrally involved when the rules are changed.

Finally, a university cannot be readily assimilated to other self-governing institutions. Current efforts to develop university-wide legislative bodies in which all constituencies will be represented are commendable, but may simply not work. The Study Commission on University Governance, composed equally of faculty members and students at the University of California at Berkeley, has cautioned:

"The heart of the problem of student participation is that a university is not a natural democracy composed of members each of whom is distinguished by an equal claim to power; it is a highly artificial community deliberately arranged so that the educational relationships among the members constitute the starkest kind of contrast to relationships based on power. Properly conceived, it is a fellowship that should prize persuasion based on reason and evidence that excludes coercion and pressure because they destroy the uncoerced agreement which is at the heart of the search for knowledge. . . ."

VII

GOVERNMENT

PROPERTY

The northeast corner of London's Hyde Park provides British orators with an open forum and a guaranteed audience. Speakers have been peddling their views there since 1855, when a carpenter addressed a small meeting, and since no one interfered, repeated his performance the next Sunday. A London bobby who has patrolled Hyde Park for the last twenty years remarked not long ago that the quality of oratory seems to have declined; contemporary speakers "talk a lot without saying much." But the vital importance of Hyde Park to British life and expression does not depend upon the intellectual caliber of the thoughts expressed there. Nor does it lie in the size of the audiences who come to listen or to heckle on a given Sunday afternoon. The key to the meaning of Hyde Park is the relative ease with which any person may mount the podium without permit or prior notice to exhort or harangue on virtually any subject. (British law actually does impose some unwritten limits on Hyde Park speakers when talk becomes "obscene, blasphemous or an incitement to a breach of the peace," or openly insults the monarchy.)

The United States really has no counterpart to the open forum of Hyde Park. One is tempted to suggest New York's Union Square, which welcomed a similarly varied array of views during World War I. But when the late George Lincoln Rockwell applied in 1960 for permission to deliver a Fourth of July speech in Union Square, his application was rejected—even though there was no other application for the occasion—because the Commissioner of Parks feared offense to the audience and perhaps violence if Rockwell spoke of racial issues in his customary manner. Rockwell took the matter to court and was eventually vindicated, but not until eight months after the day on which he wanted to speak. Nor was he offered any other podium anywhere in the city for a July 4 address. Several years later, another New York Parks Commissioner closed Central Park as a "staging area" for mass demonstrations (particularly those opposing the Vietnam war), citing some $4,500 damage that a recent war protest had done to shrubs and foliage in the park.

The absence of an American Hyde Park is but one dimension of a larger problem of limited avenues for public expression. As government at all levels, federal, state, and local, increasingly pre-empts available land for specific public purposes—through urban renewal, extension of state college and university campuses, and building of new civic centers, libraries, and hospitals—the pressures on the public forum are bound to intensify. Moreover, the facilities that are suitable for large public meetings and gatherings are increasingly built with public funds and managed by government agencies. The days of privately owned stadiums, auditoriums, and convention halls is coming to an end. The sharply declining private ownership of mass transportation systems has brought government control over access to display spaces on the sides and backs of buses, and the overhead panels in trolley and subway cars. College and university campuses, too, have been passing into the public domain at a rapid rate during the past decade; recent government acquisition of the once private, centrally located Universities of Buffalo, Pittsburgh, Houston, and other institutions has extended government control to another important segment of the speaker's forum.

Most rules regulating the use of government property raise no constitutional issues. The National Park Service, for example, is chiefly concerned with the hours during which its facilities may be used, control of fire and disposal of garbage, and the treatment of wild animals which roam the adjacent forests. Restrictions on the use of government property seldom raise constitutional questions except in densely settled regions. This chapter surveys several aspects of the emerging conflict between the constitutional liberties of the citizen and the government's role as landlord.

We shall first examine the changing constitutional character of the public forum—particularly the regulation of use of streets, sidewalks, and public parks for meetings, rallies, parades, and demonstrations. Then we shall look indoors to survey access to auditoriums and similar facilities. Particular attention will be given to the problem of the speaker ban still found on some college and university campuses. Regulation of access to mass transit facilities and newstands in government buildings deserves special consideration.

I. Changing Character of the Public Forum

Three recent legal trends mark a profound change in the constitutional dimension of government control of the public forum. First, there has been a significant narrowing of government's power to restrict access to the public forum. Second, government has been increasingly required to provide adequate protection for those who express controversial or unpopular ideas. And third, the geographical scope of the public forum—with its incumbent obligations— has been steadily enlarged to include certain areas that are technically "private" but have acquired a public character.

ACCESS TO THE PUBLIC FORUM

The recent history of the public forum begins with the ordinance passed in 1885 for regulation of meetings on Boston Common. This ordinance provided that "no person shall in or upon any of the public grounds make any public address except in accordance with a permit from the mayor." A prospective speaker who had unsuccessfully sought mayoral permission pressed the constitutionality of this ordinance all the way to the United States Supreme Court. The Justices rejected his claim that any constitutional rights were infringed. Finding the control of public parks a proper exercise of the city's police power—regardless of the purpose for which park space was sought—the court sustained the ordinance despite the unlimited and unreviewable discretion vested in the mayor's office. Such discretion was tolerable to a court that still uncritically accepted the "greater includes the lesser" reasoning: "The right to absolutely exclude all use necessarily includes the authority to determine under what circumstances such use may be availed of as the greater power contains the lesser."

It was not until 1939 that the Court had occasion to reexamine this definition of the public forum. The issue arose in the context of a bitter fight between labor unions and "Boss" Frank Hague of Jersey City, New Jersey. When the city government denied permits for organizing activities sponsored by the CIO, union leaders challenged the constitutionality of the governing ordinances and brought the question once again to the Supreme Court. The ordinance on which Hague relied was rather similar to the old Boston law in the broad discretion it gave to city officials. The Court now took a rather different view of such delegation: "Wherever the title of streets and parks may rest, they have immemorially been held in trust for the use of the public and, time out of mind, have been used for purposes of assembly, communicating thoughts between citizens and discussing public questions. Such use of the streets and public places has, from ancient times, been a part of the privileges, immunities, rights and liberties of citizens. The privilege of a citizen of the United States to use the streets and parks for communication of views on national questions may be regulated in the interest of all; it is not absolute but relative and must be exercised in subordination to the general comfort and convenience and in consonance with peace and good order; but it must not in the guise of regulation be abridged or denied."

Three lines of cases have refined the implications of this concept. First, the Court has insisted that municipalities must employ those methods of regulation which are least hostile to free expression. A city or town concededly has a valid interest in keeping the streets from being littered and cluttered by leaflets and handbills. But if the handbills carry a constitutionally protected message, the city should maintain cleanliness by hiring more sanitation workers to sweep the sidewalks rather than by barring or enjoining distribution of handbills—even if this proves substantially more expensive. With sound trucks, too, the least restrictive regulatory device must be used. Instead of banning sound trucks altogether, government must rely on such sensitive methods as regulating the hours or decibel levels at which mobile amplifiers broadcast.

The Court has not held that a speaker may never be required to obtain any type of permit before using a public facility. But if such a requirement is set, the licensing official may have no discretion to control the content of the message or to bar an applicant because of the unpopularity of the organization he represents. Nor may a speaker—even one such as George Lincoln Rockwell—be denied a permit simply because the officials fear there may be violence and disorder following the speech. Instead, the community must resort to sanctions which carry less danger of prior restraint, including police protection adequate to contain the crowd, and arresting the speaker if his words truly do create a clear and present danger of violence. A permit, therefore, can provide little more than notice to town officials when and where the speaker plans to appear, so as to prevent open conflict between two rival applicants for the podium.

Much of the law governing the public forum has evolved through criminal prosecutions of civil rights demonstrators. Most recently, the attention of the courts has been turned to anti-Vietnam war demonstrations on public property in the North and West. These cases have characteristically involved convictions for breach of the peace or trespass. Consistently, the Supreme Court has reversed such convictions in the absence of two crucial ingredients—adequate evidence of a "clear and present danger" to some strong state interest; and a sufficiently narrow law to keep the discretion of local law enforcement officials from reflecting political prejudices. The Court has also set important outer limits on the use of the public forum:

> The rights of free speech and assembly, while fundamental in our democratic society, still do not mean that everyone with opinions or beliefs to express may address a group at any public place and at any time. The constitutional guarantee of liberty implies the existence of an organized society maintaining public order without which liberty itself would be lost in the excesses of anarchy. The control of travel on the streets is a clear example of governmental responsibility to insure this necessary order. . . . One would not be justified in ignoring the familiar red light because this was thought to be a means of social protest. Nor could one contrary to traffic regulations insist upon a street meeting in the middle of Times Square at the rush hour as a form of freedom of speech or assembly. Governmental authorities have the duty and responsibility to keep their streets open and available for movement. A group of

demonstrators could not insist upon the right to cordon off a street or entrance to a public or private building and allow no one to pass who did not agree to listen to their exhortation.

The Court continued to leave open the question that lingered from the Boston Common case—"the constitutionality of the uniform, consistent and nondiscriminatory application of a statute forbidding all access to streets and other public facilities for parades and meetings." Previous decisions had implied somewhat conflicting answers to this question. (Some lower federal courts have even suggested a duty on government's part to provide access to a meaningful public forum somewhere in the community.)

The question may be only of academic interest. Political pressures are such that no municipality would attempt to prohibit St. Patrick's Day parades or American Legion rallies or picketing by labor groups. Once permission has been given for such purposes as these, it cannot be denied to others who seek access to public facilities for less popular causes. As Professor Harry Kalven of the University of Chicago Law School has written: "If some groups are exempted from a prohibition on parades and pickets, the rationale for regulation is fatally impeached. The objection can then no longer be keyed to interferences with other uses of the public places, but would appear to implicate the kind of message that the groups were transmitting. The regulation would thus slip from the neutrality of time, place and circumstance into a concern about content."

As Professor Kalven suggests, those restrictions which regulate only the time, place, and manner of expression and assembly are permissible for obvious reasons. The undoubted power to regulate sound trucks and amplification systems subsumes authority to restrict decibel levels and to forbid all broadcasting in certain places that must maintain quiet (*e.g.,* the environs of a hospital, library, or school). Where picketing and marches are concerned, the governmental interest in maintaining the flow of pedestrian and vehicular traffic implies the power to restrict the size of the group and to alter somewhat the route of march.

There is, however, a grave danger that what begins as time, place, and manner regulation will subtly shade over into discriminatory application of rules which are fair on their face, or backdoor censorship of content and message. For this reason, courts properly continue to review even the most innocuous-seeming restrictions on access to the public forum.

Until quite recently, government was obliged to do no more than leave alone those who wished access to the public forum for constitutionally protected activity. As a result of the civil rights and antiwar demonstrations of the 1960s, a wholly different dimension has been added. There is now a substantial affirmative duty to protect unpopular marchers and demonstrators from hostile onlookers. This major constitutional departure stems from the 1965 voting rights march from Selma to Montgomery, Alabama. The marchers asked a federal district judge to enjoin Alabama officials (including Governor George Wallace) from interfering in any way with the peaceful execution of the march. The judge readily granted such an order. But because he foresaw physical threats to which the marchers might be subjected, he went substantially further. Alabama officials were also enjoined from "failing to provide police protection for the [marchers], members of their class and others who may join with them in their march as presently scheduled and presently approved by this court. . . ." In response to Alabama's claim that it lacked the manpower and capacity to carry out such an obligation, the judge observed that "the United States stands ready and willing, if requested by the Governor of the State of Alabama, to assist in this regard. The only question that is now presented is whether the State of Alabama authorities are willing to employ their available resources and utilize the additional available resources of the United States Government to preserve peace and order in their compliance with this court's order." The relative calm that prevailed during the march suggests a rather high degree of compliance.

A similar case in California six months later affirmed and extended the governmental obligation. In October 1965, a large antiwar protest on the campus of the University of California inaugurated a march through Berkeley streets and into the adjoining city of Oakland. Before the marchers could reach their destination (an Army installation), they were set upon by a hostile leather-jacketed band of Hell's Angels. Undaunted, the Vietnam Day Committee planned a similar march for the next month. This time, they requested additional protection from local law enforcement authorities. But Oakland and Alameda County officials refused even to sanction the march, much less to commit their forces to the task of protection. The marchers thus went to federal court seeking a judicial imprimatur for their plans. The district judge followed substantially the precedent set down in the Alabama case. After holding that the city and county must permit the march (subject to certain restrictions on the number of marchers, the timing, and the route), the court enjoined all local officials "from refusing or failing to provide adequate police supervision for the completion of said parade and assembly . . . and from refusing or failing to take all reasonable precautions and means to protect [the marchers] and others similarly situated from attack, acts of violence or interference involving law violations during the march, assembly and disbursal thereof as hereinbefore provided." The second march went off without incident; the Hell's Angels were nowhere in sight, and supporters of the Vietnam war watched quietly from the sidewalks.

The claim that law enforcement agencies should protect the unpopular speaker from his enemies is hardly novel. Two decades ago, Mr. Justice Black sharply dissented when the Court upheld the conviction of a speaker who had been set upon by a hostile mob after he made some provocative statements. Conceding the police had both the duty and the power to prevent an incipient riot, Justice Black insisted they had done so by arresting the wrong man. "Their duty was to protect [the speaker's] right to talk, even to the extent of arresting the man who threatened to interfere. Instead, they shirked that duty and acted only to suppress the right to speak." The recent expansion of the affirmative duty concept is, however, profoundly important. If the courts have not yet held that government must provide a public forum for those who wish to assemble, protest, and petition publicly, they may well have subsumed that proposition within the more pervasive guarantee of police protection for unpopular marchers and demonstrators. If law enforcement officials in Montgomery and in Oakland can be enjoined by federal courts from failing or refusing to provide whatever protection is necessary against the White Citizens' Council and the Hell's Angels, it seems doubtful that these courts would deny a platform to the unpopular speaker if that were the only issue in the case.

The imposition of such a duty may, of course, be burdensome to local government. If the guard must be doubled or tripled along a march route or in the park where a demonstration is being held, this may stretch the blue line quite thin in other parts of the community. The resulting vulnerability of unprotected quarters may invite increased crime and make the policeman's lot an even less happy one than it customarily is. (During the open housing marches in Chicago during the summer of 1966, for example, some officials claimed that crime did rise temporarily in those corners of the city from which police were drawn to reinforce the guard along Milwaukee Avenue.) Is there any limit to the extent to which government can be compelled to provide such costly protection? The courts have said elsewhere that added expense of administrative inconvenience can never dilute the basic constitutional liberties. Yet, the point might well be reached where some balance must be struck between the right to publicize a cause, on the one hand, through marches and protests, and the interest, on the other hand, in preserving the public safety. (Federal officials reported that two days of antiwar protest in Washington during the fall of 1967 cost the government some $640,000 for police and national guard reinforcements. Some part of that sum, of course, went for protection of government buildings rather than of demonstrators.) Until the cost becomes prohibitive, or sufficient policemen simply cannot be found at any price, such talk of compromise seems premature.

EXPANSION OF THE PUBLIC FORUM—CONSTITUTIONAL RIGHTS AND "PRIVATE" PROPERTY

The third major change in the character of the public forum has been its expansion by force of law. For nearly a century, the courts have held certain types of private property to be "affected with a public interest." This characterization means only that government may regulate the rates and business practices of public utilities, innkeepers and the like without having to compensate the owners for any resulting loss of revenue. (Otherwise, such a loss might be deemed a "taking" of private property for which the government must pay under the Constitution.) In other respects, property under private ownership was virtually exempt from public responsibility. This once rigid dichotomy has been relaxed by developments in two areas: property which is generally open to the public for their use and enjoyment; and property the use of which is made possible by a government license.

The character and uses of "private" property first came under judicial scrutiny in the context of a company town owned and operated by a shipbuilding company in Alabama. A sign at the edge of the business district announced "This is private property"; visitors who exceeded the company's permission simply to walk through risked criminal prosecution. A Jehovah's Witness was accordingly arrested and convicted for distributing religious literature on the streets of the town. When his case reached the Supreme Court, doubt was cast upon the historic distinction between public and private ownership: "We do not agree that the corporation's property interests settle the question. . . . Ownership does not always mean absolute dominion. The more an owner for his advantage opens up his property for use by the public in general, the more do his rights become circumscribed by the statutory and constitutional rights of those who use it. . . . Whether a corporation or a municipality owns or possesses the town, the public in either case has an identical interest in the functioning of the community in such manner that the channels of communication remain free."

Two recent California cases have carried the concept a step further. One involved labor picketing in the parking lot of a privately owned shopping center in Torrance; the other a distribution of anti-Vietnam war leaflets in Los Angeles' Union Station, owned and operated by the Southern Pacific and Union Pacific Railroads. The California Supreme Court concluded that activities which would be constitutionally protected on the public streets or in the public park could not be proscribed on "private" property that was open to public use for all other purposes: "The picketing in the present case cannot be judged in the terms of absolute property rights; it must be considered as part of the law of labor relations and a balance cast between the opposing interests of the union and the lessor of the shopping center. The prohibition of the picketing would in substance deprive the union of the opportunity to conduct its picketing at the most effective point of persuasion: the place of the involved business. The interest of the union thus rests upon the solid substance of public policy and constitutional right; the interest of the . . . [owner of the shopping center] lies in the shadow cast by a property right worn thin by public usage."

In the railroad station case, the Court went even further in undermining the owner's proprietary claim to bar peaceful advocacy and expression: "In this respect, a railway station is like a public street or park. Noise and commotion are characteristic of the normal operation of a railway station. The railroads seek neither privacy within or exclusive possession of their station. They therefore cannot invoke the law of trespass against the [protestors] to protect those interests."

The next year the United States Supreme Court agreed with the California court and extended the rationale of the company town case to the shopping center. A state court had enjoined peaceful labor picketing in the parking lot of a center as a trespass to private property. The Court reversed that injunction on the authority of the company town case; despite obvious factual differences, a common constitutional principle was at stake: to bar access to such property used by and generally open to the public would leave the union with no effective way of enlisting consumer support in its protest against the labor policies of the center's tenants. That result would be particularly anomalous at a time when retail business is moving increasingly from the central city to suburban centers and plazas. "Business enterprises located in downtown areas would be subject to on-the-spot public criticism for their practices, but businesses situated in the suburbs could largely immunize themselves from similar criticism by creating a *cordon sanitaire* of parking lots around their stores. Neither precedent nor policy compels a result so at variance with the goal of free expression and communication that is the heart of the First Amendment."

The dimensions of the public forum have been recently enlarged in quite another direction. There is no government power more effective in guaranteeing a forum for the minority view or the unpopular cause than the authority to license radio and television stations. The broadcasting station typically holds its license for a three-year term; that term is usually renewed *pro forma* by the FCC. During the past few years, however, the Commission has been asking one question with increasing frequency: Pursuant to its obligation to serve the "public interest," how fairly has the station dealt with controversial issues? The basis of this obligation is the "fairness doctrine," imposed by a section of the Communications Act that requires licenses "to afford reasonable opportunity for the discussion of conflicting views on issues of public importance."

Suddenly in the spring of 1965, life was breathed into the fairness doctrine by the Commission's warning to a pair of Jackson, Mississippi, stations that they might lose their licenses unless they achieved better balance in their coverage of civil rights and race relations. The Court of Appeals not only supported the Commission's censure, but ordered a full hearing on the complaints of civil rights and labor organizations.

The Commission has given progressively sharper teeth to the fairness doctrine. A station cannot avoid the resulting obligations by simply hiding its head in the sand and eschewing all controversial issues. There is an affirmative obligation to seek out controversy—as well as to seek out minority points of view in opposition to those for which time has already been made available. An individual who is the victim of a personal attack on radio or television must be sought out by the station, given a transcript of the offending broadcast, and offered a chance to reply on the air. The fairness doctrine has also been extended to advertising. Stations which carry cigarette commercials must provide time for anticigarette groups to present the health hazards of smoking. This recent expansion of the affirmative obligation of radio and television licensees to deal with controversial issues, and preserve balance in dealing with public controversy, is an integral and essential component of the public forum.

The Supreme Court recently sustained the Fairness Doctrine against a constitutional challenge mounted by a group of broadcasters. So long as the supply of channels and frequencies falls short of demand, and access to the airwaves must therefore be regulated to prevent chaos, the Court affirmed that the government must ensure the availability of broadcast opportunities for all points of view. The interests of listeners and viewers, not those of broadcast licensees, must be paramount. Any use of broadcast facilities for the statement of one position creates an obligation to make time available for a response or dissent. Without the personal attack rules developed under the Fairness Doctrine, the Court concluded, "station owners and a few networks would have the unfettered power to make time available only to the highest bidders, to communicate only their own views on public issues, people and candidates, and to permit on the air only those with whom they agreed."

The United States, it is true, still has no Hyde Park. But it may be developing a substitute that will turn out to be more effective as a platform for the unpopular cause. The fusion of police protection for controversial demonstrators, access to transport stations and shopping areas, and balanced presentation on radio and television create a kind of public forum that is vastly different from Hyde Park—but is also vastly different from the alternatives offered by the British Broadcasting Corporation and the Independent Television Authority. Perhaps it is fortunate that the public forum has developed a uniquely American character and has kept pace with technological change.

II. *Controversy in the Public Forum—Access to Particular Facilities*

AUDITORIUMS, LECTURE HALLS, AND THE LIKE

There have been frequent battles over the use of public auditoriums by controversial speakers and performers. A few illustrative cases will indicate the dimensions of the problem. In 1962, the New Orleans branch of the NAACP sought to use the city auditorium for a rally opposing segregation. Such prominent national figures as Thurgood Marshall, Robert Weaver, and Adam Clayton Powell were to appear on the program. City officials withheld permission to use the auditorium chiefly on the ground that the scheduled speakers and others might urge violation of existing city and state laws (presumably those enforcing or requiring segregation). In fact, the city continued to enforce racial segregation in all functions held in the auditorium.

When the NAACP took the case to the Federal District Court, the judge had little pause in setting aside the city's decision: "Without even a pretense of requiring a showing of clear and present danger, the city conditioned the use of the auditorium on the speaker's advocating views compatible with the city's policy of segregation. In a city building intended for public assemblies, Negroes could not obtain the use of the building except by surrendering freedom of speech. The city has no power to make its license to an auditorium user depend on the licensee's giving up a constitutional right."

Two recent cases involving well-known folk singers enlarge the dimensions of the problem. In June 1965, a concert series was planned and approved by the Board of Education of East Meadow, Long Island. For the past ten years, the School Board had permitted the concert series to use the local high school auditorium—the most suitable facility in the community for such cultural and educational programs. In December, School Board officials learned that

208   THE PRICE OF DEPENDENCY

folk singer Pete Seeger was scheduled to appear on March 12. They immediately canceled their commitment for that date (despite the fact that the entire schedule had been cleared and series tickets sold): "Because he had given a concert in Moscow and because some of the songs he sings are critical of American policy in Vietnam, Seeger is a 'highly controversial figure' whose presence might provoke a disturbance with consequent danger to school property."

A state court immediately overturned the School Board's decision, noting that "the justification asserted for cancelling the permit is the unpopularity of Seeger's views rather than the unlawfulness of the [sponsoring organization's] concert. [In the absence of clear and present danger, such action is] an unlawful restriction of the constitutional right of free speech and expression."

A somewhat similar difficulty befell folk singer Joan Baez about a year later. She was scheduled to give a concert in Constitution Hall, an auditorium controlled by the Daughters of the American Revolution. (In 1939, the DAR had refused use of the auditorium for a concert by Marian Anderson; the organization's policy at that time precluded any appearances by Negroes.) After the use of the hall was withdrawn, Miss Baez' concert was rescheduled for Sylvan Theater (an outdoor stage on the grounds of the Washington Monument) with the permission of the Interior Department. But the DAR did not give up so easily. The organization's president urged Interior Secretary Stewart L. Udall, on the eve of the concert, to withdraw "the privilege of using property supported by federal taxes" because Joan Baez had withheld a portion of her own federal taxes in protest against the Vietnam war. But the concert was presented on schedule to an outdoor audience of 30,000. The Interior Department replied to the DAR that "Miss Baez' political views had not been considered in passing on her application for use of the stage."

The Federal Government is not always so generous, however, in permitting the use of facilities by politically controversial persons and groups. In February 1968, for example, a group of antiwar religious leaders asked permission to hold a "reverent and solemn" memorial service in a white marble amphitheater at Arlington National Cemetery to honor "the suffering" of Americans killed in Vietnam. The keynote of the service was to be a sermon by the Reverend Martin Luther King. The Military District of Washington, however, rejected the application because Arlington facilities may not be used "for any special pleading or for advancement of any partisan cause" but only for "services which are purely memorial in purpose, patriotic in nature, and conducted by nonpartisan patriotic groups." On the eve of the service, the ministers tried unsuccessfully to obtain a federal district court order overturning the Army's stand. The district judge found the memorial service too integral a part of an antiwar program to justify a separation. Thus, the service was held just outside the gates of the cemetery.

Another incident at Arlington involved not a memorial service, but a burial. One Robert G. Thompson was discharged from the Army at the close of World War II, having received the Distinguished Service Cross for extraordinary heroism in combat. After his return to civilian life, he became increasingly involved in left-wing political activities. In 1949, he was convicted—along with ten others—of leading a Communist conspiracy to advocate and teach the violent overthrow of the United States Government. (The conviction was subsequently affirmed by the Supreme Court in 1951.) Thompson died in October 1965. His widow requested that his ashes be laid to rest at Arlington National Cemetery because "I feel it is a symbol, a place where heroes are buried." Under existing law, his remains could have been interred there but for an Army regulation denying such honor to a person "who is convicted in a federal . . . court of a crime or crimes, the result of which is . . . a sentence to imprisonment for five years or more." Just before the burial was to take place, Florida Representative Charles E. Bennett found out about Thompson's conviction. He immediately protested on the floor of the House: "To have Arlington Cemetery . . . be-spoiled by the interment of a man dedicated to the overthrow of our beloved country, is as painful a concept as I can imagine. If this can be justified, we can justify burying there Benedict Arnold, Aaron Burr and a host of others who at one time in their lives contributed something to America but turned their back on the country that had helped them secure all the good things they had attained."

After the Defense Department withdrew its original offer of a last resting place, Mrs. Thompson brought suit in the federal court. She argued that to impose such a penalty after the death of an otherwise eligible war hero constituted both a suppression of free speech and political activity, and a bill of attainder (*i.e.,* a legislative act punishing a person without criminal process for a political offense committed in the past). The district court bypassed most of the constitutional arguments, however, and held that the Army Secretary's discretion included power to make regulations concerning burial of veterans. To the trial judge that was the end of the case.

The court of appeals reversed, however, and held that Thompson's remains were entitled to a resting place at Arlington. In applying his regulations so as to deny the widow's petition, the Secretary of the Army had clearly violated the will of Congress; "Congress conferred upon the decedent a right to burial in a national cemetery unconditioned by the Secretary's exercise of judgment."

Much of the constitutional law defining access to public facilities developed through a series of California cases. The Civic Center Act made public school auditoriums freely available to nonprofit recreational, educational, political, economic, and other organizations within the community—except to individuals or groups that sought or advocated the violent overthrow of the government. Officers of the American Civil Liberties Union applied for permission to use a high school auditorium in San Diego, but would not swear that they did not "advocate and [were] not affiliated with any organization which advocates or has as its object or one of its objects the overthrow of the present government of the United States or of any state by force or violence or other unlawful means."

The ACLU claimed that the statute and the pledge required by the Board infringed their freedoms of speech and assembly. A majority of the California Supreme Court agreed. The Court stressed that no person could be *prosecuted* because of political advocacy or activity of other members of an organization to which he belonged; a disability of that type represented the clearest form of guilt by association. The same principle was equally applicable to request for [access] to a civic auditorium: ". . . registration would be a reasonable requirement facilitating the administration of meetings and imposing no censorship on the proponents. Requirement of proof of one's convictions and affiliations, however, as a condition of exercising the rights of free speech and free assembly would compel a forfeiture of those rights by those who were unable or unwilling to submit proof that was acceptable."

The school officials had argued that use of the auditorium was a "gratuity." "It is true," acknowledged the majority, "that the state need not open the doors of a school building as a forum and may at any time choose to close them. Once it opens the doors, however, it cannot demand tickets of admission in the form of convictions and affiliations that it deems acceptable. Censorship of those who would use the school building as a forum cannot be rationalized by reference to its setting. . . . The convictions or affiliations of one who requests the use of a school building as a forum is of no more concern to the school administrators than to a superintendent of parks or streets if the forum is the green or the marketplace." Although there was no constitutional "right" to use the auditorium, the court found the "privilege" one that "was too valuable to be given lightly or lightly taken away." (Fifteen years later the California courts struck down a revised oath because it subjected auditorium applicants to a test of guilt by association. Finally in 1963 the state Supreme Court upheld a rule denying access to auditoriums to individuals who planned to use them for criminal deeds.)

In the spirit of the California decisions, the Corporation Counsel of New York City recently advised the Board of Education that it could not constitutionally deny use of high school auditoriums for meetings of the National Renaissance Party, "a neo-Nazi anti-Semitic group," even though previous public meetings of the Renaissance Party had "generally ended in violence, injuries and arrests of both bystanders and members." If the Board permits use of its facilities for any political purposes during off hours, advised the counsel (a former United States Solicitor General), "it may not condition such permission with unconstitutional limitations upon the freedom of expression. Advanced censorship of speech content or previous restraint of the free exercise of speech, based merely on prior occurrences, violates the constitutional guarantees of freedom of speech." The ruling was not universally popular, even with all liberal groups. The general counsel of the Antidefamation League of B'nai B'rith was one who objected: "The National Renaissance Party is a group of street-corner hoodlums with a membership of a baker's dozen," he charged. "To accept this lunatic fringe clique's definition of itself as a political party is to pervert the meaning of the term."

Across town, the New York Port Authority Bus Terminal on Eighth Avenue was a site of a major dispute about distribution of antiwar leaflets. Several groups (including Veterans and Reservists to End the War in Vietnam) sought permission to hand printed materials to travelers and commuters in the terminal, with the understanding that they would leave at once if the situation got out of control. But permission was denied under a Port Authority rule vesting in the manager absolute discretion over use of terminal space.

A suit in the federal courts upheld the claims of the would-be leaflet distributors. Since the Port Authority was a public agency (governed jointly by New York and New Jersey), the terminal was government property and in fact a particularly public place. So long as the proposed activities would not obstruct pedestrian traffic, and the message was constitutionally protected, it did not matter that dissemination of antiwar material was unrelated to the main functions of the terminal. "Others may quarrel with [the applicant's] choice of forum," concluded the court, "but . . . the Port Authority may not abridge his right to choose this place any more than they can control his choice of message. . . . [It is] beyond dispute that the congestion and controversy that may attend the activity in the Terminal, while pertinent to the enactment of rules and regulations to govern the activity, cannot be invoked to support a flat prohibition. . . . We should in these times be mindful that to the extent we secure legitimate and orderly access to means of communication for all views, we create conditions in which there is no incentive to resort to more disruptive conduct."

SPEAKER BANS ON COLLEGE CAMPUSES

College and university policies barring controversial off-campus speakers have posed a serious threat to academic freedoms. A recent summary of the problem suggests its dimensions: "In the mid-1940's, Howard Fast, the writer, was one of many 'contempt of Congress' persons who was denied permission to speak on the campus of New York University and elsewhere. In 1951, a Quaker pacifist was denied permission to speak on the campus at Ohio State University. In 1955, the president of the University of Washington refused to allow Robert Oppenheimer (the father of the atomic bomb) to address a conference of scientists on his campus. ". . . Reverend Martin Luther King, Jr., was denied an invitation to participate in a seminar relating religion to major current issues at Washington and Lee." A list of speakers barred from college rostra during 1968 would include Dick Gregory, Reverend William Sloan Coffin, Dr. Benjamin Spock and Allen Ginsberg—not to mention much more controversial figures like H. Rap Brown and Eldridge Cleaver.

The reasons for the persistence of speaker bans are not hard to find. In a recent survey of 225 major college and university presidents, about one third "disagreed completely" with the proposition that "Students should be allowed to invite and to hear any person of their own choosing. . . . It should be made clear to the academic and larger community that sponsorship of guest speakers does not necessarily imply approval or endorsement of the views expressed either by the sponsoring group or the institution." Another survey of 757 college presidents indicated 75 percent support for the principle of discussion of unpopular issues on campus. Yet only 32 percent of the sample would have permitted Black Nationalist leader Malcolm X; and only 28 percent would have permitted a named Communist to appear. A later survey of 189 institutions revealed that 25 percent had no campus speaker policy at all; 10 percent had a policy permitting all speakers regardless of political views; 31 percent required every speaker to be approved by an official or committee; and 24 percent allowed any speaker to appear if certain guidelines were followed (*e.g.,* having group sponsorship, registering in advance, maintaining a balance in the type of speakers invited, keeping programs orderly, insuring programs of educational value, etc.).

Why do legislators and administrators impose such sweeping bans? In 1961, the Administrative Council of the City University of New York argued a Communist speaker ban was necessary and was compatible with "the proper atmosphere for free inquiry": "The faculties and administrative officers are . . . charged with making certain that the time of students is properly spent in the examination of the various facets of human experience which can give the greatest educational value. There can be no assumption that a commitment to free expression and discussion relieves the professional staff of its duty to discriminate and choose among the welter of ideas, positions, convictions, facts and theories which present themselves for consideration."

Legislatures are themselves often subject to strong external pressures to adopt speaker bans. Early in 1966, for example, the American Legion and Veterans of Foreign Wars in Louisiana began a successful, highly organized campaign to bar Communist speakers from appearing at state-supported schools and colleges. The effort followed closely an appearance at Louisiana State University by Communist spokesman and editor Albert Nelson. Meanwhile, the majority leader of the Michigan state senate—reportedly angry over the recent appearance at Ann Arbor, Michigan State, and Wayne State of Herbert Aptheker, the Communist historian—urged his colleagues to prohibit Communist speakers from appearing at tax-supported institutions of higher learning in the state.

The political motivations for campus speaker bans are reflected in the preamble to Illinois's Clabaugh Act (which prohibits use of any facilities at the University of Illinois by "any subversive, seditious and un-American organization"): "Whereas the universities of America have been the breeding ground of a series of invidious Communist inspired organizations which have sought to instill in the hearts of American youth contempt and hatred for ideals to which the people of this great nation have been dedicated . . ." These political pressures also explain the extraordinary difficulty of repealing a speaker ban once it has been enacted. Few efforts to abolish speaker bans have succeeded except through the courts. The University of California's repeal of its rule against Communist speakers came in 1963 only after many abortive attempts to persuade both the Regents and the state courts to rescind the ban.

College and university speaker bans are, of course, constitutionally vulnerable on many of the same grounds as the high school auditorium restrictions. There are strong policy objections, also, to speaker bans. First, it is argued that a speaker ban artificially shields or insulates students from controversies for which responsible citizenship must be prepared. In defending an invitation to Communist Benjamin Davis, former President O. Meredith Wilson of the University of Minnesota declared: "We believe it would be a disservice to our students and an insult to our nation's maturity if we were to deny Mr. Davis an opportunity to speak. Overprotected students might at once assume that Davis had something to say which was too strong for our reason and our convictions. The university is the product of a free society. It is neither afraid of freedom nor can it serve society well if it casts doubts on the ability of our free institutions to meet the challenge of doctrines foreign to our own."

Second, exposure to such controversial off-campus speakers may constitute an integral part of the educational experience. If students are denied access to such views on the campus, they will be the poorer for the deprivation in an academic as well as extracurricular dimension. When a New York taxpayer sued to prevent Herbert Aptheker from speaking in a student-sponsored lecture series at the State University of New York at Buffalo, a state court rejected the argument that Aptheker's appearance at a tax-supported institution would further Communist subversion by cloaking his message in a "mantle of academic and intellectual integrity." On the contrary, concluded the court, "the tradition of our great society has been to allow our universities, in the name of academic freedom, to explore and expose their students to controversial issues without government interference."

Moreover, as Columbia historian Louis M. Hacker points out, the writings of most controversial speakers are readily available in the college library and bookstore anyway. As between reading and hearing the words of such speakers, "the latter has real advantages to satisfy a normal curiosity to see and hear persons who are espousing unpopular causes, to ask questions on matters of doctrine and policy, to match wits with and, therefore, expose the mechanical thinking of people who can but make a sorry appearance when absent from the protective screen of their massed followers and the hysteria they work up." Even Senator and former presidential candidate Barry Goldwater agrees: "If a man is a Communist and he wants to be invited to speak, let the students hear these people. The listening to these gentlemen will only broaden their knowledge and strengthen their convictions in one way or the other."

Third, a university cannot logically bar some speakers without appearing to endorse the views of all others. Macalester College President Arthur S. Flemming (formerly Secretary of Health, Education and Welfare) has warned: "The first time a university bars a speaker it will put itself in a position of either endorsing future speakers, or at least saying they are not as bad as the one who is barred. The only way in which a university can avoid putting its stamp of approval on an outside speaker is to follow the policy of permitting a faculty or accredited student group to invite anyone they desire to hear."

Fourth, the events to which controversial speakers are typically invited impose no coercion or pressure upon students to attend. While the university's position might possibly be compromised by appearance of a Communist or Fascist speaker as an integral part of a course at which student attendance was required to earn a passing grade, such dangers surely do not arise when the program is open to all, but compulsory for none.

The constitutional arguments against speaker bans parallel policy considerations. Few bans are at all specific in designating the proscribed class of speakers. Where they are precise, they almost always reach a substantial amount of speech that is constitutionally protected. Communist speakers, for example, are barred as such regardless of whether they will, on that occasion, advocate the violent overthrow of the government. Such indiscriminate prohibitions are invalid either as infringements of free speech, or as bills of attainder, or both.

The more complex and subtle problems arise under the vague speaker bans. What possible guidance can be found, for example, in the recently adopted Mississippi legislative policy barring from state college and university campuses "speakers who will do violence to the academic atmosphere of the respective institutions; and persons in disrepute in the area from whence they come, and those charged with crimes or other moral wrongs . . ." ? Or in the policy which officials at Hunter College (of the City University of New York) adopted in 1961, permitting outside speakers only when "compatible with the aims of Hunter College as an institution of higher learning" ? A New York trial court found this language was "either unconstitutionally vague" or embodied "an unconstitutional principle of selection."

It was the vagueness and invitation to arbitrary discretion which finally brought about the demise of North Carolina's perennially troublesome speaker ban. The first provision to come before a three judge federal court prohibited speeches by "known members of the Communist Party": " 'Known' to whom and to what degree of certainty?" asked the court. " 'Known' according to what standard? A 'member' in what sense? Does it include membership in a Communist 'front' organization? Is it a matter of general personal reputation or rumor, or the personal knowledge of the Chancellor? The statutes and regulations provide no clues to any of these questions. Without such answers, neither those who must obey nor those who must enforce the statutes and regulations can determine the extent of their obligation." The court found similar difficulties in that part of the statute barring visiting speakers known to advocate the overthrow of the Constitution of the United States and of the State of

North Carolina. Finally, the court invalidated provision of the law denying campus facilities to speakers who had ever pleaded the privilege against self-incrimination; any punishment for claiming that privilege was "constitutionally impermissible."

Six months later Illinois's long-contested Clabaugh Act was interred by another federal court of three judges. The substantive grounds of the decision were roughly the same as in the North Carolina case. The prohibitory terms of the statute were excessively vague, and clearly sought to muzzle some constitutionally protected forms of expression, while failing to afford any guidance to those charged with enforcing the ban. Because it omitted any provision for a hearing on a controversial speaker's application, the law lacked the "constitutional safeguards required for a form of regulation amounting to censorship."

The Illinois case presented a novel problem not found in the earlier speaker-ban suits. The speaker who had been denied access to the campus was not among the persons bringing the suit; the plaintiffs consisted entirely of students and faculty members who wanted to hear the speaker on campus. Lawyers for the University argued that only the speaker had legal standing to attack a ban of this type, and that the suit must therefore be dismissed. The court rejected this contention, and made important new law by allowing such a case to be brought by the prospective audience even if the speaker declined to challenge his own exclusion. The audience was, after all, "the principal beneficiary of the First Amendment" in the court's judgment. The constitutional right peaceably to assemble "to listen to a speaker of one's choice . . . may not be impaired by state legislatures any more than the right of the speaker may be impaired."

The application of these principles has already expanded measurably the access of controversial speakers to college rostra. When Dick Gregory and Dr. Timothy Leary were successively rejected as participants in a student-sponsored issues program at the University of Tennessee, the aid of the federal courts was sought to protect their right to speak. The University's speaker-clearance policies were held unconstitutional, even though they did not purport to forbid the range of activity covered by the more traditional speaker bans. About the same time a federal court of appeals set aside the decision of Auburn University's president to exclude Yale Chaplain William Sloan Coffin from the campus. Although the president claimed he had the authority to prohibit speeches on campus by convicted felons and antiwar advocates, there was no rule or policy that gave him such power; and had such a rule existed on paper, it would have fared no better than the broad speaker bans.

If the old-style speaker bans are now unconstitutional, as seems rather clearly the case, what conditions may be imposed on access of off-campus speakers to university facilities and audiences? First, it seems reasonable to require that some campus group (formal or informal) be eager enough to hear the speaker to sponsor his address. Second, campus facilities may be denied to speakers who plan to use them for purely commercial ends, *i.e.,* advertising merchandise or selling services. Third, a system of rotation might well be adopted to ensure the equitable allocation of scarce lecture halls and auditoriums; if demand is heavy, a particular group or speaker might be denied a return engagement until other applicants have had the use of the space. Fourth, minimal registration might be required, simply to furnish university officials with the name of the sponsor(s), the expected size of the audience, the need for any special services (including police protection), and the time at which the meeting will end so the room may be cleaned or made available to another user.

Campus speaker policies often go beyond these simple conditions without censoring the content of the speech. The constitutionality of these added restrictions seems dubious, although courts have been too concerned about bald censorship of off-campus speakers to reach these subtler issues. Speakers are sometimes required to answer questions from the floor after the speech as a condition of appearing on campus. Other institutions insist that a controversial speaker be followed by a spokesman for a contrasting or opposed view. The district court in the North Carolina case observed of such requirements: "One does not acquire an understanding of important racial problems by listening successively to a Stokely Carmichael or an H. Rap Brown and an officer of the Ku Klux Klan. Countering a Herbert Aptheker with an official of the American Nazi Party may furnish excitement for young people, but it presents no rational alternatives and has but dubious value as an educational experience." If, after all, the educational value of exposure to controversial speakers constitutes its strongest justification, then contrived or artificial arrangements should certainly be avoided.

What, finally, of the inflammatory speaker who has left a trail of bloodshed in his previous appearances? The First Amendment makes clear that "each dog is entitled to one bite." But after his first bite, it can be argued that the speaker is sufficiently dangerous to be denied further access to college campuses. Others would adopt the advice recently given by former Solicitor General Rankin to the New York City Board of Education—"Advance censorship of speech content or previous restraint of the free exercise of speech based merely on prior occurrences violates the constitutional guarantees of freedom of speech." The sounder view seems to be that the university should give the speaker another chance, but have on call enough campus police officers either to protect him from a hostile crowd or to arrest him if he crosses the constitutional line into incitement to violence.

III. *Printed Matter and Political Messages in the Public Sector*

A significant amount of highly visible, low cost advertising space exists on the sides or overhead panels of public buses, trolley, and subway cars. At about the same time, the advertising policies of the New York City Transit Authority and of the Alameda-Contra Costa Transit District in California came under court attack in strikingly similar cases. In New York, transit officials refused to approve placement by Students for a Democratic Society of anti-Vietnam war posters on subway station platforms. In California, the District refused to post in its buses antiwar advertisements submitted by the Women's Strike for Peace. The policies of the New York Authority were unclear; a letter stated simply that "the copy submitted is entirely too controversial to be posted on the stations publicly owned by the New York City Transit System. Our policy has always been to refrain from accepting business, the display of which would be objectionable to large segments of our population."

The applicable policy in the California case was somewhat more explicit. The District buses displayed mostly commercial advertising, but political advertising would be accepted "in connection with and at the time of a duly called election being held within the boundaries of the District" provided that space was made equally available to opposing candidates on opposite sides of a ballot measure.

In both cases, the antiwar groups eventually prevailed. A federal district court in New York conceded that "the authority and the advertising company could refuse to accept all posters for display in the subways." But if space had been made available for any purposes, a government agency could not constitutionally discriminate on content grounds unless the objectionable material created a clear and present danger, which had not been shown of the SDS posters. The California case presented a paradox to the state Supreme Court: "Not only does the District's policy prefer certain classes of protected ideas over others, but it goes even further and affords total freedom of the forum to mercantile messages, while banning the vast majority of opinions and beliefs extant which enjoy First Amendment protection because of their noncommercialism. . . . A cigarette company is permitted to advertise the desirability of smoking its brand, but a cancer society is not entitled to caution by advertisement that cigarette smoking is injurious to health. A theater may advertise a motion picture that portrays sex and violence, but the Legion for Decency has no right to post a message calling for clean films. A lumber company may advertise its wood products, but a conservation group cannot implore citizens to write to the president or governor about protecting our natural resources." The Court was unimpressed by several practical arguments advanced by the Transit District—the difficulty of selecting among controversial applicants if demand exceeded available space (as it seldom does in transit advertising); or the prospect that militant messages might offend substantial numbers of passengers. "Annoyance and inconvenience," said the Court, "are a small price to pay for preservation of our most cherished right."

The government risks censorship in many other contexts as well. As previously mentioned, there has been much controversy about the magazine selection policies of the General Services Administration for newsstands in federal office buildings, and by military procurement agents for P-X newsstands overseas. Several inconclusive lawsuits have resulted. The problem is less easily resolved than that of the antiwar ads in municipal buses, precisely because newsstand space is not unlimited. Moreover, the magazines most likely to be rejected on political grounds by a cautious buyer or distributor are also likely to experience limited demand. The government can effectively avoid this sort of problem—likely to arise wherever a choice or selection must be made—only by closing down all newsstands. Such a cure is surely worse than the disease.

IV. *The Future of the Public Domain*

Most of the court contests to date over the use of government property have concerned tangible, physical space. Controversies over parks, auditoriums, buses, and municipal facilities undoubtedly will continue. But the important cases of the future will more likely emerge from claims of equal access to other, less tangible forms of government property. For the public domain also includes channels of communication, vast reservoirs of information, and a host of services of growing importance to the citizen.

A few examples, drawn from recent cases, will identify the new dimension. A Southern law professor wrote an article decrying the Supreme Court's school desegregation decisions. He submitted the article to the student editors of the *Rutgers Law Review,* who declined to publish it. The professor brought suit in a federal court, claiming he had been unconstitutionally denied a forum in a state-supported journal because the editors found his political views unpalatable. Rutgers, defending the suit, pointed out that the *Review* had many more contributions than they could possibly print, and argued that the editors had rejected the particular article in spite of, rather than because of, its point of view. Two federal courts sustained the University's position, rejecting all claims of political discrimination.

Another recent case concerned nondiscriminatory access to information under government control. Reporters from a Nashville, Tennessee, newspaper were excluded from state legislative hearings because one of their colleagues had violated a state senate rule. The editor was informed that the paper's floor privileges would be restored only if he assured the Clerk of the Senate, in writing, that all members of his staff would thereafter abide by all Senate regulations.

The publisher brought a suit against the officers of the Senate, claiming the withdrawal of access to legislative proceedings violated the freedom of the press. The court agreed, holding that the legislature had abridged freedom of expression both by using access to news as a punishment for contempt of the Senate, and by threatening that "a surrender of freedom of expression may be required as the price for regaining such access."

Recent legislation, notably the Federal Freedom of Information Act, has done much to make government documents and records accessible to citizens who wish to consult them. Federal agencies must now formulate and publish regulations defining the conditions of access. Many states also have laws requiring that meetings of public bodies be open to the general public, save under exceptional circumstances where "executive sessions" may be warranted. But these laws still typically allow a degree of administrative discretion that may bar the seeker of government information who lacks influence and is unwilling to take his claim to court.

Rapid and profound changes in the technology of information storage and retrieval will also give greater importance to the issue of access to intangible government "property." There is already much talk about a single central federal data bank, into which would be fed myriad information about every citizen. Such a consolidation of diffuse knowledge would, of course, give the Federal Government an even greater control over the lives of its citizens than it now possesses. That power would be intolerable if unaccompanied by development of nondiscriminatory rules of access to the central information bank for legitimate purposes. And it seems quite certain that the dimensions of government property will be steadily enlarged by technology in many other ways as well.

The precedents developed in cases involving the use of parks and auditoriums are not readily adaptable to the anticipated contests over access to an intangible public domain. Yet the principles underlying the cases considered in this chapter seem transferable, and no less sound for computer banks than for concert halls. If the basic proposition of nondiscriminatory access to public property is well established and clearly understood, the resolution of claims of access to intangible property should be possible.

VIII

PUBLIC HOUSING

I. *Crisis in the Project*

When the first federal public housing legislation was passed in 1937, city planners, social workers, architects and others welcomed this "hopeful first step toward the goal of good housing for all." In the thirty years since that time, tens of thousands of low rent public housing units have been built. Over two million people inhabit these projects, yet the goals of both legal and architectural draftsmen clearly have never been realized. Recent years have brought a mounting chorus of dissatisfaction, hostility, and bitterness toward public housing.

Most clearly, the public housing programs of the federal, state, and local governments have not achieved their primary mission of providing "decent, safe and sanitary dwellings for families of low income." The report of the National Advisory Commission on Civil Disorders noted with alarm: "Today, after more than three decades of fragmented and grossly underfunded federal housing programs, decent housing remains a chronic problem for the disadvantaged urban household. Fifty-six percent of the country's nonwhite families live in central cities today, and of these, nearly two-thirds live in neighborhoods marked by substandard housing and general urban blight. For these citizens, condemned by segregation and poverty to live in the decaying slums of our central cities, the goal of a decent home and suitable environment is as far distant as ever."

Of course the problem of sheltering the poor in dignity and safety is not confined to *public* housing. "The poor are relegated to ghettos and are beset by substandard housing at exorbitant rents," Mr. Justice Douglas recently observed. "Because of their lack of bargaining power, the poor are made to accept onerous lease terms. Summary eviction proceedings are the order of the day. . . . Housing laws often have a built-in bias against the poor. Slum lords have a tight hold on the Nation." Public housing is clearly not the *cause* of the crisis. But it must share some blame for failing to provide the escape from the deplorable housing conditions which generated the original governmental concern; and in part, too, for having actually increased the concentration and isolation of nonwhites in the urban ghettos. Public housing projects are hated, James Baldwin has said, "because they reveal the real attitude of the white world."

Architecturally and aesthetically, public housing has been judged a disaster. *The New York Times* has attacked the bureaucratic tendency to keep building "desolate" projects which typically "carry the stigma of personal and environmental poverty and the seeds of despair. While the amount of public housing provided in American cities in thirty years has been only a drop in the bucket of need, the restrictive clauses have succeeded beyond anyone's wildest dreams in creating the 'project look,' that dismal mold that blights cities, neighborhoods and people. The impersonally cheerless barracks called 'public housing' have produced a terrifying new breed of slum—in New York as elsewhere."

Conditions inside the typical housing project have been as uncivilized as their facades have been unattractive. Harrison Salisbury made an extensive firsthand study of the public housing situation in New York a decade ago. He was "profoundly shocked" by the "stench of stale urine that pervades the elevators" in Fort Greene Houses, Brooklyn. He found the "new ghettos" created by the monolithic projects "human cesspools worse than those of yesterday." These bleak structures were "monsters devouring their residents, polluting the areas above them, spewing out a social excrescence which infects the whole of our society." They were, in short, little improvement over the slums they replaced. Thus, it is hardly surprising that 85 percent of the residents who move out of public housing projects do so quite voluntarily, because of dissatisfaction or despair with conditions there. Few of those who leave, of course, move to the suburbs. But for many, even a return to the tenement may be preferable to staying in the project.

The mounting criticism of public housing on the one hand and the urgent need to house the urban poor on the other have created an ambivalence toward new construction. The demand for increasing the rate of public housing development is heard in many quarters. The National Committee for a Confrontation with Congress —a self-styled "poor people's lobby"—has demanded an immediate commitment to construction of 600,000 public housing units. This would constitute a "first step toward closing the widening racial gap" and would also open up many new construction jobs for nonwhite groups. President Johnson's 1968 housing message sharply raised the administration's sights by calling for construction of four million new housing units and rehabilitation of two million other units within the decade ahead. Measured against past performance, these projections sound unrealistically ambitious; in the decade 1958–68, a scant half million new units were built. Yet the projections of the Kerner Commission Report were even more ambitious; the same goal (six million new or rehabilitated units) should be reached within five years rather than ten. (Housing and Urban Development Secretary Robert C. Weaver at once termed the Kerner Commission's timetable quixotic: "It's not physically impossible, but it's highly improbable. Our best judgment based on analysis of labor and the construction industry is that we've gone about as far as we can go.")

Accompanying these rising projections has been a diversification of programs to provide low-income shelter. Since 1961, there has been a burgeoning program of loans at interest rates below the regular market to assist the private construction of housing for moderate income families. Closely tied to urban renewal efforts in some communities, these subsidies have induced some of these families to stay in or near the central city.

Somewhat more promising has been the Federal Rent Supplement Program. Through such subsidies the government pays the difference between private rent and what the tenant can afford, calculated as 25 percent of his income. Early experiments under the Rent Supplement Program in Washington brought exciting results in the form of a sharp increase in the average income of the assisted tenants, and an unprecedented degree of racial integration. A similar experiment in Boston also offered promise: the tenants displayed more "social responsibility" than poor families living in public housing projects. Despite these encouraging returns, Congress sharply curtailed the appropriation for rent subsidies after the first two years; the program had run afoul of political complications and crosscurrents which jeopardized its future.

Finally, there is "Operation Turnkey" under which public housing authorities, instead of constructing low-rent units themselves, purchase units constructed by private builders.

These alternatives offer many advantages over total government financing and supervision of housing projects. Not least among the benefits is the possibility of a "mixed economy" (especially through the rent subsidy and Turnkey programs)—involving more effective collaboration between the public and private sectors. These cooperative approaches have often proved cheaper and more efficient in meeting certain types of housing needs, and seem to enhance prospects for racial desegregation. Finally, tenant morale may be substantially improved. The early rent subsidy experiments indicated that government assistance to tenants who want and can find better accommodations in private housing may so change the environment and the tenants' outlook that incomes will actually rise.

Whatever promise these substitutes may hold, however, the traditional public housing program will undoubtedly continue for a time to dominate the housing field. The constitutional conflicts and tensions that divide landlord and tenant in the public project must therefore be better understood. This has been an almost wholly neglected field of constitutional analysis. Until a few years ago, there was hardly a court decision defining the status or the rights of the public housing tenant. But the contours of tenant status are beginning to emerge, and one case involving tenant rights has already reached the United States Supreme Court. A survey of unconstitutional conditions attached to government benefits could hardly overlook the emerging implications of the public housing sector.

II. *The Lock on the Gate: Restricted Access to Public Housing*

Two neutral factors restrict access to public housing. First, demand for accommodations continues to exceed the supply of units, despite the widespread dissatisfaction with project conditions. In a typical year, the New York City Housing Authority receives over 100,000 applications but can accept only 10,000 new families. Second, there are restrictions designed to exclude families that do not need low cost shelter. From the start, the law supplying federal funds for public housing construction limited eligibility to "families of low income" who could not "afford to pay enough to cause private enterprise in their locality . . . to build an adequate supply of decent, safe and sanitary dwellings for their use." Specifically, only those families are admissible "whose net income at the time of admission does not exceed five times the rental." (The statute was recently amended to bar discrimination "against families otherwise eligible for admission to [public] housing because their incomes are derived in whole or in part from public assistance.")

There is growing criticism of these rigid income limits. The effect of restricting public housing to those who are too poor to afford anything better—and requiring them to move out as their economic position improves—is to deprive the project of those models of middle class success and responsible tenancy that might well elevate the tenor of project life in various ways. There is much to be said for greater flexibility that would permit continued occupancy of a portion of the units in each project by tenants whose low incomes once made them eligible, but whose subsequent success would otherwise force them to leave. The President's Commission on Civil Disorders recommends: "Families whose incomes increase above the public housing limit should be permitted to take over the leases of their units from the Housing Authority."

Nonincome restrictions are obviously more troublesome. The literature of public housing and project interviews contains frequent references to the "middle class mentality" of project managers and administrators: "Anxious for the program's future, housing authority officials have imposed numerous restrictions upon tenants to avoid the least appearance of harboring rowdies, derelicts, prostitutes, or subversives."

In the view of the timid or harried manager, the presence of large numbers of very poor, often unemployed tenants creates inherent and serious threats to administration. Of course restrictions can be imposed, rules enforced, and tenant behavior watched by police. Tenants who do not comply or who disrupt the normal life of the project can always be evicted—with great ease, in fact, as we shall see later in this chapter. But such problems and inconveniences can most easily be avoided by simply not admitting tenants who pose such threats. Consequently, the framing of eligibility standards on nonincome grounds has tended to work backward from the special problems the management fears, rather than working forward from either an analysis of the project's best interests or a definition of the ideal tenant. This background at least explains some of the burdensome restrictions that greet the applicant, though it does not justify their enforcement or make them valid.

III. *Eligibility and Delinquency: The Effect of a Prior Criminal Record*

Certain convicted criminals undoubtedly pose so great a danger to the community that they ought to be barred from public housing. But current restrictions go far beyond this limited need. The low income slum resident often will find that youthful misdeeds or a few minor arrests are sufficient to bar him from public housing. The case of Mrs. Manigo illustrates the problem. Her application for public housing was rejected by the New York City Housing Authority under its policy of treating a single arrest within the past five years as disqualifying evidence of "antisocial behavior." Her husband had once been adjudged a juvenile delinquent and youthful offender. Several criminal charges against him had been dismissed after arrest; his only conviction had been for disorderly conduct, resulting in a short sentence. Although New York law prohibits treatment of juvenile delinquency as "criminal behavior" or as the basis for "forfeiture of any right or privilege," the Housing Authority stressed the "extensive criminal record" of the applicant's husband.

When Mrs. Manigo sued for admission to public housing, the Authority tacitly admitted this was the sole reason for her rejection. But the court nevertheless upheld the Authority's decision. While a single act of delinquency would not "standing by itself" disqualify a person from public housing, "this does not mean that an applicant's entire behavior pattern over a period of years may not be the proper subject of scrutiny by an administrative agency before granting a right or privilege such as eligibility to public housing." An independent review of the entire record satisfied the court that the application fell short of the Authority's general "desirability" standards. (The New York Housing Authority later narrowed the disqualification: a criminal record would bar an applicant only where there was "recent serious criminal activity" or a "pattern of violent behavior.") An arrest which did not result in conviction should surely not disqualify, though if serious charges are pending at the time the application is received, the Authority might properly await the outcome. But if the charges are dismissed (whatever the reason), or if the applicant is acquitted after a trial, it is not the province of the Housing Authority to judge him "guilty" when agencies better qualified to make that decision have found him innocent.

Even where a conviction results, its bearing upon public housing eligibility should be limited in several respects: first, it should prejudice the application only when (as recently proposed by the American Civil Liberties Union of Southern California) it "suggests a continuing pattern of personal actions which reasonably could jeopardize the health, safety or morals of the project including, without limitation, rape, child molestation, or other such felonies. . . ." Second, there should be some time limit on the relevance of even serious crimes. If three years of good behavior have followed the sentence, the Housing Authority should be willing to disregard the conviction and do its part to facilitate the applicant's rehabilitation.

Finally, the effects of criminal conduct upon relatives of the offender should surely be minimized. A decade ago the manager of one large New York project systematically evicted the families of teen-age gang members without waiting for convictions or even arrests. Another New York case illustrates the cruel collateral consequences of a criminal record. The wife and children of a felon were evicted, soon after his conviction, from the project where they had lived for some time. When the family sought redress in court, a trial judge held in their favor. But the appellate court reversed this decision because the *procedures* had been regular and proper; thus, there was no occasion to examine the *reasons* for the termination. One judge of the appellate court dissented vigorously: "Plainly an eviction here runs counter to the purposes of the very statute which gave the [Authority] life. An act intended to provide housing for the poor is misused when a family is driven from its home for no better reason than that it has been sorely afflicted. Neither reason nor principle requires us to make a mockery of the law. To put this fam-

ily into the street at this time and thus bypass the social consequences . . . would be inconsistent with the avowed public policy
of this State."

IV. *Illegitimacy, Promiscuity, and Public Housing*

Housing authorities in at least twelve states are known to exclude unmarried mothers and families with illegitimate children. A
case arising in New Bern, North Carolina, first brought this practice
before the courts. Negro tenants in New Bern projects were required to sign a "covenant" in their leases forfeiting their tenancy
thirty days after the birth of an illegitimate child to the tenant or a
member of his family. The covenant was "enforced" by requiring
violators either to vacate at once or to pay a $50 fine for each illegit-
imate child. When a group of tenants protested, the Authority eliminated the fine and resorted to eviction in every case. Suit was
brought against this procedure by a group of tenants who had been
evicted or threatened with eviction because of illegitimate births,
and by several applicants who had been declared ineligible for the
same reason. The federal court granted a temporary restraining
order against further evictions pending a decision on the merits.
Meanwhile, similar restrictions were tested by suits against housing
authorities in Talladega, Alabama, Little Rock, Arkansas, and
other communities.

The Little Rock case was the first to reach a decision. The
court found unconstitutional the Housing Authority's rule that "a
family shall not be eligible for admission or continued occupancy if
any family member residing regularly with the family has a child or
children born out of wedlock." The judge acknowledged the Authority's power to prescribe reasonable criteria and to exclude applicants who threatened illegal or disorderly conduct. Moreover,
the Authority might give some weight as evidence to the presence of
illegitimate children in a family group. But the inflexible and automatic exclusion policy was "drastic beyond any reasonable necessity." The court concluded: "An indiscriminate denial of access to
public housing to families unfortunate enough to have or acquire
one or more illegitimate children would be to deprive of the real or
supposed benefits of this program many of the very people who
need it most—the poorest and most ignorant of the poor. An ad-

ministrative policy which involves such a denial does not square with the humane purpose of the low rent housing program."

Elsewhere, efforts were made through other channels to alter or remove the ban on illegitimate families. The New York State Assembly voted to prohibit local housing authorities from denying admission to families because they included illegitimate children; but the legislature adjourned before the State Senate could act. The New York City Housing Authority voluntarily abandoned its prohibition upon out-of-wedlock children and announced it would exclude or evict only in the rare case where promiscuity resulted in a conviction for rape or sexual deviation. Meanwhile, the Municipal Housing Authority in Buffalo also abandoned a long standing rule excluding unmarried mothers. A *Buffalo Evening News* editorial praised this decision as "a humane step toward assuring decent housing and possible rehabilitation for these families." The editorial vigorously maintained that "it is wrong and a denial of constructive assistance to arbitrarily exclude these women and their innocent children from what may be the only decent housing available to them. Social services provided in a setting of public housing offer greater promise of rehabilitating errant women and helping their children than an automatic exclusion policy that seems to belong to a bygone age of scarlet letters, stocks and pillories."

Despite at least one court victory and several administrative changes, the unmarried mother still fares badly at the typical public housing desk. In Detroit, for example, it is reported to be unwritten policy not even to give application forms to women known to be unmarried mothers. And if forms are inadvertently given out, they will not be favorably acted upon after they have been returned.

What constitutional arguments can be made against the exclusion of unmarried mothers? First, there is the subtle but obvious racial bias inherent in such a policy. Given the substantially higher rates of illegitimacy among low income nonwhites, such a policy strikes with particular force at Negro applicants who are already disproportionately dependent on government housing, in part because of the very lack of family solidarity that may cause their exclusion. Second, such a policy—along with other legal disabilities imposed on out-of-wedlock families—imposes the greatest hardship on the children, who have absolutely no responsibility for their condition. If it is unreasonable to discriminate against Negroes or Jews or Italians solely on ethnic or national grounds, it may be equally arbitrary to deny benefits to illegitimates because of a similar accident of birth. And it is obviously impossible to punish the mother (who can at least be held accountable for illegitimate births) without hurting the children. Finally, a ban on unmarried mothers and their children is irrelevant at best, and at worst quite damaging, to the basic objectives of public housing. Fatherless families have a particular claim to public support precisely because they lack a male head, as programs like Aid for Families with Dependent Children clearly recognize. It seems perverse for the public housing program to disqualify those families who are the objects of special solicitude from other branches of public welfare law. It should be enough for the Authority to rely upon its undoubted power to evict families whose lack of structure or discipline endangers or seriously disrupts the lives of other tenants.

Unmarried mothers have also been special victims of the practice of some housing authorities of excluding welfare recipients, or placing them at the bottom of the eligibility list. Such discrimination is never published as official policy; indeed, if it were to be announced formally as a criterion, it would conflict with federal law. Thus the only way to establish that such a policy exists is by showing a consistent pattern of discrimination against welfare recipients who are otherwise eligible for admission.

Many of the constitutional issues raised by public housing exclusionary policies may have become largely academic. The Department of Housing and Urban Development gave public housing tenants and applicants a valuable Christmas present during the final weeks of 1968—a directive to all local housing authorities revising permissible admission standards. This circular referred to the directives issued during the spring of the same year, and to court decisions in the intervening months imposing more stringent standards on some housing agencies. The heart of the new HUD directive was contained in two critical paragraphs:

> A Local Authority shall not establish policies which automatically deny admission or continued occupancy to a particular class, such as unmarried mothers, families having one or more children born out of wedlock, families having police records or poor rent-paying habits, etc.
>
> To determine whether applicants or occupants should be admitted to or remain in its project, a Local Authority may

establish criteria and standards bearing on whether the conduct of such tenants (in an applicant's present or prior housing, or in occupancy in the case of present tenants) does or
would be likely to interfere with other tenants in such a manner as to materially diminish their enjoyment of the premises.
Such intereference must relate to the actual or threatened conduct of the tenant and not be based solely on such matters as
the marital status of the family, the legitimacy of the children
in the family, police records, etc.

Two features of the directive are particularly noteworthy: first,
the insistence that each case be judged on its own facts and circumstances, and not by automatic reference to a blanket rule; and second, the principle that exclusion or eviction can only be justified
by a substantial threat of tangible harm to the project and to the
other tenants. In this respect, the law of public housing has begun
to move toward the standards we have seen evolving in other
areas of government benefits—the demand of the California courts
that restrictions on public employment not exceed the essential
needs of the civil service; and the guarantee of the University of
Oregon that students will be disciplined only for infractions that
directly and seriously affect valid university interests. It is hardly
surprising that the December 1968 HUD directive has been widely
acclaimed as a "Bill of Rights" for public housing tenants.

V. *Public Housing, Politics, and Loyalty*

The loyalty oath once required of applicants for public housing is now of little more than historic interest. The Congressional
Appropriations Act of 1952 and 1953 provided in a rider that "no
housing unit constructed under the United States Housing Act of
1937 . . . shall be occupied by a person who is a member of an
organization designated as subversive by the Attorney General."
Local housing authorities were to enforce the provisions of the rider
(which took the label "Gwinn Amendment" from the name of its
sponsor).

A student Note in the *Columbia Law Review* described the
operation of the restriction: "The local housing authorities typically
implement the Gwinn Amendment by issuing resolutions requiring

tenants to sign certificates of nonmembership in organizations listed by the Attorney General as subversive. A certificate is sent to each tenant, together with a copy of the Attorney General's list. If the tenant refuses to sign the certificate, eviction proceedings are instituted." The New York City Housing Authority adopted a similar procedure whereby each tenant received a copy of the Attorney General's list. He was told that membership in any of the listed organizations would disqualify him. He could resign from the organization, or could sign the affidavit and remain eligible.

The implementation of the Gwinn Amendment touched off a wave of constitutional litigation all over the country. Courts in California, Wisconsin, Illinois, New York, and the District of Columbia found the loyalty oath requirement either inconsistent with the public housing laws (and therefore unenforceable), or contrary to state or federal constitutions. A broad range of constitutional issues was involved. The Illinois court found, for example, that the exclusion of otherwise eligible tenants solely for refusing to sign the oath was so totally unrelated to the purposes of the Public Housing Act as to be an irrational and insupportable requirement. Moreover, the automatic reference to the Attorney General's list—without even requiring that the tenant be aware that the organization was on the Attorney General's list—constituted a denial of due process of law. (Illinois had not included the requirement that the tenant be given a copy of the list.)

But the pervasive vice of the Gwinn Amendment was its effect on freedoms of expression and association. The Wisconsin Supreme Court, in striking down the oath, found the slight governmental interest in excluding subversives from public housing clearly outweighed by the affidavit's chilling effect on beliefs and activities protected by the First Amendment. One commentator observed: "The . . . statute does not seem to be aimed at tenancy by disloyal persons because such tenancy presents a threat to American security; neither legislative history nor the statute itself reveals congressional findings of danger. It seems rather that Congress declined to extend its bounty to those whose disagreement with our government may be termed 'subversive.' In an era when federal and state aid extends into so many areas, such statutes could be used to foreclose a host of privileges." Eventually, every court that considered the question agreed the Gwinn Amendment was either contrary to prior law or contravened the Federal Constitution. It was a curious example of a doubly unconstitutional condition, operative at two levels. The original grant of federal funds for public housing imposed on local authorities the unconstitutional obligation of attaching the affidavit to their applications. When project managers did as federal law bade them, their act of requiring applicants and tenants to sign the oath was an equally unconstitutional exaction at the "retail" level.

Political activity and public housing have recently collided in a different context. Tenants who organize or head militant organizations within the project to press collective grievances against the management have been subjected to harassment and eviction with increasing frequency. Since the activity in which they are engaged is constitutionally protected in most instances, this trend has grave implications. Two recent cases illustrate contrasting approaches to the phenomenon of tenant militancy.

Curtis Holt and his wife resided at the Creighton Court project in Richmond, Virginia. In 1958, he organized the Creighton Court Civic Association and served as its first president. That position gave him power to speak for his fellow tenants in project matters; but the Authority persistently refused to deal with him on a representative basis and advised that they would talk only with individual tenants about their own grievances. Holt then sought to hold civic meetings in the project's Community Center, a building administered by the Department of Parks and Recreation, rather than the Housing Authority. When use of that facility was denied, Holt moved the meetings to a nearby Baptist church.

Increasing differences between Holt and the Authority culminated in letters which he sent to the federal Public Housing Administration and to the Mayor of Richmond, protesting the suppression of the Civic Association's activities. The federal agency referred the matter to the local Housing Authority; the Mayor requested a report from Authority officials.

Eventually, Holt and his wife received a notice terminating their tenancy. There were several rather tenuous grounds given for the eviction—for example, lack of candor in reporting income Holt had earned cutting the hair of fellow tenants and painting apartments of several neighbors. But when Holt brought suit for reinstatement, the real reason for his eviction was acknowledged: "The court finds that Mr. Holt was given a notice of termination because he was president of the Civic Association. He was treated differently from other tenants. His lease was terminated because he was organizing the tenants, because he was exercising his First Amendment rights of freedom of speech and assembly." Observing that "a tenant's continued occupancy in a public housing project cannot be conditioned upon the tenant's foregoing his constitutional rights," the court enjoined the eviction. The First Amendment liberties of Holt and his fellow tenants to organize, to hold meetings, and to discuss common grievances against the Authority and to seek collective bargaining or negotiation with the Authority were too clearly entitled to legal protection "to be frittered away under the guise of breach of contract based upon an ex parte computation of income attributed to haircutting."

Tenant leaders also incurred official wrath in the River Oaks Project in Sacramento, California. Two tenants, Ray Ortiz and Elton Field, received unexplained eviction notices, which they claimed were in response to their political activities in the project.

Some time before, Field and Ortiz had been instrumental in organizing a Steering Committee which petitioned the Housing Authority for a review of the tenants' grievances. After one member of the Authority stated he was not interested in hearing from a "bunch of rabblerousers," the Steering Committee had met again and decided to present a formal petition to the Authority, to the candidates for the City Council, and to all members of the Neighborhood Council who resided in the project. A questionnaire was simultaneously circulated to City Council candidates seeking their views on the grievances pressed by the tenants. Ortiz and Field were co-chairmen of the petition and questionnaire campaign. During the next month they received their notices of termination.

Both men brought suit in the State Superior Court alleging that "we are being evicted to punish us and to bring to an end our activities with the River Oaks Housing Committee." But the court deferred consideration of the merits until the Authority stated the reason for its action. Where tenants had met the initial criteria for admission, and their status had not subsequently changed, the court held the Authority could terminate a lease only on valid grounds reasonably related to the purposes of the Housing Act. The Authority must first serve upon its tenants a notice specifying the reason, or citing a violation of the lease and giving them an opportunity to respond. Only when the reason for the eviction was made clear could the court determine whether the tenant's constitutional rights had been infringed.

The United States Supreme Court handled its first public housing case in much the same way. The case began when an eight-year tenancy was terminated the morning after Mrs. Joyce Thorpe was elected president of a tenants' council in Durham, North Carolina. The state courts held the Authority need give no reasons for its action, and thus did not reach the lurking constitutional issue. Before the case reached the Supreme Court, the U.S. Department of Housing and Urban Development issued a circular which decreed that "no tenant be given notice to vacate without being told by the local authority . . . the reasons for the eviction, and given an opportunity to make such reply or explanation as he may wish."

On this basis, the Supreme Court sent the case back to the state court to determine whether the HUD circular was applicable to a case that preceded its issuance. The North Carolina court reaffirmed its original holding that the circular was not retroactive. The Supreme Court took a different view, however, after examining the background and objectives of the HUD directive. Not only was the circular retroactive, it was mandatory on all local housing agencies, where its predecessor had been discretionary. The Court thus sent the case back to North Carolina, declining to go further than the narrow question presented to it. Any consideration of the *merits* of Mrs. Thorpe's eviction would be premature until the *reasons* were stated.

When the Thorpe case was first before the Supreme Court, only Mr. Justice Douglas publicly expressed concern about the constitutional dimension. While urging that the Authority must give reasons for terminating the lease, and that the only reason which could be given to Mrs. Thorpe was her political activities, Justice Douglas stressed the relevance of the doctrine of unconstitutional conditions: "The recipient of a government benefit, be it a tax exemption . . . or a home in a public housing project, cannot be made to forfeit the benefit because he exercises a constitutional right. [As in other areas in which conditions imposed had been found unconstitutional], no more can a tenant in a public housing project be evicted for the exercise of her right of association, a right protected by the First and Fourteenth Amendments."

Mr. Justice Douglas acknowledged that a tenant's political activities might become so disruptive or so subversive of the welfare of the project that sanctions might be warranted: "A tenant may be evicted if it is shown that he is destroying the fixtures, defacing the walls, disturbing other tenants by boisterous conduct and for a number of other reasons which impair the successful operation of the housing project. Eviction for such reasons will completely protect the viability of the housing project without making the tenant a serf who has a home at the pleasure of the manager of the project or the housing authority."

It is conceivable, therefore, that a tenant's organizing efforts could disrupt the project or threaten destruction of its property to the point where punishment would be warranted. Suppose, for example, that the president of the tenants' association incited his aggrieved colleagues to smash and destroy the elevators or the basement washing machines in protest against failure to make regular repairs. Or suppose a sit-in organized by the association made access to and exit from the lobby impossible for other tenants. Such actions as these would presumably warrant some form of discipline by the Authority officials. Yet eviction is certainly not the only possible penalty, nor even the best one. There has been no attempt in the literature of public housing to formulate penalties less drastic than termination of the lease. If physical destruction of property results from a single incident of violence or irresponsibility, would not restitution be far more appropriate than termination? Or could not the offending tenant be denied access to common facilities within the project for a probationary term reflecting the gravity of his offense? And if a tenant is placed on probation for such offenses, could it not be made clear that a subsequent or repeated offense would probably result in eviction even though that was too harsh a punishment for a first offense? Imaginative examination of the range of available sanctions in public housing might substantially improve the entire regulatory process.

VI. *Racial Segregation in Public Housing*

Whatever the causes, there can be little doubt of the extent of racial segregation in public housing. Consider these statistics gathered in the spring of 1965: of all projects under the Public

Housing Administration, 1,213 were all white, 942 were all Negro, and 852 were integrated. Thus, nearly three quarters of the federally assisted projects were completely segregated.

The causes of segregation are many and complex. Although the Public Housing Administration has long since abandoned reliance upon race as a criterion, racial separation was a tacit policy in some areas during the early days of public housing; indeed, the Public Housing Authority deliberately encouraged segregation in some cities. Other federal agencies contributed to creation of urban ghettos. Until the late 1940s, the Underwriting Manual of the Federal Housing Administration suggested that appraisals of residential properties should be diminished by "inharmonious racial or nationality groupings . . . often to the point of rejection." Moreover, "private developers who proposed to build for interracial occupancy were treated to a variety of delaying and obstructing tactics" by FHA. The President's Commission on Civil Disorders has observed that "federal programs also have done little to prevent the growth of racially segregated suburbs around our cities. Until 1949, FHA official policy was to refuse to insure [loans for] any unsegregated housing. It was not until . . . 1962 that the Agency required nondiscrimination pledges from loan applicants."

The principal blame for creating and perpetuating segregation lies, however, at the local level. Because the Public Housing Act placed primary responsibility for the administration of the program in the hands of local authorities, projects tended often to reflect segregated living patterns in the communities in which they were constructed. Typically selection of sites involved building one project in an already predominantly black neighborhood and one in an already white neighborhood. Until 1954, of course, governmental maintenance of "separate but equal" facilities was presumably compatible with the Federal Constitution. Save for a few state court decisions banning segregated public housing, these policies went virtually unchallenged for thirty years.

Segregation in the public housing projects of the urban core areas persisted largely because alternatives or routes of escape were wholly lacking. Professor Lawrence M. Friedman notes: "Public housing is, by and large, located in Negro areas and is inhabited by Negroes . . . the granting of formal rights to Negroes to demand desegregated projects would be meaningless in many cities, not because no real abuses exist, but because the problem is so basic that only a radical solution can remedy the matter; rights are not enough." Nor has escape to the suburbs (either integrated or segregated) been feasible until recently. Thus, the racial concentration and isolation—particularly of nonwhites—has steadily increased in the huge projects of the Northern and Midwestern cities. Given the deliberate choice of location and the predictable policies of administration, one should not expect to find even a single white family, for example, in Chicago's Robert R. Taylor homes—acknowledged by officials as an "all Negro city within a city" and cynically nicknamed the "Congo Hilton" by its completely black tenant body.

There is little point in speculating at length how public housing came to be as acutely segregated as it is. The current and urgent need is for solutions, for ways of restoring some degree of racial balance. If present public housing trends continue, warns the Commission on Civil Disorders, ghetto concentration of nonwhites in the central city, and their consequent isolation from the white community, will steadily increase: "This can only continue to compound the conditions of failure and hopelessness which lead to crime, civil disorder and social disorganization."

Since 1962, some tools have been forged to meet that challenge. One year to the day before his assassination, President John F. Kennedy issued an Executive Order on Equal Opportunity in Housing. That directive took the first significant step toward ending discrimination and segregation in federally assisted housing—a step which the Congress appeared reluctant to initiate. The order banned discrimination on ground of race, color, creed, or national origin in the sale, leasing, or rental of federally assisted residential property. The order applied only to future transactions, which substantially narrowed its impact. But each appropriate federal agency was directed to use its good offices and take other suitable action, including the institution of lawsuits "to promote the abandonment of discriminatory practices" in regard to contracts entered into *prior* to the date of issuance. There was considerable dispute among lawyers as to whether the order exercised the full range of available federal power. It was argued, for example, that the Executive branch could have brought its extensive regulatory power over banks and other lending institutions to bear on the task of ending housing discrimination.

The order did, however, contain workable machinery for its own enforcement. If it found the order had been violated, any federal agency might terminate an agreement or contract with the offending party or refuse to extend further aid to any uncooperative lending institution. To bolster enforcement, the President created a Committee on Equal Opportunity in Housing—an interagency task force charged with gathering information, issuing pertinent regulations, and informally seeking to bring about compliance with the order by working with public and private agencies and contractors.

Most of the coverage of the Executive Order was superseded by the Civil Rights Act of 1964. Title VI of that law banned discrimination in federally assisted programs regardless of the date of the agreement. Thus pre-1962 as well as later public housing projects were now covered. Each federal agency was required to issue its own regulations for insuring compliance with Title VI. The Public Housing Administration has issued a set of such regulations which presuppose the power to end all discrimination in federally aided public housing, a matter which had remained in doubt under the Executive Order.

Despite the apparently ample authority that has existed since 1964, actual progress in breaking down the racial insularity of public housing has been slow and discouraging. For a while, the Public Housing Administration relied chiefly upon its "free choice plan." Under that arrangement, applicants for public housing were permitted to choose any project in which they wished to live; no tenant would be placed in a project he termed unacceptable. But against the background of governmentally approved or condoned segregation, such "free choice" may really be no choice at all. The concentration of public housing in or near the urban core may already have become a virtually irreversible trend in many cities.

After years of reluctance and hesitation, the federal courts have now begun to review claims of discriminatory site selection. The key case had been before the district court in Chicago for nearly three years until, in February 1969, the judge held that the city Housing Authority had acted unconstitutionally by maintaining racial quotas in many projects and by consistently locating new projects in predominantly black neighborhoods after rejecting available sites in predominantly white areas. The proof to support these two conclusions had taken years to compile. There were no simple statements, city council resolutions, or Housing Authority directives revealing discriminatory motives or a design to perpetuate segregation. Yet the practice of the Authority over the years convinced the court of the invalidity of its site selection policies. The judge concluded that "the statistics on the family housing sites . . . show a very high probability, a near certainty, that many sites were vetoed on the basis of the racial composition of the site's neighborhood." This sufficed to find a constitutional violation.

Several months later a federal district court in New Orleans reached a similar conclusion. While persistent location of new projects in black areas did not conclusively establish a discriminatory motive or a design to perpetuate segregation, the district judge held it did create a very strong presumption in that direction. The presumption might be rebutted if, for example, the Housing Authority could prove that no other acceptable sites were available. But that burden is an exceedingly difficult one to meet, and neither the Chicago nor the Louisiana housing officials have come close. The pattern of public housing throughout the United States suggests, moreover, that a great many such suits will be filed and will result in similar judgments. In time—and it may be a very long time— the intervention of the federal courts may bring about the realignment of public housing patterns that administrative policies have thus far failed to effect.

Quite apart from these judicial developments, the Public Housing Administration has voluntarily sought to end *de facto* segregation. Some months before the decision in the Chicago case, a new regulation was added to the *Low Rent Housing Manual:* "Any proposal to locate housing only in areas of racial concentration will be *prima facie* unacceptable and will be returned to the local Authority for further consideration . . ." Then in July 1967 the Department of Housing and Urban Development finally abandoned the "free choice" approach—taking its "most significant step so far to end discrimination in its public housing program."

The new order required local housing authorities to undertake affirmatively to reduce segregation by pursuing one of three policies. The most stringent was a requirement that applicants accept any vacancy in the city's housing projects as it became available or be moved immediately to the bottom of the waiting list. The mildest alternative would allow cities to retain existing tenant assignment procedures if they could prove to HUD that "substantial desegregation" of public housing had resulted. At the local level, New York City's Housing Authority took a major step the following spring by requiring all units to foster racial and ethnic integration through appropriate "affirmative action." Particular emphasis was to be placed upon tenant selection procedures for filling vacancies after completion of the initial tenant roster.

Whether these approaches will work where less drastic methods have failed, of course, remains to be seen. But it is increasingly clear, at national and local levels alike, that passive or permissive policies will do little to bring about desegregation of occupied projects, or to prevent total racial homogeneity in new projects. Only bold affirmative requirements seem to stand any chance of success.

Experience suggests practical responses to this demand. Some modest success has already been realized in Chicago and several other cities through the use of "vest pocket" public housing scattered in small clusters throughout the city. The Commission on Civil Disorders stressed the feasibility of reversing the trend toward "ghettoization" of public housing by focusing new programs on nonghetto areas: "Public housing programs should emphasize scattered site construction; rent supplements should, wherever possible, be used in nonghetto areas, and an intensive effort should be made to recruit below-market interest rate sponsors willing to build outside the ghettos."

VII. *The Tenant's Right to Notice and a Hearing*

The applicant who is told why his application is being rejected, or the tenant who is given reasons for his eviction, is the exception rather than the rule. Far more common is rejection or eviction unaccompanied by any explanation on the Authority's part. Existing statutes and regulations seldom require that any reasons be given, and project managers typically provide no more information than necessary. Yet effective court review of an adverse decision is available only when the applicant or tenant knows its basis. To file a complaint when no grounds can be cited is rather like trying to punch one's way out of a paper bag. Internal appeals are occasionally provided for the tenant threatened with eviction—though not

244 THE PRICE OF DEPENDENCY

to the disappointed applicant—but such recourse is seldom adequate even where it does exist. The New York City appeal procedure, for example, does not guarantee the tenant any specific information about his alleged infractions, nor an opportunity to confront his accusers or discover the sources of the charges against him.

The starting point must be to appreciate the effect of an eviction upon the tenant; there is no point talking about court review if the nature of the injury is not understood. The consequences for the tenant who is expelled, and for his family, should be obvious. A *Yale Law Journal* Note recounts them: "Suddenly ejected from one home with little or no time to find another, they suffer materially and emotionally. Loss of sanctuary and familiar surroundings, coupled with a feeling of helplessness against the dispossessor, make an eviction—especially an unjust one—a painful, sometimes traumatic experience. In relocating, the ousted tenant usually finds that he must pay more rent for less housing—frequently for substandard housing." But injury is not confined to the immediate victim. Other tenants cannot fail to take a lesson from the plight of their neighbors. Used arbitrarily, the power to evict, concludes the Yale Note, "can create a hostile, bitter atmosphere in a housing project. Tenants, made to feel insecure, begin to distrust each other as well as project officials. Any sense of community within the project atrophies; families keep to their units or form small antagonistic cliques."

Despite the damage done to the evicted tenant and to his neighbors, few courts have even questioned the manager's power to evict summarily. The earlier cases simply termed public housing a "privilege" which could be withdrawn or denied as readily as it could be extended, and with no need to explain the adverse decision. Later the courts relied chiefly on the transient character of the typical month-to-month tenancy. Under this arrangement, either party can terminate for any reason on thirty days' notice; in practice, however, the absence of a lease redounds largely to the Authority's advantage, rather than to the tenant's. Thus the courts have tended to treat the public housing management like any private landlord, who may terminate a tenancy on one month's notice when no lease exists. The governmental aspect of the relationship has been almost wholly overlooked.

Examples of this callous judicial nonintervention are legion.

In the case of the Durham tenants' council leader who received her notice the morning after her election, the North Carolina courts found it "immaterial what may have been the reason for the [Authority's] unwillingness to continue the relationship of landlord and tenant, after the expiration of the term as provided in the lease." A Pennsylvania court similarly spurned an evicted tenant's plea for a chance to contest the unstated charges against him. If reasons had to be given before terminating a tenancy, warned the court, that would "place an unreasonable restraint upon the [Authority's] powers and make it impossible for it to carry out the policies declared by the legislature." In what may be the most extreme recent case of this sort, a federal court of appeals refused to stay an eviction by the Newark Housing Authority, even though the tenant had strong grounds for a civil damage suit against the Authority. Obviously a damage claim is small solace to a penniless family that finds itself out on the streets.

Three recent developments seem to have reversed the trend of judicial indifference to the tenant's procedural interests. A federal court of appeals has sharply criticized the New York Housing Authority's failure to promulgate standards for selecting among applicants. (Applications typically exceed available accommodations by about ten to one.) The court warned that "the existence of an absolute and uncontrolled discretion in an agency of government vested with the administration of a vast program, such as public housing, would be an intolerable invitation to abuse. . . . Due process requires that selection among applicants be made in accordance with 'ascertainable standards' and in cases where many candidates are equally qualified under these standards, that further selections be made in some reasonable manner such as 'by lot or on the basis of the chronological order of application.' "

The second promising reform has been imposed by the New York state courts. Henceforth, it has been held, reasons must be given for the eviction of a tenant, and they must be constitutionally valid reasons. Since the public housing project "is not an ordinary landlord, nor its lessees ordinary tenants," special obligations inhere in the relationship. State housing laws, moreover, manifest an intent that tenants once admitted to a project should be allowed to remain unless they violate "reasonable regulations" of the Authority.

Only the duty to give reasons, concluded the court, would afford any real protection against eviction on improper grounds, or at the whim of the manager. Although New York law did not require that reasons be given, and other courts had declined to demand them, this court felt that whatever inconvenience the Authority might suffer from having to justify an eviction would be greatly outweighed by the value of such a safeguard to the tenant: "If in fact a mistake has been made in the accusation against the tenant of improper conduct or a violation of regulations, or if the reason for the ouster has no better basis than dislike or unjustified discipline, the requirement of the disclosure of the ground for the termination of the lease affords the tenant the opportunity to protest its exercise."

The other promising change has been the tightening of procedures by the federal agencies that provide funds for public housing. In 1954, the Administration concurred with the deferential attitude of the courts: "It is . . . suggested that all future notices to quit cite only the provision of the lease which permits termination within a specified time without reference to any other provision." Twelve years later, the federal agency urged a substantial shift in local policy because of "growing opposition and challenge" to the practice of "simply giving the statutory notice without stating the reason or reasons therefor." Accordingly, it was urged "as a matter of good social policy" that local authorities should hold a private conference to inform the tenant of the reasons for a termination notice.

Ten months later, the Administration moved to a much harder line: "Within the past year, increasing dissatisfaction has been expressed with eviction practices in public low-rent housing projects. . . . Since this is a federally assisted program, we believe it is essential that no tenant be given notice to vacate without being told by the local authority in a private conference or other appropriate manner the reasons for the eviction, and given an opportunity to make such reply or explanation as he may wish." In addition, the local housing authority must now keep detailed and accurate records of all terminations and evictions with reference to the appropriate reasons. Such records were to be available for inspection by HUD officials. The much firmer tone of this 1967 circular was as important as its words. Where the Administration had previously relied upon entreaties and suggestions to local officials, the new policy seemed to demand of every federally assisted project certain procedural guarantees for their tenants.

The December 1968 HUD directive codified the earlier rulings and added further safeguards, particularly for the applicant. Local authorities are now required to establish policies whereby (1) only essential information will be asked of an applicant; (2) applicants and tenants will be "treated with courtesy and consideration at all times"; (3) applicants and tenants will be the primary sources for needed information, and will be asked to produce only those documents that can be obtained without long delay or heavy expense; and (4) applicants will within a reasonable time receive "the most accurate and factual information possible concerning their status. . . ."

Nothing in these directives requires a hearing before a tenant can be evicted. But one federal court in New Orleans has taken an important step toward such a requirement. Noting the concern courts have recently shown for other government beneficiaries, the judge concluded it was anomalous to allow a tenant to be expelled from the project without procedural safeguards. "Public housing should not," he acknowledged, "be permitted to become a refuge for those who can not or will not adhere to the minimum rules required for man to live decently in community with his fellow man." Yet, like other officials dispensing government benefits, "those who manage public housing must adhere to elementary standards of fairness . . . Every public tenant, however disorderly, evil, or malevolent, is entitled to due process before he is evicted." The court stopped short of defining "elementary standards of fairness" in this context; the Housing Authority had already proposed a procedure satisfactory to the tenant, so there was no need to go further.

In the absence of any clear holdings on the point, it is worth speculating about the constitutional basis for a hearing. It must be recalled that the issue typically arises under the month-to-month arrangement as a "refusal to renew" rather than a "withdrawal" or "cancellation" of a continuing relationship. Eviction more closely resembles a decision not to extend the contract of a nontenure employee than a dismissal or discharge of a tenured employee.

Realistically, however, the period of mutual obligation is clearly longer than one month. Public housing tenants are hardly comparable to seasonal or temporary workers. The month-to-month arrangement, while occasionally beneficial to the tenant, might well be viewed as a unilateral option designed to give the authority maximum flexibility while affording the tenant neither concomitant protection nor the option of enhancing his security by negotiating a lease. On this basis, the arguments for a hearing prior to termination gain some strength by analogy to other fields of government benefits.

A rather elaborate hearing is now required, as we have seen, before expelling or even suspending a student at a publicly supported college or university. Tenancy in a public housing project and attendance at a state university are both benefits of very substantial value to the recipient; the public housing tenant is typically as anxious to keep his place as the state university student is to earn his degree. Accordingly, the premises (now universally accepted by the courts) that support the student's constitutional claim to a hearing before expulsion should also protect a tenant from summary eviction.

Moreover, if the housing authority must give reasons and if those reasons can be held up to constitutional scrutiny both in the administrative hearing and in court, then the authority's power to suppress or punish constitutionally protected activities, particularly of a political nature, will be sharply curtailed. Such protections for the tenant would thus end the anomaly which allows public housing tenants charged only with "nondesirability" to be evicted without even the safeguards available to residents in privately owned housing.

No measure of insistence on fair procedures will eliminate the second class status of public housing tenants. Many of the indignities they suffer do not violate their constitutional rights, and probably would never be overturned by a court. Yet the restrictions which cause them are demeaning and humiliating.

In the state of cold war that often prevails between tenants and managers, oppressive or silly rules and rigid, bureaucratic enforcement of reasonable rules are all too frequent. There is no ready legal remedy for the New Orleans Housing Authority that tried to evict a blind tenant because his ownership of a seeing-eye dog violated a blanket rule against pets in the project. Nor is there any obvious protection from the common rule against housing overnight guests in public housing units—"a galling reminder to [tenants] not to make themselves too much at home. . . ." Nor is there any constitutional violation in the common prohibition against conducting business or income-producing activity in public housing units, or hosting "quarter parties" at which each guest pays twenty-five cents for his share of food and drink. Such indignities and impositions, and many others like them, may be wholly beyond judicial review. But if the reasons for eviction and the regulations underlying those reasons can be forced into the open for public scrutiny, there is a good chance that a new level of humanity and sensitivity may find its way into public housing administration.

VIII. *Relief from Substandard Living Conditions*

If the plaster is falling off the walls, or the elevators don't work half the time, or the basement is infested with rats, does the public housing tenant have any alternative but to return to the old tenement where conditions are even worse? The formation of militant tenants' unions constitutes one increasingly effective form of redress—although its viability depends, as we have seen, upon legal protection against the eviction of tenant leaders. Beyond political pressure and self-help, what legal remedies exist?

The governing federal statutes require the local housing authority to maintain projects "in good repair, order, and condition." If the manager fails to do so, federal officials can inspect the premises and order remedial steps. A tenants' group in San Francisco brought a suit to enforce this obligation when, they claimed, the responsible federal agency had taken no action against premises that "are infested with rats, cockroaches, and other vermin, and buildings [that are] crumbling, need paint, leak, and lack heat." However accurate the charges, the court concluded that private citizens could compel neither the federal nor the local officials to carry out these obligations; the laws simply created no private rights or remedies.

The other possible recourse available to aggrieved tenants is to withhold rent until the repairs have been made. Several states have passed "rent strike" laws relieving tenants of their legal duty to pay rent until violations of the housing codes have been remedied—and providing a defense against eviction for nonpayment while the conditions persist. Other states allow the tenant to use the rent money to make the needed repairs on his own. The most difficult question is whether such laws apply to public housing. New York's rent strike law, which is perhaps the most sweeping of such statutes, specifically exempts public housing from its coverage.

Thus it has been possible to "break" rent strikes in public projects by threatening eviction for nonpayment of rent. This sanction was used in the fall of 1968 against a group of low-income tenants in a Bronx project who had withheld rent to protest a rising crime rate in the project and the management's failure to take adequate corrective measures. Clearly the rent strike affords public housing tenants an effective remedy against substandard conditions only if it is available on the same basis on which it is available to tenants in private housing.

A more promising approach is suggested by a law recently enacted in Michigan and signed by Governor George Romney just before he became Secretary of Housing and Urban Development. The law creates a board of tenants' affairs for public housing in Detroit. Half the board will consist of public housing tenants, and half of city appointees, with half the latter group drawn from the project neighborhood. The board has power to veto rules and regulations of the local housing commission. It also acts as a binding board of review on decisions made by the housing commission on such matters as evictions and rent increases. Clearly this law shifts a substantial power of government into the hands of the governed. It also represents a high degree of decentralization. Other cities will be watching closely to see whether Detroit has found an answer to the rising tensions between housing project managers and their tenants over many issues that cannot be satisfactorily resolved by the courts, even though they often end up there.

IX

PUBLIC WELFARE

AND

PRIVATE RIGHTS

I. *"A Second-Rate Set of Social Services"*

Welfare is the classic form of government benefit. It is welfare that draws the pejorative epithets about government benefits— "handout," "dole," "feeding at the public trough," and so on. Those who receive welfare seldom like the system upon which they are dependent; those whose tax payments support the system are not happy with it either. Yet welfare is undoubtedly the oldest form of government benefit, and probably the least easily abolished. The Roman dole, the Elizabethan poor laws, and nineteenth-century almshouses were adopted and perpetuated not because they were politically popular but because they were a necessary governmental service.

Although welfare programs in the United States are by no means new, the substantial involvement of the Federal Government in public assistance dates from 1935. Since the enactment of the Social Security Act as a depression-relief measure, the federal commitment to welfare has grown steadily and substantially. Even as unemployment has declined to near-record low levels, welfare rolls have risen; some ten million Americans now receive benefits from various relief programs.

Along with the growth in welfare programs, there has come mounting criticism of the system. The earliest critics were the spokesmen and leaders of the poor, men like the late Reverend Martin

Luther King, Jr., or Senator Robert Kennedy who called the American welfare program a "system of handouts, a second-rate set of social services which damages and demeans its recipients," and warned that unless radical changes were made soon, "the results could be the ripping asunder of the already thin fabric of American life."

Gradually the Establishment came to share this view of the welfare system—partly out of the same concern for the plight of the beneficiaries, but partly also because of the staggering costs of running a program that clearly did not satisfy those at whom it was directed. During the 1968 Presidential campaign, all the major candidates had something harsh to say about welfare; they differed only in their prescriptions for its overhaul. It was the conservative Republican Coordinating Committee that pronounced the welfare program an "ugly crisis of failure" and warned that "the creaking welfare system is daily wasting talents and funds and reducing the motivation of welfare families."

Against this background, it was hardly surprising that President Nixon chose the welfare system as the subject of his first major address on domestic policy. But the strength of his language was striking and brought home to many middle-class listeners a first realization of the pervasive dissatisfaction with welfare as it existed in the summer of 1969.

"Whether measured by the anguish of the poor themselves," said Nixon, "or by the drastically mounting burden on the taxpayer, the present welfare system has to be judged a colossal failure. . . . The tragedy is not only that it is bringing states and cities to the brink of financial disaster, but also that it is failing to meet the elementary human, social and financial needs of the poor." Two or three years earlier, this view would have been thought radical in many quarters; by fall of 1969, though, there was hardly a point on the political spectrum at which it was not shared.

Why such universal dissatisfaction with a system that had such laudable motives? The shortcomings of the American welfare program are not difficult to identify. First, there is a substantial and growing gap between assistance actually provided and the number of persons who need help from government. The President's Commission on Civil Disorders found in 1968 that current welfare policies "exclude large numbers of persons who are in great need and who, if provided a decent level of support, might be able to become productive and self-sufficient." Recent governmental estimates show that the number of persons actually receiving assistance is about one quarter of those with family incomes below the poverty line and not more than half of those actually eligible for benefits under present federal law.

There are several reasons why welfare misses so many who are truly needy. The greatest gap results from the exclusion from most welfare programs of the "working poor"—those who are employed, at least part of the time, but earn so little that they fall continually below the poverty line. It is this group that would benefit most directly from the welfare proposals offered by President Nixon in August 1969. These proposals begin by replacing the present program of Aid to Families with Dependent Children (effectively restricted to fatherless, jobless homes) with a more comprehensive program of family assistance, available to poor families regardless of employment status.

In addition to those who are needy but ineligible, there are many families who are eligible but do not seek welfare. The causes of their reticence are varied and complex. But there is one central fact about welfare that goes far to explain why many do not apply for payments to which they are entitled. Shortly before his assassination, Senator Robert Kennedy charged the welfare system with creating "a dependence on their fellow citizens that is degrading and distasteful to giver and receiver alike." Columnist Joseph Alsop argues that "the worst of the trap-producing elements in the welfare system is the simple fact that welfare clients automatically cease to be free citizens. They become 'cases' to be handled by caseworkers. They are reduced to the status of peccant children to be watched over by public governesses."

Surveys indicate that resentment of the system and its administration is widespread among welfare beneficiaries. A comprehensive study conducted in New York, including white, black, and Puerto Rican mothers receiving Aid to Families with Dependent Children, showed that 70 to 80 percent of recipients resented welfare investigations; between 30 and 40 percent were actually "ashamed" or "insulted" by inquiries that were considered routine by welfare administrators.

There is evidence, moreover, that welfare families are sometimes marked or segregated by being treated differently from other citizens—a form of discrimination that compounds the resentment. In several schools in New York City, welfare children receiving free lunches are said to be forced to stand aside while "paying" children go through the line first. During the same hearing at which this fact emerged (before the President's Commission on Income Maintenance Programs), a welfare mother complained: "Where I live children feel the stigma of being welfare recipients. A mother can't get her teen-age sons to pick up surplus food; they'd rather go hungry than let the neighbors know they're on welfare."

The welfare system has created serious inequalities within as well as without. There is a wide disparity of benefit levels provided to citizens of different states. Even though the Federal Government furnishes more than half the total budget for Aid to Families with Dependent Children, average monthly payments range from $9.30 per person in Mississippi to $62.55 in New York. For general assistance programs, average monthly payments run from Oklahoma's low of $12.00 to New Jersey's high of $129.00. President Nixon, after citing these disparate figures in his welfare speech, concluded: "So great an inequality is wrong; no child is 'worth' more in one state than another. One result of this inequality is to lure thousands more into already overcrowded inner cities as unprepared for city life as they are for city jobs."

Existing welfare laws have also had a catastrophic effect upon family integrity and solidarity. Aid to Families with Dependent Children is typically denied to homes having an employed or employable father. Senator Robert Kennedy once observed that this policy "forces men to leave their families so that public assistance can be obtained. . . ." This effect is confirmed from within; a welfare mother in Cleveland told the Civil Rights Commission after the Hough riots in 1966:

> This requirement [of Aid to Families with Dependent Children] is how me and my husband got separated when he got out of his job and went to get help, and they refused to help. . . . This is one reason we separated and divorced. He couldn't see his kids go hungry, so he just left.

Finally, there is much in the welfare system that either breeds or condones inefficiency. Economist-columnist Sylvia Porter has lamented the fact that "we have mired our welfare system in a paper jungle of forms and files. Trained welfare workers are thereby condemned to clerical work and have little time to practice their trade." An experimental self-help program in the Bronx found its first-year appropriation nearly consumed by administrative costs; only 40 percent of the funds actually reached the poor for whom they were intended. A *New York Times* survey of the city's welfare programs has found the agencies so preoccupied with threats of fraud or cheating that there has grown up "an almost impenetrable array of forms, supervisors, federal and state regulations to prevent fraud. The result is that caseworkers freely admit they lie and connive to help their clients and fill in forms with false information to save time, or that clients are denied allowances they are entitled to by law."

Understandably, the malaise among welfare recipients has brought about a wave of protest. There has been a rapid rise in sit-ins and demonstrations at welfare agency offices, invasions and bitter clashes at professional social welfare meetings, and other forms of self-help. Concurrently there has been a less dramatic but probably more telling development—a spectacular rise of welfare litigation in the courts. "Despite the time-honored admonitions that one should not bite the hand that feeds him nor look a gift horse in the mouth," notes a *New York Times* reporter, "welfare clients are suddenly suing welfare officials at a record clip. Until . . . [1965], it was virtually unknown for a person on welfare to sue the officials who were paying his bed and board. But since that time in a number of test cases that have been brought in courts across the country, welfare recipients have challenged the way in which they are being treated by those who sign their relief checks."

Several factors explain this burst of welfare litigation. First, lawyers are available and willing to handle such cases as never before. Expansion of legal aid offices and creation of a number of new legal service programs—financed both by the Federal Government and by private foundations—have provided advocates for millions who can hardly prepare and argue their own cases. And the young attorneys who staff these offices have no inhibitions about suing benign agencies as well as repressive ones. It is now quite common to find a welfare lawsuit in which lawyers on both sides are paid by the Federal Government—one to administer the welfare program and the other to keep the administration fair and equitable.

Second, there has been a growing concern for the poor on the part of the United States Supreme Court. This concern—reflected initially in decisions expanding the right of the indigent criminal defendant—has filtered down to the lower courts.

Third, the Federal Government's war on poverty has at least focused national attention upon the plight of the indigent to an unprecedented degree. Fourth, the subject of "welfare law" has recently become a respectable topic of academic concern. Today, law students, teachers, and legal research experts are devoting to that field a kind of talent and energy heretofore reserved for more traditional civil rights and civil liberties problems. Finally, the legal status of disadvantaged and minority groups is seen increasingly in terms of nondiscriminatory access to means of support, whether through employment or through public assistance.

II. *What Is "Welfare" and Who Receives It?*

We have, up to this point, discussed the "welfare system" without defining it. To describe each of the constituent programs in sufficient detail for full understanding would require a chapter by itself. Perhaps it will suffice here to rely upon a brief summary provided by J. M. Wedemayer, former director of the California Department of Social Welfare: "The American welfare system can be described as a series of provisions in each state for: (1) federally aided public assistance to specified categories of needy people; these provisions are known generally as 'old age assistance,' 'aid to the blind,' 'aid to the disabled,' and 'aid to families with dependent children' (including since 1961, families in need because the parent is unemployed); (2) a residual program financed locally or by the state or in some combination called 'general assistance,' 'general relief,' or some similar designation; plus (3) associated programs such as 'child welfare,' special state categories (for example, California's aid to potentially self-supporting blind) and other local or state programs such as those for licensing facilities, for crippled children, probation service, vocational rehabilitation and the care of children and aged.

"The system is administered either by a state department or by local departments under the supervision of a state department. The degree of supervision over local operations may vary between fed-

erally aided programs and those established solely by the state. . . .
In a few states, General Assistance is administered completely separately from federally assisted programs." This account should
make clear the complexities and subtle distinctions that are masked
by use of the single comprehensive term "welfare." In this chapter
we shall not, however, attempt to identify particular programs or
draw fine distinctions. Often it will be clear to which program particular restrictions or conditions are attached. In other cases it will
make little or no difference. Most often we shall be dealing with the
program of assistance to families with dependent children, which
has been the source of much of the recent controversy. Analogies to
other programs can readily be drawn.

One further question deserves attention before we examine
specific constitutional issues. Who are the welfare recipients? What
is known about those who seek and receive benefits? The sharp increases in the welfare rolls have come disproportionately in aid for
families with dependent children. (In fact, the number of welfare
claimants in some categories—old age assistance, for example—
has actually been declining in recent years.) The rising caseload in
this category is attributable very largely to minority groups. In New
York State, for example, there are roughly five times as many Negroes and Puerto Ricans receiving AFDC as there are in the total
population. For youths reaching age eighteen, approximately one
white child in ten has at some time been supported by AFDC. For
nonwhites, the comparable figure is six children in ten.

To what extent are welfare beneficiaries "lazy people who
have chosen the easy alternative to honest work"? Surveys show
that the vast majority of recipients are simply not readily employable. Of the 600,000 New Yorkers on the welfare rolls, 79 percent
are children and adults caring for children, and 15 percent are persons unable to support themselves because of age, sickness, or disability. Only 2,600 men of the entire group "have enough occupation ability to move into employment without considerable training
and rehabilitation."

Of the more than seven million persons on welfare, federal
officials estimate that no more than 50,000 are "capable of being
given job skills and training that will make them self-sufficient."
Thus fewer than 1 percent of the total welfare pool appear capable
of getting off the relief rolls through their own efforts. Yet many
mothers of dependent children seem to be willing to work if suitable

jobs could be found. A poll conducted by the City University of New York disclosed that nearly 70 percent of welfare mothers would prefer gainful employment to staying at home, but lacked information about job opportunities.

For the employable men on welfare, the prospects of eventual self-sufficiency are good. In Erie County (Buffalo), New York, for example, 80 percent of the able-bodied male recipients were back to work and off welfare within a three-year period. But three fourths of the county's welfare cases were too old, too young, or too sick to accept employment.

The prognosis for mothers of dependent children is far less hopeful. Only 8 percent of the mothers on welfare in New York City in the spring of 1966 were off the rolls a year later. (Where both father and mother were present in the home, the rate of re-employment was substantially higher—18 percent—during the same period.) About 15 percent of the welfare mothers in New York are "second generation beneficiaries," at least one of whose parents had been on welfare. And nearly half the 1968 recipients had first applied for welfare before 1960 (although not all had been on the rolls continuously since that time).

There may be significant geographic and ethnic variations in welfare dependency. In sharp contrast to the New York experience is a survey of predominantly Mexican-American welfare recipients in Northern California. Three fifths of those interviewed were seeking welfare for the first time. They regarded public assistance as a temporary bridge between regular jobs. For most, the expectation was accurate; roughly half the sample drew total benefits of less than $100 after their applications were cleared.

What are the long-range prospects for the welfare caseload, in both size and composition? After a career of studying American public assistance, Professor Eveline M. Burns of the Columbia University School of Social Work recently offered some projections: ". . . it is unlikely that the numbers currently in receipt of public assistance will substantially decline. . . . as the public at large becomes better off, there is a tendency to raise the income level which is regarded as being intolerable and denoting poverty or the need for public support.

"An increasingly large proportion of the current public assistance caseload consists of broken families. This very fact suggests that the mere improvement in economic conditions will not substantially reduce the assistance rolls. Only changes in behavior patterns will make much difference. But the problem of the growing number of families headed by a woman with no adequate support from a responsible male and where the woman's earning power is restricted by the claims of her children has so far resisted social diagnosis and prevention. . . . the out-of-wedlock birth is not a phenomenon peculiar to the poor. It occurs at all income levels, although its incidence is higher among the very poor and presumably reflects changing attitudes to sexual relationships and to the supposed shame associated with illegitimacy."

This summary of the welfare system and overview of its clientele provide the context within which to study the recent rash of lawsuits. Some attention must also be given to restrictions and conditions on welfare benefits that have not yet been brought to court. The first limitation we consider—the means test—is of that type. For decades, there have been attacks upon the means test in various forums, but it has been virtually impossible to launch against it a viable constitutional attack.

III. *The Means Test: "A Principle That Eats Like an Acid into the Homes of the Poor"*

Aneurin Bevan, the British Labour leader of the 1930s and 40s, thus characterized the means test a quarter century ago. The Labour Party was firmly committed to barring the use of a means test in the British Welfare State. When a financial standard of eligibility is applied, Bevan continued, "In the small rooms and around the meager tables of the poor, a hell of personal acrimony and wounded vanities arise."

Recent economic trends have brought a curious reversal of policy toward the means test. The British, facing a severe economic crisis, have seriously considered reviving strict financial eligibility standards. In the United States, by contrast, acceptance of the means test as a welfare criterion is being undermined for the first time. The current interest in the negative income tax and guaranteed annual income has drawn substantial momentum from recent concern about the intrusive and demeaning character of the means test.

The means test is traditionally justified as a necessary evil to determine eligibility. There must be some assurance that public assistance programs intended for the poor actually reach the poor. There must be checks against cheating, dishonesty, and misrepresentation. It is also said that the means test pries no more deeply into the applicant's personal life than does the federal or state income tax return.

The arguments against the means test do not reject these governmental interests. Instead, they stress the overriding importance of the welfare recipient's privacy and individual dignity. Fifteen years ago, Professors Jacobus ten Broek and Richard B. Wilson argued forcefully against the use of the means test. "Under it," they claimed, "the individual recipient soon loses control of his daily activities and the whole course and direction of his life. The capacity for self-direction presently atrophies and drops away. It is the welfare agency rather than the individual which decides what wants shall be taken into account. It is the welfare agency which decides what needs shall be budgeted. If the recipient does not live up to the conditions and do so with alacrity, he may be removed from the rolls or have his budget reduced. The alternatives are thus obedience or starvation. . . . With each new item budgeted or eliminated, with each new resource tracked down and evaluated, the social worker's influence increases. This is an inevitable concomitant of the means test. . . . Dignity is jeopardized by the initial investigation, by the searching inquiry into every intimate detail of need, living habits, family relations, by the setting up of a detailed budget of expenditures subject to repeated examination and review, by the continuously implied and often explicit threat that if behavior is uncooperative or unapproved, aid will be reduced or stopped . . . and finally, by the constant tendency of the whole system to push living standards down below a minimum of decency and health.

"Means test aid is fundamentally antithetical to the idea of equality. A system which makes so much depend upon a minute examination of every aspect of the individual's situation necessarily involves personalized judgments by officials and invites arbitrary and whimsical exercises of power. . . ."

The means test thus presents a continuing and corrosive threat to privacy in its most basic sense. While a single question by a social worker about a single item of income or particular expenditure obviously need not violate the client's constitutional interests, the cumulative effect may be as subversive of individual dignity as a violent physical intrusion. Moreover, it is the means test more than any other element of the welfare system that motivates physical and psychological invasions of the client's privacy—midnight raids, lie detector tests, detailed financial questionnaires, and the like. If the means test were no longer applied as a criterion for welfare recipients, the incentive to use many other objectionable practices might well disappear.

There are two other important objections to the means test. In many states, welfare applicants must show not only that their *incomes* fall below the poverty line, but that their total *assets* do not exceed a minimal level. In Connecticut, for example, a family seeking aid for dependent children may have no property (including even the cash value of life insurance) above $250. An AFDC applicant in Illinois may not keep assets in any form with a total value exceeding one month's assistance grant. Although these restrictions are most stringent in the Aid to Dependent Children program, they are found in some form in the welfare systems of every state.

The means test also has a stifling effect on efforts to escape the cycle of dependency. Since any income earned by the beneficiary or assets available to him must be used to meet his current needs, welfare payments are usually reduced by a corresponding amount. The effects on the beneficiary's initiative are predictable. As the Commission on Civil Disorders observed, the deduction of earnings or income from the welfare check "appears to have taken away from many recipients the incentive to seek part or full-time employment."

Several unsuccessful lawsuits have been brought against state laws that strip welfare beneficiaries of income and assets. A federal court in New York recently rejected a barrage of constitutional challenges to the statute requiring recipients to assign to the welfare department the proceeds of insurance policies, judgments for personal injuries, and certain claims to property that may materialize in the future. This procedure assumes that the beneficiary should eventually "repay" his benefactors if he becomes financially able to do so, and may thus be compelled to agree to repay by assigning such assets as a condition of welfare. Social workers argued before the court that such provisions deter some needy persons with modest assets from seeking welfare in the first place, and inhibit others from becoming self-sufficient by taking away their means of escape from dependency.

The majority of the court found no violations of the constitutional rights of welfare clients in the repayment obligation. But one of the three judges dissented. In his view, the state's interest in demanding repayment was substantially outweighed by the adverse effects on the beneficiary: ". . . the Constitution . . . does prohibit the State from placing obstacles in the path of efforts to become independent of welfare bounty or to maintain independence already achieved. The social benefit of public assistance would come to naught if this were not so."

Much attention has recently been given to the question of incentives (or lack of them) in the welfare system. Instead of docking a welfare recipient a dollar for every dollar he earns, New York City has sought to encourage employment by permitting some beneficiaries to keep their earnings up to $85 a month without jeopardizing their welfare checks. They may even earn above that figure, although the welfare payments will be reduced by two-thirds of the amount of additional wages.

President Nixon has now proposed that incentives of this sort should be built into the federal welfare program. Under his philosophy that "outside earnings [should] be encouraged, not discouraged," a worker could earn $60 a month with no loss of welfare payments; earnings above that figure would "cost" him fifty cents on the dollar in welfare. (The 1967 amendments to the Social Security Act included a very modest federal incentive arrangement, whereby working welfare clients could keep the first $30 a month, and one-third of any additional amounts.)

New York has tried to mitigate the corrosive effect of the means test in another way. The city's welfare commissioner recently announced the substitution of a simple affidavit of need for the old "time-consuming and degrading questionnaire" that probed assets and financial position in depth. The new form works rather like an income tax return. Fraud and cheating are to be curbed by spot checks of recipients. The change is intended to serve two purposes: first, to cut down needless paper work required by the old form, thus giving caseworkers more time "to give the help that clients really need"; second, the simpler form "will stop robbing clients of their sense of dignity and worth. It will say to them that we think they're responsible and valuable, and we can hope that it will make them feel that way, too."

Such simplifications do not, however, strike at the heart of the means test or alter the demeaning relationship it creates between caseworker and client. Nor do limited incentives afforded by earning-retention schemes ensure self-respect or self-sufficiency. "Even at best," comments *The New York Times,* they "are linked to the means test and other dehumanizing aspects of the old-line relief apparatus." It may well be that only a radical reform of the eligibility standards, such as that envisioned by the proponents of the guaranteed income or the negative income tax, will materially improve the second-class status of the welfare client.

The deepening concern about the means test has intensified interest in the guaranteed annual income, the flat welfare grant, and the negative income tax. There are numerous devices for simplification of welfare disbursements, of which these are the best known. Widespread support has developed for such alternatives—from conservative economist Milton Friedman, the original proponent of the negative income tax, to Senator Eugene McCarthy, who championed the guaranteed income during his 1968 Presidential campaign. To the extent these alternatives may furnish solutions for the dilemma of the means test, they deserve consideration here.

Some of the advantages of the income guarantee are obvious; others are subtler, and require close examination. Clearly the proposal has administrative virtues. By drastically simplifying the determination of eligibility, it would free social workers to provide much needed personal assistance and counseling rather than committing the bulk of their time to budgeting and investigation. Much of the reduced paper work load could be assumed by the Internal Revenue Service, which is already set up to perform this kind of task, leaving state and local agencies free for social service work. Such efficiencies would undoubtedly make the system much cheaper to administer on a per capita or per dollar basis than the cumbersome welfare system.

But the psychological and humanitarian advantages of the guaranteed income far exceed its purely administrative virtues. The elimination of the means test would be a most significant achievement, made possible by basing eligibility upon a simple statement of need, and relying on spot checks (as the income tax system does for other taxpayers) against fraud and concealment of income. The scrapping of the means test would presumably bring the abandonment of its most demeaning and corrosive concomitants, such as the midnight raid, the man-in-the-house rule, work requirements, and other offensive restrictions and conditions.

Basing eligibility on a simple statement of need would improve the beneficiary's morale, by transferring from the caseworker to him the essential decisions about family budgeting and purchases. Creation of a subsistence guarantee might also help to lift many of the chronically poor out of the depths. Under the present welfare system, argues Milton Friedman, "we are getting two kinds of people: those who are free, and those who are wards of the state and must do what the state says. On the negative income tax, some would choose not to try. That is part of the loss you take; but the proportion would be small and would decline."

These arguments—probably those of Friedman in particular—have been influential in shaping the Nixon administration's welfare program. The proposals presented to the country by the President on August 8, 1969, clearly do not go as far as a guaranteed income. But they do represent two important steps in that direction.

First, the Nixon proposals call for a uniform federal standard of welfare payments, at least uniform *minimum* levels, with the states free to provide higher benefits if they wish. The dollar amounts projected for the start of the new program are below those of many of the Northern industrial states, but substantially above the appallingly low benefit levels of most Southeastern and some border states. For the moment, the level at which uniformity is to be achieved is perhaps less important than the mere fact of equalization. Given the present crazy-quilt of welfare payments, and the extreme disparities, the installation of a federal floor is the first step.

Second, the new program would place that floor under the income of all families, whether or not the father lived in the home and regardless of whether he was employed. The heart of the new program is the elimination of the corrosive distinction between the unemployed poor—the beneficiaries of the present AFDC program—and the working poor, for whom general assistance has been typically unavailable.

There should be no misunderstanding on one point: these proposals do not call for a guaranteed annual income. The level of support envisioned by the Nixon administration program would be available only to employable heads of families actually working, or willing to work or accept job training—the latter to be provided by another part of the projected federal program. In Nixon's view, "a guaranteed income would undermine the incentive to work; the family assistance plan increases the incentives to work."

The critical question about the operation of this part of the program, of course, is who determines (and under what standards) when a person in financial need is unable to work or even to take job training. The proposals recognize there will be some such persons. Indeed, it specifically excludes mothers of preschool children. Beyond that limited group, no standards are provided for deciding when a person who is not physically disabled is nonetheless incapable of effective employment. In the absence of such standards, not only is the proposal no income guarantee; it may even constitute a kind of trap by which regressive local welfare agencies can deny aid to needy families because a parent refuses to accept training for a job he deems menial or degrading. The implementation of the program will have to be watched closely.

IV. *Residence Tests: Fencing Out the Needy*

In the summer of 1966, Mrs. Vivian Marie Thompson moved with her baby from Boston (where her husband had abandoned her) to Hartford, in order to live near her mother. In Boston, she and the child had been supported by Aid to Dependent Children payments from the city welfare department. By September, her name was removed from the Massachusetts welfare rolls since she had left the state. She sought assistance from the Connecticut welfare office. Her application met all the eligibility criteria save one: she had not resided in the state for the one-year period required of newcomers who had no visible means of support or a promise of a job immediately after arrival. (The Thompson family were in fact sustained from month to month by contributions from the Catholic Family Services of Hartford.)

Mrs. Thompson would have encountered a similar obstacle in any of thirty-nine other states to which she might have moved. Of the major Northern and Western industrial states, only New York and Rhode Island (and for some programs, New Jersey) have no absolute waiting period. In many states, moreover, a new arrival would not have been so fortunate as Mrs. Thompson in finding a private charity to tide her over the interim.

Connecticut's law is neither the harshest nor the mildest residence test. Many states require a three-year waiting period, and one (New Hampshire) sets a five-year term. On the other hand, some states with residence tests also make emergency provision for destitute and otherwise eligible newcomers. But for most indigent migrants, the hardship is obvious. The Commission on Civil Disorders noted that residence tests have "frequently served to prevent those in greatest need—desperately poor families arriving in a strange city—from receiving the boost that might give them a fresh start."

Some attempt must be made at this point to understand why forty states have adopted such seemingly harsh restrictions on access to welfare benefits. One obvious explanation for the waiting period is that federal law specifically sanctions it; the AFDC portion of the Social Security Act, for example, allows states to impose waiting periods of up to one year. It would be surprising if many states had not responded to this explicit invitation. But there are other, less obvious pressures that have fostered the widespread use of residence tests.

A major factor is the combined impact which declining agricultural employment and regressive welfare policies in the Southeastern states have had upon migration patterns of the poor. The failure of the Federal Government to raise the benefit levels in the poorer states, it is said, has caused most Northern industrial states "to adopt laws excluding newcomers from the relief rolls until they have been residents for a year. . . ." Legislators have probably assumed, as Connecticut's Attorney General predicted recently, that "if all residency requirements were eliminated, there would be an influx of welfare clients, and Connecticut would be penalized for having established high welfare standards." Thus the Commission on Civil Disorders surmised that residence qualifications "were enacted to discourage persons from moving from one state to another and to take advantage of higher welfare payments."

If welfare seekers are compelled to wait a substantial time before becoming eligible for benefits, then one of two things will happen (assuming they do not simply starve, as actually happened to indigent newcomers in several instances). They might, on the one hand, return to the state of origin, which would reduce the burden on the industrial state and allow it to maintain high benefit levels. Or a newcomer might remain, seeking nongovernmental sources of support. He might find employment somewhere, or might rely (as did Mrs. Thompson) on private charity. In either case, the financial burden on the state would, of course, be reduced. The migrant who was able to survive his first year in the new state would thus quite likely have found some durable alternative to welfare.

Although it has been argued that there simply is no reliable correlation between migration patterns and presence or absence of residence tests, there is some fragmentary support for the states' position—for example, a report that some 30 percent of welfare recipients in Elizabeth, New Jersey, were recent arrivals. And the Governor's Commission investigating the Watts riots of 1965 suggested that many Negroes on relief in Los Angeles had migrated to the state because California's welfare payments are higher than in the Southcentral and Southeastern states.

There is much persuasive evidence to the contrary. The Northern California survey of a Mexican-American community found that the typical welfare applicant "is not a stranger to this city. Chances are that he has lived in this community for ten years or more . . . and he has lived in the state over fifteen years." In New York City, which has long had virtually no residence test and high welfare benefit levels, the welfare commissioner noted that "only 2.2% of those on the welfare rolls had been in the city for less than one year, and that of those, more than half applied for relief six months after they arrived." Connecticut welfare officials estimated that the extra cost of public assistance programs without a residence test would probably not exceed 2 percent of the total annual budget (of which the Federal Government would absorb about half).

Several strong constitutional arguments have been mounted against welfare tests. First, there is an inherent inequality: the residence test discriminates against one group of needy persons solely because they have recently arrived in the state. It is not arbitrary or unreasonable for a state to deny welfare to those who are self-sufficient, for the purpose of welfare is to aid those who cannot support themselves. But length of residence is an irrational criterion, wholly unrelated to the purposes of the program.

In fact, in the judgment of the federal court that struck down Delaware's residence test, a waiting period actually frustrates the goals of welfare; it "prevents prompt assistance to some of the state's needy and distressed, and to that extent, it is the antithesis of 'humane.' " Economy could surely not justify such a discrimination against the needy newcomer: "The protection of the public purse, no matter how worthy in the abstract, is not a permissible basis for differentiating between persons who otherwise possess the same status in their relationship to the State of Delaware."

A federal court in Wisconsin held that state's residence test unconstitutional because it arbitrarily assumed all indigent newcomers migrated solely to obtain welfare: the waiting period "not only exerts the duress of the denial of the necessities of life upon people who have been so motivated, but also upon others who have come for different reasons and upon children who have exercised no choice in the matter."

A residence test may also deter the exercise of the constitutional right of movement and travel from one place to another within the United States. In 1941, the Supreme Court struck down a California law prohibiting any person from bringing an indigent into the state. To the majority, the law violated the interstate commerce clause of the Federal Constitution, which necessarily included the right to move and travel freely between states.

Four Justices suggested that the right of interstate movement was also a "privilege" of national citizenship protected by the privileges and immunities clause of the Constitution. This suggestion supplied the basis of the federal court decision striking down Connecticut's residence test in Mrs. Thompson's case: ". . . the right of interstate travel embodies not only the right to pass through a state, but also the right to establish residence therein. . . . Denying to [Mrs. Thompson] even a gratuitous benefit because of her exercise of her constitutional right effectively impedes the exercise of that right . . . because [the residence test] has a chilling effect on the right to travel."

Whatever legitimate interests the states may be seeking to serve by residence tests and waiting periods might be served in other ways. The state could probe an applicant's sincerity in claiming residence: And if it can be shown that a migrant came to the state for the sole purpose of getting public assistance, stricter standards might well be applied to him. But a state may not justly employ the easy shortcut of an automatic one-year presumption of ineligibility.

When Mrs. Thompson's case reached the Supreme Court, it

was decided in her favor. The rationale of the decision was simple and clear: Residence requirements created "two classes of needy resident families indistinguishable from each other except that one is composed of residents who have resided a year or more, and the second who have resided less than a year. . . ." Such a classification violated the Fourteenth Amendment's guarantee of equality, since the interests asserted by the state in support of it were insufficient to justify such harsh discrimination.

Speaking through Mr. Justice Brennan (for a 6-3 majority) the Court went on to review the various asserted bases for the residence period. To the extent the state sought simply to conserve public funds by deterring needy migrants, such a restriction represented an illegitimate attempt to cut itself off from responsibilities of membership in the federal system. The residence requirement also inhibited the right to travel guaranteed by the Commerce Clause (for reasons we have already developed at some length, and which figured only incidentally in the Supreme Court's opinion).

Whatever state interest there might be in excluding needy migrants who came solely to get higher benefits than were offered in their home states, the residence requirement went far beyond it. The waiting period was all-inclusive, deterring those who (like Mrs. Thompson) came for legitimate reasons as well as those who sought only higher benefits.

The states had also advanced a number of practical administrative justifications for the waiting period. Whether the concern was budget predictability, prevention of fraud, making an objective determination of residence, or encouraging newcomers to join the labor force promptly, the Court concluded that all such administrative needs could be served—and in many states were already being served—by less drastic measures. The classification imposed by the residence test went substantially beyond any of the justifications advanced by the states. It was invalid, therefore, because it was irrational and arbitrary—the more so because of its harsh effect on the constitutional right to travel freely across interstate lines.

The decision is a profoundly important one for several reasons. There is of course the obvious fact that some forty states enforced residence requirements which are now invalid. But the practical impact of the decision upon welfare administration may be greatly reduced by the proposals of the Nixon administration to create uniform federal payment levels; with the removal of the wide interstate disparities in welfare benefits, a major incentive for migration is gone, and with it has gone also the principal asserted need for waiting periods and other deterrents to migration.

Far more important is the philosophy of the decision as a cornerstone of the constitutional protection for the rights of the poor. *The New York Times* commented editorially the morning after the Court had spoken: "It is as reprehensible to deny welfare assistance to needy newcomers as it would be to save on school taxes by keeping indigent children out of school or to deprive the poor of police and fire protection. . . . The decision is an impressive victory for lawyers in the antipoverty program and demonstrates that the judicial system can be an instrument of social justice even for the poorest."

The scope of the Thompson decision was soon clarified by an important development in the lower courts. Before the Supreme Court had spoken, the New York legislature sought to take advantage of a loophole that might survive whichever way the case came out. A new section of the state Social Service Law created a presumption that any person applying for benefits within a year of his arrival in New York had come there for the sole purpose of getting welfare. (In 1960 Governor Rockefeller had vetoed a regular one-year residence law. This time he signed the new law designed more subtly to achieve the same end.) The three-judge federal court made short shrift of this statute, finding that the loophole it sought to exploit never really existed. The court perceived no constitutional difference between a presumption against welfare migration and an absolute barrier, where the statutory purposes and the state interests were the same. The Thompson decision had unequivocally foreclosed a state from discouraging entry of indigent persons, regardless of their reasons for entering.

V. *Welfare and Loyalty: "The Subversive Octogenarian"*

The loyalty oaths and other tests that have plagued public employment and public housing have not been completely absent from the welfare field. The Economic Opportunity Act of 1965 barred any expenditure to any individual who had not formally renounced "any organization that believes in or teaches the overthrow of the United States Government by force or violence or any illegal or unconstitutional methods." Before any test case could be brought, Congress repealed that dubious provision of the law. State legislatures have employed similar welfare restrictions. Ohio, for example, still requires a loyalty oath of applicants for unemployment compensation.

The most notable loyalty issue in the welfare field arose over the political disclaimer required of all applicants for Medicare. When the statute was enacted in 1965, it barred any person otherwise eligible (but not covered by Social Security) who "is at the beginning of the first month in which he meets [the other requirements] a member of any organization [registered or required to register with the Subversive Activities Control Board] . . ." The Department of Health, Education and Welfare read this restriction as a mandate to fashion a loyalty oath. Accordingly the applicant was required to swear "that I am not now and during the last twelve months have not been a member of any organization" required to register as a Communist action or Communist front organization under the Internal Security Act of 1950. (The Agency later accepted applications without the certificate, and sent them to the Justice Department for a search of the applicant's political record.)

Many Congressmen were indignant over this method of enforcement and set about to repeal the underlying portion of the law. Senator Javits warned that "the very persons whom we worked so hard to include will be disqualified unless the requirement for this particular kind of affidavit shall be removed." An Ohio Congressman deplored the oath as "absurd and humiliating" to elderly applicants. Representative Ryan of New York asked his colleagues: "[Does the oath] not tell millions of our aged that unless they are guarded about whom they associate with that they run the grave risk of losing their eligibility for this new government health program? And is this not a patent infringement of the rights of the individual?"

The New York Times thought the disclaimer "an affront to individual dignity," and a futile, pointless prerequisite: "for what genuine subversive would hesitate to swear loyalty if to do so served his purpose? Only the conscientious are likely to be the victims." The *Cincinnati Enquirer* ridiculed the oath: "Now, in its majesty, the U.S. Government has added a new burden to the ordinary indignities and ills to which aging flesh is heir. . . . To protect this mighty nation from the legions of the aged and the sick, crafty legislators wrote into Medicare a joker requiring the signing of such a Communist disclaimer. . . . It is estimated there are about two million such oldsters whose fighting days one would presume are over." Before test cases could even be filed against the disclaimer, the Commissioner of the Social Security Administration joined the opposition and urged that the requirement in the law be repealed.

The first test case that reached the constitutional issue was decided in favor of the applicants, a sixty-five-year-old woman and her ninety-year-old mother, both of whom refused to take the oath. The Court first discarded the option theoretically afforded by not signing the certificate and allowing the Justice Department to run a security check. The applicant who took this route would, for one thing, encounter a delay of several months while his political past was being scoured. Moreover, the applicant who failed (even inadvertently) to reveal membership in a listed organization ran the risk of a criminal prosecution in addition to forfeiture of Medicare benefits.

Thus there was no realistic choice except to sign the disclaimer or forego medical assistance. The vagueness of the certificate's language became critical, as did the absence of any element of knowledge about suspect political associations. An applicant approaching sixty-five might well "be deterred from joining an organization which states it is opposed to the war in South Vietnam for fear that it may be or may become a proscribed organization. . . . Others, rather than inquire at an office of the administration as to the organization covered by [the law] might disassociate themselves from any unpopular group even though they are completely loyal to the Constitution of the United States." There was also much uncertainty as to what groups were already on the Attorney General's list, and what criteria those groups might use for determining membership.

The court concluded that Supreme Court loyalty oath decisions made the Medicare disclaimer unconstitutional "unless it be saved by the fact Medicare benefits are a 'gratuity' as to persons not covered by Social Security or Railroad Retirement." Surely it was too late in the day to accept that distinction. The Supreme Court's view of the deported Bulgarian's claim for Social Security had resolved that issue.

Two federal courts reached substantially opposite conclusions about the constitutionality of the Medicare certificate. The government would ordinarily have appealed the adverse decision in order to resolve the judicial conflict. But the impact of the Supreme Court loyalty oath cases made further proceedings appear futile. Accordingly, in the first weeks of 1967 Solicitor General (now Justice) Thurgood Marshall officially abandoned the government's pursuit of the subversive octogenarian, and allowed the oath requirement to die a natural death in the district courts.

VI. *Welfare and Physical Privacy: Midnight Raids and Searches*

The physical privacy of the welfare recipient may be endangered in several ways. The most dramatic and recurrent threat is, of course, the celebrated "midnight raid." Such intrusions are most prevalent in administration of Aid to Families with Dependent Children; as AFDC rolls expanded, midnight raids increased. Professor Charles Reich has described the procedure as follows: "In many states and in the District of Columbia, it has become common practice for authorities to make unannounced inspections of the homes of persons receiving public assistance. Often such searches are made without warrants and in the middle of the night. . . . The searches are sometimes based upon particular evidence known to investigators beforehand, but on occasion there have been mass raids designed as general checks on eligibility. The demand for entry may carry with it the threat, explicit or implied, that refusal to admit will lead to discontinuance of public assistance."

Such raids rarely involve the actual breaking down of doors or the forcing of entry. In fact, the caseworkers who execute such operations are usually warned not to force their way into the home over the recipient's protest. Force is seldom necessary, because of the client's natural fear about his relationship with the caseworker. Indeed, Professor Reich observes that "the mere demand for admission by one in authority is likely to be considered as coercive . . . [Therefore] it seems clear that the opening of a door by a welfare recipient in response to a demand by official investigators is not consent to a search."

If there is any doubt about the sanction behind the caseworker's demand for entry, that sanction can easily be made explicit. A suit in the District of Columbia attacking the practice of unannounced nighttime welfare searches alleged that the "consent" which welfare mothers gave to caseworkers knocking at the door before dawn was clearly not voluntary: "They had not actively opposed these acts, demands and intrusions, and had submitted to [the caseworkers'] assertions of authority because [the caseworkers] had led them to fear that any other course would result in termination of the benefits they had received under the AFDC Program of the District of Columbia."

An entry gained through threats of termination or withdrawal of benefits seems as much a violation of the client's constitutional right to privacy as one gained by beating down the door. To force a client to choose between assistance and privacy constitutes a patently unconstitutional condition attached to the welfare program. Only recently has the practice been tested in the courts, and only one court has ruled squarely on the constitutionality of surprise nighttime welfare raids. In the case involving dismissal of a California welfare worker who refused to participate in such raids, the state courts readily concluded that the liberties of the clients had been violated: the threat which a predawn demand for admission by the caseworker carried with it nullified any consent implied by the client's acquiescence. "In light of the resulting pressure upon welfare recipients to sacrifice constitutionally protected rights," the court concluded that the county could not condition receipt of welfare benefits "upon a waiver of rights embodied in the Fourth Amendment." Whatever legitimate interest the county might have in preventing fraud or concealment of assets must be served by other methods of surveillance.

The constitutional issue may well have been rendered academic by a recent shift in federal administration policy. Mounting criticism of midnight raids and unannounced searches brought about a tightening of federal standards over state and local welfare practices. Since July 1967, every federally aided state plan must "respect the rights of individuals" and must avoid "practices that violate the individual's privacy, or personal dignity, or harass him, or violate his constitutional rights." Specifically, welfare agencies "must especially guard against violations in such areas as entering a home by force, or without permission, or under false pretenses, making home visits outside of working hours, and particularly making such visits during sleeping hours; and searching in the homes . . . to seek clues to possible deception."

The welfare client's privacy has been further protected by a recent federal court decision in New York. The state and city welfare regulations required that caseworkers visit clients' homes at least once every three months (or once every six months in the case of blind, aged, and disabled recipients). Mrs. Barbara James, a Bronx mother, refused to allow an investigator to visit her home. The city welfare department promptly terminated welfare payments to Mrs. James for her support and that of her child. She brought suit in the federal district court for the restoration of benefits, claiming that the investigator's demand invaded the privacy of her home in violation of the Fourth Amendment.

The court granted Mrs. James a preliminary injunction pending a review of the merits of her claim by three judges. The full panel ruled in her favor in late August 1969 and enjoined further enforcement of the mandatory visit policy. The judgment reflected clearly the developing law of unconstitutional conditions on government benefits: "The city and state may not condition the initial and continuing receipt of . . . [welfare] upon a waiver of rights embodied in the Fourth Amendment." Though hoping that the great majority of clients would continue voluntarily to allow the caseworker to visit the home, the court concluded that "when entry is barred, benefits may not be denied or terminated solely on that basis." Whatever information the welfare department might need for its records, and would ordinarily gather through home visits, could be obtained in other ways that less directly threatened the client's privacy. And regular meetings between caseworker and client could always be held at the welfare office.

This decision clearly goes far beyond the "midnight raid" cases. It holds not merely that investigators cannot demand entry at irregular hours or without prior announcement, but that at no time and for no purpose may they use the threat of terminating benefits as the key to a client's door that he wishes to keep locked against official entry. This extension of the client's privacy has broad implications. Professor Edward Sparer, a leading expert on welfare law, has termed the result "a major decision that goes to the dignity of people on the welfare rolls." On the one hand, he points out that forcing a client to admit a caseworker who is seeking evidence of wrongdoing really violates his right not to incriminate himself as well as his privacy. And if the caseworker refuses to schedule an interview at the welfare office when the client balks at a home visit, "that proves that they are looking for something—looking over the home."

VII. *"Obligations" That Go with Welfare: Employment and Other Forms of "Cooperation"*

As we have already observed, the dynamics of the caseworker-client relationship impose a pervasive but subtle coercion upon the welfare recipient. But the system does not rely for cooperation solely upon these implied pressures. There are, in addition, various formal and explicit responsibilities incurred by receiving assistance, of which the most common is the obligation to accept employment or job training.

The demand that a welfare client work if he is able to do so is a quite traditional one. "Whether a welfare recipient must work to obtain assistance, and what work he may be compelled to do," notes Professor Charles Reich, "have . . . been issues since the days of the Elizabethan Poor Laws." But a once local controversy has now acquired national scope. Recent federal legislation requires states that participate in AFDC to establish work and training programs for parents and children sixteen and over who are not in school and who can "appropriately receive training or accept jobs." The law leaves it to the individual states to decide whether mothers with small children are "appropriate" persons for jobs or training; federal funds must be used to set up day care centers for children of mothers who are at work or in class. Beneficiaries who refuse employment or training deemed "suitable" for them are to be cut off welfare. While this legislation was pending, it came under heavy attack in Congress and among social workers. Senator Joseph Tydings implored his colleagues: "We cannot take children from their mothers and place them with thirty or fifty other children into bare prison-like rooms where they are warehoused like so many cardboard boxes all day while their mothers work in order to remain on the welfare rolls." New York's Welfare Commissioner Mitchell Ginsberg and representatives of more than forty organizations active in the welfare field warned that mothers would be "forced to leave their children and to go out to work against their own best judgment." They urged that prime consideration should be given to the welfare of the children.

The "employable mother" policies have also been attacked in the courts. A group of AFDC mothers in Georgia late in 1966 filed suit in the federal courts against that state's employment requirement. The Georgia Manual of Public Welfare Assistance compels able-bodied mothers to accept "suitable" work save under certain exceptional circumstances (for example, when needed to care for infants or sick persons). When the mother is actually employed, or refuses to accept a full-time job offered to her, she receives no AFDC payments—even though the income she receives from the job may be substantially below the benefit levels she would otherwise receive. In this respect Georgia's policy is far harsher than those of most other states that require beneficiaries to accept work. Elsewhere, the welfare recipient is at least no worse off for taking a job the welfare agency compelled him to take. That is, the amount of his earnings is simply deducted from the regular benefit payments up to the statutory level. In some states, in fact, relatively benign policies actually reward more industrious beneficiaries by allowing them to keep a portion of their earnings without a corresponding reduction of benefits. The recent federal amendments contain a very modest incentive provision of this sort.

Georgia's policy is constitutionally objectionable in another respect that distinguishes it from work requirements of most states. Georgia welfare officials regularly classify field labor and domestic service as "suitable" for Negro beneficiaries but not for whites. Negro mothers who refuse to accept such menial employment are cut off welfare altogether, while white mothers, even in rural areas, do not forfeit benefits unless they refuse to accept somewhat better-paying positions, since field work is "unsuitable" for them.

This practice, it is said, builds into the Georgia work requirement a heavy racial bias. Moreover, it assures Georgia planters and growers of a ready supply of field hands at low wages—since the welfare recipients for whom field work is "suitable" have no effective choice but to accept it when it is offered. In practice, the choice is often even more limited. Some county welfare boards simply determine the duration of the planting and harvest seasons, and automatically terminate welfare payments for *all* field-employable beneficiaries during that period. Because of the "suitability" policies, the beneficiaries affected by such draconian decisions are almost exclusively black. Negro mothers in Georgia are thus regularly forced to choose between extreme deprivation and menial work, if they have a choice at all. And even where a choice does exist, it is loaded against them; not only are the wages typically lower than AFDC benefits in the jobs into which they are forced, but adequate provision is seldom made for the care of young children during the workday.

The federal court rendered a decision that cuts both ways. On the one hand, the court upheld that basic policy of the Georgia employable mother rule—assuming adequate safeguards such as suitable child care facilities—on the ground that a welfare recipient has no constitutional right to "refuse employment while receiving assistance and remaining at home with her children." The court did, on the other hand, strike down that part of the Georgia law that prohibits supplementation of wages derived from full-time employment. This restriction was found discriminatory, since it worked to the "financial disadvantage" of welfare recipients solely because of the source of their income and the character of their employment. A proposed substitute policy was equally invalid for the same reasons; it would arbitrarily leave persons having some *employment* income with less in AFDC benefits than welfare mothers receiving income from other sources. During the trial of the case, Georgia's welfare director agreed not to terminate aid in the future without a showing of a bona fide offer to suitable employment; provision would also be made for the mother to show good cause for rejecting specific employment and a hearing would be held if requested.

Obligations other than employment have undermined the dignity of welfare recipients. A Catholic mother in California recently sued to enjoin the county welfare department from forcing her to institute divorce proceedings against her estranged husband by threatening to terminate her payments. A California law forbade payments to children of parents separated or deserted unless they had been apart for three months, or a divorce suit had been filed. The couple had been separated less than three months; the mother claimed that as a good Catholic she could not seek a divorce.

This case recalls the case of the Seventh Day Adventist who was denied unemployment compensation because her religion prevented her from working Saturdays at a time when only six-day work was available in her field. The Supreme Court decided, it will be recalled, that an applicant for a benefit could not be put to so cruel a choice between livelihood and religion.

The case of the California Catholic mother may be less compelling than that of the South Carolina Adventist in two respects. First, the California law makes benefits available, without filing for a divorce, after a three-month separation period. The South Carolina disability, by contrast, was immediate and permanent. Yet three months may be a sufficiently long time to create very serious hardship. If a state residence test or waiting period for newcomers seeking welfare is unconstitutional, a three-month waiting period would be no more valid than a twelve-month term.

There is another possible distinction. Working on Saturday strikes at the very heart of the Seventh Day Adventist creed. The mere filing of a divorce suit is less vital to Catholic belief and practice. Yet the drawing of such distinctions is not the business of the courts. If claims of religious infringement are to be accepted at all, so long as the basis for the claim is not wholly frivolous or subjective, the courts should give it substantial deference. Thus there seems little constitutionally valid difference between the California Catholic who refuses to sue for divorce, and the South Carolina Adventist who refuses to work on Saturday.

The obligation to "cooperate" with the welfare department may raise other constitutional issues. Another California AFDC mother refused to submit to a lie detector test during a district attorney's investigation of the paternity of her child. The agency thereupon withdrew her welfare benefits, under a statute terminating payments if one parent refuses "reasonable assistance" to law enforcement officers seeking to enforce the duty of support against the other parent. But an appellate court held that the mother's refusal to take a lie detector test did not, as a matter of law, constitute that refusal of "reasonable assistance" which the statute contemplated. The court did not, however, invalidate the statute. It apparently continues to be invoked despite an opinion of the California legislative counsel that "the use of such a device . . . suggests a refusal on the part of the county to accept an applicant's statements as truthful and certainly does not demonstrate respect for the integrity and self-esteem of the applicant."

Such a demand for "cooperation" subjects the welfare recipient to a dilemma akin to that of the government employee compelled to make possibly incriminating statements under threat of losing his job. Clearly, mere resort to the self-incrimination privilege could not by itself be made a ground for terminating benefits. But the harder question persists in both areas: Can the use of a rubric such as "noncooperation" obscure the relationship between a claim of privilege and a loss of benefits so as to legitimize this suspect penalty? The welfare agency clearly has a valid interest in obtaining certain information from those to whom it provides assistance. But that interest cannot justify the enforced surrender of so basic a constitutional liberty as freedom from self-incrimination— here any more than in government employment.

VIII. *Morality, Legitimacy, and Welfare*

The American legal system and the welfare system in particular discriminate against illegitimate children and their parents in a variety of ways. Until the Supreme Court declared the practice unconstitutional, for example, Louisiana denied to illegitimates the right to sue for the wrongful death of their mothers. In some states a woman may be prosecuted for the crime of child neglect if she bears two or more illegitimate children. A California trial court recently required a young Mexican-American mother to submit to sterilization as a condition of probation after being convicted of a narcotics offense; the rationale was that she had had extramarital relations and borne an illegitimate child while receiving welfare. And, as we have seen, women may be excluded or evicted from public housing because they have children out of wedlock.

The manifestation of morality that is of chief concern here is the "substitute father" or "man in the house" rule. With minor interstate variations in definitions and procedures, some forty states have terminated assistance because of illegitimate births or extramarital relationships involving the applicant mother.

What factors explain the widespread adoption of such provisions? "The search for the 'phantom father,' " commented Mr. Justice Fortas, "suggests a motivation other than concern for the state or federal fisc. It is much more suggestive of the days when the stocks and pillory and public disgrace were considered suitable for the women caught in illicit love." A student of the American welfare system finds the origins in the historic bias against vagrants: "The vagrant as a prostitute or person of dissolute character is a notion reflected in the rules relating to the AFDC mother who invites a man into her house, fails to keep a suitable home or resorts to park or county lane for purposes of extramarital relations."

The termination of aid to mothers suspected of "immoral" conduct first attracted national concern because of the harsh enforcement in the early 1960s of Louisiana's "suitable home" requirement. The families of more than twenty thousand dependent children were deprived of all welfare by the retroactive application of a law denying aid to homes harboring illegitimates. An appeal was promptly made to the federal Social Security commissioner for a hearing at which Louisiana officials were called upon to defend the conformity of their policies with the underlying federal acts that supplied a substantial share of the state's welfare funds. The hearing brought about a significant change in federal Social Security regulations. Effective July 1, 1961, "a state plan for aid to dependent children may not impose an eligibility condition with respect to a needy child on the basis that the home conditions in which the child lives are unsuitable while the child continues to reside in the home." Thus, for a time, it appeared that one stroke of the federal pen had abolished state use of illegitimacy as a condition of welfare.

Soon, however, Southern states devised subtler ways of stigmatizing the illegitimate family: ". . . mothers of illegitimate children may be dissuaded from applying for assistance," Professor Reich reports, "by threats of neglect proceedings leading to loss of custody of the child or children."

The direct descendant of the "unsuitable home" policy was the "substitute father" rule. Its operation may be illustrated through the case of Mrs. Sylvester Smith, who lived in rural Alabama with her four children aged fourteen, twelve, eleven, and nine. For several years prior to October 1966, the family received AFDC payments. Suddenly Mrs. Smith was informed that the welfare department had learned from an anonymous source that she was "going with" a Mr. Williams; he would henceforth be considered a "substitute father" so as to disqualify her for further aid unless she could disprove the inference of support. Although Mr. Williams lived with his wife and nine children, for whom he was the sole source of support, Mrs. Smith was unable to satisfy the welfare officials that her intimacy with him had no economic significance. Her AFDC benefits were accordingly terminated, leaving her family dependent upon roughly $20.00 a week she earned as a waitress.

The welfare department's action rested upon the state's substitute father regulation. The rule provides: "An able-bodied man, married or single, is considered a substitute father of all the children of the applicant-recipient mother living in her home, whether they are his or not, if: (1) He lives in the home with the child's natural or adoptive mother for the purpose of cohabitation; or (2) Though not living in the home regularly, he visits frequently for the purpose of cohabiting with the child's natural or adoptive mother; or (3) He does not frequent the home, but cohabits with the child's natural or adoptive mother elsewhere. Pregnancy or a baby six months or under is prima facie evidence of a substitute father . . ." The regulation thus terminates benefits whenever there appears to be an intimate relationship between the mother and the man; no standards are prescribed for determining such an "appearance."

This inference of support may cut the mother off from welfare when the man is, in fact, not the father of any of her children, never visits the home nor furnishes any actual support to the children, nor is even under any legal obligation to furnish such support to the children or the mother. The presumption may thus rest on a purely social relationship. The notice of termination, moreover, does not advise the mother of the facts that led to the withdrawal of aid. Nor is there any hearing prior to the termination.

After her benefits were cut off, Mrs. Smith brought suit in the federal district court on behalf of herself and other Alabama mothers affected by the substitute father regulation. She argued that the substitute father rule discriminated arbitrarily and irrationally among needy and dependent children, contrary to the federal law that provided a substantial portion of the funds. It was the purpose of AFDC to benefit all "dependent children"—that is, those who were "deprived of parental support or care by reason of the death, continued absence from the home, or physical or mental incapacity of a parent." Congress had defined as "parents" only those persons who were under a legal duty to support the children. Alabama's reason for cutting off certain needy and dependent children—a social relationship between the mother and a man who was not, in fact, the children's father—was thus beyond the authorization of the federal law.

Moreover, Mrs. Smith argued that the Alabama rule had a clear and deliberate built-in racial bias. Both the reasons for adopting the substitute father rule and its effect attested to this anti-Negro animus. Among the alleged goals of the policy were reduction of aid to Negroes on welfare rolls, penalizing Negro children of allegedly promiscuous mothers (whether the children were legitimate or illegitimate), and discouraging mothers from acting in an "immoral manner" and having illegitimate children. The state had subtly achieved these ends, argued Mrs. Smith, because of the disproportionately higher rate of illegitimacy among Negroes in Alabama. (The number of black illegitimate children receiving aid in the state is sixteen times the number of whites although the total ratio of illegitimates in Alabama is estimated at 45:1.) Thus a denial of welfare to families with illegitimate children is discriminatory in effect without saying a word about race.

The Supreme Court held the Alabama rule invalid on a nonconstitutional ground. To the extent Alabama determined eligibility on the basis of a "substitute father" rather than the actual need of the children, its policies conflicted squarely with the federal Social Security Act which furnished a substantial portion of the state's welfare funds. Whatever interest the state might have in deterring illegitimacy and promoting family solidarity "should be dealt with through rehabilitation measures rather than measures that punish dependent children, [since] protection of such children is the paramount goal of AFDC." Without reaching any of the constitutional issues, the Court concluded that "destitute children who are legally fatherless cannot be flatly denied federally funded assistance on the transparent fiction that they have a substitute father."

This case dealt only with laws such as Alabama's that denied *eligibility* for any benefits because of the presence of a substitute father. Many other states, including some in the North and West, recognized the presence of a male friend of the mother, but only to the extent of reducing the mother's benefits by the amount of the man's income, or by some other amount he was presumed to contribute to the family's expenses (whether or not he actually did so). The Smith decision said nothing about these restrictions. Shortly, however, new standards for state programs were issued by the Department of Health, Education and Welfare. These rules prohibited the inclusion in the family of a person not a parent or spouse (or other person legally obligated to support the children) for purposes of determining eligibility "or for assuming the availability of income." This regulation reaffirmed an earlier directive that states could consider "only such net income as is actually available for current use on a regular basis. . . ." Thus most man-in-the-house rules, including those not invalidated by the Smith decision, now appear to be inconsistent with federal law.

Subsequent developments suggest the Smith case may have raised new problems as difficult as the old ones it solved. Shortly after the Supreme Court's decision, a test case was filed to challenge California's treatment of the man-assuming-the-role-of-spouse (MARS). The state law under attack obligates a MARS to support the children in the house if he is financially able. The amount of assistance to the family is reduced by the amount of income which the welfare department computes (according to a complex formula) is available from the MARS. Clearly this policy conflicts with the new HEW regulations, which permit reduction of welfare benefits only to the extent the MARS actually does contribute to the family's support. Thus the federal court had to choose between the California statute and the federal regulations by deciding which better reflected the policies of the Social Security Act. The three judges unanimously held those policies were better served by California's presumption of support than by HEW's exclusion, since the legislative history of the Social Security Act revealed a design to defer to state law on such vital matters as obligation of support. The court then went on to find the California policy consistent with the Supreme Court's Smith decision—because of the stringent requirement that must be met before a man other than the real father could be classified as a MARS for support purposes. Several other constitutional attacks on the statute were also rejected in the course of the decision. Quite clearly neither the Smith decision nor the HEW regulations—even if they are valid—solve all the problems in this field where welfare law, family law, criminal law and social policy intersect in often bewildering fashion. It will be some time before the courts even perceive the vast array of questions that lurk below the surface.

IX. *Adequacy of Welfare Payments: The Question of Floors and Ceilings*

The courts have given no answer to the bare question whether there is a constitutional right to welfare benefits adequate for survival under decent living conditions. There are, however, several recent developments in the law which come at that question obliquely, and suggest that a more direct answer may not be too far away. Meanwhile, of course, the question may be rendered academic by legislative action—if, for example, Congress enacts the essence of the Nixon administration's proposals to place a uniform federal floor under the welfare program.

The most significant development has been the striking down of a host of state "maximum grant" laws. These laws (often administrative regulations) typically provide for the amounts of benefits that a needy family may receive per week or month, with a fixed dollar ceiling above which no family grants may be made. The computed budget of a small or medium-sized family will seldom exceed the ceiling. But for the large family—five or six children or more —the budgeted needs may be substantially higher than the ceiling —with the result that members of large families will receive somewhat smaller *per capita* welfare payments than the members of a small family.

These maximum grant rules have been attacked on both constitutional and statutory grounds. The constitutional challenge rests on the equal protection clause; welfare lawyers have argued that no valid interest of the state justifies this sort of economic discrimination against the large family. It has also been argued that welfare ceilings are inconsistent with the federal Social Security Act—but the content of the argument is rather technical and need not be developed here.

Federal courts have held the maximum grant provisions of Arizona, Maine and Maryland, and similar provisions of California, invalid on constitutional or statutory grounds or both. Several asserted state interests have been held insufficient to support the discrimination created by such welfare ceilings. Clearly a legislative desire to save money no longer warrants an infringement of constitutional rights. Nor does the maximum grant serve either to deter desertion by fathers of needy children, or to encourage parents to seek work, as some states have claimed. There is no logical relationship between either of these policies and family size. There exist, moreover, alternative ways of serving both interests that are far less oppressive to the indigent family. Finally, it cannot be said that these maximum grant rules are valid because they discourage people on welfare from having large families. Even if this were a legitimate goal for the state to pursue, which is doubtful in itself, the maximum grant does not necessarily serve that goal; one of the families in the Maryland case, for instance, already had all eight children before the father became disabled and was forced to seek welfare. If none of these asserted state interests bears a rational relationship to the maximum grant, then the state's power to penalize a needy family in this way for having more than a fixed number of children seems doubtful.

Another factor reinforced the constitutional judgment. In most states, the "extra" child in a large family would receive benefits if he were moved to the home of an eligible relative with no children or few. Thus, the court concluded in one maximum grant case, the state "impermissibly conditions [that child's] eligibility for benefits upon the relinquishment of the parent-child relationship." Thus the provision might well operate to push families apart—an anomalous result within a legal framework ostensibly designed to keep families intact.

All three courts added one important caution to this judgment: The striking down of the maximum grant provision in no way obligates a state to appropriate more funds—or indeed any particular amount—for welfare payments. The holding in these cases means only that whatever funds the state does commit to welfare must be allocated in a way that does not irrationally discriminate among needy persons who are similarly situated. The extent of the state's commitment to welfare programs remains the concern of the state (and perhaps of Congress), not of the courts.

It was inevitable, though, that this conclusion would soon be challenged. The opportunity for challenge arose later the same spring when New York instituted across-the-board reductions of about 8.5 percent for all recipients. Welfare lawyers promptly brought suit in the federal court, claiming these reductions were both unconstitutional and against the spirit (if not the letter) of the Social Security Act, from which the federal share derived. A district judge at first enjoined these reductions until he could review and decide the merits of the suit. But the court of appeals reversed the injunction, and the Supreme Court refused to act in time, with the result that the cuts went into effect on August 1, 1969. The lawyers who filed the suit acknowledged they had never been hopeful of success, but felt the effects of the reductions so drastic to their clients, and the legal issues so imminently in need of resolution, that a legal challenge had been made in the best of faith.

Is there a constitutional right to "adequate" welfare payments? The courts have given no answer, and most likely will give none for the forseeable future. Professor Edward Sparer of the University of Pennsylvania argues, however, that a constitutional "right to live" is implicit in other liberties that courts traditionally recognize and protect. "The guarantee of life," he maintains, "is as essential as the right to dissent, as essential as the guarantee of free speech or the free exercise of religion." Indeed, he adds that the traditional liberties cannot survive without recognition of a right of subsistence: "Let the unemployed man lie starving, let the sick woman die because an affluent society won't provide her with minimal medical treatment, and you have killed off the speaker, the writer and the worshipper. You have preserved those rights only for the comfortable and the affluent. The reason we need a constitution is to protect the rights of the weak, the powerless and the dispossessed."

Although most constitutional scholars still reject so sweeping a claim to public assistance, Sparer points to a recent decision by three federal judges in New York. Acknowledging that "welfare benefits may not at the present time constitute the exercise of a constitutional right," the court found "basic concepts of humanity and decency" implicit in the "general welfare" clause of the Constitution. One of those concepts "is the desire to ensure that indigent, unemployable citizens will at least have the bare minimums required for existence, without which our expressed fundamental constitutional rights and liberties frequently cannot be exercised and therefore become meaningless." If the courts are ready to make pronouncements of this type, it is surely not too early to ask whether a right to some public assistance can be found implicit in the framework of our Constitution.

X. *The Right to a Hearing—Before or After?*

There is no longer any question whether a welfare recipient has a right to a hearing to contest a termination of payments. Whether or not the constitution would independently require such an opportunity, federal regulations demand a "fair hearing" on a disputed question of eligibility. The contents of the hearing vary somewhat from state to state, but basic procedural interests are safeguarded by the federal requirements.

There is one critical problem about the fair hearing—the question of timing. The usual practice is to remove the beneficiary from the rolls by administrative action and then notify him that he may request a hearing if he wishes to reestablish his eligibility. It is hardly surprising that rather few recipients actually do demand hearings after the fact. (In Illinois, the number who seek hearings runs about one third of 1 percent of those taken off the welfare rolls each year.) The welfare laws are now almost as complex as the income tax laws, even for a legal expert. And the services of a lawyer are not always available. Some states allow a layman to accompany and represent the beneficiary at a hearing; in California, having even a friend along doubles the chances of success. But this option is far from universal.

By far the more serious obstacle is the financial plight of the recipient whose payments have been terminated. He is presumably without other adequate sources of income; indeed, the very process of applying for welfare may have caused him to surrender assets that might otherwise have tided him over. The hearing may take as long as four or five months to run its course. Although retroactive amends are made by a few enlightened states, federal law limits recovery of back benefits to two months, even when the beneficiary is completely vindicated. The very fact of having to keep himself and his family alive following termination is likely to cripple the claimant's ability to pursue the remedy that is theoretically available. "Every day without the necessities of life," it has been said, "creates an immediate and irreparable injury."

It remains to be seen whether the government's interests are adequate to justify the typical procedure. Surely there are situations in which government must act first and hold the hearing later, as the courts have recognized. Where a load of poisoned or spoiled food is about to reach the market, local officials can of course impound or destroy the shipment and remit the owner to a damage suit—even though wholesome produce may be mistakenly destroyed by precipitous action. Where a fraud is about to be perpetrated on unsuspecting securities buyers, a stop order may be issued without a hearing—so long as there is a subsequent chance to contest the decision and have the order dissolved.

These cases are different from the welfare situation in two essential respects. First, the governmental interest is substantially weaker where no "emergency" exists; surely there seems to be none when a welfare recipient is suspected of a disqualifying change in status. While the cost of continuing doubtful recipients on the rolls for several months longer may be substantial, nothing more than money is involved. The government does have other remedies to move quickly against fraud or collusion, and even to recover payments erroneously made. Moreover, the delays that presently worsen the claimant's plight would quite likely be reduced if the cost of procrastination fell on the agency rather than on the recipient.

The second distinction, of course, relates to the impact of a summary or one-sided government action upon the citizen who is affected by it. A businessman denied a license at the eleventh hour may suffer heavily when the government wipes out a potential market before holding a hearing. Subsequent recovery of damages (if, indeed, they are recoverable) may be inadequate to compensate for the loss. But such misfortunes are, after all, risks of doing business and can presumably be covered by insurance. For the welfare client, life is precarious enough, even when the payments arrive regularly every month. The only kind of "insurance" that might help the beneficiary has typically been already assigned to the welfare department, or at least put beyond reach as a condition of eligibility. So the welfare system itself destroys the very force that mitigates the effect of a decision before hearing in the business world.

Where emergency conditions do not justify the termination of a government benefit before the beneficiary is heard, the courts have increasingly recognized a prior hearing as a constitutional right. The state university student cannot be expelled or suspended without a prior hearing; it is well recognized that a hearing after the fact—after the examination period, for example—would be wholly inadequate. The civil servant, too, is protected against a discharge without a hearing; in some states, in fact, the government must not only hold a hearing but must seek review in court before a dismissal can be effected. Even in public housing, the right to a prior hearing is being accepted as a protection for the tenant. It would be anomalous if the welfare recipient—who is the most completely dependent of all government beneficiaries, and has the fewest alternatives in the private sector—were denied the basic procedural safeguards to which his counterparts in other fields are entitled.

Two subsequent developments promise a more effective guarantee of an adequate prior hearing. On the judicial side, the Supreme Court has agreed to review a conflicting pair of federal district court decisions dealing with the character and content of the hearing. One trial judge upheld California's provision for an informal conference prior to termination of benefits, noting that an adversary hearing could be demanded after termination. In New York, however, a federal court held that welfare clients could not constitutionally be denied a chance to appear in person before a hearing officer prior to termination. The three-judge panel declared that "due process requires an adequate hearing before termination of welfare benefits, and the fact that there is a later constitutionally fair proceeding does not alter the result." Not only must the beneficiary be permitted to appear in person; equally important, he must have "a chance, if he so desires, to be fully informed of the case against him so that he may contest its basis and produce evidence in rebuttal." Under some circumstances, though not all, the client must be able to confront and cross-examine those who have brought the charges; there have been "too many case histories in which welfare recipients have allegedly been cut off on the basis of untrue rumors and reports. . . ." Yet the court qualified this announcement just as courts have qualified the newly defined right to a hearing of other government beneficiaries: There need not be a formal trial with all the safeguards that would be required in a criminal court. It would be neither feasible nor appropriate to bring all the formalities of the criminal trial to bear upon the administrative hearing, no matter how vital the consequences. What is required, and is within the competence of agencies administering government benefits, is a hearing that gives the beneficiary at least as much chance to know why he is in trouble, to explain his side of the story, and to challenge the basis of charges against him as a regulated businessman or commercial licensee receives when his status is in jeopardy.

On the administrative side, there has been an equally important development. Shortly after the district court decision in New York, the Department of Health, Education and Welfare amended the federal regulations to require state and local welfare agencies to continue payments during appeal "when a fair hearing is requested because of termination or reduction of assistance, involving an issue of fact, or judgment relating to an individual case." The new rule took effect October 1, 1969. It also requires that lawyers be provided at welfare hearings for beneficiaries who wish counsel. While this new regulation does not mandate the content of the hearing, it does go a long way toward ensuring that the beneficiary will not be left destitute while the process of the law takes its often tedious course.

X

"FOR THE POOR, IT'S A DOLE,

FOR THE RICH, SUBSIDIES—

BUT IT'S ALL WELFARE"

The American system of government benefits has largely failed to reconcile dignity and dependency. Most benefit programs provide support for those who need it but at a cost of undermining self-reliance. More than anything else, it is the restrictions on government benefits that thwart this accommodation of vital interests. The fault lies both with conditions that are relevant to the goals of the program, such as the means test in welfare, and with irrelevant restrictions such as loyalty oaths.

The situation might be substantially improved if the extent of dependency upon government benefits in the United States were more widely acknowledged. Early in 1969, Washington newsmen discovered that Mississippi Senator James Eastland was a government beneficiary to the extent of $157,930 he received from the Agriculture Department in 1967 for withholding farmland from production. Some accounts facetiously termed Eastland a "welfare recipient." One reporter wrote a story contrasting Eastland's relationship to government with that of an unmarried Mississippi mother near starvation because of inadequate welfare payments. His article was headlined: "For the Poor, It's a Dole, For the Rich, Subsidies—But It's All Welfare." To the headline writer, and probably to most of his readers, the chief message of the article was the stark contrast between powerful people who are enriched by government benefits and the weak and dependent who are sometimes literally impoverished by their dependency.

The Washington reporter also thought he had discovered something novel about government's relations with its citizens: many more Americans receive benefits than most of us realize. This insight is important, but hardly original. Yet it does provide a point around which to review much of what has been discussed in this book. A detailed consideration of specific problems arising under different benefit programs runs the risk of obscuring the common elements that bind the subject together. At the outset, we tried to identify some of those recurrent themes that justify a homogeneous treatment of distinct and superficially unrelated government programs. This final chapter tries to bring those themes together on the basis of the raw material now available for assimilation. The chapter concludes by offering some comprehensive remedies within, and alternatives to, the present benefit system that may alleviate some of its worst features.

I. *Recurrent Themes and General Observations About Government Benefits*

The first observation that emerges from this study is deceptively simple and actually quite misleading. It is the almost tautological comment that the relationship between government and beneficiary is voluntary and optional on both sides. For government, almost every benefit program represents a deliberate legislative choice among several options—including the option to create no benefits. There is hardly a government program that is really indispensable. Even most public employment, at least most of the civil service roster, is not essential. Government can theoretically perform almost any function through private business; if the United States can operate Job Corps training camps for unemployed youth in California by contracting them out to Litton Industries, there is no limit to what can be handled by the private sector. War can be waged with mercenary armies, and the Constitution actually provides for issuance of letters of marque authorizing private vessels to engage in naval warfare. Government can provide education by subsidies to private schools and scholarships to their students, as several Southern states actually did in hopes of avoiding desegregation. Even the Capitol and government office buildings could be run by a private real estate management firm if necessary. Some may assume that a government must have courts, and so the United States Constitution appears to require. But if we were to start again, there would be no intrinsic reason why much adjudication could not be left to arbitration; in fact, the time may not be far off when automobile negligence cases, which occupy half or more of the docket of most civil courts, will be handled in precisely that way.

The relationship also appears voluntary from the beneficiary's side. No one has to work for the government if he has skills usable in the private sector; most students can get an education at some private college; and if one can stand slums, public housing is not the only source of shelter. Even welfare benefits are seldom the only hedge against starvation, as the number of beggars—essentially private entrepreneurs bypassing the public welfare system—on the streets of any major city indicates. Thus, the relationship is technically voluntary on both sides.

Yet this analogy to other voluntary relationships stops on paper. In practice, few of the other attributes of voluntariness follow. Seldom is the applicant for a government benefit free to write the terms of his own contract, or bargain over any of its incidents; government salaries, like public housing rent and welfare payment levels, are typically based on a printed schedule of grades and dollar amounts that seem as immutable as the scriptures, even at top grades. The terms of the relationship are typically determined by a body that does not administer the program—the Congress, the State Legislature, or some superagency in Washington—or by a lower-level body that may be just as remote in practice because of the beneficiary's inability to bargain with it. Terms of public housing occupancy, for example, are set partly by Congress, partly by Housing and Urban Development, and partly by city or county council. Some incidental matters are left for the project manager, with whom—or with whose immediate subordinate—the tenant deals directly. But that proximity is of little comfort because the typical applicant would be in no position—because of limited education, experience, or simple knowledge of what is at stake—to bicker over the terms even if he thought they were negotiable. Thus the conditions of tenancy might as well be set in Washington, as far as his ability to revise or adjust them is concerned.

This disparity of bargaining power affects all beneficiaries, but most acutely it affects the poor. There is a kind of double stan-

dard at work within the broad class of government beneficiaries—
reflected by the difference between the treatment of Senator Eastland
and the rural black Mississippi welfare mother. Professor Lawrence
Friedman has offered some thoughtful and critical insights into
the implications of this double standard:

> Over the long run, welfare programs tend to polarize.
> When a "middle-class" population demands inclusion in a
> government service, conditions tend to be removed or dimin-
> ished. Hence, the demand may be met in the form of an en-
> tirely new program, rather than through some classic form of
> relief . . . The hard-core poor, who do not qualify, or for
> whom these programs are not adequate, are still covered by
> the residual programs. But these residual programs have now
> lost many of their "middle-class" customers. The middle class
> has graduated into the new programs. Along with them, the
> old programs have lost whatever political appeal they might
> have had, which had been one of the major restraints against
> bad administration. AFDC and public housing are programs
> that illustrate what happens when the "middle class" poor
> move up and out.

There is a related factor of some importance. Seldom does the
beneficiary have an opportunity to participate in the drafting of the
conditions or restrictions which may govern his activities and affairs. The physical remoteness of the policy-making process is one
serious obstacle to participation. In addition, conditions and restrictions—loyalty oaths and other antisubversive clauses,
especially—are often surreptitiously tucked in or tacked on to
bills as they move rapidly through the final stages of enactment.
And these riders have a way of attaching themselves to bills to
which they relate only vaguely, which further confuses even the
alert lobbyist. If the experienced observer cannot always see what is
happening in time to stem the tide, how likely is it that the average
public housing tenant or welfare client could resist in any meaningful way?

The case may be overstated a bit. Opportunities for participation are not always absent. When Congress was thinking about
withdrawing fellowships of students who broke campus rules or destroyed university property, the President of the National Student

Association was given an opportunity to forecast consequences for a Senate subcommittee. The severity of the sanction was modified a bit thereafter. In the same month, however, Congress passed a rider denying NASA funds to colleges and universities that barred military recruiters from the campus. The case for the bill rested almost entirely on a list of twenty-odd institutions said to have excluded representatives of the armed services. The bill passed before anyone had a chance to examine the list. Within a week, however, most of the cited institutions proved they had been erroneously included; among them were two women's colleges, Barnard and Sarah Lawrence, whose relationship to military recruiting might well have been questioned by anyone with even a passing knowledge of higher education. The immediate error was attributable to a careless clerk in the Defense Department. The underlying fault lay, however, with the Congressional process, which afforded no opportunity for any of the listed institutions or a national organization representing them to participate before enactment of the bill.

The relative weakness of the beneficiary, and the lack of an opportunity to react to conditions before they affect him, reflect other common disabilities. Most government beneficiaries are substantially unaware of the degree to which they share a second class status with thousands of others who are similarly situated. Meaningful contacts and associations that coalesce interest groups are largely absent. Welfare clients seldom hold weekly or even monthly meetings. Only very recently have state college students and public housing tenants begun to organize. And when they seek to use group strength to press common grievances, they face another serious obstacle: their beneficial status is often so temporary, the beneficiary class so transient and fluid, and the beneficiaries so reluctant to identify themselves as such for class purposes, that the roots necessary for effective organization can seldom be developed. (The same is not true of public employees, of course, among whom the most effective organization has taken place.)

College students, public housing tenants, and welfare clients (not to mention occasional users of public property) face organizational problems comparable to those of airline stewardesses, whose economic interests are protected only to the extent the powerful Pilots' Association becomes their spokesman. The rate of turnover, the physical separation, and lack of opportunity to meet regularly, and the characteristic absence of career commitment militate against effective organization for redress of grievances among the stewardesses much as they do among project occupants, college students, welfare clients, and park or auditorium users.

The absence of procedural safeguards is a major disability that affects virtually all government beneficiaries, although the situation seems to be improving under pressure from the courts. Even the government employee has only the formal, skeletal safeguards of the civil service system to protect him from arbitrary discharge, while the private worker usually has a strong union to press his claim through the grievance and arbitration machinery. The welfare recipient has a right to a "fair hearing," but no guarantee that he will be heard before benefits are terminated. The public housing tenant now must be given the reasons for his eviction—but has no assurance he can answer the charges at a hearing that means anything. The state college student cannot be expelled or dismissed without a hearing (if he can persuade a court to order the college officials to act as the law requires), but there is no guarantee that he cannot be suspended summarily for a long enough term to interrupt his education seriously.

Thus, the administrative safeguards that exist in theory should provide a measure of security and redress they do not always provide in practice. Unavailability or exhaustion of internal remedies leads naturally to external channels of review, principally to the courts. Here, too, opportunities for redress that are available in theory often prove in fact to be remote or tortuous. The most pervasive deterrent to effective judicial review, of course, is the difficulty and expense of obtaining legal counsel. The government employee may be able to retain a private attorney, although the cost of legal and court fees will burden him at a time when he can least afford to pay. Other groups of beneficiaries are less fortunate. Those who happen to live near, or know about, a legal aid office may obtain counsel; but for the vast majority, and for a variety of reasons, the remoteness of a lawyer to press such a claim reflects a psychological more than a geographical distance. We shall have more to say about this problem later.

Even if legal counsel is available to handle the suit, there are other barriers to court review. The "voluntary" character of government benefits, which has only rhetorical significance elsewhere, still causes some courts to dismiss suits brought by beneficiaries, and especially by mere applicants. Some courts still hold that one who loses (or even more, is denied) a government benefit because of conditions or restrictions attached to it, lacks legal "standing" to complain, which he would have if he were the subject of a criminal prosecution or an action to condemn his real estate. Equally serious, the case may be declared moot and dismissed if the beneficiary accepts reinstatement or alternative aid while the suit is pending, even though he may have no practical alternative if he is to survive in the meantime.

The worst part of distinctions between government beneficiaries and other persons is their essentially arbitrary nature. Sometimes the beneficiary is better treated than his counterpart in the private sector. (A student at a private university, as we have seen, has no constitutional right to a hearing, and can seldom ask a court to review his dismissal.) But whichever way the distinctions cut, they are essentially irrational; that is, they are unrelated to any substantial governmental interest peculiar to the process of conferring benefits, or to the activity of the beneficiaries. Workers performing identical tasks, in adjacent communities, or even adjacent plants, can strike if they serve a private employer but not if they serve the state. Private apartment tenants can have overnight guests or children out of wedlock, while public project occupants cannot. Recipients of private charity are not forced to take lie detector tests, or to sue absent spouses, or to accept unsuitable employment. The list of such contrasts could be multiplied indefinitely.

The point is clear enough, and it is central to understanding what makes government beneficiaries second class citizens: the government is seldom called to account for the rationality of or justification for the differences between those who receive its bounty, and those who either receive similar benefits from private sources or do not need them. It is not only the arbitrariness of the distinctions, which is bad enough. Far worse is the virtual immunity of governmental decisions that produce and perpetuate these distinctions.

A further observation is relevant: the second class status of dependence on government demeans a steadily expanding portion of the American population. Such growth is an inevitable corollary of the spread of government benefit programs—although it is hardly intended by those who view such programs as sources of advancement and betterment for the beneficiary class. The second class status, moreover, is by no means confined to the poor. In some respects, the high ranking civil servant who cannot take an active part in politics is affronted much more severely—because the disability is so out of keeping with the other perquisites of his socioeconomic class—than is the welfare client who cannot associate too freely with men to whom she is not married. Both restrictions are, however, equally irrational.

The pressures for change may be coming, and quite rapidly. The rising tide of militancy among beneficiaries cannot be dismissed idly or regarded as a passing phase of maturation in the public sector. Campus riots and demonstrations are not new, of course. But a new era of direct action by students began with Berkeley's 1964 sit-in.

Militancy elsewhere in the public sector, however, is a new phenomenon. Rent strikes by public housing tenants were unknown until the mid-1960s. Sit-ins by hungry clients at welfare agencies, and strikes by aggrieved public employees, are also contemporary phenomena to which the system has not yet adapted comfortably. The rising tide of dissatisfaction throughout the public sector and its growing resort to direct action provide one justification for understanding more clearly the root causes and concerns.

The vast majority of beneficiaries are probably not deeply aggrieved, or at least not enough so to mount the barricades. Even at Berkeley or Columbia, the average student is either apathetic or patient enough to accept gradual, peaceful change. The average public housing tenant (even in Newark) and the typical welfare client (even in New York) may hate the bureaucracy, but is not moved to militancy. But this relative calm should not make administrators complacent. It takes only a small band to make a revolution, as many college presidents have now discovered. A movement within the ranks that is somewhat less than revolutionary can force the resignation of an administrator who thinks he understands the grievances, but in fact does not. So the storm warnings are clearly up. Only the unwary or the foolhardy will fail to heed them.

The correlation between the rising militancy and the conditions we have analyzed in this book is uncertain at best. Government employees have never walked off or sat down on the job because of a loyalty oath or a ban on political activity—although many have refused such jobs in the first place because they could not brook these restrictions. Public housing tenants do not withhold rent, or jam the elevators, or misplace the garbage, because unmarried mothers are denied admission or tenants with criminal records are evicted. (In fact, *residents* of the project often may be just as happy to see such policies enforced.) The current protests cannot, therefore, be traced directly to the encumbrances we have studied.

There may, however, be an indirect relationship of greater significance than the direct causes. May not the administrator's knowledge that he can evict or expel summarily, or fire employees who strike or engage in political campaigns, really be rather close to the heart of the problem? Take away the arbitrary, unreviewable power over the beneficiary, or control it in these areas, and you begin to balance the relationship between benefactor and beneficiary. Restrict the authority to expel a student or evict a tenant without a hearing, and you may make the president or the manager cautious about exercising other powers in the smug and insensitive fashion that does provoke protests and lead to the barricades. At the same time, you give the student or the tenant a degree of self-respect and dignity that may make him realize that direct action is not the only remedy when he is abused or mistreated by the establishment.

These common elements are important for a variety of reasons. They clearly reveal the important similarities that bind the various problems together for analytical as well as legal purposes. The identification and understanding of these recurrent themes is vital as a prelude to the framing of solutions that will have general applicability. Piecemeal solutions may help individual beneficiaries, if they are lucky, to get back what has been taken away, or to claim what they believe they deserve. But such remedies do not alter or ameliorate the system. They leave untouched the plight of the great mass of persons who are dependent on the government for employment, education, shelter, or survival. It would be quite irresponsible for us to stop there.

II. *Safeguards for the Beneficiary: Controlling the Administration of the System*

The ultimate protection for the beneficiary's interests may lie in the machinery available to redress grievances. Substantive guarantees, through statutes and regulations, are only as effective in practice as the remedial channels through which they are enforced. Without such channels the gap between the practice and the theoretical prescription is likely to widen as the system becomes larger and more complex. Without fair procedures, harried administrators, facing expanding caseloads and rising demand for the benefits they dispense, are likely to take the easiest, shortest way out. It is most often taken at the beneficiary's expense rather than that of the system. Fair procedures, in short, are essential because (to paraphrase an aphorism about the criminal law) few men are angels. Even the few government administrators who have achieved this state of grace occasionally make mistakes. The average bureaucrat strays more often.

Although the problem may be partly attributable to the administrator's workload, it is certainly more complex than this factor alone. Changes in the governing law, through legislation and new regulations, often face long delays in implementation—either because they are inadequately communicated to the local level or because they are imperfectly understood. One might recall, illustratively, that Texas state college and university students had to keep signing a loyalty oath for thirteen years after the law had been repealed. Such long delays are unusual, but shorter time lags are recurrent in welfare and public housing; anachronistic practices may and do persist long after the law has been reformed.

Delays and inequities of this sort typically result from innocent maladministration. But there are less pure motives behind other problems to which procedural safeguards are addressed. As was frequently the case in the South after a decision requiring an end to official segregation or discrimination, informal practice sometimes replaces an untenable formal rule—thus making the restriction much harder to attack because it is no longer in the open for all to see. (When a Housing Authority is told, by either a court or a superior agency, that it can no longer reject unmarried mothers, it may continue to impose a code of morality through an unwritten but no less rigorously enforced policy of exclusion.)

Finally, uniformity and equality in administration of government benefit programs demand accessible remedies. The tendency toward disparity in the absence of such procedures is obvious from what has just been said here—the heavy pressures upon the administrator, the natural human tendency to take shortcuts, and the communication delays. Even review at the local level can standardize practices considerably; the mere prospect of review at a higher level, in appellate courts or in a superior administrative body, enhances still more the probability of uniform treatment. Any civilized, responsible system of government benefits must at least try to eliminate inequality and disparity.

THE RIGHT TO A HEARING

If the case for some kind of fair procedure is established, then we must examine more closely what remedies are available. The first and most obvious safeguard is the right to a hearing. It enables the beneficiary to answer charges against him, and to resist the government's claim of ineligibility or disqualification. But the paper guarantee of a hearing is of little value to the beneficiary without some assurances as to both its character and its timing. A proceeding that is perfunctory or after the fact may in fact be worse than no remedy at all—because it will allow the administrator to plead in court, with a persuasive ring, "But he had a hearing." To be meaningful, a hearing must take place before the termination of benefits —before eviction from the project, before expulsion of the student (or a long term suspension), before the recipient is cut off the welfare rolls. While a subsequent hearing may be justified under emergency conditions (e.g., eviction of a tenant who contracts a highly contagious disease), it has been the rule rather than the exception in many agencies. Surely if a prior hearing is usually afforded in the business context before a benefit can be terminated, no less should be assured where fundamental human rights are at stake.

The grounds of the hearing are as important as its timing. Above all, the agency threatening to withdraw the benefit should bear the burden of proof—just as the claimant should bear the burden of proof if his application is initially rejected. This means that if the agency cannot prove its charges, the beneficiary will succeed even if he submits no evidence in his own behalf. Thus, if the welfare agency claims that an AFDC mother is actually receiving support from a man with whom she associates, and seeks to reduce her payments accordingly, it must prove just that at the hearing. To require the mother to prove the contrary, or disprove an inference of support that arises from friendship, would only compound the inequity that is inherent in the dependency of welfare.

JUDICIAL REVIEW: THE BENEFICIARY IN COURT

Most of the cases we studied here reached public notice only because someone brought them to court. Yet only the tiniest fraction of grievances subject to court review ever do reach the courts, because of several obstacles. Chief among these is the unavailability of legal services.

In other ways, the disparity between the plight of the welfare client or the public housing tenant and the treatment of the business licensee is striking. Decisions of most regulatory agencies are readily reviewable in the courts by any person who is adversely affected. Not so for the welfare or housing recipient; the path of review is by contrast often narrow, dimly lit, and poorly marked. It is sometimes a labyrinth, and may not even be entered until the beneficiary has "exhausted" internal remedies of which he may be unaware and cannot pursue in the time before his next crisis. And if the beneficiary does find some alternative support, employment or shelter to tide him over, he may well be told that his case is "moot" because he is no longer in need of the benefit.

The remedies seem obvious from a brief analysis of the obstacles. The channels of review should be at least as clearly marked for the individual beneficiary as for the business claimant. This might be achieved by extending to the welfare, housing, employment, and student fields the systematic review provided by the Federal Government and most states by the Administrative Procedure Acts, conferring on the court automatic jurisdiction over adverse decisions by administrative agencies, at the instance of any aggrieved person. Exhaustion of remedies should be sparingly required, and should not be pursued at the cost of exhausting the beneficiary instead. Finally, the right to review should not automatically be thwarted even if the benefit is restored or if the beneficiary finds an alternative means of support, so long as an honest dispute persists.

AVAILABILITY OF LEGAL SERVICES

Volumes have been written about the need of the poor for legal services in civil cases, and about ways of obtaining such services. Only the briefest discussion is possible here. The nature of the need is obvious: the average welfare recipient or public housing tenant, or even college student, is quite unlikely to know very much about his legal rights without advice from a lawyer. The need for representation is, in many ways, as great here as in the criminal area, though far less clearly recognized. A variety of obstacles deter access to such legal services—the poor man doesn't realize that a lawyer can help him; or if he does realize, he doesn't know where to find one; or he fears that consulting a lawyer may bring reprisal from his employer or from the welfare or housing agency; or when he does seek aid he finds either a long waiting line at the Legal Aid office, or finds that office so remote (in physical distance or in atmosphere) as to deter him from seeking counsel at all.

Both the organized bar and the government have recently recognized their responsibility to counsel the poor in noncriminal cases. Their needs cover a broad range of public and private disputes—consumer problems, landlord-tenant controversies, domestic relations issues, as well as welfare and public housing matters. Legal Aid bureaus have existed for a half century and more, in the large metropolitan areas, and do provide a limited source of advice and counsel. But the manpower of these offices is heavily committed to divorce, custody, adoption, and landlord-tenant cases, neglecting the newer legal problems of the type we have explored here. Many civil rights and civil liberties groups occasionally bring suits that vindicate the interests of government beneficiaries. But these organizations have a special and historic concern with the core constitutional rights and liberties—freedom of speech and religion and racial equality for the most part—and are not easily diverted to the newer fields of litigation. Thus the combined efforts of the Legal Aid bureaus and the civil rights-civil liberties groups fall short of the rising need of government beneficiaries for legal services.

The Federal Government has gone far to meet this need through its extensive program of neighborhood law offices of the Legal Services Program within the Office of Economic Opportunity. Unlike the traditional Legal Aid bureaus, these offices are usually located in the ghetto, and their staffs are willing to tackle the greatest grievances and most urgent needs of the poor, whether or not these present familiar legal problems or civil rights-civil liberties claims. Nor are they reluctant to use federal funds to bring suit against government benefit programs. In fact, the first OEO legal service case to reach the Supreme Court was the challenge to

Connecticut's welfare residence test, brought by OEO attorneys on behalf of Mrs. Vivian Thompson.

There is an expanding range of legal service programs, some using federal funds, others relying on private funds, and still others combining sources of support. For the first time, attorneys have been available to migrant farm workers in the San Joaquin, Sacramento, and Napa valleys through the California Rural Legal Assistance Program, which maintains a string of offices in the farm regions of the state. Although CRLA, which is federally funded, has been attacked by Governor Ronald Reagan and by conservative lawyers' groups, it has survived and prospered. Perhaps its most notable victory was the decision of the California Supreme Court enjoining the state from reducing medical care payments under the Medi-Cal program.

Private funds have been selectively used to supplement government support. The Ford Foundation created a Mexican American Legal Defense and Education Fund, based in San Antonio, to bring to the Spanish-speaking people of the Southwest legal services comparable to those which CRLA has provided in California. The Carnegie Corporation supports a Community Law Office in an East Harlem storefront, through which fifty young lawyers from Wall Street devote time released by their firms to the problems of indigent Harlem residents. Channels of this type must be utilized and expanded if the legal problems of the poor, especially those involving disputes with government, are to be met.

Several supplemental steps may facilitate achievement of this goal. First, the underrepresentation of minority groups in the legal profession, and the greater confidence that minority group clients have in their own attorneys, make it imperative to expand the number of lawyers who are nonwhite and Spanish-speaking. Several groups, including the American Bar Association and the predominantly Negro National Bar Association have joined forces to attack the problem by forming a Council on Legal Education Opportunity. Supported both by the Office of Economic Opportunity and by private foundations, CLEO brought 100 additional minority students into law schools in its first year (1968), and approximately 400 in the second year.

These needs cannot be met without the services of paraprofessionals, persons who have some legal training but are not qualified to practice on their own or belong to the bar. Professor David

Cavers of the Harvard Law School notes that, with even a year of special education, such persons could serve as lawyers' aides at least as effectively as many legal secretaries now do with no law training. "Moreover," he adds, "the extension of legal services to more and more people with low and middle incomes will multiply the occasions for rather routine operations performable by the para-lawyer."

Finally, access to legal services must be improved for government beneficiaries who are not technically indigent and thus do not qualify for legal aid, but who nonetheless are unable to retain a lawyer for major litigation. The college student on a scholarship, the low-level civil servant, and the employed public housing tenant, fall into this category. They have legal problems and need counsel but as matters now stand they may have a harder time getting effective representation than the truly indigent person who readily qualifies for legal aid and neighborhood law office help. Recent Supreme Court decisions have removed doubts that for decades hampered development of group legal service programs for labor union and other common interest group members. Student associations at some universities have retained law firms to handle institutional cases, and may expand the retainer to cover individual grievances as well. The American Bar Association is seriously considering a proposal for legal insurance, which would work rather like medical insurance and would meet the legal needs of the middle and lower middle class client by diffusing the costs. Thus the expansion of legal services to government beneficiaries just above the poverty line is already in prospect.

The total unmet need for legal services cannot be accurately measured. The recent wave of test cases and the change they have wrought in the substantive law suggest the dimensions of the need. Only an attorney can bring a test case to court. And only a lawyer can police the day-to-day practices of administrative agencies to ensure compliance with the decisions in test cases. The total unmet need for legal services among government beneficiaries is vast even if inestimable.

THE OMBUDSMAN: SPOKESMAN FOR THE MAN ON THE STREET

Several European nations have created "ombudsmen," or citizens' advocates. The ombudsman has been defined as an independent, high level officer who receives complaints, pursues inquiries into the matters involved, and makes recommendations for suitable action. He may also investigate on his own motion. He makes public reports periodically. His remedial weapons are persuasion, criticism and publicity. As a matter of law, he cannot reverse administrative action.

Public officials, legal scholars, and professional groups have urged the creation of ombudsmen in the United States. But to date such a position exists in only a very few communities, such as Nassau County, New York, and the cities of Buffalo and Honolulu. (The Nassau ombudsman is actually a county official already holding another position, and supported by regular county funds; the Buffalo office receives direct federal support from the Office of Economic Opportunity and is beholden to no local official.) In both areas, political opposition to the ombudsman has been substantial. A Nassau County election in the fall of 1967 withdrew official recognition and support for the experimental program; in Buffalo, the Common Council (after initially supporting the ombudsman) voted to ask OEO to cancel its grant. Yet the results of these undertakings have been significant and impressive; both ombudsmen had a substantial and rapidly rising caseload; among the complaints have been a substantial share from welfare, public housing, and other government benefit programs.

It is much too early to judge the success of either experiment. The ombudsman may provide the independent channel through which the citizen can complain, or seek redress for a grievance, without summoning the heavy artillery of hearing or lawsuit. Often the grievance may be corrected simply by better understanding of the problem, or by additional information on one side or the other. Yet the limits to the ombudsman's powers are important: on the one hand, the survival of the office depends upon assurances that it will not compete with the bar, with political channels, or with local agencies that do have power of review and enforcement; on the other hand, the ombudsman's relative impotence may undermine the confidence of those who are accustomed to getting prompt and effective action from their City Councilman or ward boss. The problem therefore is to find ways of building confidence in a rather sophisticated institution with inherently limited power.

EXTERNAL REVIEW BOARDS

Few contemporary institutions have been more maligned and misunderstood than civilian police review boards. Municipal elections have been fought over the creation or dismantling of such boards. Civil rights and civil liberties groups urge adoption of machinery to check police abuses through external review. Police officers, on the other hand, perceive civilian review boards as a threat to the autonomy of law enforcement and to the exercise of professional judgments about police practices. (Many departments will accept, indeed welcome, *internal* review boards appointed by, or composed of, professional police officers.)

Whatever the case against the civilain review board in the police setting, the concept need not be as controversial in other areas. Might not welfare abuses be checked to some extent by a welfare review board, composed of citizens and caseworkers, sitting to pass upon complaints from beneficiaries? Could not a public housing review board exercise a similar function, without raising the hackles of the manager or the authority to the same degree that external review makes policemen bristle? Even in the college and university setting, there may be some advantage in independent, external, civilian (i.e., nonadministration, nonfaculty) boards to review proposed student regulations and investigate charges of illegal enforcement of existing rules. The concept may be novel, and is tainted by its association with the police review board experience; but its greatest potential may well lie outside law enforcement.

INTERNAL GRIEVANCE MACHINERY

In the industrial world, a large volume of complaints, grievances, and charges are resolved amicably through recognized grievance and arbitration machinery. Government beneficiaries are emulating factory workers in their resort to collective action. Not only are government employees forming unions (whether authorized by law or not) but, as we have seen, militant student organizations, public housing tenants' associations, and welfare rights groups are beginning to act like unions—even if uncertain how they want to exercise their power. These groups have functioned sporadically and have negotiated with administrators largely on a hit-or-miss basis. But within the structure may lie the seeds of an

effective grievance machinery. What works in the industrial setting
—several levels of review leading finally to arbitration by an impartial referee or umpire—might be equally adaptable to areas of
government largesse where the problems and the channels are both
comparable.

If this assessment of the potential of collective action in the
public sector is accurate, the growing militancy among beneficiaries
need not be viewed with fear. With the maturing of such organizations, the filing of a formal complaint may well replace the rent
strike, the sit-in, the disruptive demonstration, and the walkout.
Not all causes can be isolated or resolved as individual or group
grievances, but the great majority of them probably can. And even
those issues that transcend the grievance machinery may be more
easily and amicably resolved, with much less resort to the barricades, if the channels do exist for expeditious handling of individual cases.

POLITICAL MACHINERY

The utility of the ward boss, the city councilman, and the local
legislator as problem solvers and expeditors cannot be overlooked.
They are there, expect to perform that role for constituents in trouble with the government, and would be quite opposed to any substitute channel that tried to usurp this prerogative. Indeed, concern
that such usurpation might take place was a key factor behind the
Buffalo Common Council's lopsided vote against the embryonic
ombudsman project. Equally important is the large caseload the
political channels already process. (One of the few Buffalo Coun-
cilmen who supported the ombudsman reported that on a busy Sunday he probably received more complaint-type calls at home than
the ombudsman received in his first month of operation.)

There is no question that the newer, more sophisticated channels have a hard time gaining acceptance in the poor areas. A recent
field study has shown that "even when an ideal recourse is presented . . . many disadvantaged persons shun the culturally approved system of legal institutions," and rely, instead, on access to a
"power patron." In his second quarterly report, the Buffalo
ombudsman, Professor John Hollands, recognized that "digging
channels of communication to the poor has proved harder than was
anticipated. . . . The explanation is partly distrust, which only

time and familiarity can overcome, and which has not, and may never be, fully dispelled."

III. *Safeguarding the Beneficiary's Interest: Participation as an Independent Value*

There is no assurance that the interests of a particular group of beneficiaries will be protected by inviting them to participate in developing the laws and rules that regulate their relations with government. But there is a good chance that the worst abuses and inequities will be checked by allowing involvement or at least consultation during the drafting stage. The experience in seeking to stimulate participation among beneficiaries has been spotty, of course. In the Poverty program, as Daniel Patrick Moynihan has shown recently, the experience has been discouraging if not disastrous. Some college and university presidents have given up hope of effectively involving students after finding student seats on committees empty or irregularly occupied. But it is much too early to give up because practical obstacles frustrate achievement of a goal that has such philosophical merit. In any case, nothing is lost if overtures of this type do not initially bring participants flocking to the conference table.

There are encouraging signs on many fronts. The academic year 1968–69 has probably seen the addition of more students to more faculty, administrative, and university-wide committees on more campuses than were added in the preceding half century. The change is not simply numerical. More important is the degree to which students, really for the first time, have been invited into the inner councils of the university. During the year, a student was added to the Board of Trustees at Vanderbilt University. The search committee for the new President of the University of Oregon included one student. Princeton University in 1969 added two graduating seniors—one white and one black—to its powerful Board of Trustees. The evidence of effective and active student participation in shaping the institutional environment is dramatic. Students as a class or group are also gaining opportunities for participation. A spokesman for the National Student Association was invited to testify on the "riot-ban" bills when they were pending in Congress. NSA has also been allowed to participate for the first time in an administrative hearing affecting the interests of students —the CAB proceeding to review the airline youth standby fares. There are attempts at participation in public housing as well. Quite apart from the indigenous tenants' unions, which bring pressure on the management from without, one first step has been made toward representation from within. The new Michigan public housing law creates a board of tenants' affairs for Detroit projects. Each board will be composed equally of tenants and of city appointees, and half the latter must live in the project neighborhood. The board has power to veto rules and regulations of the local housing commission. It also acts as a final body for internal appeals from decisions of the housing commission on such matters as evictions and rent increases. The Detroit experiment may well provide a model that can be used in many other cities.

Perhaps the most exciting development in this field, which will affect most of the government benefit programs we have studied, is the adoption by the Administrative Conference of the United States of a set of recommendations for "representation of the poor in agency rulemaking of direct consequence to them." The proposals from which these recommendations derived were drafted by Professor Arthur E. Bonfield of the University of Iowa. They resulted from an extensive survey of the practices of federal agencies as regards participation of the poor in the development or revision of regulations affecting their interests. Professor Bonfield found in the results of the survey an ample basis for action: ". . . the poor of our society have been inadequately represented in federal rulemaking. . . . About one third of the agencies claiming to administer programs substantially affecting the poor indicated that they had not previously attempted to ascertain the views of economically underprivileged persons with respect to rules and policies proposed by the agencies to implement those programs. . . . In fact, the interests of the poor have rarely had any continuous and systematic affirmative representation in the federal rulemaking process." On the basis of these findings, Professor Bonfield proposed, and the Administrative Conference adopted in substance, a set of remedies, including a clearinghouse coordinator organization, and an independent poor people's counsel with a full-time staff to represent the interests of the poor in all federal rulemaking proceedings affecting those interests. The proposals include detailed provisions for the financing, authority, and operations of the office, and for its relations with the constituent community. Professor Bonfield argues that if these proposals are adopted, they will improve the administration of government and its responsiveness to the needs of a hitherto neglected class of citizens. In addition, they may "eliminate one source of unnecessary tension between the poor and the federal establishment" by creating "procedures whereby the poor can get a fair hearing on the formulation of significant policies affecting them."

In these and other ways, the interests of government beneficiaries are coming to be better understood and better represented in the making of laws and rules that affect the beneficial relationship. Some channels of participation have come about in response to pressures from the beneficiaries; this is undoubtedly the case with collective bargaining in public employment and most student representation on university committees. In other instances, a benevolent administration—or one that sees consultation as an antidote to militancy—has created channels before they are demanded. The motive or reason for seeking participation should, however, be unimportant in light of its intrinsic value and the contribution it can make to responsible government.

IV. *Safeguarding the System: The Legal Standards Governing the Beneficial Relationship*

No matter how scrupulous the machinery, there is a limit to the efficacy of *procedure* as a guarantor of fairness for government beneficiaries. Part of the blame for the inequities and indignities we have examined here still lies with bad substantive law. Any ultimate assurance of dignity for the beneficiary must come through changes in the governing legal precepts. What is most urgently needed is new models for the benefactor-beneficiary relationship.

The most viable model is that developed by Professor Hans Linde of Oregon. He contends that government has the power to restrict a public beneficiary only to the extent it can control his private counterpart. The argument runs as follows: "The relevant measure of the constitutionality of government action is not the analogy of public management and private management. It is the comparison of governmental decisions in a public operation with governmental regulation of the analogous operation in private hands. The rele-

vant question is not whether the complainant—be he an employee,
a contractor, a student or an insurance beneficiary—could make
his claim against the action of the public managers if they were private. It is whether he could object if that action had been imposed
upon comparable private managers by governmental decision."
Linde concludes by urging that the test of government power in the
private sector, where constitutional liberties are at stake, should be
"effects rather than devices."

The test is intriguing in principle, and works well in practice.
Consider the case of the private employee. There are many regulations that government can constitutionally impose on him and his
employer: they may be required to contribute to Social Security, to
pay and to receive minimum wages, to bargain collectively over a
variety of issues, to limit the hours of work, and so on. If the place
or type of work warrants, government can undoubtedly impose certain health and safety standards such as the chest X ray required of
private as well as public school teachers in many states. But the
scope of governmental power over private employees stops long
before one reaches the host of restrictions that chip away at the liberties of public workers. Clearly government cannot exclude any
group of private employees from partisan politics. Nor can it demand that a private employer fire workers who criticize the government's foreign policy—or, for that matter, who are equally critical
of the way the private employer runs his business. Few states have
attempted to exact loyalty disclaimers as a condition of private employment. All these conditions would be invalid in the public sector, Linde argues, because government could not force them upon
the private sector. The degree to which this formula resolves hard
cases is the measure of its utility. The courts could not do better
than to consider its adoption and work out its implications. Yet it is
not likely that will take place very soon or very easily.

If some progress may be achieved by insisting that government
treat the recipient of public benefits no differently from the private
person subject to government regulation, there is another reform
that would also measurably enhance the beneficiary's lot. The procedures for withholding benefits from individual recipients or
claimants should be at least as elaborate and as rigorous as those to
which institutional and business beneficiaries are entitled. This is
not to say that recipients of subsidies, government contracts, fran-
chises and the like always receive complete due process. But they

usually have the influence, or the legal talent, or the money to demand—and get—somewhat greater protection for their interests than is typically given the individual (and often indigent) beneficiary.

One example may suggest the inclination and capacity of government to respond with impeccable procedures where the interests appear to require due process. Shortly after the 1968 running of the Kentucky Derby, the president of Churchill Downs ruled that the winning horse, Dancer's Image, had been drugged before the race in violation of Derby rules. The owner of the horse immediately demanded a hearing before the Churchill Downs Stewards, and such a hearing was held within a week. Meantime, the purse money and the official record of the race were held in abeyance. The Stewards upheld the president, and their decision was promptly appealed to the Kentucky Racing Commission, which scheduled, in accordance with its rules, another and more elaborate hearing. Before the Commission, attorneys for Peter Fuller, owner of the horse, cross-examined witnesses representing Churchill Downs, introduced expert testimony of their own, and amassed a transcript of over three thousand pages. Together with the transcript of the hearing before the Stewards, and depositions and affidavits taken earlier, the record of the case reached some six thousand pages. But Fuller's remedies did not end with the Commission's adverse decision. His lawyers immediately announced they would seek judicial review, confident that the court would review the judgment on the merits.

Of course the case of Dancer's Image is a cause célèbre. Few horses disqualified at the finish line would fare so well. Even many licensees and franchise holders are not nearly as fortunate, largely because they are unable or unwilling to commit the human resources that Peter Fuller could muster for a contest of this type. Beyond that, however, the rules of the Kentucky Racing Commission (if not of Churchill Downs) do appear substantially more rigorous and solicitous of the beneficiary's interests than the rules for eviction from the Louisville Housing Authority or the regulations of most welfare agencies. If the courts will simply insist that procedures followed in welfare termination, student dismissal, and public housing eviction cases be no less scrupulous than procedures for canceling subsidies, disqualifying government contractors, or race horses, or terminating business licenses, much will be gained for the beneficiary.

V. *Alternatives to the System: Dignity Through Choice*

None of the remedies suggested here can solve all the problems in the public sector. Some of what we have found fault with is really inherent in any system of public benefits, and becomes increasingly dangerous as the power of government expands and its activities multiply. In most areas, there are probably fewer private sector alternatives available—at least comparatively—than there were fifty years ago. With two thirds of all students attending publicly supported colleges and universities, the number of private elementary and secondary schools shrinking each year, all but a handful of transit systems (once mostly privately owned) now under government control, auditoriums, stadiums, and other facilities increasingly built by governmental rather than private promoters, and government health care programs preempting a field once handled entirely by private insurers, there are fewer and fewer opportunities available in the private sector for the person who finds a public benefit unacceptable or inaccessible because of restrictions.

A long-range solution may lie in more effective cooperation between public and private institutions. The concept of the mixed economy seeks a balance between complete nationalization of facilities on the one hand, and total dominance of private enterprise on the other. Theoretically, as we have seen earlier in this chapter, government could go either way on almost any activity. There is hardly anything that government could not nationalize and remove entirely from the private sector; conversely almost any activity can be performed by contract with private business. The rationale of the mixed economy is to differentiate those activities that are most suitably private, and others that are optimally governmental, with the residue open for joint participation.

A central aspect of the mixed economy is competition between public and private enterprise. Such competition is more common outside the United States. Railway transportation in Canada provides a perfect illustration: the government's Canadian National competes on certain important routes with the privately owned, though regulated, Canadian Pacific. The government furnishes air transportation through Air Canada, but allows Canadian Pacific Airlines to compete on some of the choicest routes. Air transportation and television broadcasting in Great Britain similarly involve competition between an arm of the government and a privately owned concern seeking the same audience (although the BBC does not, of course, compete for the advertising market, to which the Independent Television Authority has exclusive access).

In the United States, there are some tentative thrusts toward such a mixture under government sponsorship and direction. In a few major cities, municipally owned radio stations broadcast in competition with private outlets; but the governmental share of the market is so small that there is not yet any meaningful sharing. In television, the division may be more realistic as the government-supported Public Broadcasting Corporation begins to compete with private commercial channels and foundation-sustained educational stations. In at least one state, the government runs a retail liquor business, with a series of local outlets, but also permits limited competition by private distributors and sellers. In some communities, municipally owned transit systems compete with privately owned (though closely regulated) bus companies.

In some sectors, such public-private competition in the United States has been conscious; indeed, the survival of the private competitors may frequently depend upon public subsidy or stipend. This is increasingly the case in two fields to which we have given considerable attention in this book—low-income housing and higher education. Faced with the inability of public housing projects to meet the nation's needs for low-rent residential units, the government has turned increasingly to the private sector. The below-market interest-rate program, direct subsidies to private housing construction, and other programs reflect an increasing preference for public sponsorship of private programs in lieu of exclusive reliance upon public construction and management.

In higher education, the model is somewhat more sophisticated. Every American state has a state university, and in most there is also a private four-year college or university. There has long been active rivalry between the public and the private institutions, at the local as well as statewide level. And because of the diversity of sources of support, including student tuition, the private institutions have been able to compete quite effectively. Increasingly, though, the continuance of the competition is dependent upon direct government support to private institutions. New York State, which has the newest of the major state universities, has also been the first to recognize this public responsibility for the survival of the private colleges and universities. This pattern is quite likely to be repeated in other states as the plight of the private sector becomes clearer. And private higher education is already the beneficiary of major federal programs designed to relieve rapidly rising financial pressures.

There are other manifestations of the mixed economy in higher education, too: on the one hand, presently twelve of the twenty largest collegiate recipients of federal funds for research and development (which is not earmarked for particular types of institutions) are private universities. On the other hand, three of the top ten institutional fund raisers from *private* sources (corporations, foundations, alumni, etc.) are state universities. A few major institutions, like the University of Texas, already draw very heavily from both private and public sources. Thus, the mixed economy has reached a high degree of complexity in higher education—not because it was initially planned that way, but because institutional needs and fiscal realities have combined to create a pattern of growing interdependence.

There is another field of activity in which competition is beginning to exist, quite without official sanction. An enterprising young man in Oklahoma has founded a strikingly successful private mail delivery service, the Independent Postal Systems of America. By achieving economies not possible in the huge and beleaguered United States Post Office, he boasts faster and more efficient local mail deliveries in certain cities and at lower rates than the government charges. The founder explains that he is "proving . . . that free enterprise can do a better job than any government in business." The government, he adds, has been doing a "lousy job because it doesn't have any competition."

The initial support for a mixed economy has little to do with unconstitutional conditions. The beneficial effects of competition in the private sector are already well known, and are reflected in strong national mandates such as those enjoining monopolization of commerce and fixing of prices. Public-private competition, in addition to reinforcing these mandates, may foster experimentation and change in ways that would not be possible in a government monopoly context. More effective utilization of resources, both physical and human, is quite likely to follow diversification. These benefits should flow even though the government may, in a sense, be subsidizing the private competition as well as the public program. (In the case of the private postal system, for example, the government subsidy is readily apparent; only the high level of third class mailing rates, which could easily be reduced if governmental priorities were altered, allows such private competition to exist at all.)

To the extent that meaningful alternatives in the private sector can be restored, through a mixed economy or other means, the beneficiary's lot will be commensurately improved. The ability of government to conduct certain business through private channels, or to promote public-private competition in other areas, is virtually unlimited. The use of artificial methods to stimulate such competition and alternatives would not be unthinkable; after all, the government sometimes requires private firms to set up essentially artificial means of preserving competition in an industry that tends toward monopoly. Whatever may be the economic cost or loss of efficiency resulting from a commitment to a mixed economy, the compensating advantages to beneficiaries of many types would be immeasurably greater.

REFERENCES AND

BIBLIOGRAPHY

Important references to court decisions, documents, and other materials cited in the text have been grouped here under appropriate chapter headings. No attempt has been made, however, either to furnish a complete bibliography on the subjects with which this book is concerned, or to provide the reference for each individual item of information. A law review article would, of course, contain such precise references, as would a legal treatise. But it was felt that such detail would impair the readability of this book and would misrepresent its purpose. Accordingly, only essential documentation has been provided.

A few introductory notes about citation of legal materials may facilitate the use of this section. Many court decisions have been summarized or referred to in the text, and are identified in these notes. All but a handful of these cases were decided by appellate courts, reviewing the decision of a trial court or of a lower appeal court. Many are decisions of the United States Supreme Court, recognizable by the citation to a volume of the *United States Reports*. (Such a citation is in the form "100 U.S. 200," which indicates that the case cited, or the opinion of the Court in that case, is in Volume 100 of the *United States Reports*, beginning at page 200. Dating from the first year of the Supreme Court, the series is now approaching its four hundredth volume.) The same system of page and volume references is used below in references to articles in journals and reviews.

There are also decisions of the lower federal courts. These appear in two series of reports, both issued by the West Publishing Company rather than by the courts or the government. Decisions of Federal Courts of Appeals appear in the *Federal Reporter*, Second Series, which is also nearing its four hundredth volume. (The form would be "100 F.2d 200" and would typically include the circuit in which the case was decided. There are ten federal circuits, numbered roughly from East to West across the country, and one in the District of Columbia.) Decisions of the Federal District (trial) Courts appear in the *Federal Supplement,* which has run to almost three hundred volumes. They are cited in the form "100 F. Supp. 200," usually followed by a reference to the judicial district—about one hundred throughout the United States—in which the case was decided. (Although nearly all decisions of Federal Courts of Appeals are published in the *Federal Second,* only those district court decisions appear in the *Federal Supplement* that have been submitted by the judge as having special merit or novelty.)

Finally, there are references to a smaller number of state court decisions. Only in New York are state trial court opinions reported regularly. For all other states, the decisions of the highest court appear in regional reporter series—Northeast, Northwest, Pacific, Southern, etc. —all in the second series. Opinions of intermediate appellate courts appear for some states but not all. Until recently every state also published an "official" report of its high court decisions. That practice has been declining, however, with increasing reliance on the "unofficial" (but often the only) report that appears in the West Company regional reporters. A typical citation would be "100 N.E.2d 200 (Mass. 1965)" for a case decided by the Supreme Judicial Court of Massachusetts in 1965 and reported in the hundredth volume of the *Northeast Reporter,* second series, page 200.

Some of the cases cited here have not yet been reported in either official or unofficial volumes, and others (for example, trial court decisions in states other than New York) never will be. Information about such cases is gleaned from various sources. Usually cases of importance involving government benefit programs will at least be noted in *The New York Times* the following day. Within two or three weeks, an abstract of the opinion may well appear in the *United States Law Week,* published in Washington weekly by the Bureau of National Affairs. This loose-leaf service distributes promptly the full text of U.S. Supreme Court decisions and of selected congressional enactment; it also culls the state and lower federal court advance sheets (preliminary reports) for cases of special importance. These are abstracted or summarized and distributed in the weekly supplement.

There are several other sources for information about unreported cases in the subject areas of this book. Since 1966, all court decisions relating to student rights and university law have been noted and summarized—often reported in full—in the *College and University Reporter,* a publication of the Commerce Clearing House in Chicago. Cases in the welfare and public housing area have been noted monthly in the *Welfare Law Bulletin,* a most useful publication of Project on Social Welfare Law at New York University. (The *Bulletin* also includes in each issue a bibliography of current law review articles, books, and pamphlets dealing with the rights of welfare clients, public housing tenants, and poor people generally.) Regrettably, the *Welfare Law Bulletin* ceased publication with the June 1969 issue, noting that its major objectives had been achieved. The recent inauguration of a comprehensive loose-leaf service, the *Poverty Law Reporter* (published by the Commerce Clearing House in Chicago), fills much of the gap. But the rapidity and diversity of developments in this area makes a careful reading of the daily newspaper essential.

There is a growing volume of books and articles dealing with these timely subjects. Indeed, hardly a week passes that news magazines, pulp weeklies, and slick monthlies do not focus on some aspect of teacher strikes, college student demonstrations, welfare protests, or public housing tenants' unions. Any attempt to include materials of this sort would lengthen this section to a book of its own. It must be assumed that the reader, if he is sufficiently interested in the subject matter, will find ways of building his own bibliography. Moreover, any attempt to make a single listing of publications current or even timely would be foredoomed to failure by the rapidity with which new works appear, and the speed at which the subject matter and emphasis change.

A list of abbreviations used in this appendix follows:

American Pol. Sci. Rev.	*American Political Science Review*
C.D.	Central District
Cal. App.	*California Appellate Reports*
Cal. Rptr.	*California Reporter*
Cir.	Circuit
Ct. Cl.	Court of Claims
Dist. Ct.	District Court
E.D.	Eastern District
F. Supp.	*Federal Supplement*
F.2d	*Federal Reporter,* Second Series
Law & Contemp. Prob.	*Law and Contemporary Problems*
L.J.	Law Journal
L. Rev.	Law Review
L.Q.	Law Quarterly
M.D.	Middle District
N.E. (N.W., etc.) 2d	*Northeast (Northwest,* etc.) *Reporter,* Second Series
N.Y.S. 2d	*New York Supplement,* Second Series
N.Y. Supp.	*New York Supplement*
P.2d	*Pacific Reporter,* Second Series

S.D.	Southern District
U.S.	United States Reports
W.D.	Western District
W.L.B.	*Welfare Law Bulletin*

Chapter I

A number of cases are mentioned in Chapter I. All but a handful of these appear at greater length in subsequent chapters. Thus in order to avoid duplication and repetition, specific references will be reserved for the notes for the chapters in which these cases are discussed in detail.

Chapter II

The general subject of conditions on government benefits—"unconstitutional conditions" is the phrase that most often appears in legal literature—has given rise to many scholarly articles. The most comprehensive and insightful of these might well be overlooked by the casual reader because of its modest title. It is a two-part article by Professor Hans A. Linde, "Constitutional Rights in the Public Sector," 39 Washington L. Rev. 4 (1964); 40 Washington L. Rev. 10 (1965). Also valuable and recent is Professor William Van Alstyne's "The Demise of the Right-Privilege Distinction in Constitutional Law," 81 Harvard L. Rev. 1439 (1968). An early treatment of the subject, which has at least historical interest, is Robert L. Hale, "Unconstitutional Conditions and Constitutional Rights," 35 Columbia L. Rev. 321 (1935). Useful reviews of the field are found in John French, "Comment: Unconstitutional Conditions: An Analysis," 50 Georgetown L. J. 234 (1961); and in a student Note, "Unconstitutional Conditions," 73 Harvard L. Rev. 1595 (1960). Some of the material in this chapter was adapted from Robert M. O'Neil, "Unconstitutional Conditions: Welfare Benefits With Strings Attached," 54 California L. Rev. 443 (1966), although the present treatment is substantially expanded and somewhat differently oriented. There are two articles, rather specially concerned with the welfare benefit area, that contain such thoughtful treatments of the general problem of unconstitutional conditions that they should be mentioned here. Alanson W. Willcox, former general counsel of the Department of Health, Education and Welfare, wrote most sensitively about the programs his agency administered, in "Invasions of the First Amendment Through Conditioned Spending," 41 Cornell L.Q. 12 (1955). Professor Charles Reich of the Yale Law School has devoted much time and thought to this area, and has offered some striking insights in "Individual Rights and

Social Welfare: the Emerging Legal Issues," 74 Yale L.J. 1245 (1965).

The classic statement of the unconstitutional condition theory comes from Professor Thomas Reed Powell, who promptly went on to refute it, in "The Right to Work for the State," 16 Columbia L. Rev. 99 (1916). The Supreme Court decision on partial closing of a business to forestall labor organizing was Textile Workers Union v. Darlington Mfg. Co., 380 U.S. 263 (1965). Decisions involving the concept of cruel and unusual punishment as a check on "the greater includes the lesser" are Trop v. Dulles, 356 U.S. 86 (1958) (denaturalization of a deserter); and Louisiana ex rel Francis v. Resweber, 329 U.S. 459 (1947) (death by slow torture after a death sentence).

The early cases allowing states virtually unlimited power to exclude nonresident corporations were Paul v. Virginia, 75 U.S. 168 (1869), and Doyle v. Continental Ins. Co., 94 U.S. 535 (1877). It was in the latter case that Justice Bradley announced his notable dissent. The overruling case was Frost & Frost Trucking Co. v. Railroad Commission, 271 U.S. 583 (1926), of which Terral v. Burke Construction Co., 257 U.S. 529 (1922) was an important precursor. These cases are reviewed at some length in the Willcox and French articles cited above, and in the 1960 *Harvard Law Review* student Note.

The contest about the mayor's power to condition access to the Boston Common resulted in Commonwealth v. Davis, 162 Mass. 510, 39 N.E. 113 (1895), affirmed by the U.S. Supreme Court in Davis v. Massachusetts, 167 U.S. 43 (1897). The New Bedford policeman's case was McAuliffe v. Mayor and Board of Aldermen, 155 Mass. 216, 29 N.E. 517 (1892). The two post office mailing privilege cases were Milwaukee Social Democratic Publishing Co. v. Burleson, 255 U.S. 407 (1921); and Hannegan v. Esquire, Inc., 327 U.S. 146 (1946), the latter effectively overruling the former. One of the last vestiges of the old conditioning theory was in the decision sustaining New York's loyalty oath for teachers, Adler v. Board of Education, 342 U.S. 485 (1952). A somewhat different approach was evinced in the case of the Bulgarian deportee, Flemming v. Nestor, 363 U.S. 603 (1960), and much more clearly revealed in the case of the South Carolina Seventh Day Adventist, Sherbert v. Verner, 374 U.S. 398 (1963). The persistent use of the "privilege" terminology is illustrated by the decision in a welfare case of a District judge, since retired, in Harrell v. Board of Commissioners, 269 F. Supp. 919 (D.D.C. 1967).

The series of California cases developing a strong protection for the beneficiary against unconstitutional conditions began with Fort v. Civil Service Commission, 38 Cal. Rptr. 625 (Cal. 1964), and continued through three important cases in late 1966 and early 1967. The opinion most often quoted as a statement of the California law on this question is that of the majority in Bagley v. Washington Township Hospital District, 55 Cal. Rptr. 401 (Cal. 1966), followed closely by Rosenfield v. Malcolm, 55 Cal. Rptr. 505 (Cal. 1967), and Parrish v. Civil Service Commission, 57 Cal. Rptr. 623 (Cal. 1967)—the last of these the case of the Alameda County Social Worker who refused to participate in "Operation Bedcheck."

The quotation from Justice Douglas about the dubious connection between a doctor's politics and his medical ability is from a dissenting opinion in Barsky v. Board of Regents, 347 U.S. 442 (1954). The later, more sympathetic view of the Court appeared in the case of denial of the California veteran's tax exemption for refusal to file the disclaimer oath, Speiser v. Randall, 357 U.S. 513 (1958). The recent Supreme Court decision breaking down the technical barriers to a taxpayer's suit is Flast v. Cohen, 392 U.S. 83 (1968).

Chapter III

There are surprisingly few general studies of the differences between public and private employment. The financial, functional, and psychological disparities seem not to have been of great interest to sociologists and students of public administration until rather recently. A most useful and timely collection of articles is found in the December 1967 issue of *Public Administration Review*. Notable are H. George Frederickson, "Understanding Attitudes Toward Public Employment," p. 411; Frank Gibson and George James, "Student Attitudes Toward Government Employees and Employment," p. 429; Alan Schechter, "The Influence of Public Service on Businessmen's Attitudes Toward the Federal Government," p. 452. There is some information in earlier works, e.g., Marver H. Bernstein, *The Job of the Federal Executive* (Washington: The Brookings Institution, 1958); W. Lloyd Warner, *The American Federal Executive* (New Haven: Yale University Press, 1963); and Franklin Kilpatrick, *The Image of the Federal Service* (Washington: The Brookings Institution, 1964).

The old case involving restrictions on employment of aliens was Heim v. McCall, 239 U.S. 175 (1917), with which should be compared Truax v. Raich, 239 U.S. 33 (1917); in the latter case the Court held that Arizona could not bar aliens from *private* employment in the state. The Santa Barbara (California) trial court decision declining to follow Heim is reported in *The New York Times,* December 3, 1967, p. 86, col. 8. That decision was affirmed by the California Supreme Court in Purdy & Fitzpatrick v. California, 456 P.2d 645 (Cal. 1969).

A quite tolerant view of the effect of a criminal record on eligibility for government employment is reflected in the California Supreme

Court decision, Hallinan v. Committee of Bar Examiners, 55 Cal. Rptr. 228 (Cal. 1966).

The most definitive study of privacy—not only in government employment but in many other areas, is Professor Alan Westin's exhaustive work, *Privacy and Freedom* (New York: Atheneum, 1967), the result of a five-year study sponsored by the Association of the Bar of the City of New York. Also useful is a symposium in the spring 1966 issue of *Law & Contemporary Problems* (a quarterly journal published by Duke University Law School), dealing with the whole field of privacy. Especially pertinent is an article by the former Chief Counsel and Staff Director of the Subcommittee on Constitutional Rights of the U.S. Senate Judiciary Committee, William A. Creech, "The Privacy of Government Employees," 31 Law & Contemp. Prob. 413 (1966). The article summarizes many of the most relevant findings of Senator Ervin's subcommittee investigating invasions of the privacy of public workers. The several quotations from the subcommittee findings are taken from this article. The two pertinent California cases involving the private lives of public employees, both teachers, are Board of Trustees v. Hartman, 55 Cal. Rptr. 144 (1966) (the case of the invalid Mexican divorce); and Finot v. Pasadena City Board of Education, 58 Cal. Rptr. 520 (1967) (the bearded teacher). For a recent review of congressional investigations of public employee privacy, together with a summary and detailed critique of legislation introduced by Senator Ervin, see Note, 37 Geo. Wash. L. Rev. 101 (1969).

The series of Supreme Court cases involving compulsion or obligation to testify began with Slochower v. Board of Higher Education, 350 U.S. 551 (1956), setting aside the Brooklyn College professor's dismissal, and was followed closely by two cases upholding discharges for "insubordination": Lerner v. Casey, 357 U.S. 468 (1957) (the New York subway conductor); and Beilan v. Board of Education, 357 U.S. 399 (the Philadelphia teacher). More recent cases include Nelson v. County of Los Angeles, 362 U.S. 1 (1960), which is consistent with Beilan and Lerner, and several decisions that point the other way. The interests of the employees or licensees were upheld in Spevack v. Klein, 385 U.S. 511 (1967); Garrity v. New Jersey, 385 U.S. 493 (1967); Gardner v. Broderick, 392 U.S. 273 (1968); and Uniformed Sanitation Men Association v. New York Sanitation Commissioner, 392 U.S. 280 (1968). The only recent case going the other way involved a government contractor firm disqualified because of the recalcitrance of one of its officers; the Court held that the privilege was personal, in Campbell Painting Corp. v. Reid, 392 U.S. 286 (1968).

The two leading cases involving the obligation to perform an allegedly unconstitutional act are Parrish v. Civil Service Commission, 57

Cal. Rptr. 623 (Cal. 1967), which we have already encountered in another context. This was the case of the California social worker. The other case, involving the New York school teacher who refused to lead the pledge, has been reported only as a decision of a trial examiner appointed by the New York City Board of Education. The summary of his decision is found in *The New York Times,* September 7, 1968, p. 1, col. 1; p. 19, col. 4–5.

Chapter IV

The case of the discharged New Bedford policeman, as previously cited, is McAuliffe v. Mayor and Board of Aldermen, 155 Mass. 216, 29 N.E. 517 (1892). Surprisingly, there were no reported cases of that type from McAuliffe's day until rather recent times.

There have been many books written about loyalty oaths and disclaimers, and other forms of security testing. Among these are Harold M. Hyman, *To Try Men's Souls: Loyalty Tests in American History* (Berkeley: University of California Press, 1959); and Ralph S. Brown, *Loyalty and Security* (New Haven: Yale University Press, 1958). Much of the important litigation has, however, taken place since these very thorough works appeared. Among the most helpful of the recent articles are Professor Jerold Israel's "Elfbrandt v. Russell: The Demise of the Oath?," 1966 Supreme Court Review 193 (1966); and Professer Arval A. Morris's two contributions, "The University of Washington Loyalty Oath Case," *AAUP Bulletin,* Autumn, 1964, p. 221; and "Academic Freedom and Loyalty Oaths," 28 Law & Contemp. Prob. 487 (1963). (Professor Morris played a key role in the lawsuit that invalidated the Washington State oath in 1964.)

The first oath cases, right after the Civil War, were Cummings v. Missouri, 71 U.S. 277 (1867); and Ex Parte Garland, 71 U.S. 333 (1867). Father Cummings was a priest and Garland a lawyer, and both cases involved Reconstruction government oaths directed against former Confederates or Confederate sympathizers. Justice Traynor's observations on the futility and demeaning character of loyalty oaths appeared in his dissent in First Unitarian Church v. County of Los Angeles, 311 P.2d 508 (1957). The essence of his view was accepted when the Supreme Court reversed a companion case, Spesier v. Randall, 357 U.S. 513 (1958). The opinion of Mr. Justice Douglas about guilt by association was taken from his dissent in Adler v. Board of Education, 342 U.S. 485 (1952).

The more recent loyalty oath cases were reviewed in the text substantially in chronological order. The California case was Garner v. Board of Public Works, 341 U.S. 716 (1951); this decision was sharply qualified by the Oklahoma oath case, Wieman v. Updegraff, 344 U.S. 183 (1952). The same year the Court sustained the New York Feinberg law in the Adler case, cited just above. Little happened in the oath field until 1961, when the Court struck down a vague Florida oath in Cramp v. Board of Public Instruction, 368 U.S. 278 (161). The modern era of oath cases really began with the striking down of the Washington disclaimer in Baggett v. Bullitt, 377 U.S. 360 (1964). Taking a slightly different approach to the constitutional issue the following year, the Court invalidated the Arizona oath in Elfbrandt v. Russell, 384 U.S. 11 (1966), which set the stage for the demise of New York's Feinberg Law in Keyishian v. Board of Regents, 385 U.S. 589 (1967), and Whitehill v. Elkins, 389 U.S. 54 (1967). Since that time several state and lower federal courts have invalidated similar oath requirements, but there has been no further activity at the Supreme Court level.

J. Edgar Hoover's observations about the frequently guiltless membership in the Communist Party and other allegedly subversive organizations appeared in testimony before the House Committee on UnAmerican Activities during the 80th Congress, 1st session, and were reprinted in the *FBI Law Enforcement Bulletin* in 1952.

The doctrine of the least onerous alternative is well established in Supreme Court law. A lengthening series of cases has insisted that government use that method of regulation that is least injurious to or subversive of individual liberties. The first such case was Lovell v. City of Griffin, 303 U.S. 444 (1938), the theme has recurred in more recent cases such as Shelton v. Tucker, 364 U.S. 479 (1960); and Aptheker v. Secretary of State, 378 U.S. 500 (1964).

A good deal has been written about the Hatch Act and parallel restrictions on the political activities of civil servants. Particularly useful are James W. Irwin, "Public Employees and the Hatch Act," 9 Vanderbilt L. Rev. 527 (1956), Dalmas H. Nelson, "Public Employees and the Right To Engage in Political Activity," 9 Vanderbilt L. Rev. 27 (1955); Henry Rose, "A Critical Look at the Hatch Act," 75 Harvard L. Rev. 510 (1962); and Milton J. Esman, "The Hatch Act—A Reappraisal," 60 Yale L.J. 986 (1951). A most useful survey of the constitutional arguments surrounding the Hatch Act is contained in a memorandum prepared by Richard P. Sims, then a Columbia University law student, for the Free Speech/Association Committee of the American Civil Liberties Union during the summer of 1967. For recent developments see the Report of the Commission on Political Activity of Government Personnel (1968); and Note, "The Public Employee and Political Activity," 3 Suffolk Univ. L. Rev. 380 (1969).

Representative recent Hatch Act cases are Democratic State Central Committee v. Andolsek, 249 F. Supp. 1009 (D. Md. 1966); and Jarvis v. Civil Service Commission, 382 F.2d 339 (6th Cir. 1967). A summary of the recent enforcement of the Hatch Act is found in *The New York Times,* December 13, 1965, p. 22, col. 3–6. The Supreme Court decision sustaining the Hatch Act against constitutional challenge was United Public Workers v. Mitchell, 330 U.S. 75 (1947). The California Supreme Court has taken a quite different view of county and municipal restrictions on political activity so similar to the Hatch Act as to be legally indistinguishable. The Oregon Supreme Court has adopted a similar view in Minielly v. State, 411 P.2d 69 (1966). The foreign experience, particularly in Great Britain, is summarized in James B. Christoph, "Political Rights and Impartiality in the British Civil Service, 51 American Pol. Sci. Rev. 67 (1957).

The American Civil Liberties Union announced its stand on the alleged muzzling of Peace Corps volunteers in a telegram to Peace Corps director Jack Vaughn, with a copy to President Johnson, on June 13, 1967. The case of the outspoken Berkeley fireman is Belshaw v. City of Berkeley, 54 Cal. Rptr. 727 (Cal. App. 1966). The Cedar Rapids firemen prevailed in Klein v. Civil Service Commission, 152 N.W.2d 195 (Iowa 1967). The two federal cases are Swaaley v. United States, 376 F.2d 857 (Ct. Cl. 1967) (the Brooklyn Navy Yard Worker); and Meehan v. Macy, 392 F.2d 822 (D.C. Cir. 1968).

In the late spring of 1968, the Supreme Court resolved many of these issues in Pickering v. Will County Board of Education, 391 U.S. 563 (1968). The Court sent the Alaska case back to the state court for reconsideration in light of the Pickering decision.

The materials dealing with collective bargaining (and peripherally with the right to strike) in public employment are burgeoning rapidly. Probably the most useful publications are those of the Cornell University School of Industrial and Labor Relations—including a series of reprints covering many aspects of the problem, and several books, such as Professor Kurt Hanslowe's *The Emerging Law of Labor Relations in Public Employment* (Ithaca: New York School of Industrial and Labor Relations, 1967); and *Teachers, School Boards and Collective Bargaining* (Ithaca: New York School of Industrial and Labor Relations, 1967), by Professors Walter E. Oberer and Robert E. Doherty. From the same source come the periodic *Public Employee Relations Reports.* Report No. 2, by Andrew Thompson, deals with "Strikes and Strike Penalties in Public Employment"; No. 3, by Richard S. Rubin, contains a summary of state laws on collective bargaining in the public sector. There are also a number of law review articles, e.g., Daniel P. Sullivan, "How Can the Problem of the Public Employees Strike Be Resolved?," 19 Oklahoma L. Rev. 365 (1966).

The two federal court of appeals decisions upholding the right of a public worker not to be discharged for joining a union are McLaughlin v. Tilendis, 398 F.2d 287 (7th Cir. 1968); and American Federation of

State, County and Municipal Employees v. Woodward, 406 F.2d 137 (8th Cir. 1969). The two state cases that present contrasting views on the right to strike are the New York case rejecting it out of hand, City of New York v. DeLury, 243 N.E.2d 128 (N.Y. 1968); and the California decision leaving the question open, In re Berry, 65 Cal. Rptr. 273 (Cal. 1968). The recent Superior Court decision refusing to enjoin the Los Angeles public school teacher strike is reported in *Los Angeles Times,* September 17, 1969, p. 1.

The question of a civil servant's right to a hearing or other remedy, both in the United States and abroad, is the subject of several articles. Particularly germane are Ivor Richardson, "Problems in the Removal of Federal Civil Servants," 54 Michigan L. Rev. 219 (1955); and Mark Joelson, "Legal Problems in the Dismissal of Civil Servants in the United States, Britain and France," 12 American Journal of Comparative Law 149 (1963). The cause célèbre in this country is Bailey v. Richardson, 182 F.2d 46 (D.C. Cir. 1950), which was affirmed without opinion by an equally divided Supreme Court, 341 U.S. 918 (1951).

The suggestion that due process may compel a government employer to give an applicant an opportunity to rebut an unfavorable inference resulting from refusal to sign an oath comes initially from Slochower v. Board of Higher Education, 350 U.S. 551 (1956), and was refined by a three judge district court in Heckler v. Shepard, 243 F. Supp. 841 (D. Idaho 1965). The recent decision holding a public employee entitled to due process prior to dismissal, regardless of civil service procedures, is Olson v. Regents of Univ. of Minn., 301 F. Supp. 1356 (D. Minn. 1969).

Chapter V

It is hard to know where to begin in describing the swelling literature on the rights and responsibilities of college students. There are now a number of studies devoted primarily or exclusively to the legal aspects of student-institutional relations. The current volumes of M. M. Chambers *Colleges and the Courts* (Danville, Ill.: Interstate Pub. Co., 1969) summarize the recent cases. Professor George M. Johnson's *Education Law* (East Lansing: Michigan State University Press, 1969) contains much useful and pertinent material. There have been several law review symposia devoted to this topic—notably the March 1966 issue of the *California Law Review* (Vol. 54, No. 1), and the Special 1968 issue of the *Denver Law Journal* (Vol. 45, No. 4). There is a thoughtful section on student rights in "Developments in the Law—Academic Freedom," 81 Harvard L. Rev. 1045, 1143–56 (1968). Apart from the long symposia, perhaps the best contributions have been those dealing particularly with procedures in student discipline cases: William Van Alstyne, "Procedural Due Process and State University Students," 10 U.C.L.A. L. Rev. 368 (1963); Michael T. Johnson, "The Constitutional Rights of College Students," 42 Texas L. Rev. 344 (1964); and a long unsigned student Note, "Private Government on the Campus—Judicial Review of University Expulsions," 72 Yale L.J. 1362 (1963). Two other articles particularly deserve mention, though they do not deal with disciplinary procedures. One of the first discussions of the substantive legal limits on university rule making was Professor William Van Alstyne's "Student Academic Freedom and the Rule-making Powers of Public Universities: Some Constitutional Considerations," 2 Law in Transition Quarterly 1 (1965). Also noteworthy for its analysis of the various bases of university authority over students, and of student safeguards against the institution, is Professor Alvin Goldman's "The University and the Liberty of Its Students—A Fiduciary Theory," 54 Kentucky L.J. 643 (1966). A recent and quite comprehensive treatment of the emerging law in this field is an article by Professor Charles Alan Wright, "The Constitution on the Campus," 22 Vand. L. Rev. 1027 (1969).

There is a much broader and richer literature containing the raw material from which the cases derive. Every major student upheaval has produced at least one major book; the Berkeley protest movement of 1964–65 has brought forth probably eight to ten works, of which the most comprehensive is *The Berkeley Student Revolt* (Garden City: Anchor Books, 1965), edited by Seymour M. Lipset and Sheldon S. Wolin. Columbia has already produced the remarkable report of the Fact Finding Commission chaired by Professor Archibald Cox, under the title, *Crisis at Columbia* (New York: Vintage Books, 1968). An earlier, but still useful, collection is *The Troubled Campus* (Boston: Little Brown & Co., 1965), taken from the pages of the *Atlantic Monthly*. From the same period is the collection of papers from the 1965 Institute for College and University Self-study, entitled *Order and Freedom on the Campus* (Boulder: Western Interstate Commission for Higher Education, 1965). The list could be lengthened indefinitely, but this brief sample must suffice.

The statement of Dr. Bruno Bettelheim is from an interview with a Chicago reporter the day after students left the Administration Building, with their demands for the rehiring of a popular young faculty member unmet. The interview appears in *Chicago Sun-Times,* February 16, 1969, Section II, pp. 1–3.

Thomas Jefferson's encounters with student radicals at the University of Virginia are described in *Writings of Thomas Jefferson,* Library Edition (Washington: The Thomas Jefferson Memorial Edition, 1904), Vol. 18, pp. 341–48. The international perspective on student protest, and the prognosis for the future, come from the summary of the report to the U.N. Commission for Social Development, *The New York Times,* February 16, 1969, p. 10, col. 1.

The opinion giving considerable latitude to the university administration as late as 1956 did involve a private university, Brandeis, to be specific. The case was Deehan v. Brandeis University, 150 F. Supp. 626 (D. Mass. 1956). Professor Seavey's critical comments about the indifference of courts toward students were in "Dismissal of Students: 'Due Process,' " 70 Harvard L. Rev. 1406 (1957). The recent, sharply contrasting views of the Presidents of the American Council on Education and of the American Association of University Professors are found in James A. Perkins, "The University and Due Process," pamphlet printed by the American Council on Education, Washington, D.C., 1967; and Clark Byse, "The University and Due Process: A Somewhat Different View," Address Delivered at the 54th Annual Meeting of the American Association of University Professors, April 26, 1968.

As late as 1959, the federal courts still seriously doubted their jurisdiction to review disciplinary actions of publicly supported colleges and universities. The Brooklyn College case is Steier v. New York State Education Commissioner, 271 F.2d 13 (2d Cir. 1959). The dramatic change was brought about by two Southern cases, Dixon v. Alabama State Board of Education, 294 F.2d 150 (5th Cir. 1961), and Knight v. State Board of Education, 200 F. Supp. 174 (M.D. Tenn. 1961). The comment about the importance of continuing one's education is from "Note, Private Government on the Campus—Judicial Review of University Expulsions," 72 Yale L.J. 1362 (1963).

The excerpts from the Cox Commission report are drawn from Chapter I of *Crisis at Columbia,* the chapter dealing generally with "Student Attitudes and Concerns" as background for analysis of the specific issues that troubled the Columbia campus.

The California ROTC case, Hamilton v. Regents, 293 U.S. 245 (1934), has never been overruled, although the rather rapid decline in ROTC credit-bearing programs (much less compulsory participation) has made the issue substantially moot.

The statements attributed to Cornell University President James A. Perkins are taken from the speech to the American Council on Education, cited above. To a limited degree, Dr. Perkins's fears may find confirmation in the case of Connelly v. University of Vermont, 244 F. Supp. 156 (D. Vt. 1965), holding that if a student could make out a case of prejudice or improper bias in the award of a failing grade, he would then have a federal claim. Obviously, though, such a claim is not easily established. As Professor Byse explained in his address to the annual convention of the American Association of University Professors (cited above), the dangers of judicial intervention are easily exaggerated on the basis of a few cases.

The insistence on a direct relationship between offending student behavior and special university interests is embodied most clearly in the University of Oregon Code of Student Conduct. The background and operation of the Code is explained, and some of its provisions set forth, in Hans A. Linde, "Campus Law: Berkeley Viewed From Eugene," 54 California L. Rev. 40 (1966). The same philosophy is found in the *Proposed Code of Student Conduct and Discipline Proceedings in a University Setting* (New York: New York University Law School, 1968).

The Cornell Commission report is properly termed the report of the University Commission on the Interdependence of University Regulations and Local, State and Federal Law, which was appointed by President Perkins in May 1967 and reported its recommendations to him in September.

The question of on-campus advocacy or organization of off-campus political activities was discussed at some length in a report prepared for the Academic Freedom Committee of the Academic Senate at Berkeley just before the crucial vote of December 8, 1964. The report is contained in Lipset and Wolin, *The Berkeley Student Revolt* (Garden City: Anchor Books, 1965), pp. 273–80.

The initial cases on the application of constitutional constraints to "private" colleges and universities were the two from Tulane. The first of these, Guillory v. Administrators of Tulane University, 203 F. Supp. 855 (E.D. La. 1962) held in favor of the Negro students seeking admission. When the case was reconsidered by another judge, a different result was reached in Guillory v. Administrators of Tulane University, 212 F. Supp. 674 (E.D. La. 1962). The next case on the point was a very brief, unsigned opinion in Hammond v. University of Tampa, 344 F.2d 951 (5th Cir. 1965). The two recent and important cases are from Columbia, Grossner v. Trustees of Columbia University, 287 F. Supp. 535 (S.D. N.Y. 1968), and Powe v. Miles, 407 F.2d 73 (2d Cir. 1968). Two other recent cases, reaching the same result on slightly different facts, are Browns v. Mitchell, 409 F.2d 593 (10th Cir. 1969); and Torres v. Puerto Rico Junior College, 298 F. Supp. 458 (D.P.R. 1969).

The preliminary report on campus disorders of the National Commission on the Causes and Prevention of Violence was released in June 1969 and appears in *The New York Times,* June 10, 1969, p. 30. President Nixon's major speech on campus disturbances appears in *The New York Times,* April 30, 1969, p. 29.

The recommendations of the Bundy Commission for direct subsidies to private colleges and universities in New York State are in *Report of the Select Committee on the Future of Private and Independent Higher Education in New York State* (1968). Professor William Cohen's observations on the changing character of "private" universities are in

"The Private-Public Legal Aspects of Institutions of Higher Education," 45 Denver L.J. 643 (1968).

Chapter VI

The discussion of the student's right to a hearing draws essentially upon materials already cited in connection with Chapter V—Professor Seavey's article, the Dixon and Knight cases, and Professor Van Alstyne's article (the latter containing the survey of actual practice in university discipline cases). The ideal is found in statements such as those of the American Association of University Professors and the American Civil Liberties Union. The AAUP "Statement on the Academic Freedom of Students" is significant in part because it recognizes that students do enjoy academic freedom. After many successive drafts, the statement was adopted by the AAUP Council on recommendation of Committee S, and appeared in the Winter 1965 *AAUP Bulletin,* pp. 447–49. The ACLU statement has also undergone successive revisions. The current version appears as a pamphlet published in September 1966 by the National ACLU office—"Academic Freedom, Academic Responsibility, Academic Due Process in Institutions of Higher Learning."

Professor Heyman's comments on the importance and character of the disciplinary hearing are from "Some Thoughts on University Disciplinary Proceedings," 54 California L. Rev. 73 (1966). Additional ground rules for discipline cases have been set by the judges of the United States District Court for the Western District of Missouri, sitting en banc, in an extraordinary "General Order" which appears in 45 Federal Rules Decisions 133 (1968). This statement distinguished between those incidents of the hearing that are constitutionally mandated and those that are optional for the institution (though perhaps desirable).

A number of specific cases are cited in the text of this chapter. The South Carolina demonstration case is Hammond v. South Carolina State College, 272 F. Supp. 947 (D.S.C. 1967). The case arising from the Berkeley "dirty word" incident is Goldberg v. Regents of the University of California, 57 Cal. Rptr. 463 (Cal. App. 1967). The recent case invalidating Wisconsin's use of "misconduct" as a standard for expulsion, is Soglin v. Kauffman, 295 F. Supp. 978 (E.D. Wis. 1968). The two decisions finding insufficient evidence in the record to sustain the university's disciplinary action are Zanders v. Board of Education, 281 F. Supp. 747 (W.D. La. 1968); and Scoggin v. Lincoln University, 291 F. Supp. 161 (W.D. Mo. 1968).

The two recent Wisconsin federal cases on the right to a prompt hearing are Marzette v. McPhee, 294 F. Supp. 562 (W.D. Wis. 1968);

and Stricklin v. Regents of the University of Wisconsin, 297 F. Supp. 416 (W.D. Wis. 1969). The first involves the denial of a hearing of the Oshkosh students, the second concerns the use of interim suspensions at Madison.

In the area of substantive student rights, there are several important new cases. The Supreme Court decision involving the wearing of armbands to protest the Vietnam war is Tinker v. School District, 393 U.S. 503 (1969). The federal district court case on the constitutional aspects of wearing one's hair longer than school authorities allow is Breen v. Kahl, 37 U.S. Law Week (W.D. Wis. February 20, 1969). The views of the American Civil Liberties Union on the increasingly violent forms of student demonstrations are reproduced in *The New York Times,* April 4, 1969, pp. 1, 18.

On the question of student organizations and membership lists, the California case is Eisen v. Regents of the University of California, 75 Cal. Rptr. 45 (1969). The Columbia litigation brought by SDS is reported in *The New York Times,* June 4, 1969, p. 24; June 26, 1969, p. 7.

The text of the letter from the Department of Health, Education and Welfare to officials at Antioch College, permitting the continued operation of the Afro-American Studies Institute, may be found in *College and University Reporter,* ¶14,881 (May 2, 1969).

The tribulations of the DuBois Club at Illinois are reviewed in the *Chicago Tribune,* February 10, 1967, p. 1, col. 3; the editorial appears on p. 16 of that edition. The running battle between the Colorado Regents and the SDS chapter is recounted in Circular Letters No. 36 and 37 of the National Association of State Universities and Land Grant Colleges, December 17 and 27, 1968. On the question of the extent to which membership in the Communist Party can be made illegal, see Scales v. United States, 367 U.S. 203 (1967); and for the present status of the party, see Communist Party v. Subversive Activities Control Board, 367 U.S. 1 (1961).

Several references to student press problems are in order. The survey of students editors is reported in the *San Francisco Chronicle,* April 7, 1965, p. 3, col. 5–8. The contrasting views of college presidents are reflected in a survey summarized in *College Management,* May 1966, pp. 44–46. The leading case on the freedom of the student press is Dickey v. Alabama State Board of Education, 273 F. Supp. 613 (M.D. Ala. 1967). The restrictive view of student journalism, and of the latitude for criticism of the administration, is in "Developments in the Law— Academic Freedom," 81 Harvard L. Rev. 1045, 1130 (1968).

The discussion of nonresident tuition charges invokes the general question of privileges and immunities under the constitution. The case of the high fee for the out-of-state shrimp fisherman is Toomer v. Witsell,

334 U.S. 385 (1948). The one student's suit against the tuition differential that has reached trial and produced a reported decision is Clarke v. Redeker, 259 F. Supp. 117 (S.D. Iowa 1966). Several other cases have been filed, but apparently have not been decided on the merits.

The Supreme Court case upholding California's ban on quota picketing is Hughes v. Superior Court, 339 U.S. 460 (1950).

The survey of college and university practices regarding required living accommodations is found (among many other surveys) in *Institutional Policies on Controversial Topics: A Special Report*, Monograph No. 1 of the National Association of Student Personnel Administrators, January 1968. The two cited dormitory search cases are Moore v. Student Affairs Committee of Troy State College, 284 F. Supp. 725 (M.D. Ala. 1968); and People v. Cohen, 292 N.Y. Supp. 2d 706 (Dist. Ct. 1968). The high school locker case is People v. Overton, 229 N.E.2d 596 (N.Y. 1967), vacated and remanded by the Supreme Court for further consideration in light of a subsequent Supreme Court decision on search and seizure. The Louisiana case holding invalid a requirement that all unmarried female students under twenty-one live in the dormitories to help the college pay its overhead costs, is Mollere v. Southeastern Louisiana College, 38 U.S.L. Week 2217 (E.D. La. 1969).

In the concluding section of this chapter, the comments of Secretary Finch are taken from his testimony before a House Education subcommittee in the spring of 1969, abstracted in *The New York Times*, April 19, 1969, pp. 1, 16. The observations of President Martin Meyerson are from an interview with a *New York Times* reporter, appearing in *The Times*, March 31, 1969, p. 45. The excerpts from the preliminary report of the Violence Commission may be found in *The New York Times*, June 10, 1969, p. 30.

Chapter VII

A most valuable and insightful general discussion of regulations and restrictions on access to public facilities for the exercise of constitutional liberties is found in Professor Harry Kalven's article, "The Concept of the Public Forum: Cox v. Louisiana," 1965 Supreme Court Review 1 (1965). There are other commentaries, but this will suffice as a guide to the subject matter of this chapter.

The Boston Common case, which we have encountered before, is Davis v. Massachusetts, 167 U.S. 43 (1897), which affirmed the decision of the state court in Commonwealth v. Davis, 39 N.E. 113 (1895), giving the mayor absolute discretion over access to the Common for speeches and meetings. A significant change came with Hague v. CIO, 307 U.S. 496 (1939), allowing much greater access to public places for speech and political activity. This trend was reinforced by the handbill cases of the late 1930s, which expanded access to the public forum in another direction. The principal case of that group was Lovell v. Griffin, 303 U.S. 444 (1938). Most recently, there has been a series of cases involving civil rights demonstrations in public places, notably Cox v. Louisiana, 379 U.S. 536 (1965). It is this decision that provides the focal point for Professor Kalven's article cited earlier.

The series of cases involving the unpopular speaker, and the need for police protection, really begins with Justice Black's dissent in Feiner v. New York, 340 U.S. 315 (1951), where he urged that the police should have arrested the antagonist in the crowd rather than the speaker if violence threatened. This view seems increasingly to have prevailed. It is reflected in the decision ordering police protection for the civil rights marchers in Alabama, Williams v. Wallace, 240 F. Supp. 100 (M.D. Ala. 1965); and a similar guarantee of police protection for the Vietnam Day marchers in Oakland, Hurwitt v. City of Oakland, 247 F. Supp. 995 (N.D. Calif. 1965).

The transformation of certain kinds of private property as a result of extensive public use began with the Supreme Court decision in Marsh v. Alabama, 326 U.S. 501 (1946), involving a company-owned town that sought to exclude distributors of religious literature. Later the California Supreme Court extended this concept to commercial shopping centers in Schwartz-Torrance Investment Corp. v. Bakery & Confectionery Workers Union, 40 Cal. Rptr. 233 (Cal. 1964); and the Supreme Court accepted this extension in its recent decision of Food Employees' Local 590 v. Logan Valley Plaza, Inc., 391 U.S. 308 (1968).

There had been several federal court of appeals cases concerning the constitutionality of the FCC's Fairness Doctrine, beginning in 1965. A conflict of holdings between two circuits brought the issue to the Supreme Court. The high Court resolved the issue in the Commission's favor in Red Lion Broadcasting Co., Inc. v. FCC, 395 U.S. 367 (1969).

Several cases are cited involving use of auditorium facilities under governmental control. The Pete Seeger case is reported as East Meadow Community Concerts Association v. Board of Education, 272 N.Y.S.2d 341 (N.Y. 1966). The similar case involving the New Orleans public auditorium is Bynum v. Schiro, 219 F. Supp. 204 (E.D. La. 1963). The most notable of these cases was the series of California decisions under the state's Civic Center Act—the source of the requirement of proof of loyalty on the part of users of public facilities. The development of the law is ably recounted by one of the participants, in Blease, "The Civic Center Act and the Freedom of Speech," 2 Calif. Commission on Law & Social Action Law Commentary 43 (1964). The cases are Danskin v. San Diego Unified School District, 171 P.2d 885 (1946), American Civil Liberties Union v. Board of Education, 359 P.2d 45 (1961), and American Civil Liberties Union v. Board of Education, 379 P.2d 4 (1963). The Port of New York Authority Bus Terminal case, involving a slightly different but obviously related issue, is Wolin v. Port of New York Authority, 392 F.2d 83 (2d Cir. 1968).

On the subject of speaker bans, one of the most thorough and thoughtful works is the one quoted in the text, Pollitt, "Statutory Comment: Statute Barring Speakers From State Educational Institutions," 42 North Carolina L. Rev. 179 (1963). Also important is Van Alstyne, "Political Speakers at State Universities: Some Constitutional Considerations," 111 U. of Pennsylvania L. Rev. 328 (1963). A most interesting case study on speaker bans is Eric Solomon, "Free Speech At Ohio State," in *The Troubled Campus* (Boston: Little, Brown & Co., 1965), p. 63. The major recent cases in the speaker ban area are those striking down the North Carolina ban, Dickson v. Sitterson, 280 F. Supp. 486 (M.D.N.C. 1968), and the Illinois Clabaugh Act, Snyder v. Board of Trustees, 286 F. Supp. 927 (N.D. Ill. 1968). The most recent developments in this field, also in the federal courts, are Brooks v. Auburn Univ., 412 F.2d 1171 (5th Cir. 1969) (involving Rev. William Sloane Coffin); and Smith v. University of Tennessee, 300 F. Supp. 777 (E.D. Tenn. 1969) (involving Dick Gregory and Dr. Timothy Leary).

The two leading cases on the use of advertising space on or adjacent to public transit vehicles are Wirta v. Alameda-Contra Costa Transit District, 64 Cal. Rptr. 430 (Cal. 1967), and Kissinger v. New York City Transit Authority, 274 F. Supp. 438 (S.D. N.Y. 1967).

The decision upholding the *Rutgers Law Review* in rejecting the article by the Southern author is Avins v. Rutgers, State University of New Jersey, 385 F.2d 151 (3d Cir. 1967). The reporter for the *Nashville Tennessean* was vindicated in Kovach v. Maddux, 238 F. Supp. 835 (M.D. Tenn. 1965). The concluding quotation, which notes the changing character of the public forum and recognizes the need for new guarantees of access to it, is from Barron, "Access to the Press—A New First Amendment Right," 80 Harvard L. Rev. 1641 (1967).

Chapter VIII

There is a rapidly growing body of literature on the law of public housing. Most notable and useful is a publication of the Project on Social Welfare Law—*Housing for the Poor: Rights and Remedies,* (New York: New York University Project on Social Welfare Law, 1968) an entire book devoted to these issues. A symposium in the Summer 1967 issue of *Law and Contemporary Problems,* dealing generally with the federal role in housing, included several articles devoted specifically to public housing. An excellent student Note, "Government Housing Assistance to the Poor," 76 Yale L.J. 508 (1967) covers many aspects of the subject quite readably. The relevance of the Kerner Commission report cannot be overlooked; the President's Commission on Civil Disorders devoted substantial space to the shortcomings of present public housing programs, and possible correctives. Finally, Professor Lawrence Friedman has written a most useful article, "Public Housing for the Poor; An Overview," in *The Law of the Poor* (San Francisco: Chandler Publishing Co., 1966).

Most of the specific cases that are not officially reported are found in the *Welfare Law Bulletin,* which will hereafter be cited "WLB" in these notes.

The effect of a criminal record on eligibility for public housing has been considered by several courts. The case discussed in the text is Manigo v. New York City Housing Authority, 273 N.Y.S. 2d 1003 (Sup. Ct. 1966). Compare the eligibility policies proposed by the ACLU of Southern California for adoption by the Los Angeles Housing Authority, in WLB, No. 11, p. 6 (January 1968). The New York case in which a relative's criminal record brought the eviction of an otherwise eligible applicant was New York City Housing Authority v. Watson, 207 N.Y.S. 2d 920 (Appellate Term 1960). The circular issued by the Department of Housing and Urban Development to all local housing authorities on December 17, 1968, is printed in full in CCH Poverty Law Reports ¶9280.

The principal case on the eligibility of unmarried mothers, which held Little Rock's exclusionary policy invalid, is Thomas v. Housing Authority of Little Rock, 282 F. Supp. 575 (E.D. Ark. 1967). The editorial commending a voluntary removal of such a barrier is from the *Buffalo Evening News,* February 14, 1968, p. 36, col. 1.

The decision enjoining discrimination against welfare recipients who are otherwise eligible for admission to housing projects is Colon v. Tompkins Square Neighbors, Inc., 294 F. Supp. 134 (S.D. N.Y. 1968).

The development and application of the Gwynne Amendment (requiring public housing applicants to sign a loyalty oath) are reviewed in two good student notes. One is at 53 Columbia L. Rev. 1166 (1953), and the other at 69 Harvard L. Rev. 551 (1956). The cases invalidating the Gwynne Amendment are Chicago Housing Authority v. Blackman, 122 N.E. 2d 522 (1954); Peters v. New York City Housing Authority, 121 N.E. 2d 529 (1954); Housing Authority of Los Angeles v. Cordova, 279 P.2d 215 (1956); and Lawson v. Housing Authority of Milwaukee, 70 N.W. 2d 605 (1955).

The principal case on eviction of a tenant for antimanagement activity such as tenant union leadership is, of course, Thorpe v. Housing Authority of Durham, which has now been twice before the Supreme Court—although both times on the procedural question whether and when Mrs. Thorpe shall receive a hearing at which she may contest the basis for her eviction. At least one case decided on the merits of this issue, against the tenant, is Holt v. Richmond Redevelopment and Housing Authority, 266 F. Supp. 397 (E.D. Va. 1966). The case of the two tenant leaders in Sacramento is reported in the Northern California ACLU News, January 1966, p. 3, and in the 1963–66 Report of the ACLU of Northern California, p. 31. The Thorpe case is reported at 386 U.S. 670 (1967); 393 U.S. 268 (1969).

The Executive Order barring discrimination in future housing built with federal funds was President's Executive Order 11063, issued by President John F. Kennedy on November 24, 1962. The principal case on discrimination in selection of public housing sites is Gautreaux v. Chicago Housing Auth., 265 F. Supp. 582 (N.D. Ill. 1967) (on a preliminary hearing); 296 F. Supp. 907 (N.D. Ill. 1969) (on the merits). The Bogalusa, Louisiana, case is Hicks v. Weaver, 302 F. Supp. 619 (E.D. La. 1969).

The Newark eviction case, decided by the Court of Appeals for the Third Circuit, is Randall v. Newark Housing Authority, 384 F.2d 151 (3d Cir. 1967). At the time of the decision there was no clear federal requirement of procedural safeguards for the tenant. Examination of the new Michigan housing law, summarized in *The New York Times,* July 28, 1968, p. 64, col. 3, indicates how much progress has been made in protecting the tenant's interests in a very short period.

The case in which the Court of Appeals came down rather hard on the New York Housing Authority for failure to publish and define its standards of admission is Holmes v. New York City Housing Authority, 398 F.2d 262 (2d Cir. 1968). The New York state court decision, requiring the housing authority to state its reasons for an eviction, is Vinson v. Greenburgh Housing Auth., 288 N.Y.S.2d 159 (App. Div. 1968). The federal case strongly suggesting a right to a hearing prior to termination of tenancy is Ruffin v. Housing Authority of New Orleans, 301 F. Supp. 251 (E.D. La. 1969).

Chapter IX

As recently as five years ago there was hardly any literature on welfare law, law and poverty, or the law and the poor. What has been published during this very short period would now fill several shelves. In large part these materials are the result of symposia called to consider the special legal problems of the poor, and especially of those who are on welfare. Conferences of this type have often focused on the teaching of poverty law, and have made contributions to the development of new course materials for law school classes in this field. One of the most notable contributions from this direction is the volume of papers from the Berkeley conference in the spring of 1966, published under the title *Law of the Poor* (the contents appeared initially as a special issue of the *California Law Review,* later being revised for book form). There have been more specialized compilations, such as the volume *The Law and the Low Income Consumer* (New York: New York University Project on Social Welfare Law, 1968). There have also been symposia on legal services for the poor, and many related concerns. Any bibliography on welfare law, or law of the poor, would almost certainly be dated by the time it appeared. One who wishes to be currently informed about publications in this field would be well advised to review the bibliographical sections in each *Welfare Law Bulletin.*

The introductory definition and description of the American welfare system is from Wedemeyer and Moore, "The American Welfare System," in *The Law of the Poor.* The lengthy comment about the problems and prospects of the welfare system is from Dr. Eveline M. Burns of the Columbia University School of Social Work, addressing the (New York) Governor's Conference on Public Welfare held at Arden House in the fall of 1967. The published proceedings of that conference make a most useful addition to the literature on the social welfare side of the liaison with law.

The strong indictment of the means test is from Ten Broek & Wilson, "Public Assistance and Social Insurance—A Normative Evaluation," 1 U.C.L.A. L. Rev. 237 (1954).

The case sustaining the repayment provisions of the New York welfare law is Snell v. Wyman, 281 F. Supp. 853 (S.D. N.Y. 1968). Since the decision was that of a three judge federal district court, it was appealable directly to the Supreme Court; that court declined to overturn the judgment of the district court.

Residence tests of several states have been attacked in federal district courts, and the decisions have uniformly favored the welfare claimants. In Green v. Department of Public Welfare, 270 F. Supp. 173 (D. Del. 1967); Waggoner v. Rosenn, 286 F. Supp. 275 (M.D. Pa. 1968); Smith v. Reynolds, 277 F. Supp. 65 (E.D. Pa. 1967); Ramos v. Health & Social Services Board, 276 F. Supp. 474 (E.D. Wis. 1967); and Thompson v. Shapiro, 270 F. Supp. 331 (D. Conn. 1967), the courts held the residence tests unconstitutional on a variety of grounds. Only in the District of Columbia has the residence test been upheld, Harrell v. Board of Commissioners, 269 F. Supp. 919 (D.D.C. 1967). Many of these cases were appealed to the Supreme Court, where they were argued in the spring of 1968. No decision was reached that term. They were accordingly held over to the following term, when they were decided in a single opinion, Shapiro v. Thompson, 394 U.S. 618 (1969).

The Medicare loyalty oath, though short-lived, produced an interesting conflict of decision between the two district courts that passed upon its constitutionality. Three judges in California held the oath to be a violation of First Amendment liberties, Reed v. Gardner, 261 F. Supp. 87 (C.D. Cal. 1966); while three other judges at about the same time held the oath valid, in Weiss v. Gardner, 66 Civ. 498 (S.D. N.Y., Oct. 11, 1966). Ordinarily such a conflict would bring the case rapidly before the Supreme Court, but in this instance the government chose not to fight.

On the question of privacy and welfare, see a most thoughtful article, "Privacy in Welfare: Public Assistance and Juvenile Justice," 31 Law & Contemp. Prob. 377 (1966), by Professors Margaret Rosenheim and Joel Handler. On the more specific issue of midnight raids and searches by welfare officials, see Reich, "Midnight Welfare Searches and the Social Security Act," 72 Yale L.J. 1347 (1963). While the Smith case described in the text was pending, other suits had been filed against the District of Columbia practice of midnight searches of clients' quarters. The first such case to come to decision in the federal district court resulted in a signal victory for the client, and permanently enjoined the practice of terminating benefits because of refusal to "cooperate" with a caseworker seeking entry for inspection purposes. (Steward v. Washington, WLB No. 14, September 1968, p. 7). The Department of Health, Education and Welfare had already adopted a new rule, binding on all programs receiving federal funds, that seemingly stopped unannounced midnight searches and other "practices that violate the individual's privacy or personal dignity. . . ." WLB No. 9, p. 4 (July 1967).

Several suits have been brought against the "employable mother" policies of many states' welfare programs. For the range of arguments advanced in these cases, and the uncertain results to date, see WLB, No. 13, pp. 4–6 (June 1968). The district court decision in the Georgia case is Anderson v. Burson, 300 F. Supp. 401 (N.D. Ga. 1968).

The case of the Catholic mother given her choice between instituting divorce proceedings and losing her welfare payments is reported in the San Francisco *Chronicle,* January 3, 1968, p. 4, col. 8. The lie detector case is summarized in WLB, No. 1, p. 5 (December 1965). The trial court decision putting the unmarried Mexican-American mother to the choice between sterilization and loss of welfare was reversed on appeal. Neither decision was officially reported; the appellate judgment is in re Hernandez, No. 76757, Superior Court for Santa Barbara County, June 8, 1966.

The "man-in-the-house" case reached the Supreme Court and was decided in the spring of 1968, King v. Smith, 392 U.S. 309 (1968). HEW rules were promptly revised to conform to the Supreme Court mandate, WLB, No. 14, p. 2 (September 1968). The federal court decision striking down the HEW regulations on attribution of income, and sustaining the California MARS statute, is Lewis v. Stark, CCH Poverty Law Reports ¶9299 (N.D. Cal. 1968).

The three principal decisions invalidating state maximum grant rules, are Dews v. Henry, 297 F. Supp. 587 (D. Ariz. 1969); Williams v. Dandridge, 297 F. Supp. 450 (D. Md. 1969); and Westberry v. Fisher, 297 F. Supp. 1109 (D. Me. 1969). The case involving the reduction of New York welfare payment levels is Rosado v. Wyman, 414 F.2d 170 (2d Cir. 1969). All four cases were granted by the Supreme Court for consideration during the 1969–70 Term.

There have been significant developments toward strengthening the welfare recipient's right to a hearing before benefits are terminated. Most important are the decision of the three judge federal court in Kelly v. Wyman, WLB, No. 15, p. 8 (December 1968), and the parallel decision of a state trial court in Michigan. For general background on the right to a prior hearing, and the arguments on both sides of the question, see Note, "Withdrawal of Public Welfare: The Right to a Prior Hearing," 76 Yale L.J. 1234 (1967); Note, "Federal Judicial Review of State Welfare Practices," 67 Columbia L. Rev. 84 (1967). With the Kelly case compare McCullough v. Terzian, 80 Cal. Rptr. 283 (Cal. Ct. App. 1969). For the regulations issued by the Department of Health, Education and Welfare, see CCH Poverty Law Reports ¶9334, 10,246 (HEW 1969).

Chapter X

Most of the materials cited or referred to in this chapter have already been discussed in earlier notes. A few additional citations are, however, appropriate to complete the presentation. The particular newspaper story about Senator Eastland's federal bounty, from the heading of which the chapter title was taken, appeared in the Buffalo *Evening News*, February 19, 1969, p. 36, col. 1–2.

Professor Lawrence Friedman's observations on the double standard in government benefits are found in his recent article, "Social Welfare Legislation: An Introduction," 21 Stanford L. Rev. 217, 229 (1969).

There is a wealth of material on the need for, and availability of, legal services for the poor. An important document is the Report to the National Conference on Law and Poverty in June 1965, which appeared under the title *Law and Poverty*. The following year the Department of Health, Education and Welfare issued a report on Neighborhood Legal Services, under that title, prepared by Professor Joel Handler (Washington: U.S. Government Printing Office, 1966). There are symposia in 41 Notre Dame Lawyer 843 (1966); 66 Columbia L. Rev. 247 (1966); 12 U.C.L.A. L. Rev. 279 (1965); and 12 New York Law Forum 55 (1966). New discussions of the legal service question appear almost monthly.

The ombudsman, too, has been a subject of much scholarly attention despite the paucity of implementation in the United States. The two major works, by Professor Walter Gellhorn of Columbia Law School, are *Ombudsmen and Others* (Cambridge: Harvard University Press, 1967); and *When Americans Complain* (Cambridge: Harvard University Press, 1966).

Professor Bonfield's article appeared in 67 Michigan L. Rev. 511 (1969) under the title, "Representation for the Poor in Federal Rulemaking." It contains, in an appendix, the text of the recommendations offered to, and those adopted by the Administrative Conference.

INDEX